D1259166

HARMLESS SOULS

Karmic Bondage and Religious Change in Early Jainism with Special Reference to Umāsvāti and Kundakunda

W.J. Johnson

MOTILAL BANARSIDASS PUBLISHERS
PRIVATE LIMITED • DELHI

First Edition: Delhi, 1995

© MOTILAL BANARSIDASS PUBLISHERS PRIVATE LIMITED
All Rights Reserved

ISBN: 81-208-1309-x

Available at:

MOTILAL BANARSIDASS

41 U.A. Bungalow Road, Jawahar Nagar, Delhi 110 007
120 Royapettah High Road, Mylapore, Madras 600 004
16 St. Mark's Road, Bangalore 560 001
Ashok Rajpath, Patna 800 004
Chowk, Varanasi 221 001

PRINTED IN INDIA

BY JAINENDRA PRAKASH JAIN AT SHRI JAINENDRA PRESS,
A-45 NARAINA, PHASE I, NEW DELHI 110 028
AND PUBLISHED BY NARENDRA PRAKASH JAIN FOR
MOTILAL BANARSIDASS PUBLISHERS PRIVATE LIMITED,
BUNGALOW ROAD, DELHI 110 007

CONTENTS

Preface

This book is a revised version of my thesis, 'The Problem of Bondage in Selected Early Jaina Texts', approved for the D.Phil. degree at Oxford University in 1990.

I am grateful to Wolfson College, Oxford, where the original thesis was written, for electing me Michael Coulson Research Fellow in Indology from 1991-1992, thus enabling me to begin work on the revised version. I am also most grateful for the support of the Boden Fund, without which I would have been unable to complete the original thesis, and which also made a grant towards the cost of producing the typescript. The Bhogilal Leherchand Institute of Indology, Delhi, provided me with a research scholarship to study in their library during the early stages of revision in 1990. I take this opportunity to thank Mr. Narendra Prakash Jain of Motilal Banarsidass, Mr. Raj Kumar Jain, and the administrators and staff of the Institute for their hospitality.

My intellectual and academic debts are many - to Alan Williams and Partha Mitter, who encouraged me as an undergraduate at Sussex to believe I could go on to do research, to Jim Benson who taught me elementary Sanskrit so intensively, and to Alexis Sanderson who taught me more Sanskrit and gave generous advice on many subjects. I should also like to thank the examiners of the thesis, Friedhelm Hardy and Roy Norman for their criticisms and suggestions, which I have attempted to incorporate into the revised version. My principal and overriding debt is to Richard Gombrich, who taught me Prākrit and gave me a level of encouragement, advice and support far in excess of the most rigorous standards of professorial responsibility. I could not have hoped for a better supervisor or to have worked under a more inspiring scholar.

My greatest personal debt is to my wife, Patricia, who has more than once suspended her own academic work to enable me to press on with mine. To her, and to our son, Jonathan, I dedicate this book.

Cardiff 1994

Abbreviations

[material in square brackets refers to entries in the Bibliography]

AN	*Aṅguttara Nikāya*
Ātmakh	*Ātmakhyāti* [see Kundakunda (4), *Samayaprābhṛtaṃ*]
Āy	*Āyāraṃga Sutta* (unless otherwise stated, references employ Jacobi's numbering system, duplicated by Schubring and Bollée)
CPD	*A Critical Pāli Dictionary*
Das	*Dasaveyāliya Sutta* (references are to Leumann's ed., unless otherwise stated)
DN	*Dīgha Nikāya*
JGM	Jaina Grantha Mālā ed. of *Samayasāra* [see Kundakunda (4), *Samayaprābhṛtam*]
JPP	*The Jaina Path of Purification* [see Jaini, P.S. (1979)]
MN	*Majjhima Nikāya*
Niy	*Niyamasāra* [see Kundakunda (1)]
PTS	Pali Text Society
Pañc	*Pañcāstikāya* [see Kundakunda (2)]
Pravac	*Pravacanasāra* [see Kundakunda (3)]
Sam	*Samayasāra* [see Kundakunda (4)] (references are to Chakravarti's ed., unless otherwise stated)
SBE	Sacred Books of the East
SBJ	Sacred Books of the Jainas
SN	*Saṃyutta Nikāya*
SS	*Sarvārthasiddhi* [see Pūjyapāda]
Sūy	*Sūyagaḍaṃga Sutta* (unless otherwise stated, references employ Jacobi's numbering system, duplicated by Schubring and Bollée)
TD	*Tattvadīpikā* [see Kundakunda (3)]
TS	*Tattvārtha Sūtra* (numbers in brackets indicate the Śvetāmbara text, otherwise reference is always to the Digambara version, as employed in the *Sarvārthasiddhi*)

TV *Tātparya-vṛtti* [see Kundakunda (4), *Samayaprābhṛtaṃ*]
Utt *Uttarajjhayaṇa Sutta* (references are to Charpentier's ed., unless otherwise stated)
Vin *Vinaya*
Viy *Viyāhapannatti* (numbering is that employed by Deleu [1970])
YS *Yoga Sūtras* [see Patañjali]

PART I

EARLY JAINISM

Introduction

The ascetic practices of early Jainism are conditioned by three different but intertwined concepts or beliefs. First, that virtually all matter is alive, in the sense of containing life-monads or souls. Second, that doing harm to living beings is wrong. Third, that actions inevitably have results which affect the future condition and future births of the actor.

If souls (*jīva*) are ubiquitous, then it is clearly very difficult to do any action at all without harming them. Such harming action (*hiṃsā*) is believed to result in karmic bondage; that is to say, the soul is invaded and weighted down by subtle matter which ensures that at death the *jīva* is reborn in this or another world (*saṃsāra*), rather than rising to a state of liberation and omniscience at the top of the universe. Consequently, the more harm one does, the heavier the bondage and the worse the rebirth. In short, according to these beliefs, an ordinarily active life in the world will almost inevitably involve too much *hiṃsā*, and therefore bondage, for the actor to have any realistic hope of even a good rebirth, let alone liberation.

On the other hand, to avoid such bondage, it is essential to observe the vow of non-injury (*ahiṃsā*) towards all creatures. The central concern of Jaina practice, therefore, is to establish a means of conducting oneself which (ideally) entails no *hiṃsā* and thus no further bondage. (An important secondary concern is, of course, to get rid of the karma one has already accumulated.) Given the above conditions, this is clearly a very difficult undertaking, requiring special, ascetic restraints. It is particularly problematical for ordinary householders; in fact, *prima facie*, 'lay Jainism' would seem to be a contradiction in terms.

But Jainism did develop as a religion, as opposed to a personal soteriology - a religion which acquired lay followers and then (numerically, at least) came to be dominated by them. Therefore, it is my purpose in the first part of this work to consider the manner in which this religion developed, and I shall do so by examining both the ways in which the needs and circumstances of the laity were reconciled (in so far as they were) with early, purely ascetic doctrines, and the further problems to which such an enterprise inevitably gave rise.

The first textual synthesis of Jaina doctrine, Umāsvāti's *Tattvārtha Sūtra*, attempts just such a reconciliation of ascetic and lay concerns. It does so, as we shall see, through a mixture of doctrinal reformulation, doctrinal rejuxtaposition, and doctrinal expansion. Crucial to the new synthesis is the postulation and development of a proper (i.e. technical) doctrine of the mechanism of bondage. That is to say, the way in which karmic matter is attracted and bound to the soul is precisely delineated for the first time. This, however, gives rise to some internal contradictions: the new doctrine is apparently incompatible with certain aspects of canonical teaching. But it is precisely through the examination of these contradictions that it becomes possible to infer what is significantly new about the *Tattvārtha Sūtra*'s mechanism of bondage. (For the content of that canonical teaching, and the ascetic practices which are founded on it, I shall refer to the earliest parts of the Śvetāmbara canon, contrasting the doctrines found there with their reformulation and transformation in the *Tattvārtha Sūtra*.)

In short, by examining the question of what is perceived to be the immediate cause of bondage, and considering how the answer changes throughout Jainism's early history, it is possible to chart the way in which the religion grew beyond the extreme asceticism of its roots and delineate some of the incompletely resolved tensions to which that growth gave rise. The ways in which apparently insuperable theoretical contradictions are overcome, or evaded, in the actual practice of ascetics and laity, will be discussed in the conclusions to Part I.

I begin, however, with an account of the earliest detectable Jaina view of the causes of bondage, as found in the most ancient parts of the Śvetāmbara canon.

1

Bondage and liberation according to the early Śvetāmbara canon

1.1 *Early Jainism - Primary sources and chronology*

To determine the earliest Jaina view of the mechanism of bondage, I have referred to the *Āyāraṃga, Sūyagaḍaṃga, Dasaveyāliya,* and *Uttarajjhayaṇa Suttas,* although some reference is also made to later canonical texts, especially to the fifth Aṅga of the Śvetāmbara canon, the *Viyāhapannatti* (*Bhagavaī*).[1]

The Jaina canon presents considerable problems of chronology; of the texts named above, however, the *Āyāraṃga* and the *Sūyagaḍaṃga* are almost universally agreed to be the oldest on grounds of language and metre. And within these two, the first *suyakkaṃdha* (*śrutaskandha*) of each text is thought to contain the earliest material in each case.[2] There is less agreement about the *Dasaveyāliya* and *Uttarajjhayaṇa,* although both Schubring and Alsdorf accept them, at least in part, as the oldest texts in the canon, along with the two already named.[3] Alsdorf remarks that nothing really contradicts the idea that the doctrines contained in these most ancient Jaina texts go back to the time of Mahāvīra, and that even there one does not get to their roots.[4] Any precise dating,

---

1 When I use the term 'canon' I am, of course, referring to the Śvetāmbara texts. The Digambaras, as is well-known, deny that a canon survives. See, for instance, *JPP* pp. 49-52.

2 See, for example, Schubring 1962, p. 81; *JPP* p. 53; cf. Alsdorf 1965, p. 28, and in general Alsdorf's analyses of *āryā* metre to establish chronology: *āryās* indicating more recent material, *śloka* or *triṣṭubh* that which is earlier (e.g. 1966 and 1962-63). On the history of the early canon, see also Alsdorf 1977.

3 Schubring 1962, p. 81; Alsdorf 1965, p. 28.

4 Alsdorf 1965, p. 28.

however, is clearly not possible. It is not even known when the Śvetāmbaras first began to write down their canon. P.S. Jaini suggests some time prior to the second council at Mathurā in the fourth century CE. But the final redaction was not made and committed to writing until the end of the fifth or beginning of the sixth century.[5]

Later canonical texts raise similar problems of chronology, which I shall not consider here. However, further research into these works may well help to lay bare the process of doctrinal change which occurs between the *Āyāraṃga Sutta* and Umāsvāti. For my present purposes it is sufficient to show that such a change has taken place, and the longer the period to have elapsed between the canonical material and the *Tattvārtha Sūtra* the more clearly that change is delineated. For that reason I have chosen here to compare the teachings of the *Tattvārtha Sūtra* with those in what are generally acknowledged to be the earliest extant canonical texts.

1.2 *The force of activity (yoga) in bondage: action and intention*

K.K. Dixit, characterising *Āyāraṃga* 1 and *Sūyagaḍaṃga* 1, which are generally admitted to be the earliest surviving Jaina texts, says that they put an unconditional emphasis on world-renunciation, extol the life of the monk, and have 'nothing but condemnation for the life of the householder'.[6] Under such conditions it is difficult, if not impossible, for any community of monks 'to forge special links with any community of householders'.[7] The ascetic's life, which is so hard to follow, is designed to reduce monks to a minimum of dependence upon lay society. The texts connect *parigraha* (attachment to worldly things / 'possession') with *ārambha* ('violence') and treat them as

---

[5] See *JPP* pp. 51-52; Doshi pp. 26-27.

[6] Dixit 1978, p. 4.

[7] Ibid. p. 5.

the two most fundamental sins; the former is the proximate cause of sinful activity and the latter the immediate cause.[8]

The objects of *parigraha* may be either animate or inanimate - 'material goods and social relatives'.[9] To satisfy the demands of this attachment to worldly things, *ārambha* is undertaken. The objects of *ārambha* are the six types of living beings (i.e. the totality of transmigrating *jīva*s): 1) *trasa* - 'mobile' *jīva*s with more then two senses (including humans, animals, birds, insects, etc.), and 2-6) *sthāvara* - 'static' *jīva*s with only one sense (i.e. those in earth, water, fire, air, and plants).[10]

As Dixit remarks, this understanding must have accentuated the strong ascetic tendency of Jaina speculation.[11] That is to say, one cannot undertake activity which manipulates earth, etc.; indeed, given the ubiquity of *jīva*s, almost any activity is liable to be harmful in some way or other. The later idea formulated to accommodate the laity - that violence done to the *sthāvara* beings is less sinful than that done to *trasa* beings - is not found in these texts.[12]

In the earliest Jaina textual treatment of 'ethical' problems, it is said of the evil-doer that, typically, he either commits a particular evil act, or has it committed by someone else, or approves of it when it is committed by someone else. Thus at *Sūyagaḍaṃga* 1.1.1.3. we read: 'If a man kills living creatures himself, or causes them to be killed by others, or authorises / allows / approves their killing, animosity will increase for himself'[13]

---

8 Ibid. *Ā √rabh* has the basic meaning of 'to undertake', but in Middle Indo-Aryan dialects it falls together with *ā √labh*, 'to kill'. So there is an ambiguity in Prākrit and a tendency for *ārambha* to mean 'killing'. For a further discussion, see pp. 38-39, below.

9 Dixit 1978, pp. 6, 18-19.

10 See *Āy*. 1.1.2-7.

11 Dixit 1978, p. 6.

12 Ibid.

13 *sayaṃ tivāyae pāṇe aduvā annehiṃ ghāyae |*

Dixit speculates that this formulation of the characteristic behaviour of the evil-doer went through a series of changes in the following manner.[14] In the *first* formulation, the evil-doer either:

1) commits a particular (evil) act, or
2) has it committed by someone else, or
3) approves of (or allows?) an (evil) act when it is committed by someone else.

In the *second* formulation, the evil-doer commits an (evil) act either:

1) through body - he does it himself, or
2) through speech - he employs an agent to do it, or
3) through mind - he approves of an (evil) act when it is committed by another.

The relationship between the two formulations was, according to Dixit, eventually 'forgotten', and it became 'customary to speak of a triple evil act committed in a triple manner'.[15] That is to say, an (evil) act committed through:

	-	by oneself
1) body	-	by one's agent
	-	by someone else with one's approval

(This corresponds to the second formulation in its entirety.)

	-	by oneself
2) speech	-	by one's agent
	-	by someone else with one's approval

---

hanaṃtaṃ vāṇujāṇāi veraṃ vaḍḍhei appaṇo || *Sūy*. 1.1.1.3.||
Bollée's edition, 1977. Tieken 1986, p. 12ff., offers a different interpretation of this; cf. Bollée's trans., 1977, p. 54. Bollée also gives an alternative translation for *veraṃ vaḍḍhei appaṇo* - 'his "sin" increases'. Cf. *Āy*. 1.1.1.5.

[14] Dixit 1978, p. 88.

[15] Ibid.

- by oneself

3) mind - by one's agent

- by someone else with one's approval.

What is the precise meaning of this? Is an evil act a triple act - does it require all three components to be evil - or is each component evil in itself? Crucially, is component 3), 'mind', a necessary condition for an *evil* act to take place?

This becomes clearer if we look in more detail at one of the texts cited by Dixit, *Dasaveyāliya* 4.[16] In Prākrit this reads:

> *iccesiṃ chaṇhaṃ jīva-nikāyāṇaṃ neva sayaṃ daṇḍaṃ samārambhejjā nevannehiṃ daṇḍaṃ samārambhāvejjā daṇḍaṃ samārambhante vi anne na samaṇujāṇejjā*

The key word here is the ambiguous *samaṇujāṇejjā.* (Skt. *samanujānīyāt* - (*sam-*) *anu-√jñā*) - 'to fully permit, or allow or consent to, wholly acquiesce in, or approve of'.[17] Dixit translates this term with the sense of approval - i.e. one should not approve of a violent action which has been

---

[16] Leumann's ed., bottom of p. 6.

[17] Monier-Williams, *Sanskrit Dictionary.* Cf. Pāli *samanuññā* - 'approval' - used, for example, at *Saṃyutta Nikāya* 1.1 and *Majjhima Nikāya* 1.159. Also cf. Pāli *anujānāti* - 'to give permission', 'grant', 'allow' (e.g. *Vinaya* IV, 225, 25: *ekaṃ me itthim anujānātha*, 'allow me the power over her'); but when the Buddha speaks in *Vinaya*, the meaning is near to 'to ordain or prescribe' - see *CPD* and, for example, *Vin.* II, 254, 6: *na Bhagavā anujānāti mātugāmassa ... pabbajjaṃ.* Compare also the formulation of the first *pārājika* offence in the *Suttavibhaṅga*: e.g. 1.10.26:

sādiyi tvaṃ bhikkhū 'ti
nāhaṃ bhagavā sādiyin ti
anāpatti bhikkhu asādiyantassā 'ti
'Monk, did you consent?'
'I did not consent, lord,' he said.
'There is no offence, monk, as you did not consent.'
(Horner's trans. p. 62, etc.)

committed by someone else.[18] Schubring, however, translates *na samaṇujāṇejjā* as '(the monk) should not allow others who perform a violent action to do so'.[19] The complete passage reads:

> Towards these six groups of souls (i.e. all *jīvas*) he should not perform any act of violence himself, nor cause it to be performed by others, nor allow others who perform it to do so.

Schubring's version is clearly the more uncompromising of the two. In his reading a proper act of 'mind' is not simply a matter of disapproval (which is internal, a question of attitude), rather it is a matter of not *allowing* other people to perform *hiṃsā*. It is possible that the Jains themselves, or some Jains (the ambiguity of the term permits different interpretations and so different responses to the violence of others), started with the uncompromising sense - one should not allow others to commit violence if one is aware of their action - and later internalised the idea to a matter of attitude, of approval or disapproval. (Just how a monk could prevent others committing violence without causing violence himself, even if, as is possible, the injunction applies only to preventing his fellow *monks* from transgressing, is clearly problematic.)

In this respect, the evidence of textual passages relating the Jaina attitude to Brahmanical ritual is interesting. As P.S Jaini points out, Jaina attacks on Vedic sacrifice have at times 'reached the proportions of a crusade'.[20] In contrast to incidents in the Buddhist texts, where Brahmans seek out the Buddha to engage him in debate, Jaina stories frequently tell of some kind of active protest against, or interference in, Brahmanical rites. This indicates that the

---

[18] Dixit 1978, pp. 88-89. Cf. Norman p. 14, who, in translating *Utt.* 8:8, renders *na ... aṇujāne* as: 'One should not approve ...'.

[19] Leumann's ed., p. 84.

[20] *JPP* p. 169.

uncompromising reading of *sam-anu-√jñā* may have been that of some early Jaina ascetics.   For unless the Brahmanical rite was responsible for an influx of karma into the Jaina beholder of the ritual simply through the fact of his witnessing it, why should he be so vehement in his protest?   If it were merely the Brahmans' act of violence, causing influx of karmic matter (*āsrava*) into them (the Brahmans), the Jaina could have let it pass.   But it is clear that there is some sense in which the Jaina considers himself personally responsible for it.   Belief that an evil act can be committed through the activity of mind explains this. (It may also be the case that the ascetic's attitude is based on compassion for the suffering *jīva* which is the sacrificial material, although such a reason is not prominently advanced in the texts.)

The passage from *Dasaveyāliya* 4 continues:

> While I live I (shall) not act (violently) in any of three ways, i.e. with mind, speech, and body, nor shall I authorise such action, nor allow another person to act so.[21]

In contrast to the suggested original meaning of the formula - that acts of body, speech, and mind all referred ultimately to particular physical actions -, this passage introduces a properly mental element.   However, this is still a long way from the idea that it is mental attitude alone which is really instrumental in bondage.   It is not necessary for all three components, the physical, the vocal, and the mental, to be present for an evil act to be committed; any one of these alone constitutes such an act. Violence is still evil and thus binding, whatever the mental attitude or intention of the actor.   Nevertheless, if, as seems likely, the uncompromising reading of *sam-anu-√jñā* as 'allowance' was eventually relinquished entirely in favour of 'approval',

---

[21] *jāvajjīvāe tivihaṃ tivihenaṃ maṇeṇam vāyāe kāeṇaṃ na karemi na kāravemi karentaṃ pi annaṃ na samaṇujāṇāmi* - Leumann's ed. pp. 7-8.

then a precedent was established (albeit initially only with regard to the actions of others) in which attitude or intention alone was enough either to cause bondage or, more importantly, to evade it, regardless of what happened physically. A mental event was judged to have soteriological significance regardless of what happened in the external world. Thus, as in the passage cited above, which constitutes the first great vow (*Dasaveyāliya* 4), it became possible to speak of performing a *mental* act of violence.

Prima facie, this would seem to increase the difficulties involved in undertaking the vow of *ahiṃsā*, since now not only actually accomplished physical acts but also mere 'evil' thoughts are defined as *hiṃsā*. However, once a mental element is introduced into *hiṃsā*, the way is open to introduce the further idea that acts are only 'evil' - and so karmically binding - *when* there is an element of intention: a mental component (viz. 'passion') has to be present. And as will be made clear, this was precisely what happened as Jainism expanded into a religion with a strong lay following. This process will be examined below, along with its doctrinal and social ramifications, but first of all it is necessary to consider in more detail what counts as a harming action according to the earliest Jaina texts.

1.3 *Some early Buddhist and early Jaina attitudes to bondage compared*

It is useful to begin by examining the contrasting attitudes of Buddhists and Jains to what is really instrumental in bondage. Such a comparison reveals very clearly what is most important in this respect according to the earliest Jaina canonical texts, namely, physical action. Consequently, it also throws light on the original meaning of *'yoga'*, which in the *Tattvārtha Sūtra* is given as the technical term for all forms of physical, vocal and mental action.[22]

In the *Upālisutta* of the *Majjhima Nikāya* (56), which describes the conversion of Upāli, a lay disciple of Mahāvīra, by the Buddha, a dispute arises over whether the sins of the mind, as the Buddha teaches, or the sins of the body, as the Nigaṇṭha Nātaputta (Mahāvīra) contends, are the heaviest. The Buddha asks Tapassī (a Jain) how many kinds of acts 'effect and start Demerit, according to Nātaputta the Nigaṇṭha'. Tapassī replies: 'It is not his usage, Gotama, to employ the term "acts"; he speaks of "inflictions" (*daṇḍa*)' (namely, those of body / deed, word and mind).[23]

Each of the three kinds of *daṇḍa* is agreed to be distinct from the other two. Mahāvīra is reported by Tapassī to state that, of the three, those of deed (*kāyadaṇḍa* - i.e. of body) are the heaviest. But the Buddha replies that those of mind are the heaviest; and rather than *'daṇḍa'*, he prefers to use the term *'kamma'*. Thus, according to the *Majjhima Nikāya*, the Jains give a negative gloss to the word for activity itself. (Although, as Jacobi points out, the word *kamma* occurs in the Jaina *sūtras* too, in the sense of 'deed';

---

[22] See p. 47ff., below.

[23] Pāli: *kati pana Tapassi Nigaṇṭho Nātaputto kammāni paññāpeti pāpassa kammassa kiriyāya pāpassa kammassa pavattiyā ti ... Na kho āvuso Gotama āciṇṇam Nigaṇṭhassa Nātaputassa kammaṃ kamman-ti paññāpetum, daṇḍam daṇḍan ti kho āvuso Gotama āciṇṇam Nigaṇṭhassa Nātaputtassa paññāpetun ti - Majjhimanikāya* 1, 372.

The sense of *daṇḍa* here would seem to be 'hurtful physical acts', i.e. 'violence'. Cf. *Dhammapada* 129:

sabbe tasanti daṇḍassa sabbe bhāyanti maccuno |
attānaṃ upamaṃ katvā na haneyya na ghātaye ||

'All men tremble at violence, all men fear death. Likening others to oneself, one should neither kill nor cause to kill.'

According to Chalmers (PTS ed. of *MN*, p. 267), Buddhaghosa 'says that the Jain idea was that *citta* (the *mano-daṇḍa*) did not come into bodily acts or into words, - which were irresponsible and mechanical, like the stirring and soughing of boughs in the wind'.

daṇḍa, however, is at least as frequently used.)[24]

The term preferred by the Buddhists - *kamma* - is in essence a more neutral term than *daṇḍa*, in that action is either sinful or not, depending upon intention, i.e. the karmic quality of any action is determined by the quality of volition (*cetanā*) underlying it. Nothing can be called karmically wholesome (*kusala*) or unwholesome (*akusala*) independently of volition; acts in themselves are karmically indeterminate (*avyākata*).[25] Whether a particular volitional state is karmically binding or not depends on the absence or presence of *lobha* (greed), *dosa* (hate), and *moha* (delusion) - perhaps comparable to the 'passions' (*kaṣāyas*) of classical Jaina thought. For this reason, the Buddha can state explicitly that 'volition, O monks, is what I call action (*cetanāham bhikkhave kammam vadāmi*), for through volition one performs [significant] action by body, speech or mind'.[26]

From the above, it is clear that for the early Jains physical activity is, by definition, 'hurtful' and thus binding, whereas for the Buddhists it is only binding if accompanied by the mental factors of *lobha*, *dosa* and *moha*. And it is perhaps significant that it is a lay disciple of Mahāvīra's who is converted by the Buddha, since the Buddha's view of what is karmically binding, as represented in the *Upālisutta*, is clearly more compatible with lay life than the view attributed to Mahāvīra.

It is also interesting to note that *'yoga'*, the Jaina term

---

24 Jacobi 1895, intro. p. xvii. See, for instance, *Sūy*. 2.2 (p. 357ff. in Jacobi's trans.), where thirteen ways of 'committing sins' are treated of, and where the first five are *daṇḍa-samādāne* and the rest are *kiriyāṭhāne* (i.e. *kriyāsthāna*). Cf. also *Sthānāṅga Sūtra* (third *uddeśaka*) where, according to Jacobi (ibid. p. xvii), the doctrine of the three *daṇḍa* is expressed in nearly the same words. Norman p. 15, translating *Utt*. 8:10, renders *daṃḍa* as 'punishment'.

25 See *Buddhist Dictionary*, p. 122ff.

26 *Aṅguttara Nikāya* 6.63, quoted in *Buddhist Dictionary*, p. 92.

for 'activity', is used by Buddhists, in the sense of 'yokes' or 'bonds', as a synonym for the four *āsavas*, the four 'cankers' or 'corruptions' - viz. *kāmāsava* - the canker of sense desire, *bhavāsava* - of (desiring eternal) existence, *diṭṭhāsava* - of (wrong) views, *avijjāsava* - of ignorance.[27] Thus *yoga* is that which binds for both the Buddhists and the Jains; however, for the former, it is clearly mental events which bind (*kāmāsava*, etc.), whereas for the latter, it is physical action which is important, for it is physical action which causes the influx of karmic matter (*āsrava*).

Alsdorf has suggested, convincingly, that the use of the term *'āsava'* by both Buddhists and Jains, is not a case of one heterodox tradition borrowing from the other, but that when the Buddhists use the term it is a remainder from an ancient, 'primitive' form of a common Indian doctrine concerning the effect and expiation of action - a doctrine which the Jains preserved whereas the Buddhists 'modernized' and 'spiritualized'.[28] In other words, the 'original' belief was that the instrument of bondage, of *āsrava*, was physical activity; the Jaina monks retained this idea, whereas the Buddhists redefined *yoga* and *āsrava* in terms of mental or 'internal' events.

Etymologically, however, *yoga* must be the juncture of two things. Caillat defines it as 'the attraction and conjunction' of the material particles which form karma with 'the spiritual monad'.[29] P.S. Jaini, referring to the fully developed doctrine of the *Tattvārtha Sūtra,* says that karma generates a vibration (*yoga*) in the soul which brings

---

[27] See *Dīgha Nikāya* 16, quoted in *Buddhist Dictionary*, p. 27.

[28] Alsdorf 1965, p. 4f.

[29] Caillat 1974, p. 30; cf. Caillat 1987, p. 511, where she defines *yoga* as the attraction of subtle matter to the soul through the vibration of its 'soul-points', presumably following the *SS* on *TS* 6:1: *ātmapradeśaparispando yogaḥ*. See below, p. 47ff., for my comments on *TS* 6:1.

about the influx (*āsrava*) of new karmic matter.[30] He goes on to say,

> The vibrations referred to here actually denote the volitional activities of the individual. Such activities can be manifested through either body, speech, or mind; hence the soul's vibrations are said to be of three types, each corresponding to one of these modalities.[31]

As will be made clear, I differ from Jaini on the importance of volition as an element in bondage, particularly in early Jainism; nevertheless, we may readily infer from the above that, in this context, the primary meaning of *yoga* is the juncture of the soul and matter (which then becomes karma), i.e. bondage. The meaning is then referred back to the *cause* of that bondage, either vibration of the space-points of the soul or the bodily, vocal and mental activities associated with it. However, since activity is the ultimate cause of vibration, it is the activity of the individual which comes to be synonymous with *yoga*.

For reasons which will become clear, I further suggest that in these earliest Jaina texts the influx of karmic particles and their bondage to the soul is seen as being the *inevitable* result of activity. In other words, activity is considered binding simply by virtue of its being activity; and the fact that both meanings, 'bondage' and 'activity', can be carried by the same term, *'yoga'*, bears this out.

In this, I have again followed the *Majjhima Nikāya* (56) and assumed that for early Jainism volition is not a relevant factor in bondage. But is the account of Mahāvīra's attitude to activity given in the Buddhist text really an accurate reflection of the early Jaina position?

In the *Sūyagaḍaṃga* (2.6.26-42), the Buddhists are

---

30 See *JPP* pp. 105, 112.

31 *JPP* p. 112.

ridiculed for saying (according to the Jains) that it is no sin to cause harm believing that one is not doing so.[32] In other words, the Buddhists maintain that mistaking the object of harmful actions relieves the actor of the consequences of his act. Thus killing a man without knowing that he *is* a man is not sinful; unintentional harm incurs no guilt. For the Jain, however, it is axiomatic that the well-controlled man, one who is careful, does not make such mistakes. He takes care not to harm living creatures whether intentionally or unintentionally. Thus at *Sūyagaḍaṃga* 2.2.3 thirteen kinds of karmas or activities are enumerated, including 'accidental' (*akasmāt*) sin, and sin committed through an error of sight. And bad karma accrues to people sinning in either of these ways (2.2.11-13).

Similarly, at *Sūyagaḍaṃga* 2.4.1, Mahāvīra teaches that, 'Even the fool who is unaware of the workings of his mind, speech, and body, and does not see (i.e. register) even a dream, performs evil actions'.[33] This is asserted throughout *Sūyagaḍaṃga* 2.4 against the opponent's (Buddhist's) view that:

> If his mind, speech, and body are free from evil, if he does not kill, if he is mindless (i.e. without an internal organ or organ of consciousness), if he is unaware of the workings of his mind, speech, and body, and does not see even a dream, he does not perform evil actions.[34]

The passage goes on to say that a 'mindless' person still

---

[32] See the passage beginning: *piṇṇāgapiṇḍīmavi...* Jacobi's trans. (1895), pp. 414-417.

[33] *bāle aviyāramaṇavayakāyavakke suviṇam avi ṇa passai pave ya se kamme kajjai* - *Sūy*. 2.4.1

[34] *asaṃtaeṇaṃ maṇeṇaṃ pāvaeṇaṃ asaṃtiyāe vaīe pāviyāe asaṃtaeṇaṃ kāeṇaṃ pāvaeṇaṃ ahaṇaṃtassa amaṇakkhassa aviyāramaṇavayakāyavakkassa suviṇam avi apassao pāvakamme ṇo kajjai* - *Sūy*. 2.4.2

commits sins of violence, etc., and is thus bound by his actions. Taking the argument a step further, Mahāvīra then states that even *ekendriyas*, viz. earth-bodies, etc.,

> though these beings have neither mind nor speech, yet as they cause pain, grief, damages, harm, and injury, they must be regarded as not abstaining from causing pain, etc. (2.4.9) .... Thus even senseless beings are reckoned instrumental in bringing about slaughter of living beings ... (2.4.10).[35]

In other words, injury is injury, whatever the motive or lack of motive which accompanies it: what counts is the harmful effect on the object, the injured, not the subjective state of the actor responsible for the injury. Here the ethical, compassionate roots of early Jainism are laid bare: injury is bad in the first place because it is injury to *others*. It is only with the development of a consistent theory of bondage and liberation that the stress switches from the fact of injury to others to its consequence, namely, self-injury through bondage. Consequently, the *Sūyagaḍaṃga* does not make it completely clear whether the consequences for the *jīva* of committing a sin of the kind outlined above are the same whatever embodiment it happens to be in.[36]

According to the pan-Indian (although not the Buddhist) doctrine of karma and later Jaina theory, karma is only accrued in a human birth; existence in other births is just the reflex of human action. But the *Sūyagaḍaṃga*

---

[35] Jacobi's trans., p. 404, of: *jāva ṇo ceva maṇo ṇo ceva vaī pāṇāṇaṃ jāva sattāṇaṃ dukkhaṇayāe soyaṇayāe jūraṇayāe tippaṇayāe piṭṭaṇāyāe paritappaṇayāe ... iti khalu se asaṇṇiṇo vi sattā ... pāṇāivāe* ...

[36] But see *Sūy*. 2.4.11: 'The venerable One has declared that the cause (of sins) are the six classes of living beings, earth lives etc.' - Jacobi's trans., p. 404 of: *tattha khalu bhagavayā chajjīvaṇikāyāheū paṇṇattā taṃ jahā puḍhavīkāiyā jāva tasakāiyā.*

appears to be saying that, since intention is irrelevant to sin, and thus to karmic bondage, therefore just as the 'mindless' man binds himself by his actions alone so do *jīva*s in all other conditions down to *ekendriyas* (i.e. beings who have no organs through which they can experience passion or intention). This would certainly be consistent with the view that it is action and not intention which is instrumental in bondage, and is a further indication that the instrumentality of passion (*kaṣāya*) is a relatively late addition to Jaina belief.

Thus the ideal Jaina monk, according to *Sūyagaḍaṃga* 2.4.11, is one who abstains from the five cardinal sins and all the vices, who 'does not act or kill'; he is 'well-controlled and restrained, avoids and renounces sins, is not active, but careful and thoroughly wise'.[37] Comparing this with the standard formula given, for instance, at *Sūyagaḍaṃga* 2.1.50 - 'A monk who does not act, nor kill, who is free from wrath, pride, deceit, greed, who is calm and happy,' etc.[38] - the implication would seem to be that wrath, etc. (the four kinds of passion or *kaṣāya*) are not directly instrumental in bondage as such, but that they lead to violent action (or action of any kind?) which is binding. This probably reflects the original connection of *kaṣāya* with bondage.[39]

Colette Caillat, in her study of the *Cheya Suttas*,[40] states that Jaina teachers are anxious to 'redeem and reform even the very impulses and intentions' of the monks. Consequently, they take trouble to 'divine these intentions

[37] Jacobi's trans., p. 405 (with minor alterations), of: ...*akirie alūsae ... saṃjayavirayapaḍihayapaccakkhāyapāvakamme akirie saṃvuḍe egantapaṇḍie ...*

[38] Jacobi's trans., p. 352, of: *se bhikkhū akirie alūsae akohe amāṇe amāe alohe uvasaṃto pariṇivvuḍe ....*

[39] See pp. 35-36, below, for a discussion of this.

[40] Caillat 1975.

correctly and to appreciate exactly the responsibility of the offender'. She concludes that 'One cannot then take the accusations of the Buddhists literally when they accuse the *nirgrantha* of not according any value to the intentions which motivate the individual'.[41] She also says that passages in the *Sūyagaḍaṃga*, such as 2.6.26 and 2.2 (quoted above), 'are not conclusive'.[42]

Without entering here into the relative chronology of the *Cheya Suttas* and their commentaries (from which Caillat draws her evidence) and the earliest portions of the Śvetāmbara Canon, I would point out that, according to the early texts, intention is significant in so far as it may lead to or away from physical *hiṃsā*, but in terms of the mechanism of bondage it is action or restraint from action that counts. For, in any given case, the intention may be good but the fact of physical *hiṃsā* is incontrovertible evidence that it is not good enough. In other words, the emphasis in the earliest texts is not on intention or lack of it as such, but on the degree of direct involvement with *hiṃsā*. Actions are judged, in the first place, according to their result, not according to the intention of the actor. The latter may be significant before the act, but afterwards it is irrelevant. It is external harm or lack of harm that matters when the soteriological consequences of an action are calculated.

Caillat herself corroborates this in her comments on the *Vavahāra Pīṭhikā*, which analyses the acts of the monk into their constituent elements in order to determine to what extent he has sinned.[43] As a typical example, she cites the

---

41 Ibid. p. 108.

42 Ibid. fn. 1, referring to La Vallée Poussin's fn. 3, p. 2 in his edition of *L'Abhidharma de Vasubandhu*, IV 155, Paris 1923-31, where such passages are cited to support the *Abhidharmakośa*'s interpretation of the Jaina attitude.

43 See Caillat 1975, p. 104ff.

case of a monk who picks up, or puts down, a stick. He is totally innocent if in taking hold of it or in laying it down he acts with attention and cleans it. Conversely, he deserves five days of austerity (*tapas*) if he is guilty of negligence on the first or second point, or on both. Nevertheless, *it is still necessary that no creature should have been injured* [my emphasis]. Months of *tapas* have to be observed for harm done to a living creature when one spits, for instance, or if one receives alms in a wet bowl; and the death of a living creature involves complete loss of seniority.[44]

1.4 *Hiṃsā and the ascetic*

From the above, it is clear that in the earliest Jaina texts *yoga* refers primarily to physical action, and that when it is harming it is 'sinful' (i.e. evil action - *pāvakamma*), and thus binding, regardless of intention or consciousness. For this reason the behaviour of the Jaina monk is characterised above all by physical inactivity and restraint. An early text dealing with ascetic behaviour, the *Dasaveyāliya Sutta*, makes this very clear.

Dasaveyāliya 4.1 reads: 'He who walks, (stands, sits, and lies down, eats and speaks) carelessly, will hurt living beings. He binds evil karman, that is his bitter reward.'[45] And *Dasaveyāliya*.4.8 states: 'He should walk, stand, sit, and lie down carefully; if he eats and speaks carefully, he does not bind evil karman'.[46]

Nothing is said about binding 'good' *karman*; the important thing is not to bind *karman* at all (i.e. all *karman*

---

[44] Ibid. p. 105.

[45] Trans. by Schubring, Leumann's ed. 1932, p. 87, of:
ajayaṃ caramāṇo u pāṇa-bhūyāi hiṃsaī |
bandhaī pāvayaṃ kammaṃ taṃ se hoi kaḍuyaṃ phalaṃ ||

[46] *jayaṃ care jayaṃ ciṭṭhe jayaṃ āse, jayaṃ sae* |
jayaṃ bhuñjanto bhāsanto pāvaṃ kammaṃ na bandhaī ||

is evil in so far as it leads to further bondage). The attitude is that of *Āyāraṃga* 1.3.1.4, where killing (*chaṇaṃ*) is described as the root of karma (*kammamūlaṃ*) and rebirth; that is to say, *karman* is profoundly negative according to these earliest texts.

It is clear that, for the *Dasaveyāliya*, *hiṃsā* of any kind results in bondage, regardless of whether such 'harming' is intentional or unintentional; that is to say, there is no such thing as an 'accident' for the Jaina monk, all *hiṃsā* is due to carelessness. So at *Dasaveyāliya* 5.1.5 a monk is warned to be careful at all times on his begging tour, since, 'By falling or stumbling a (monk, however) self-controlled, would injure moving or unmoving beings'.[47] And at *Dasaveyāliya* 6.10, it is explicitly stated that, 'As many moving or unmoving beings as there are in the world, (so many of them) a monk should not injure or cause to be injured, *either consciously or unconsciously*'.[48] Thus, among many other restrictions, 'he should duly (and) with exertion inspect (his) alms-bowl and cloth, his bed, the place of excretion, straw or seat' (*Dasaveyāliya* 8.17), and 'Excrement, urine, mucus, phlegm, (and) filth, he should put away, having, by inspection, found out a pure place' (*Dasaveyāliya* 8.18).[49]

Throughout the *Dasaveyāliya Sutta*, the necessity for the monk to act in a manner which does not cause

---

[47] *pavaḍante va se tattha pakkhalante va saṃjae* |
hiṃsejja pāṇa-bhūyāiṃ tase aduva thāvare ||
See also *Das*. 5.1.57-64 for the prohibition on food and drink which might have been mingled with blossoms, seeds, plants, dust and mould, fire, etc.

[48] Emphasis added to Schubring's trans. (with alterations) of:
jāvanti loe pāṇā tasā aduva thāvarā |
te jāṇam ajāṇaṃ vā na haṇe no va ghāyae ||

[49] Schubring's trans. (with minor alterations) of:
dhuvaṃ ca paḍilehejjā jogasā pāya-kambalaṃ |
sejjam uccārabhūmiṃ ca saṃthāraṃ aduvāsaṇaṃ ||8.17||
uccāraṃ pāsavaṇaṃ khelaṃ siṅghāṇa jalliyaṃ |
phāsuyaṃ paḍilehittā pariṭṭhāvejja saṃjae ||8.18||

intentional or unintentional *hiṃsā* is repeatedly stressed (see 4.1-9). This is combined with a constant awareness of the extreme difficulty of treading such a path. At *Dasaveyāliya* 6.4, it is described as 'the hard, difficult conduct of the Free Ones'.[50] And, even more explicitly, in the following verse it is said (perhaps even boasted) that,

> In no other (system) has been taught anything which, among worldly people, is (so) hard to carry out; a man may adhere to a great many tenets, (but there has) never been (taught), nor will be (taught to him) anything like our principles.[51]

The *Āyāraṃga Sutta* is more laconic: 'A very severe religion has been proclaimed'.[52]

In all these early monastic rules, nothing is said about intention or attitude as such; for what counts for salvation is physical harm itself; what causes the harming action to arise is of secondary concern. In other words, it is harmful action (*hiṃsā*) which is directly instrumental in bondage, not attitude. Attitude is only significant in so far as it leads to or away from *hiṃsā*; it does not cause karmic bondage in itself.

---

50 Schubring's trans. of: *nigganthāṇaṃ ... āyāragoyaraṃ ... durahiṭṭhiyaṃ*

51 Schubring's trans. of:
nannattha erisaṃ vuttaṃ jaṃ loe parama-duccaraṃ |
viula-ṭṭhāṇa-bhāissa na bhūyaṃ na bhavissaī || *Das.* 6.5 ||
The precise meaning of this verse is obscure. Lalwani (1973) gives an even freer translation:
'This sort of highly difficult conduct
For the world of human beings
Is delineated nowhere save in *nirgranṭha* philosophy.
For those covetous of *mokṣa*
Such conduct has nowhere been prescribed in the past
Nor will it ever be prescribed in the future.'
The general meaning, however, is not in doubt.

52 *Āy.* 1.6.4.2: *ghore dhamme udīrie.*

1.5 *The householder in the earliest texts*

i) The status of the householder

Although the doctrine of karma, with the doctrine of rebirth and liberation (*mokṣa*) as its corollary, is the most prominent feature of the earliest Jaina texts, it is not developed systematically and there is no discussion at all of its precise mechanism.[53] Moreover, the earliest detectable stream of doctrine holds an uncompromisingly negative view of the householder *because* he is a householder. The prospect of a better rebirth in heaven or on earth, as a result of good activity which attracts good karma, is hardly admitted, and the four possible births (*gatis*) seem to have only a theoretical significance at this stage.[54] As Dixit puts it, all action leads inevitably to a 'more or less inauspicious' rebirth, and is *ipso facto* bad.[55] This contrasts with the position found in later doctrinal layers where the pious householder and the good monk who is not yet good enough to attain *mokṣa* are promised auspicious rebirths.[56]

Given that the ultimate soteriological goal of Jainism is total liberation from *saṃsāra*, the idea that any rebirth is relatively undesirable remains a constant component of doctrine. However, what is largely absent from the earliest texts is the idea that there is any gradation or progression through a series of births to ultimate liberation. Instead, what is emphasised is the critical nature of the present birth and, necessarily (since these texts are addressed to ascetics), those kinds of ascetic restraint which will ensure that there is no further rebirth. Thus *Āyāraṃga Sutta* 1.6.2, for instance, apparently considers that there are only two possibilities after death: 1) birth among hellish beings

---

[53] See Dixit 1978, p. 9.

[54] References to the *gatis* in the very earliest parts of the canon are few and far between and cannot be dated with any certainty. See, for example, *Sūy*. 1.2.3.13, 2.2.60ff. and *Utt*. 5.19ff.

[55] Dixit 1978, p. 9.

[56] See ibid.

and animals, and 2) *mokṣa*. The latter will be the condition of the *jīva* of the ideal monk, and the former that of the *jīva*s of everyone else, whether householder or monk.[57] *Āyāraṃga* 1.6.2.1 reads:

> Though some know the misery of the world, have relinquished their former connections, have given up ease, live in chastity, and, whether monk or layman, thoroughly understand the law, they are not able (to persevere in a religious life). The ill-disposed, giving up the robe, alms-bowl, blanket, and broom, do not bear the continuous hardships that are difficult to bear. He who prefers pleasures will, now or after a short time, be deprived (of a human body, not to recover it) for an infinite space of time. And thus they do not cross (*saṃsāra*), for the sake of these pleasures which entail evil consequences and are associated with others of their kind.[58]

It is clear from this that anything short of full mendicancy will entail a long series of miserable, non-human rebirths. Similarly, as Dixit points out,[59] at *Āyāraṃga* 1.3.4.4, in a sequence which begins with anger (*koha*) and ends with pain (*dukkha*), re-birth is described not only as entry into a womb (*gabbha*), a new birth (*jamma*), and a new death (*māra*), but also as characterised by a birth among hellish beings (*ṇaraya*), animal existence (*tiriya*) and pain (*dukkha*).

In this respect, it is significant that the *Dasaveyāliya Sutta*, for instance, states that for a monk to return to the life of a householder apparently necessarily entails (among

---

57 See ibid. p. 16.

58 Jacobi's trans., with minor alterations, of:
āuraṃ logam āyāe caittā puvva-saṃjogaṃ hiccā uvasamaṃ vasittā baṃbhaceraṃsi vasu vā aṇuvasu vā jāṇittu dhammaṃ ahā-tahā ah' ege tam accāī kusīlā vatthaṃ paḍiggahaṃ kaṃbalaṃ pāya-puñchaṇaṃ viosijjā aṇupuvveṇa aṇahiyāsemāṇā parīsahe durahiyāsae. kāme mamāyamāṇassa iyāṇiṃ vā muhutte vā aparimāṇāe bheo, evaṃ se aṇtarāiehiṃ kāmehiṃ ākevaliehiṃ; aviṇṇā c' ee - *Āy*. 1.6.2.1 - Schubring's text (1910).

59 Dixit 1978, p. 16.

other disadvantages) a worse re-birth after death. *Dasaveyāliya* 11.7 reads: '(To return) means going down (after death)'.[60] Such a fate could hardly be construed as some kind of punishment *simply* because he has given up being a monk, because, since influx of karmic matter (*āsrava*) is tied to *hiṃsā*, there is no karmic result from such a change of status in itself: rather, rebirth in hell is here portrayed as the inevitable result of leading the life of a householder.[61] For, as Dixit points out, the idea that acts involving the employment of human or animal labour were particularly 'sinful' (i.e. binding) and others less so, does not appear in the earliest texts.[62] That is to say, all acts which harmed any of the six types of living beings, whether *trasa* (mobile) or *sthāvara* (immobile), were considered to be equally binding. (To be clear about this, the ethical attitude is not so much that a man is as worthless as a mango or a louse, but that a mango or a louse is as important as a man, all *jīva*s having equal value.) Such a distinction between the binding effects of doing harm to *trasa* beings on the one hand, and *sthāvara* beings on the other, only emerged in later Jaina speculation, where the concept of the 'pious householder' is defined as 'one who abstains from all violence done to the trasa beings', that done to *sthāvara* ones being tolerated.[63] As P.S. Jaini puts it, the vow of *ahiṃsā* in its partial, i.e. lay, form applies

---

60 Schubring translates *aharagai-vāsovasaṃpayā* as '(To return) means to reach a (place in hell (after death)'. Cf. *Āy*. 1.6.4.1: 'When they (the disciples) feel the hardships (of a religious life) they slide back, for their love of life. Their leaving the world is a bad leaving' - Jacobi's trans. of *puṭṭhā v' ege ṇiyaṭṭanti jīviyass' eva kāraṇā. ṇikkhaṇtaṃ pi tesiṃ duṇṇikkhaṇtaṃ bhavai.*

61 Cf. *Sūy*. 1.3ff. on the potentially fatal temptation to return to lay life. *Das*. 11 also stresses the social disadvantages of being an ex-monk: see, for example, 11.6. See also Olivelle 1974, p. 20, on the general revulsion felt by Indians for the *parivrājaka* who attempts to return to a society where there is no place left for him.

62 Dixit 1978, p. 6.

63 Dixit 1978, p. 6.

'only to beings with two or more senses (*trasa*), it is extended for the monk or nun to include the infinitely larger group of single-sense beings (*ekendriya*) and element bodies (*sthāvara*)'.[64] In later Jainism, it is this complete vow concerning *ahiṃsā* which marks the real distinction between the advanced lay-person and the mendicant. In the earliest texts it had similarly distinguished the practice of the Jaina monks from that of all others, but there the distinction was absolute.

Thus, in the early texts, there are passages such as *Āyāraṃga* 1.1.2.2-4:

> Take note - there are innumerable tiny beings individually embodied in earth. Take note - there are some men who truly control themselves, safeguarding even these beings, while others, (such as the monks of other sects) fail to do so and thus are only pretending to be renunciants.[65]

In such a context the life of the householder inevitably entails *hiṃsā*, bondage, and a bad rebirth.

ii) Merit and Rebirth

As we have seen, the very earliest texts (i.e. the earliest parts of the *Āyāraṃga*, *Sūyagaḍaṃga* and *Dasaveyāliya Suttas*) are dominated by the idea that virtually all action is harming and therefore binding, since harming is the root of karma.[66] Typical in this respect is *Āyāraṃga* 1.3.1.3, which asserts that 'action results in misery' (*āraṃbhajaṃ dukkhaṃ*). In other words, the possibility of some kind of *meritorious* activity scarcely arises; it is only by restraint from action that one can hope to improve one's condition

---

64 *JPP* p. 241.

65 P.S. Jaini's trans. (*JPP* pp. 241-242) of: *santi pāṇā puḍho siyā, lajjamāṇā puḍho pāsa; aṇagārā 'motti ege pavayamāṇā jaṃ iṇaṃ virūvarūvehiṃ sattehiṃ puḍhavikammasamārambheṇaṃ* ... *aṇegarūve pāṇe vihiṃsai.*

66 *Āy.* 1.3.1.4 - *kammamūlaṃ* ... *chaṇam.*

(i.e. one is working towards a smaller quantity of bad karma). Such continuous restraint, however, is only possible at the ascetic extreme inhabited by the Jaina renouncer; for the householder it is, by definition, impossible.[67] It is not surprising, therefore, that references to merit (*puṇya*) or to activity which leads to a better rebirth in heaven or on earth, as opposed to rebirth in hell or as an animal, are hard to find in this earliest stream of doctrine, and that when they do occur they have an unemphatic and adventitious quality. And it is clear that although, according to some strands of thought, there may be a theoretical possibility of a relatively better rebirth (and perhaps in some cases a practical one for ascetics),[68] for householders there is no real possibility of accumulating anything other than more bad karma and the promise of a bad rebirth.

In this connection it is important to remember that what is being reported here is the ascetic's view - the view of the texts. We have no way of telling what views householders may have held. But since the specific category of 'Jaina householder' would seem to be an anachronism if applied to the period in question - for the very reasons being outlined here - then that consideration plays no part in a reconstruction of the earliest layers of Jaina doctrine. This is borne out by passages such as *Sūyagaḍaṃga* 1.7.24-27, where the connection between the giving and receiving of alms and the giving and receiving of the teaching seems to be minimal. Least of all should the monk actually teach the Jain Dhamma, or promise to do so, *in order to* obtain

---

[67] See *parigraha* section, p. 31ff., below.

[68] See, for instance, *Das*. 3:14:

dukkarāiṃ karettāṇaṃ dussahāiṃ sahettu ya |
ke ettha devalogesu keī sijjhanti nīrayā ||

'Having done that which is difficult to do, having forborne what is difficult to forbear, some of them [pass] to the worlds of the gods, others attain perfection unburdened [by Karman].' - Schubring's trans. Cf. *Sūy*. 2.2.74, for example.

alms.[69] This is interesting because it implies that there was some expectation on the part of householders that alms *should* be repaid with teaching, combined with the Jaina ascetic's view that any prolonged contact with householders (such as might take place during a sermon) was fraught with potential danger for him. It seems likely, in these circumstances, that the first Jaina ascetics made use of the general (i.e. pan-Indian) cultural perception that it was 'the duty of the householder to feed anyone who came to his door',[70] without subscribing to the additional idea that such giving was a means by which the householder acquired merit. Indeed, as we have seen, the earliest detectable Jaina doctrine of karma leaves no room at all for the idea of meritorious action.

In this connection, there is an interesting verse at the end of a section in the *Dasaveyāliya Sutta* where the two ideas - the pan-Indian one that there is merit in giving, and the early Jaina one that there is none - are apparently brought together in some kind of compromise. (It should be noted that this verse, *Dasaveyāliya* 5.1.100, is the last one in a long chapter and could well be a later addition.) This states that, rare as it is to find such people, he who gives for nothing (i.e. the householder) and he who lives for nothing (the monk) both have a good rebirth.[71] This

---

[69] See *Sūy*. 1.7.24: 'He who visits houses where he gets nice food, who professes the Law, desirous only of filling his belly, and brags (of himself) for the sake of food, is not equal to the hundredth part of an Arya.' - Jacobi's trans. of:

kulāiṃ je dhāvai sāugaiṃ āghāi dhammaṃ ayarāṇugiddhe |
ahāhu se āyariyāṇa sayaṃse je lāvaejjā asaṇassa heū ||.

Cf. 1.7.26: 'The servile man says pleasing things for the sake of food, drink, and other things: but wrong belief and bad conduct are worthless like chaff.' - Jacobi's trans. of:

aṇṇassa pāṇassihaloiyassa aṇuppiyaṃ bhāsai sevamāṇe |
pāsatthayaṃ ceva kusīlayaṃ ca ṇissārae hoi jahā pulāe ||

[70] Gombrich 1988, p. 75; and see ibid. for reconstruction of contact between early Buddhist monks and householders.

[71] *dullahā u muhā-dāī, muhā-jīvī vi dullahā* |
muhā-dāī muhā-jīvī do vi gacchanti soggaiṃ || *Das*. 5.1.100||

seems to mean that householders will only benefit from giving alms if they have no intention of benefiting from them: only alms given with the understanding that the gift is not merit-making *are* merit-making.[72] There is also an ambiguous verse in the *Dasaveyāliya Sutta* which may suggest that the ascetic should not even accept alms which he knows to have been given for the purpose of obtaining merit (perhaps itself a reflection of the monks' awareness that it is possible to make use of lay misconceptions about the result of giving).[73]

None of this, however, need seem so paradoxical if it is remembered that the *Dasaveyāliya Sutta* is a text composed by and for ascetics, and reflects their wariness of any kind of social intercourse. Thus *Dasaveyāliya* 5.1.100 (see above), rather than teaching a doctrine of motive or intention, simply reflects the monks' concern lest they themselves may come to believe that they are providing, directly or indirectly, something in return for alms, and that they might thereby encourage householders actively to seek them out, or follow them, in an attempt to obtain merit. Such behaviour would inevitably bring them into closer contact with lay life, with its concomitant temptations and *hiṃsā*-fraught relationships; when possible, it was far safer, therefore, to accept only from those expecting nothing in return. This attitude, enforced by rules of monastic discipline, ensured that it was difficult, if not impossible, for any community of monks, as Dixit remarks, 'to forge special links with any community of householders'.[74]

---

72 Cf. *Aṅguttara Nikāya* IV, 60-3, where it is said that the lowest motive for giving alms is with thought of reward in the next life. Quoted by Gombrich 1971, p. 252.

73 See *Das*. 5.1.49:
asaṇaṃ pāṇagaṃ vā vi khāimaṃ sāimaṃ tahā |
jaṃ jāṇejja suṇejjā vā puṇṇatthā pagaiṃ imaṃ ||
Schubring translates this, referring to other verses, as: 'When a monk knows or is informed that food (of any kind) was prepared for the purpose of acquiring merit, he should refuse it', etc.

74 Dixit 1978, p. 5.

Indeed, it is clear that the monks went out of their way to avoid the conditions which might lead to such a relationship.

To summarise, we may suppose that meritorious action and a better rebirth on earth or in heaven as a result of it were concepts familiar to the householders with whom the early Jaina ascetics had their minimal contact; such ideas were part of the general cultural furniture. And although the earliest Jaina doctrine apparently denies the possibility of these consolations to the householder, nevertheless, Jaina mendicants had to take that general cultural view into account when regulating their own relations with lay persons. While their ties with the laity remained so loose, however, it was not necessary for them to make any systematic doctrinal concessions to that view. For the real possibility of a better rebirth for an ordinary lay person to be theoretically established, some doctrine of intention or motive as being, at some level, more karmically significant than action alone would have been required. And as we have seen, in the earliest texts motive is regarded either as totally irrelevant or only important in so far as it helps to engender or inhibit action. (Ideas such as the Buddhist one that there can be karmically wholesome or recommended action [*puṇya-karma*] are, of course, entirely absent, as is the related idea that individual monks and the Saṅgha in general are the 'unsurpassable field of merit' for the laity.)[75]

Only in *Sūyagaḍaṃga* 2 (intermittently) and the *Uttarajjhayaṇa* are there enough references to the self-restrained householder who achieves rebirth in heaven or as a human to give the impression that this possibility is becoming doctrinally established.[76] This is not to claim that there are no references whatsoever to merit and a better rebirth in the very earliest texts; when they do occur,

---

[75]See *Buddhist Dictionary*, '*puñña*', p. 80; cf. Collins p. 219.

[76] See, for example, *Sūy*. 2.1.13, 2.1.17, 2.2.60ff., 2.2.74, 2.2.78, 2.5.16, 2.7.36, and *Utt*. 5.19ff., 7.20ff., 10.15, 12.12-17, 21.94, 36.50-53.

however, they are isolated and, for the most part, ambiguous.[77] Moreover, to talk of a 'pious' or 'meritorious' *act* remains largely a contradiction in terms, since 'merit', in this context, is usually taken to mean a relative lack of (bad) karma - the result of *abstaining* from action.[78]

The references to merit and the development of the idea in early Jainism would make an interesting independent study, but there is no need here to consider the relative dating of particular sections of any one text to make my point, since the overall tenor of these works (*Āyāraṃga* 1, *Sūyagaḍaṃga* 1, *Dasaveyāliya*) is self-evidently and uncompromisingly anti-householder, as I have demonstrated. That is to say, only from the secondary layers of early material is it possible to adduce firm evidence for particular lay followers who associate themselves specifically with Jaina ascetics (as opposed to all kinds of *śramaṇa*s) in the expectation of gaining merit. But even here, the doctrine of merit still lacks a clear, specifically Jaina rationale.

1.6 *Parigraha and the origins of the kaṣāya doctrine*

i) *Parigraha*

As we have already noted,[79] Dixit has drawn attention to the fact that in the earliest canonical texts the two worst sins are *ārambha* (violent activity) and *parigraha* (possession).[80] That is to say, they perform the same function as that performed by *kaṣāya* (passion), and by the major vows (*mahāvratas*), in later texts - they 'provide a frame work for the fundamental classification of moral virtues and vices'.[81] Moreover, the two are intimately

---

[77] See, for instance, *Sūy*. 1.2.3.13, 1.7.16, 1.11.17-21.

[78] See, for instance, *Āy*. 1.4.22, Suy. 1.2.13, 1.8.1-2, 1.15.10, and even the relatively late *Utt*. 29.37.

[79] p. 5, above.

[80] Dixit 1978, p. 5.

[81] Ibid. p. 7.

connected, for *parigraha* includes that complex of sins which involve a positive attitude towards a particular object, while *ārambha* comprises those sins which involve a negative attitude.[82] Thus *parigraha* may be translated as 'attachment to worldly things' or 'possessiveness', as well as 'possession' itself. And such an attitude directed towards a particular object or person necessarily entails an attitude of *ārambha* towards other objects or persons. Thus all *ārambha* may be traced back to some case of *parigraha* . Or as Dixit puts it,

> Taken as a whole *parigraha* signifies attachment for things worldly - where things include both the material goods and the social relatives, and *ārambha* the acts injurious to others undertaken with a view to satisfying the demands of this attachment.[83]

(Like *kaṣāya* in its earliest sense [see below], *parigraha* leads to violence and thus to bondage, but it is not the direct cause of the latter - i.e. it is the cause of violence but not the direct cause of bondage.) *Parigraha* is thus clearly associated with the life of the householder, for it is the householder who is attached to worldly things. It is a life, moreover, which is inextricably bound up with violence, actual and potential. Thus the *Sūyagaḍaṃga* characterises householders as *sārambhā* and *sapariggahā*- 'killers' and 'acquirers of property' in Jacobi's translation.[84]

---

[82] Ibid. p. 5.

[83] Ibid. pp. 18-19.

[84] Jacobi 1895, p. 350. See *Sūy*. 2.1.43-46. *Sūy*. 2.1.43 reads:

iha khalu 'gāratthā sāraṃbhā sapariggahā, saṃtegaiyā samaṇā māhaṇā vi sāraṃbhā sapariggahā, je ime tasā thāvarā pāṇā te sayaṃ samāraṃbhanti aṇṇeṇa vi samāraṃbhāveṃti aṇṇaṃ pi samāraṃbhataṃ samaṇujāṇanti

'Here, indeed, householders are killers (of beings) and acquirers of property, and so are even some Śramaṇas and Brāhmaṇas. They themselves kill moving and unmoving living beings, have them killed by another person, or consent to another's killing them.' - Jacobi's trans.

The Jaina mendicant, on the other hand, is one who 'disowns all things not requisite for religious purposes', or who 'disowns attachment',[85] since 'he who possesses anything sentient or insentient, however slender, or allows / approves of others doing so, will not be delivered from suffering'.[86]

In other words, such a person goes on killing and binding new karma.[87] Similarly, *Sūyagaḍaṃga* 1.2.2.9-10 states that:

> A monk should be completely familiar with the Law, and at the same time no longer be engaged in (worldly) actions (*ārambha*). (People) who are entangled in thoughts of possessions take care of those possessions; they attain, however, no permanent property. (9)
>
> Know that (property) causes suffering in this world, and that such suffering continues in the next world. Who, knowing this, would be a householder? (10)[88]

In the *Dasaveyāliya Sutta*, this is made even more explicit in the statements: 'He who desires to hoard (things) is a householder, not a monk',[89] and 'the Great Sage has

---

with minor alterations.

85 Alternative translations of *pariggaha* suggested by Jacobi at *Āy*. 1.2.5.3.

86 *cittamantaṃ a-cittaṃ vā parigijjha kisām avi |*
annaṃ vā aṇujāṇāi evaṃ dukkhā na muccai || *Sūy*. 1.1.1.2 ||
Bollée's ed., Vol. I 1977, p. 14. Tieken 1986, p.10ff., offers a very different translation of this; cf. Bollée's trans. (1977), pp. 53-54.

87 See *Sūy*. 1.1.1.3-5.

88 Based on Bollée's trans. Vol. II 1988, pp. 55-6 of his ed. of *Sūy*. 1.2.2.9-10:
dhammassa ya pārae muṇī ārambhassa ya antae ṭhie |
soyanti ya ṇaṃ mamāiṇo no labbhanti niyaṃ pariggahaṃ ||9||
iha-loga duhāvaham viū para-loge ya duhaṃ duhāvahaṃ |
viddhaṃsana-dhammam eva taṃ ii vijjaṃ ko 'garam āvase ||10||.
Cf. Jacobi's trans. 1895, p. 254.

89 *je siyā sannihī-kāme gihī pavvaie na se* - *Das*. 6:19b, Schubring's trans.

said that property means delusion'.[90] The desire to hoard or store things is to experience greed (*lobha*),[91] and *lobha* is not simply the worst of the four sins, it in fact includes the other three: 'Anger destroys kindness, pride civility, deceit drives away friends, [but] greed destroys all.'[92]

It is clear from this that *lobha* (greed) is synonymous with one meaning of *parigraha*, and that it is also an inclusive term for the four sins or passions which are later understood as the components of the technical term *kaṣāya*.[93]

ii) *Kaṣāya*

The four 'moral vices' or passions - anger, pride, deceit and greed (*krodha*, *māna*, *māyā*, and *lobha*) -, which are later called *kaṣāya* (literally, 'stains'), do appear as a set in both the *Āyāraṃga Sutta* and the *Sūyagaḍaṃga*, although they are never given any common designation, and there is no extended treatment of them.[94]

---

[90] *mucchā pariggaho vutto ii vuttaṃ mahesiṇā* - *Das*. 6:21, Schubring's trans.

[91] *Das*. 6:19a.

[92] *koho pīiṃ paṇāsei, māno viṇaya-nāsaṇo* |
māyā mittāṇi nāsei, lobho savva-viṇāsaṇo || *Das*. 8:37||.

[93] See below; Cf. *JPP* p. 177.

[94] See Dixit 1978, pp. 7, 15, 19. In *Sūy*. 1 there are, however, a number of instances where four vices appear under what Dixit calls 'rather peculiar and obscure designations' (Dixit 1978, p. 19). For instance, at 1.1.2.12, the Prākrit terms *savvappaga*, *viukkassa*, *nūma*, and *appattiya* appear. Jacobi reads these as (Sanskrit) *sarvātmaka* (= *lobha*), *vyutkarṣa* (= *māna*), ... (= *māyā*), and *appattiya* (= *krodha*?) respectively. Thus his translation reads: 'shaking off greed, pride, deceit and wrath, one becomes free of karman'. (Cf. Bollée, Vol. I [1977], pp. 89-92, on these). Again, at *Sūy*. 1.1.4.12, a wise monk is enjoined to leave off *ukkasa*, *jalaṇa*, *nūma*, and *majjhattha*. Jacobi renders these as (Sanskrit) *utkarṣa* (= *māna*), *jvalana* (= *krodha*), ... (= *māyā*), and *madhyastha* (= *lobha*?) respectively. (Cf. Bollée [1977], p. 129.) And at 1.9.11, *paliuṃcana*, *bhayaṇa*, *thaṇḍilla*, and *ussayaṇa* are named as the causes of sin. Jacobi renders these as (Sanskrit) *parikuṃcana* (= *māyā*), *bhajana* (= *lobha*), ... (= *krodha*), and *ucchraya* (= *māna*), adding the note that 'these four passions are named here

At *Sūyagaḍaṃga* 1.6.26, for instance, it is said of the Arhat that, having expunged the passions which defile the soul, viz. wrath, pride, deceit and greed, he does not commit any wrong, nor does he cause it to be committed.[95] This is typical in that although it sees the four passions as the instigators of wrong (i.e. harmful) behaviour they are not tied directly to bondage in any technical sense, but to *hiṃsā*; and it is *hiṃsā* that causes the soul to be bound by karma. This is borne out by passages such as *Āyāraṃga* 1.3.4.1, where the conquest of anger, etc. is described as the 'doctrine of the Seer who does not injure living beings and has put an end (to acts and to *saṃsāra*)'.[96] In other words, motivation is still not seen as directly binding in itself; it is the act (killing, etc.) which remains soteriologically crucial. The important thing is control: control of physical action and therefore also control of the passions which may lead to the loss of such physical restraint and the consequent destruction of living creatures.

In the *Dasaveyāliya Sutta*, the term *kaṣāya* is applied to the four vices (*krodha*, etc.). Dixit argues that because *kaṣāya* is used in a technical sense here, a *relatively* late date should be assigned to the passage.[97] However, whether Dixit is right about the dating or not - and *prima facie* his argument seems to be at best circular - *kaṣāya* still has no direct connection with bondage in the sense of providing conditions for karmic matter to stick to the *jīva*, which is the later technical sense of the term (see below). Thus at *Dasaveyāliya* 7:57 there is the passage:

---

from the way in which they are supposed to act upon the soul' (1895, p. 302 fn. 5). These are passages which clearly need further investigation.

[95] See Jacobi's trans. (1895, p. 291) of:
kohaṃ ca māṇaṃ ca taheva māyaṃ lobhaṃ cautthaṃ ajjhattadosā |
eyāṇi vantā arahā mahesī ṇa kuvvaī pāva ṇa kāravei || *Sūy*. 1.6.26 ||

[96] Jacobi's trans. (1884, p. 33) of:
se vantā kohaṃ ca māṇaṃ ca māyaṃ ca lobhaṃ ca eyaṃ pāsagassa daṃsaṇaṃ uvarayasatthassa paliyantakarassa.

[97] Dixit 1978, p. 29.

> (He who) speaks after consideration, controls his senses well, has overthrown the four passions, (and) is without (worldly) support, purges (his soul) of the dirt resulting from previous evil deeds (and) may gain this world and the next.[98]

And at *Dasaveyāliya* 8:36-39, the four 'passions' and the ways to subdue them are analysed in more detail as part of a long description of the way in which a monk should behave:

> When he wishes that which is good for him, he should get rid of the four faults anger, pride, deceit, and greed which increase evil... Anger and pride, when not suppressed, deceit and greed, when arising: all these four black passions water the roots of rebirth.[99]

It should be noted that the metaphor here is of passions 'watering' the 'roots of rebirth', not of causing the *jīva* to become 'sticky'.[100] There is no specific link with karma, and in this case passions (*kaṣāya*) are again clearly considered to be a contributory factor in bondage and not directly instrumental: the term is evidently not yet being used in its technical sense (i.e. in the sense employed in the *Tattvārtha Sūtra* - see below).

iii) *Kaṣāya* and *parigraha*

Richard Gombrich has pointed out the close association in Indian religious thought between asceticism and the idea

---

98 Based on Schubring's trans. of:
parikkha-bhāsī susamāhiindie caukkasāyāvagae aṇissie |
sa niddhuṇe dhutta-malaṃ pure-kaḍaṃ ārāhae logam iṇaṃ tahā paraṃ || *Das.* 7:57 ||.

99 Schubring's trans., with alterations, of:
kohaṃ māṇaṃ ca māyaṃ ca lobhaṃ ca pāva-vaḍḍhaṇaṃ |
vame cattāri dose u icchanto hiyam appaṇo || *Das.* 8:36||
koho ya māṇo ya aṇiggahīyā māyā ya lobho ya pavaḍḍhamāṇā |
cattāri ee kasiṇā kasāyā siñcanti mūlāi puṇabbhavassa || 8:39 ||.

100 Cf. p. 47ff., below.

that emotion stands as the main obstacle to salvation.[101] Jainism is exemplary in that respect. For any system which seeks to regulate physical action to the extent that early Jainism does must also seek to regulate passion or emotion. The two are so closely related as to be virtually interdependent: emotion expresses itself in physical indiscipline, physical indiscipline implies some loss of inner control, whether it be full-blown passion or mere carelessness. Physical and emotional control is therefore paramount. (Again it should be noted that, in terms of karma and avoiding it, it is the physical which takes priority here: one is seeking to control the emotions in order to avoid harmful, and thus karmically binding, actions.)

For the Jaina ascetic, the distinguishing characteristic of the householder's life, with its possessions and the emotions aroused by having and wanting possessions (*parigraha* and *lobha*), is lack of control. And as we have seen, according to the *Dasaveyāliya Sutta*, *lobha* ('greed') comes to subsume all those emotions which are virtually synonymous with lack of control. This interdependence of 'possessions' (being a householder) and 'possessiveness' (thinking and acting like a householder) are seen as the *hiṃsā*-causing and thus binding factors par excellence. In this respect, an inadequate monk can all too easily behave like a householder, but a householder cannot (yet) be like a monk. However, the very distinction between 'possessions' and 'possessiveness' does open up at least a theoretical possibilty of non-attachment to possessions, an attitude or intention, having a significant part to play in liberation from karma. And as we shall see, although the interdependence of the two - of possessiveness and the householder's life - continues to hold good from the ascetics' perspective, for the laity a gap begins to open up.

Parigraha thus becomes an all-inclusive term for the inner, emotional reaction to the external world - a reaction

---

101 Gombrich 1988, pp. 44-45.

which ensures that one remains bound in *saṃsāra*. The beginnings of this internalisation were probably subject to Buddhist influence. For *parigraha* as 'possessiveness' is very like *taṇhā* ('thirst', 'craving', or 'grasping'), which for early Buddhism is the karmically significant (i.e. binding) factor.[102] In the Buddhist case, of course, karma is fully internalised to volition; for the Jains it is still ultimately a matter of physical action. Nevertheless, we can see here the beginnings of what later becomes a crucial doctrine for the Jaina lay person. It is only with Umāsvāti, however, as will be made clear, that a technical explanation in terms of the mechanism of bondage is given for the widely held perception that passion is somehow very closely linked to violence and so to continuing bondage.

1.7 *Activity and karma before Umāsvāti*

i) *The meaning of ārambha*

Monier-Williams gives *√rabh / rambh* as an early form of the root *labh / lambh*. *Ā √rabh* has the basic meaning of 'to set about', 'begin', 'undertake', whereas, although *ā √labh* can also have the meaning 'to commence', it also has the sense of 'taking hold of (in a physical sense)', and 'to kill', especially 'to sacrifice'.[103] In eastern Middle Indo-Aryan dialects *rabh* and *labh* fall together (r > l). Thus there is an ambiguity in Prākrit and Pāli, and for both Jains and Buddhists there is a tendency for the word to mean 'killing'. For the Jains, however, there may have been a doctrinal as well as a linguistic reason for this ambiguity. *Ārambha* originally meant 'undertaking' / 'beginning', but, given the fact that *jīva*s were believed to be almost everywhere (vide the sixfold objects of *ārambha*),[104] for the earliest Jaina ascetics virtually any activity was probably perceived as

---

[102] On *taṇhā*, see Rahula pp. 29-34, and *Buddhist Dictionary*, pp. 218-219.

[103] Monier-Williams, *A Sanskrit-English Dictionary*.

[104] See p. 6, above.

causing *hiṃsā*; and thus *ārambha* as 'undertaking an action' and *ārambha* as 'killing' or 'violence' were very likely considered synonymous.

This is probably how the term *ārambha* is to be understood in such passages as *Āyāraṃga* 1.3.1.3 (*Suttāgame* 172):

> *āraṃbhajaṃ dukkham iṇaṃ iti ṇaccā, māī pamāī puṇar ei gabbhaṃ, uvehamāṇo saddarūvesu ujjū, mārābhisaṅkī maraṇā pamuccai*

> Knowing the suffering born of action,
> The deluded and careless person enters a womb again;
> Indifferent to sounds and forms, upright,
> Anticipating / fearing Māra one is liberated from death.

Ujjū (Sk. *ṛju*) means 'straight' (Sk. √*arj* - 'to stand firm'), and so literally and figuratively 'upright'. Thus, although it can mean 'ethically upright' or 'sincere', aligned here with indifference to *sadda* (*śabda*) and *rūva* (*rūpa*), *ujjū* may have the primary meaning of being *physically* straight or upright (cf. *ṛju-kāya* - 'having a straight body'). In other words, it refers to the typical Jaina meditative posture, *kāyotsarga* - literally, 'abandonment of the body', standing or sitting motionless.[105] If that is the correct reading, then, since the remedy for rebirth as a result of action is total stillness, the implication is that *ārambha*, in this context, does mean *any* action.[106]

---

[105] See *JPP* pp. 190, 192, 225.

[106] Compare, however, *Suttanipāta* 8 (*Mettasutta*) where *ujjū* (= *ṛju*) has the sense of morally upright::

karaṇīyam atthakusalena
yan taṃ santaṃ padaṃ abhisamecca:
sakko ujjū ca sūjū ca
suvaco c'assa mudu anatimānī

'Whatever is to be done by one who is skilful in seeking (what is) good, having attained that tranquil state (of Nibbana): - Let him be able and upright and conscientious and of soft speech, gentle, not proud.'

ii) *Ascetic and non-ascetic actions and karma*

'*Ārambha*', however, soon begins to acquire a more technical meaning, denoting 'purposive', 'deliberate' or 'premeditated action'. This is particularly evident in the fifth Aṅga of the Śvetāmbara canon, the *Bhagavaī Viyāhapannatti (Bhagavatī Vyākhyāprajñapti)*.[107] There, actions (*kiriyā*, Sk. *kriyā*) are described as being:

> (1) purposive *(ārambhiyā kiriyā)*, (2) appropriative (*pariggahiyā kiriyā)*, (3) emotional *(māyā-vattiyā kiriyā)*, (4) implying non-renunciation *(apaccakkhāṇa-kiriyā)* or (5) implying heresy *(micchādaṃsaṇa-kiriyā)*.[108]

In other words, *kiriyā* is here used as a term for all actions, while *ārambha* is reserved for purposive, harming activity directed towards other beings.[109] In spite of the negative nature of the above list (5.6.2), it is clear from other passages in the *Viyāhapannatti* that *kiriyā* is in itself a karmically neutral term. That is to say, we are now presented with a perception that all action is not necessarily harming, and thus binding, simply because it is action (i.e., the position I inferred to be the earliest ascetic one has now been modified). This is made explicit at *Viyāhapannatti* 7 7.1, which reads, in Deleu's summary:

> When a monk who is closed [against karmic influx] *(saṃvuḍa aṇagāra)* moves and handles his equipment in an attentive way (*āuttam*) he commits an action in agreement with his religious duties (*īriyāvahiyā kiriyā*), not a profane action (*saṃparāiyā*

Text PTS, eds. D. Andersen & H. Smith, 1913; trans. V. Fausboll, SBE Vol. X, Pt. 2, p. 24 (Oxford 1881).

[107] The *Viyāhapannatti* is a long, incoherent compilation of material, some of which is probably very early - see Deleu (1970).

[108] Deleu's (1970) summary of *Viy*. V 6.2; cf. Schubring 1962, p. 199.

[109] See Deleu (1970) on *Viy*. V 7.7. On *kiriyā* being employed when concrete actions are referred to, see Schubring 1962, para. 99 (p. 198).

> *kiriyā*) [see explanation below], because in him the four passions are extinguished (*vocchinna*) and he acts in agreement with the precepts (*ahā-suttaṃ eva rīyai*).[110]

Furthermore, this is not simply a distinction between harming and non-harming activities, it is also an institutional distinction between ascetics and laity: just as *īriyāvahiyā kiriyā* is the action of a monk conforming to the monastic rules, so *saṃparāiyā kiriyā* is the action of a non-ascetic or lay person. And while it is considered impossible, by definition, for a non-ascetic or layman to perform an *īriyāvahiyā* action,[111] it is very easy for an inattentive monk to perform a *saṃparāiyā* action.[112] Thus, with monks, actions are said to result either from 'carelessness' (*pamāya*, Sk. *pramāda*) or from 'activity' (*joga*, Sk. *yoga*).[113] *Yoga*, therefore, is the minimal action undertaken by a monk following the monastic rule. And, crucially, the karma bound by a monk as the result of this *yoga* - as a result of 'discharging his religious duties (*īriyāvahiyā kiriyā)*' - 'is consumed within two samayas' (i.e., virtually instantaneously).[114]

Deleu remarks that 'Mahāvīra's idea of the *īriyāvahiyā* action seems to have met with a great deal of incomprehension on the part of his contemporaries', and sometimes even puzzled his own disciples.[115] He goes on to say that the Jaina conception of *iriyā-samii* / *īryā-samiti* ('care in walking') was often attacked by rivals, particularly the Ājīvikas, although (in Deleu's opinion) 'Mahāvīra's explanation of its real tenor sounds reasonable enough: if a monk hurts some small living being while walking in the prescribed way, the action is still in agreement with his

---

110 Deleu (1970). Cf. *Viy*. VII 1.6; I 10.2.

111 See Deleu (1970) on *Viy*. VII 1.3a.

112 See ibid. on *Viy*. VII 1.6.

113 See ibid. on *Viy*. III 3.1c.

114 See ibid. on *Viy*. III 3.1d.

115 Deleu 1977, p. 190.

religious duties'.[116] Furthermore, according to Deleu, such passages as this 'somehow put the old controversial issue regarding the unconsciously committed sin (that divided as is well known the Jainas and the Buddhists) in quite a different light'.[117]

There are a number of points to consider here. First, it is not certain that the *Viyāhapannatti* reports the actual words or doctrines of Mahāvīra. Even if it does, it is clear that the oldest canonical texts (*Āyāraṃga* 1, etc.) contain material which is less sophisticated doctrinally and is probably even older. (If that is the case, it may be that here Mahāvīra is reforming a previous Jaina or proto-Jaina position, or simply excluding, through unambiguous formulation, what had been a matter for debate in earlier practice.) Moreover, regarding the controversy with the Buddhists, the Jain view is that if a monk is following the discipline properly he cannot, by definition, unconsciously commit a sin. For *hiṃsā* done while the monk is conforming to *īryā-samiti* is tolerated, not because it is unconscious, but because it is a special case, sanctioned by the monastic rule. The total amount of karma accrued from such actions is agreed to bind for a short enough time to do no real damage to a monk's prospects of liberation, providing he continues to adhere to the discipline. This, of course, allows ascetics a realistic chance of achieving liberation, and may represent the loosening of some previously very tight rule.

The idea that unavoidable injury perpetrated while following the monastic rules, i.e. while acting with rigorous carefulness or awareness, is less karmically significant than injury perpetrated through neglect of the monastic rules, i.e. done out of carelessness, can be found in isolated passages in the early canon. For example, *Āyāraṃga* 1.5.4.3 states that:

---

116 Ibid., referring to *Viy*. XVIII 8.1.

117 Ibid. Cf. pp. 11-20, above.

On occasion, living beings are destroyed by contact with the body of a virtuous monk walking in the prescribed fashion; he will get his punishment in this life. But if it was done contrary to the rules, he should repent of it and do penance for it. Thus he who knows the sacred texts recommends penance combined with carefulness.[118]

Again, this is not the same thing as saying that monks are allowed to commit what might be normally understood as 'accidental' injury. The reference is to unavoidable injury done in highly controlled circumstances; this still has karmic consequences, but of a short-term, and thus manageable nature. Although it may be noted that the consequences envisaged in this early text are apparently more serious and longer-lasting than the almost instantaneous entry and exit of karma portrayed in the *Viyāhapannatti* (see above).[119]

The invention of categories of action and karmic 'bondage' which have negligible consequences in effect makes both action and the inflow of karma neutral in themselves. The development of this is perhaps traceable from a passage in the second book of the *Sūyagaḍaṃga*. There, at *Sūyagaḍaṃga*. 2.2.1, thirteen kinds of activity

---

118 Jacobi's trans. 1884, p. 48, with alterations of: *egayā guṇasamiyassa rīyao kāyasaṃphāsam (sam)aṇuciṇṇā egaiyā pāṇā uddāyanti, iha logaveyaṇavejjāvaḍiyaṃ, jam āuṭṭikayaṃ taṃ pariṇṇāya vivegam ei, evaṃ se appamāeṇaṃ vivegaṃ kiṭṭai puvvavī** - *Āy*. 1.5.4.3 (*Suttāgame* 307). *Schubring's ed. prints *veyavī, Suttāgame puvvavī.*

119 Note also *Das*. 5.1:87-89, where a monk who has collected alms and returned with them to where his guru is, should approach the latter with 'the airyāpathikī formula'. This is Schubring's understanding of *iriyāvahiya* at *Das* 5.1:88 (his trans., p. 93, Leumann's ed.). The formula referred to here is probably the third of the *āvassaya* / *āvaśyaka* formulae, *vandaṇaga*, which is the prescribed way of respectfully addressing a superior upon entering a place (see Schubring 1962, p. 269). Here it is clearly connected with returning from the begging round, i.e. returning from a permitted monastic activity (*iryāvahiya*). On the 'ritualisation' of monastic discipline, see below.

(*kiriyā*) are named. The last of these is *iriyāvahiya* (translated by Jacobi as 'actions referring to a religious life').[120] These 'subtle' or 'insignificant' (*suhumā / sūkṣma)* activities of the ascetic, governed by the *samiti* and *gupti*, are described in detail at *Sūyagaḍaṃga* 2.2.23.[121] Moreover, the influence of the karma attracted to the soul by these actions is said to be only momentary, lasting but three *samaya*.[122]

This passage on *iriyāvahiya-kriyā* is, however, concluded by the refrain which has accompanied the other twelve kinds of activity, viz. 'Through that something blameable is produced for him' (or as Jacobi translates it, 'Thereby bad karma accrues to him').[123] And the inappropriateness of this here suggests that this kind of *iriyāvahiya* activity may have been a later, somewhat mechanical addition to an original list of twelve bad actions. This conjecture is further borne out by the fact that this passage views the karma acquired from *iriyāvahiya* actions as being more or less instantaneously destroyed, in contrast to the apparently longer process envisaged by *Āyāraṃga* 1 (see above).

Through this kind of development we are brought close to Umāsvāti's distinction between passionate, binding activity and non-passionate, non-binding activity. (The *Viyāhapannatti* does not, however, contain a '*kaṣāya* doctrine' in the technical sense developed in the *Tattvārtha Sūtra*, although passages like *Viyāhapannatti* 7 7.1, quoted above, contain all the necessary components.)[124]

---

[120] Jacobi 1895, p. 356.

[121] Jacobi, in his translation of *suhumā kiriyā iriyāvahiyā nāma kajjai* (ibid. p. 365), takes *iriyāvahiya* to refer to subtle actions other than those followed in the discipline, but that seems confused.

[122] Cf. *Viy*. III 1.d, above, and *Utt*. 29.71 (Jacobi 1895, p.172).

[123] *vaṃ khalu tassa tappattiyaṃ sāvajjaṃ ti āhijjai* - *Sūy*. 2.2. *passim*.

[124] See also *Viy*. VIII 8.3a, b, where *iriyāvahiya*- and *samparāiya-kamma* (as opposed to just -*kiriyā*) are specifically referred to.

The soteriological and social implications of such a distinction are far-reaching, and in order to examine these at greater length I shall now turn to the teachings of the *Tattvārtha Sūtra* on the subject of long and short-term karma.

PART II

UMĀSVĀTI'S JAINISM

2

The mechanism of bondage according to the *Tattvārtha Sūtra*

2.1 *Umāsvāti's Jainism - Primary sources and chronology*

As it represents the first real synthesis of Jaina doctrine, I have, for this part of my argument, used the *Tattvārtha Sūtra* of Umāsvāti as my point of reference. This is the earliest extant Jaina work in Sanskrit, written between 150 C.E. and 350 C.E.[1] Indeed, as P.S. Jaini points out, it 'manages to synthesize virtually the entire Jaina doctrinal system in a mere 350 sūtras'.[2] Furthermore, it is not only the one text that both Digambaras and Śvetāmbaras recognize as authoritative, but the commentaries on it, whether by Digambara or Śvetāmbara authors, 'present almost identical explications of Jaina doctrine'.[3] (In any case, the differences between Śvetāmbara and Digambara doctrine are not significant for the present discussion, which deals with problems fundamental to both traditions.) For that reason I have used the earliest extant Digambara commentary, the *Sarvārthasiddhi* of Pūjyapāda (Devanandin) (c. fifth century C.E.), in conjunction with the *Tattvārtha Sūtra*, rather than the alleged autocommentary, the *Tattvārthādhigama Bhāṣya* (also known as the *Svopajña Bhāṣya*). There is in fact

---

[1] See Bronkhorst p.178; also Dixit 1971, pp. 5-8. Ohira pp.135-137, dates Umāsvāti to the end of the 5th century, but that seems to be too late - see Bronkhorst and Zydenbos, below.

[2] *JPP* p. 82.

[3] Bronkhorst p. 178.

considerable doubt whether the 'autocommentary' was written by Umāsvāti himself; indeed, Bronkhorst has presented a convincing case for attributing it to a Śvetāmbara of the fourth century C.E. (at the earliest) who, in the manner of the *Yoga Sūtra* and *Yoga Bhāṣya*, incorporated the *sūtras* into his own work, the *Tattvārthādhigama Bhāṣya*.[4] Furthermore, the *Sarvārthasiddhi*, although composed perhaps a century later than the *Tattvārthādhigama Bhāṣya,* may be using a version of the *Tattvārtha Sūtra* which is at times closer to the original than that used in the *Bhāṣya*.[5] There is also some evidence that the *Tattvārtha Sūtra* itself was composed in a Digambara milieu, while the *Bhāṣya* has marked Śvetāmbara features.[6] In any case, since the commentaries only differ on a few sectarian issues which are not significant for the present discussion,[7] one may take either as authoritative, in the sense that each represents Jaina doctrine in a non-controversial manner which is not at variance with the *prima facie* meaning of the *Tattvārtha Sūtra* itself. The *Sarvārthasiddhi*, however, often develops the logical implications of doctrines which are merely stated or formulated in the *Tattvārtha Sūtra*, as will become apparent.

2.2 *The mechanism of bondage according to the Tattvārtha Sūtra*

Tattvārtha Sūtra 6:1-4 (= 6:1-5) states that:

> *Yoga* is the activity of body, speech and mind. [6:1]
> It is influx. [6:2]

---

[4] Bronkhorst p. 179. See also Zydenbos pp. 9-12, who dates the *Tattvārthasūtrabhāṣya* to the 5th century; for the *Sūtra* itself, he suggests the end of the 3rd century.

[5] Bronkhorst p. 172.

[6] Ibid. p. 177; see also R. Williams pp. 2-3.

[7] See *JPP* p. 82.

Good activity is the cause of (the influx of) meritorious (karmic matter), and bad activity is the cause of (the influx of) demeritorious (karmic matter). [6:3 (3/4)]
(There are two kinds of influx, namely) that of persons with passions, which brings about rebirth, and that of persons free from passions which has no effect on rebirth. [6:4 (5)][8]

To expand this: Umāsvāti teaches that *yoga* is the vibration of the soul caused by the activity of speech, the mind and the body.[9] This vibration is in turn the cause of the attraction of groups of karmic particles (although, strictly speaking, this matter only becomes karma as such when it adheres to the soul). Thus, when activity occurs, influx (*āsrava*) is inevitable: *yoga* causes the soul to act like a magnet, drawing in karmic matter. All three instigators of *yoga* can be either good or bad, potentially the causes of the influx of meritorious as well as demeritorious karma.

There are two kinds of *āsrava*, depending upon whether one acts out of passion or not: that activity accompanied by *kaṣāya* (passions) results in the influx of *sāmparāyika karma* (rebirth-causing karma), that activity which is free from passions results in the influx of *īryāpatha karma* (short-term karma which has no effect on rebirth). In other words, *yoga* attracts (karmic) matter to the soul, and *kaṣāya* causes that matter to adhere to the *jīva* and to bind it.[10]

The source materials used in *Tattvārtha Sūtra* 6 (concerning *yoga*, *āsrava*, etc.) are widely dispersed in the canon, deriving from passages in the *Bhagavaī*, the

8 *kāyavāṅmanaḥkarma yogaḥ* [*TS* 6:1]
sa āsravaḥ [*TS* 6:2]
śubhaḥ puṇyasyāśubhaḥ pāpasya [*TS* 6:3 (3/4)]
sakaṣāyākaṣāyayoḥ sāmparāyikeryāpathayoḥ [*TS* 6:4 (5)]

9 Cf. *SS* on *TS* 2:25:
yogo vānmanasakāyavargaṇānimitta ātmapradeśaparispandaḥ
'*Yoga* is the vibration of the space-points of the soul caused by the group speech, mind and body.'

10 See *TS* 8:2 (2/3), quoted p. 55, below.

Ṭhāṇaṃga, and the *Uttarajjhayaṇa*, among others.[11] These show that at *Tattvārtha Sūtra* 6:1 Umāsvāti changed the traditional sequence of the threefold *yoga* (*manas, vāc, kāya)* into *kāya, vāc,* and *manas*. According to Ohira, he probably did this because he attached most importance to *kāyikakriyā*.[12] But leaving aside the likelihood that the most important element would in fact be placed last, all the evidence points in the opposite direction: in the canonical texts the emphasis is on the physical and material, and it is Umāsvāti who starts to switch the emphasis to 'internal' action. The change in order is therefore probably not significant. (Devanandin, commenting on *Tattvārtha Sūtra* 2:25, uses the order *vāc, manas, kāya.*)

More importantly, Ohira points out that the definition of *āsrava* as threefold *yoga* is given for the first time in the *Tattvārtha Sūtra* (at 6:2).[13] (*Tattvārtha Sūtra* 6:2 can mean that *yoga* is either the cause of *āsrava* or that it is itself *āsrava*; but there is no real ambiguity here, since it is clear that *yoga* and *āsrava* are pragmatically synonymous, in the sense that any activity automatically causes the influx of karmic matter.) A further innovation of Umāsvāti's is to classify *yoga* as *śubha* ('virtuous' or 'good'), giving rise to *puṇya* (merit), or *aśubha* ('wicked' or 'bad'), giving rise to *pāpa* (demerit) (*Tattvārtha Sūtra*. 6:3).[14]

---

[11] See Ohira p. 61. The identification of Umāsvāti's sources in what follows relies mostly on this work.

[12] Ibid. p. 62.

[13] Ibid.

[14] See ibid. Ohira claims that *yoga* belongs theoretically to a 'neutral category', but that Umāsvāti reads it in terms of *śubha-aśubha* on the basis of the absence or presence of *kaṣāya* [ibid.]. However, this analysis seems to be wrong on both counts, since, first, it is Umāsvāti himself who makes *yoga* into a 'neutral category' precisely through the introduction of the *kaṣāya* doctrine. The underlying feeling of early canonical Jainism, as has been made clear, is that virtually all *yoga* leads to *āsrava* and bondage, and is thus ipso facto to be avoided. Only when the *kaṣāya* doctrine (that the binding power of action depends upon the internal state or attitude of the individual) is introduced, is it possible to conceive of *yoga* as being either binding or not (i.e.

The *Sarvārthasiddhi*, commenting on *Tattvārtha Sūtra* 6:4, states that karma is of two kinds:

1) *sāmparāyika* , leading to *saṃsāra*, and
2) *īryāpatha,* caused by vibrations.

Śāmparāyika is caused by *yoga* and *kaṣāya* combined, and *īryāpatha* by *yoga* alone. However, it is evident that what are being referred to here are not two different types of karma as such, but two different conditions of the *jīva* whether it has, or is associated with, *kaṣāyas* or not. Particular karma or karmic matter is not inherently more or

---

'neutral'). This statement of Ohira's is also wrong in that it claims that Umāsvāti reads *yoga* in terms of *śubha* and *aśubha* on the basis of the absence or presence of *kaṣāya*, i.e. that *śubha yoga* leads to *īryāpatha karma* and *aśubha yoga* to *sāmparāyika karma*. But it is clear that the two categorizations of karma are not synonymous. At *TS* 8:25, *puṇya karmas*, the result of *śubha yoga*, are listed as:

1) *sadvedya* - pleasure bearing karma
2) *śubhāyu* - good age-karma
3) *śubha-nāma* - good body-making karma
4) *śubha-gotra* - high family-determining karma.

(These are divided into forty-two sub-classes of *aghātiyā* or 'non-destructive' karmas.) [On *aghātiyā-karmas,* see *JPP* p.132.]
All other karmas are *pāpa* (*TS* 8:26).

This list shows that *puṇya* karmas are those which determine a good rebirth. So they cannot be synonymous with *īryāpatha* karma, since that has no karmic effect and is certainly not a cause of rebirth. Rather, both *puṇya* and *pāpa* karma are forms of *sāmparāyika* karma. That is to say, both *śubha* and *aśubha yoga* lead to rebirth of some kind; they are actions motivated by some kind of *kaṣāya*. What is new about Umāsvāti's thought here is the idea that there can be such events and categories as *śubha* yoga and *puṇya* karma; such a technical division of *yoga* and karma was inconceivable in the ascetic milieu which is reflected in the doctrines propounded in the earliest parts of the canon. (As we have seen, in the earliest passages virtually all *yoga* is *aśubha* and causes *pāpa* karman; i.e. all activity binds and so threatens a lower rebirth.) So, for Umāsvāti, the category of *sāmparāyika* karma contains *puṇya* as well as *pāpa* karma, a concept which brings the Jaina view of karma into line with the view held by other Indian religions. This, as we shall see, is essentially a lay rather than a monastic or ascetic doctrine. The ascetic is not so much concerned with the possible effects of various *types* of karma, but with stopping the influx of any kind of karma whatsoever.

less binding than any other karma; rather, it is passion which is instrumental in bondage. (A possible explanation for this puzzling terminology will be discussed below.) Thus the emphasis is not on activity as such, but on the accompanying mental or emotional state - on the internal rather than the external.

The reason why 'short-term' (*īryāpatha*) karma is posited at all, since it has no effect, will emerge later. Here, I suggest that while to begin with virtually all activity caused bondage, for reasons connected with the growing importance of the laity it eventually became necessary to differentiate the relative amount of bondage caused by different actions.[15]

How does the *Tattvārtha Sūtra*'s contention that the decisive instrumental factor in bondage is *kaṣāya* fit with the main teaching of the earliest canonical texts, namely, that to cause harm (*hiṃsā)*, by any means whatsoever, to any of the innumerable *jīva* which populate the physical world, is the binding sin *par excellence*?

At *Tattvārtha Sūtra* 7:13 (8), *hiṃsā* is defined as *pramattayogāt prāṇavyaparopaṇam,* 'the destruction of life due to an act involving negligence'.[16] The *Sarvārthasiddhi* comments:

> *Pramāda* connotes passion. The person actuated by passion is *pramatta*. The activity of such a person is *pramatta-yoga*.[17]

Thus the *Sarvārthasiddhi* differentiates between activity engendered by passion, which results in *hiṃsā*, and

---

[15] S.A. Jain echoes this historical and institutional divide when he remarks, 'From the real point of view, it is no doubt true that all activities are undesirable, as every kind of activity is the cause of influx and bondage. But from the empirical point of view there is a difference.' - p. 168, fn. 2.

[16] Sukhlalji's trans., p. 267.

[17] S.A. Jain's trans., pp. 196-197, of:
pramādaḥ sakaṣāyatvaṃ tadvānātmapariṇāmaḥ pramattaḥ pramattasya yogaḥ pramattayogaḥ.

passion-free activity, which does not (i.e. *hiṃsā* is only *hiṃsā* because it has been engendered by passion).

This interpretation is clearly tendentious; the technical meaning of *pramāda* is 'heedlessness', 'carelessness', or 'negligence', derived from √*mad* + *pra*, 'to be intoxicated'.[18] Here, therefore, the use of *pramāda* is comparable to its use in, for instance, the *Yoga Sūtras* (for example, at 1:30, where *pramāda* is included in a list of *citta-vikṣepas*, 'distractions of the mind-field'). And as we have seen, the stress in the earliest canonical sources is on physical 'carefulness', in contrast to the Buddhist concept of *appamāda*, which has the connotation of 'mindfulness'.[19] In the *Sarvārthasiddhi* , however, the whole emphasis of *hiṃsā* is shifted on to the internal state of the agent, i.e. on to passion and its effect on the agent: *hiṃsā* is always *hiṃsā* to oneself. This goes much further than a literal reading of the *sūtra* allows; however, as will be seen later, the space for such an internalised doctrine of bondage is cleared by Umāsvāti in the *Tattvārtha Sūtra*, if not completely developed there. The *Sarvārthasiddhi* simply takes Umāsvāti's thought a step further. Mere injury, according to the *Sarvārthasiddhi*, even killing, does not stain one with the sin of *hiṃsā;* i.e. it is not *hiṃsā* as such, and does not bind.

Apparently quoting from Kundakunda's *Pravacanasāra*, Pūjyapāda (Devanandin), in his commentary on *Tattvārtha Sūtra* 7:13, affirms that:

> When a monk goes on foot with carefulness, sometimes small insects get crushed under his feet and die. Still there is not the

---

[18] Cf. *TS* 7:4, where the five observances of the vow of *ahiṃsā* are all couched in terms of 'carefulness'; and the *SS* itself (on *TS* 8:1) defines *pramāda* as 'misinterpreting' injunctions, and indifference in relation to *kriyā* (action).

[19] See, for instance, the Buddha's last exhortation (*Dīgha Nikāya* 16): ... *appamādena sampādetha* - 'strive diligently'; also see *Buddhist Dictionary* p. 22: 'In the commentaries (*appamāda*) is often explained as the presence (lit. "non-absence") of mindfulness (*satiyā avippavāsa*)'.

slightest bondage of sin in this case. ['Carefulness' being the opposite of *pramāda* or 'negligence'.][20]

The emphasis here is clearly on the state - what amounts to the mental condition - of 'carefulness', not on the physical injury as such. This is confirmed by Pūjyapāda when he goes on to express the converse argument that a 'mere passionate attitude even without the severance of vitalities constitutes violence'.[21]

Again the *Sarvārthasiddhi* quotes a verse that also occurs in the *Pravacanasāra* which summarises this line of argument:

He who acts with negligence commits injury whether death is caused to organisms or not. And he who proceeds with proper care

---

[20] S.A. Jain's trans., p. 197, of:
uccālidamhi pāde iriyāsamidassa ṇiggamaṭṭhāṇe |
āvādejja kuliṃgo marejja tajjogamāsejja ||
ṇahi tassa taṇṇimitto baṃdho suhumovi desido samaye ||
This is to be found in Jayasena's recension of the *Pravacanasāra* at 3:17 (1-2), Upadhye's edition (see Appendix 3, *Pravacanasāra* 3.17b). Given the compilatory nature of the *Pravacanasāra* (see below), it cannot be certain that such quotations originate there. The attribution is made by P.S. Shastry (ed. *SS*, Banaras 1955), but it is possible, even likely, that Pūjyapāda and Kundakunda are quoting from a common source. Indeed, Upadhye in his translation of *Pravacanasāra* 3;17 (1-2) assumes that this is a quotation without identifying the source. In fact, Upadhye speculates that these are very old traditional gāthās, belonging to both Digambaras and Śvetāmbaras (1935, p. liiiff.). Moreover, the fact that Pūjyapāda also quotes here a verse which appears as *Pravacanasāra* 3:16 in Amṛtacandra's recension (see below), indicates that he had access either to an earlier version of the *Pravacanasāra* than Amṛtacandra's (the earliest we possess), i.e. the one from which Jayasena drew as well, or that he is quoting directly from Kundakunda's source. (See also *Viy*. XVIII.7.1, where the same idea is presented in a more technical way.) It is therefore not desirable to draw conclusions about the dating of the *Pravacanasāra* from this coincidence.

[21] S.A. Jain's trans., p. 197, of:
prāṇavyaparopaṇābhāve 'pi pramattayogamātrād eva hiṃseṣyate - *SS* on *TS* 7:13.

> does not contract bondage of karma by mere injury.[22]

Pūjyapāda concludes:

> He who has passions causes injury to himself by himself. Whether injury is then caused to other living beings or not, is immaterial.[23]

This argument is derived from the assertion that *hiṃsā,* the activity which binds, is actually *produced* by passions. Similarly, P.S. Jaini, using the *Sarvārthasiddhi* as his source, notes that the subtlest forms of the passions are called *saṃjvalana* ('the smouldering'). These are not sufficiently strong to prevent one entering the mendicant's path, but they induce 'an insidious state of apathy or inertia (*pramāda*), a lack of drive with regard to the actual purificatory practices enatailed by that path'.[24]

To summarise, Pūjyapāda is claiming that 'negligence' (*pramāda*), and thus *hiṃsā*, is only produced when passions are involved. Consequently, bondage can only occur when there is some kind of volitional activity motivated by passion.[25] This is essentially in agreement with the definitions of bondage given by Umāsvāti at *Tattvārtha Sūtra* 8:

> Wrong belief, non-restraint, carelessness, passions and

---

22 S.A. Jain's trans., p. 197, of:
maradu va jiyadu va jīvo ayadācārassa ṇicchidā hiṃsā |
payadassa ṇatthi baṃdho hiṃsāmitteṇa samidassa ||
Pravacanasāra 3:17 ||
See *Pravacanasāra* 3:16; and see p.156ff., below, for a further discussion of this gāthā.

23 S.A. Jain's trans., p. 197 of:
svayam evātmanā "tmānam hinasty ātmā pramādavān |
pūrvaṃ prāṇyantarānāṃ tu paścāt syād vā na vā vadhaḥ ||
This is in fact a quotation from a Sanskrit source which I have not been able to identify.

24 *JPP* pp. 120. See *SS* on *TS* 8:9; cf. *TS* 10:1.

25 See *JPP* pp. 112-113.

activities are the causes of bondage. [8:1]

Because of its connection with passion, a soul takes on particles of matter liable to become karma. This is bondage. [8:2 (2/3)]

Bondage is of four kinds, according to the nature of karmic matter (*prakṛti*), the duration of karma (*sthiti*), the intensity of the fruition of karma (*anubhāva*), and the quantity of space-points of karma (*pradeśa*). [8:3 (4)][26]

According to the commentaries, *prakṛti* and *pradeśa* are caused by *yoga*, *sthiti* and *anubhāva* by *kaṣāya*. It is *yoga* which attracts karma to the soul in the first place, deciding its type and quantity, and *kaṣāya* which causes it to adhere, deciding its duration and intensity. Thus, according to *Tattvārtha Sūtra* 8:2, it is *kaṣāya* which underlies all bondage (i.e. it is the cause of all *hiṃsā* and thus the cause of all *pramāda* as well).

However, in the list of the five causes of bondage given at *Tattvārtha Sūtra* 8:1, *kaṣāya* and *pramāda* are listed as *independent* causes of bondage.

According to a modern commentator, there are three traditions regarding the number of the causes of bondage: viz. there are either five causes, as given above, or four (*pramāda* is excluded), or there are just two, *kaṣāya* and *yoga*.[27] But these traditions can be harmonised by taking *pramāda* as a type of either *avirati* or *kaṣāya*, and then by viewing *mithyādarśana* and *avirati* as not essentially different from *kaṣāya*. This leaves *kaṣāya* and *yoga* as the only distinct causes of bondage, which is Umāsvāti's conclusion.

In some canonical texts the five causes of bondage

---

26 *mithyādarśanāviratipramādakaṣāyayogā bandhahetavaḥ* [*TS* 8:1]
sakaṣāyatvāj jīvaḥ karmaṇo yogyān pudgalān ādatte sa bandhaḥ [*TS* 8:2 (2/3)]
prakṛtisthityanubhāvapradeśās tadvidhayaḥ [*TS* 8:3 (4)]

27 Sukhlalji's trans. and commentary on *TS*, p. 298f.

(*bandhahetavaḥ*), enumerated at *Tattvārtha Sūtra* 8:1, occur as *āsravadvāras* - causes of (literally, 'entrances for') *āsrava*.[28] As Ohira points out in connection with this, theoretically there is no difference between the root causes of *āsrava* and of *bandha* ,[29] but Umāsvāti took *yoga* to be the root cause of *āsrava* (on the basis that the threefold *yoga*s are present in all the other causes), and then classified *yoga* as causing both *īryāpatha āsrava* and *sāmparāyika āsrava* while placing the rest of the canonical *āsravadvāras* (viz. *mithyādarśana, avirati, pramāda*, and *kaṣāya*) in the category of *sāmparāyika āsrava* only. The crucial alteration here, however, is Umāsvāti's division of *yoga* into that which stems from *kaṣāya* and involves *mithyādarśana*, *avirati*, and *pramāda*, and that which is free from *kaṣāya,* i.e. it is only one kind of *yoga* which causes bondage - the other (passionless) kind does not bind. Thus Umāsvāti has in effect made a distinction between the causes of *āsrava* and the causes of bondage: whereas both kinds of *yoga* (passionless and passionate) cause *āsrava*, only one kind causes bondage.

The canonical idea that *mithyādarśana*, *avirati*, *pramāda*, *kaṣāya*, and *yoga*, as the causes of *āsrava*, are indistinguishable from the causes of bondage, makes it clear that before Umāsvāti there is no technically formulated conception of any kind of *āsrava* which does not bind.[30]

At *Tattvārtha Sūtra* 8:9 (10) the four *kaṣāya* are included in a list of twenty-eight deluding karmas (as *cāritra-mohanīya,* 'right-conduct deluding karmas'), but they are not mentioned there as the specific cause of karmic matter adhering to the *jīva*. It is clear that Umāsvāti is here

---

28 See, for example, *Sthāna* 5.2.517, and *Samavāya* 16, cited by Ohira, p. 62.

29 Ibid.

30 See the discussion, p. 14, above, of the ancient meaning of *āsrava* according to Alsdorf (1965), indicating that *āsrava* was probably originally synonymous with bondage.

taking over an earlier list without any attempt to integrate it with later doctrines.[31] That is to say, the four *kaṣāya* are functioning here as they did before Umāsvāti collated them with the principle of instrumentality. The relevant source-passage from the *Uttarajjhayaṇa* makes this clear:

> The two kinds of *mohanīya* referring to conduct are: 1) what is experienced in the form of the four cardinal passions (*kaṣāya*); 2) what is experienced in the form of feelings different from them (*no-kaṣāya* or 'subsidiary passions').[32]

According to the *Sarvārthasiddhi*, the *cāritra-mohanīya* karmas both cause the passions and are caused by them (i.e. the passions are at the same time both the result of delusive conduct and what lead to further delusive conduct).[33] But even within the circularity of this later commentarial gloss, it is clear that the passions are understood as leading to bondage only through the indirect route of conduct which is deluded - i.e. activity which is harmful in some way.

2.3 *Sāmparāyika and īryāpatha karma in the Tattvārtha Sūtra*

As has been seen above,[34] *yoga* accompanied by *kaṣāya* gives rise to the influx of *sāmparāyika karma,* i.e. karma which binds and thus leads to rebirth - literally, it is the 'passage to the other world' (*samparāya*). At *Tattvārtha Sūtra* 6:5 (6), Umāsvāti subdivides *sāmparāyika karma* into four types, corresponding to the five causes of bondage at *Tattvārtha Sūtra* 8:1. Thus *sāmparāyika karma* is caused

---

[31] In fact this passage is probably directly derived from *Utt*. 33 - see Ohira p. 64, and below.

[32] Based on Jacobi's trans. (1895, p.194) of *Utt*. 33.10:
cārittamohaṇaṃ kammaṃ, duvihaṃ tu viyāhiyaṃ |
kasāyamohaṇijjam tu nokasāyaṃ taheva ya || 10 ||

[33] See *SS* on *TS* 8:9 (10) and S.A. Jain's trans., p. 223-224.

[34] See above, p. 47ff.

by the activity of:

1) the 5 senses (*indriya*) - touch, taste, smell, sight, hearing,
2) the 4 passions (*kaṣāya*) - anger, pride, deceitfulness, greed,
3) the non-observance of the 5 vows (*avrata*),
4) the 25 activities (*kriyā*).

These correspond to the 5 causes of bondage (*Tattvārtha Sūtra* 8:1) in the following way:

1) the 5 *indriyas* correspond to *pramāda* (*indriya*, as Ohira points out, is explained in the *bhāṣya* on 6:5 (6) as *pañca pramattasyendriyāṇi)*,[35]
2) the 4 *kaṣāyas* correspond to *kaṣāya*,
3) *avrata* corresponds to *avirati*,
4) the 25 *kriyās* correspond to *mithyādarśana* (*mithyādarśana* is included as the twenty-fourth of the twenty-five *kriyās*, and *mithyātva* occurs as the second of the twenty-five).[36]

The fifth cause of bondage, *yoga*, is, as has been shown, defined by the other four (i.e. it is *yoga* with 'passion'), and it is activity (*yoga*) in the four categories enumerated which gives rise to *sāmparāyika karma*.

Comparing these two classifications, the question arises why it is that, when he comes to list the causes of *sāmparāyika karma* (*Tattvārtha Sūtra* 6:5 (6) = the 5 causes of bondage [*Tattvārtha Sūtra* 8:1]), Umāsvāti substitutes a list of 25 *kriyā* for *mithyādarśana*, which is only one item on that list.

According to Ohira, *kriyā* is repeatedly propounded in the early canonical works as the cause directly inviting *āsrava*, 'so Umāsvāti must have wanted to lay emphasis on it by counting twenty-five in all in place of *mithyātva* which is just part of them'.[37] But as Ohira herself has

---

35 Ohira p. 62.

36 See J.L. Jaini's list in his trans. of *TS* (1920) p. 126.

37 Ohira pp. 62-63.

already pointed out,[38] the inventory of *kriyā* 'has been worked out independently in the long Āgamic period', so this list is not Umāsvāti's invention. Rather, he is trying to integrate canonical material into his own division between binding and non-binding *yoga* - *yoga* with and without *kaṣāya*.[39] This process is revealed when the list of 25 *kriyā* is examined in detail, for not all the activities listed are compatible with their classification as giving rise to *sāmparāyika āsrava* and further bondage in *saṃsāra*.

The fourth *kriyā* in the list is given as '*īryāpatha*'.[40] The term '*īryāpatha*' has first occurred in this context in the previous aphorism (6:4 [5]) as the kind of *āsrava* which does not lead to transmigration, viz. that kind experienced by persons free from passions (in opposition to *sāmparāyika āsrava*, it gives rise to short-term karma). What then is its meaning at *Tattvārtha Sūtra* 6:5 (6), where it appears among the list of *kriyā* which give rise to *sāmparāyika karma*? If the meaning is the same, the two sūtras contradict each other.

Īryāpatha is derived from the root *īr* (II), meaning 'to go', 'to move'. Thus the *Sarvārthasiddhi* on *Tattvārtha Sūtra* 6:4 (5) comments, '*Īraṇam* means *īryā*, *yogo* or movement (vibrations). That karma which is caused by vibrations is called *īryāpatha*',[41] i.e. it is that (non-binding) karma which is caused by *yoga* alone, as opposed to that (binding) karma which is combined with passions (*kaṣāya*). Similarly, Sukhlalji comments:

> The reason why this *karma* of a duration of one *samaya* is called *īryāpathika* is that in the absence of all passion it is bound down merely through the *patha* or instrumentality of *īryā* or acts like

---

[38] Ibid. p. 62.

[39] On *kiriyā* / *kriyā*, cf. p. 40ff., above.

[40] See J.L. Jaini, (TS 1920) p. 125, on *TS* 6:5.

[41] S.A. Jain's trans., p. 169, of:
īraṇam īryā yogo gatir ity arthaḥ |
taddvārakam karma īryāpatham.

coming and going.[42]

However, when he comes to deal with *īryāpatha-kriyā* at *Tattvārtha Sūtra* 6:5 (6), Sukhlalji glosses it in exactly the same way, as '*kriyā* which causes either the bondage or the experiencing of *īryāpatha karma* - that is, *karma* of a duration of one *samaya*'. Such a reading leads to the incompatibility between the two sūtras outlined above (i.e. how can this be included in a list of *sāmparāyika karma* / *āsrava*, when it is apparently of the other type of *āsrava* / *karma* - *īryāpatha*?). Sukhlalji is aware of the problem, but is unable to resolve it. He comments on the exceptional position of *īryāpatha kriyā* on this list:

> Of the *kriyā*s ...(mentioned above)... there is only one - viz. *īryāpatha kriyā* - that is not *āsrava* for a *sāmparāyika karma*: as for the remaining ones since they are all impelled by *kaṣāya* they are all cause-of-bondage for *sāmparāyika karma*. And when all these *kriyā*s are here called *āsrava* for a *sāmparāyika karma* that is done simply because most of them (really all of them except *īryapathikī*) are in fact so.[43]

In other words, he can offer no explanation at all. But this does highlight the problem, and indicates that the list of *kriyā* was probably taken over in its entirety from an earlier source which does not fit the later division into *sāmparāyika* and *īryāpatha āsrava*.

In the context of a list of *kriyā*, the correct interpretation of *Tattvārtha Sūtra* 6:5 (6) is probably that of the *Sarvārthasiddhi*, viz. '*īryāpathakriyā* is walking carefully, by looking on the ground (for living beings which may be trodden and injured)'.[44] But this in turn raises two problems: 1) why does the same term apparently

---

[42] Sukhlalji (*TS* 1974), p. 233.

[43] Ibid. p. 236.

[44] S.A. Jain's trans., p. 170 (cf. J.L. Jain (1920) p. 125) of: *īryāpathanimitteryāpathakriyā* - *SS* on *TS* 6:5.

have two different technical meanings? 2) what does *īryāpatha kriyā* ('walking carefully') have to do with *kaṣāya* and bondage? (How can 'care in walking' be said to be characteristic of a *jīva* which has passions?)[45]

Suhklalji attempts to solve the first problem by running the two meanings together (as discussed above), but at the cost of making the two sūtras incompatible. The *Sarvārthasiddhi* 's commentary on *Tattvārtha Sūtra* 6:5 (6), that the 5 senses, the 4 passions, the 5 kinds of vowlessness, are the causes of influx, and that the 25 kinds of activity (*kriyā*) are the effects, similarly fails to remove the incompatibility between the two sūtras.[46] Again *īryāpathakriyā* as defined (and *samyaktva kriyā*) is out of place in such a list. One incoherence is replaced by another.

This incompatibility of *Tattvārtha Sūtra* 6:4 (5) with 6:5 (6) indicates that Umāsvāti is attempting to run together two different categories or lists, one developed later than the other (i.e. one containing the term *'īryāpatha'* as used at an earlier date and with a different meaning). In other words, Umāsvāti is taking over lists of *kriyā* from earlier sources - as Dixit remarks, all four categories of activities listed at *Tattvārtha Sūtra* 6:5 (6) were in 'more or less extensive use' independently of each other in the texts available to Umāsvāti[47] - without attempting to make them fit his definition of *sāmparāyika āsrava* (that pertaining to persons with passions), which he merely superimposes.

It is interesting to note that at *Tattvārtha Sūtra* 9:5 *īryāsamiti*, 'proper care in walking', is named as one of the

---

[45] There is a similar problem in explaining the presence *of samyaktva kriyā* - 'that which strengthens right belief' - in the list of *kriyā* (no.1). The other 23 *kriyā* are at least negative, although they are by no means obvious characteristics of the 'passionate'.

[46] See S.A. Jain p. 171: *etānīndriyādīni kāryakāraṇabhedādbhedamāpadyamānāni* - *SS* on *TS* 6:5.

[47] Dixit in the preface to Sukhlalji (*TS* 1974) pp. 7-8.

five types of *samiti* ('carefulness' or 'awareness'),[48] and that *samiti* is listed at *Tattvārtha Sūtra* 9:2 as one of the means to *saṃvara*. The latter is defined at *Tattvārtha Sūtra* 9:1 as *āsravanirodhaḥ* 'the stoppage of inflow' - presumably of that karmic matter which binds, since all activity causes *āsrava* as such. Thus the types of *samiti* clearly cannot belong to the category of *sāmparāyika karma* / *āsrava*. This provides further evidence that the linkage of *Tattvārtha Sūtra* 6:4 and 6:5 by Umāsvāti is incoherent, and that the original meaning of *īryāpatha* was 'care in walking', and only at a later date acquired the general meaning of 'short-term karma'.

It is perhaps significant that in Buddhism *īryāpatha* (Pali: *iryāpatha*) is more or less a technical term for 'the four postures' - walking, standing, sitting and lying.[49] If we apply this to the Jain case, it is easy to see that *īryāpathakriyā* would be care in all bodily movements, since the four postures cover all eventualities. Of the four, walking would of course be the most dangerous, but the others are presumably included as moments when a monk might easily do harm. Consequently, as *īryākriyā* refers to all an ascetic's movements, then it covers all the physical harm he might do, and thus it is responsible for the totality of his karma.

From this it is possible to see how *īryāpatha*'s change in meaning may have taken place. 'Care in walking', a term which includes all controlled ascetic activities, causes so little *hiṃsā* (although some is inevitable given the distribution of souls), and gives rise to such slight *āsrava*, that the quantity of karma accrued in this way is small enough to be shed in a single lifetime, and thus it does not lead to another birth (*sāmparāyika*). A distinction is therefore made between activities which lead to the influx of long-term karma, which is binding, and

---

48 See p. 69, above, for the other kinds of *samiti*.

49 See *Buddhist Dictionary* p. 81. They form a subject of contemplation and an exercise in mindfulness in the *Satipaṭṭhāna Sutta*.

those which lead to an influx of short-term karma, which is not. Such activities are all related directly to *hiṃsā* and non-*hiṃsā*, and especially to physical activity. That is to say, the behaviour of the ascetic is being distinguished absolutely from that of the non-ascetic or lay-person in terms of soteriological consequences.[50]

There are, therefore, two types of *āsrava*: that which occurs to *jīva*s in lay bodies, and that which occurs to those in the bodies of monks. The difference arises from the difference in behaviour between ascetics and others. Similarly, *īryāpatha* and *sāmparāyika* are, strictly speaking, two different quantities of karma, one accrued by mendicants and the other by householders. But the distinction is considered to be so fundamental that they become in effect two different types: short-term, and that which leads to a further rebirth. And in these soteriological terms, the division is absolute.

In this way *īryāpatha* acquires the general meaning of 'short-term karma'. At a later stage, it is given a specific technical definition, by Umāsvāti, as that influx of karma which is short-term because it is free from passion; it is therefore no longer directly linked to the amount of (physical) *hiṃsā* caused, but to internal states, motivation, etc. In other words, Umāsvāti's definition of *hiṃsā* - 'Injury is the destruction of life out of passion'[51] - bears witness to the development of a less exclusive, i.e. more lay-compatible ethic in the intervening period.[52] If this modei is correct, then the concept of *īryāpatha karma* developed in the period when *āsrava* and the resulting bondage of the *jīva* by karmic matter were still seen as the results of physical activity alone. In that case the instrumentality of *kaṣāya* would be a later accretion, based upon the

---

50 See the passages quoted from the *Viy*., etc., p. 40ff., above.

51 *pramattayogāt prāṇavyaparopaṇaṃ hiṃsā* - *TS* 7:13 (8) and *SS*.

52 Cf. *SS* on *TS* 7:22, where *TS* 7:13 is quoted as a justification of lay *sallekhanā*.

supposition that 'passion' or 'intention' can to some extent be controlled by someone who goes about his worldly business (i.e. it is a matter of attitude), whereas restraint of physical activity demands a particular kind of 'extra-worldly' ascetic discipline. And as will now be made clear, the practice of monks and nuns remains unaffected by this internalisation, which effectively comes to function as a means of giving the laity a theoretical foothold on the path to salvation.

2.4 *'Activity' in the Tattvārtha Sūtra*

According to *Tattvārtha Sūtra* 6:7, *jīva* (what is sentient, i.e. the soul) and *ajīva* (what is insentient) constitute the *adhikaraṇāḥ* - the 'substrata' - of influx; in other words, the causes of influx. Or as the *Sarvārthasiddhi* puts it, being *adhikaraṇa* is 'the condition of being the instruments of injury and so on', and thus the condition of being instrumental in the influx of binding karmic matter.[53] Commenting on this, Sukhlalji says that 'both *jīva* and *ajīva* are called *adhikaraṇa* - that is to say, a means, implement or weapon of karmic bondage'.[54] This seems to make 'karmic bondage' the active principle which needs the *adhikaraṇa* in order to express itself, rather than the *jīva* being the active principle. But by the very fact of being available for *āsrava*, the *jīva* is in a sense instrumental in its own bondage. Karmic bondage can only become 'active' if the *jīva* behaves in certain ways (enumerated at *Tattvārtha Sūtra* 6:8), and it is in this sense that the *jīva* is the 'substratum' - a reading which is compatible with the usual meaning of *adhikaraṇa* as 'that in which anything happens'.

The ways in which a *jīva* can cause injury are numbered as 108, as follows:

> The substratum of the living is planning to commit violence,

---

[53] S.A Jain's trans., p. 172, of: *hiṃsādyupakaraṇabhāva.*

[54] Sukhlalji's commentary on *TS*, p. 239.

preparation for it and commmencement of it, by activity, doing, causing it to be done, and approval of it, and issuing from the passions, which are three, three, three and four respectively. [*Tattvārtha Sūtra* 6:8 (9)][55] (These are the causes of the influx of karma in general; specific types of karma have, of course, the same general causes but also have specific causes which are subtypes of the general causes.)[56]

With the help of the commentaries,[57] *Tattvārtha Sūtra* 6:8 (9) can be presented in a schematic form [see Table]. The notably new thing about this schema or formulation, compared with those associated with its component parts (which, as we have seen, are scattered throughout the early Śvetāmbara canon), is that whichever way one reads it, left to right or right to left, passion (*kaṣāya*) is instrumental in causing violence, and thus *āsrava* and bondage. Note that nothing is said here of action without passion; it is clear that for Umāsvāti *ārambha* means premeditated, violent action (*hiṃsā*). In other words, the action which binds is violent action *engendered by passions*; from which it may be inferred that passionless, non-violent action does not bind (although it does cause an influx of matter into the soul in the form of *īryāpatha karma*). And it is clear from *Tattvārtha Sūtra* 6:4-6 that this enumeration of the 108 ways in which influx can be caused to a *jīva* refers specifically to the person who is actuated by passions (*sakaṣāya*) (*Tattvārtha Sūtra* 6:4).

This is further clarified by the *Sarvārthasiddhi* on *Tattvārtha Sūtra* 6:8 which, taking for its example 'bodily impulsion' (*kāya-saṃraṃbha*), i.e. the determination to do violence through bodily activity (one of the three *yoga*s),

---

[55] S.A. Jain's trans., p. 172, fn. 1, with minor alterations of: *ādyaṃ saṃrambhasamārambhārambhayogakṛtakāritānumatakaṣāya-viśeṣais tristristriścatuścaikaśaḥ* [*TS* 6:8 (9)].

[56] See *TS* 6:10f.

[57] See *SS*, J.L.Jaini (1920), Sukhlalji (*TS* 1974).

subdivides it as follows:

Bodily impulsion performed (*kṛta*) by anger (*krodha*)
Bodily impulsion performed by pride (*māna*)
Bodily impulsion made by deceitfulness (*māyā*)
Bodily impulsion made by greed (*lobha*)
(i.e. all done by oneself)

Bodily impulsion instigated (*kārita*) by anger
.... by pride
.... by deceitfulness
.... by greed
(i.e. done by one's agent)

Bodily impulsion approved (*anumata*) by anger
.... by pride
.... by deceitfulness
.... by greed
(i.e. done by others with one's approval).

It is also interesting to note that it is no longer simply the act of doing violence which is binding, but also the impulsion or intention to do it, and the preparation for it (*saṃrambha* and *samārambha*) (*Tattvārtha Sūtra* 6:8). This threefold division of *hiṃsā* may be seen as the logical corollary of, or complement to, the development of the idea of the instrumentality of *kaṣāya* as the binding agent, for passion may be as strong or stronger in intention and preparation as in outcome (actual violence).[58]

Tattvārtha Sūtra 6:9 (10) deals with the *adhikaraṇa* of

---

58 These three - *saṃrambha*, *samārambha*, and *ārambha* - are also to be found at, for instance, *Utt.* 24.19ff., although their meaning there may be somewhat different if Jacobi's trans. (1895, p. 135) is followed. Schubring quotes the commentary which understands the terms to mean - as in the *TS* - 'two stages of preparation and the performance of forbidden thinking, speaking and acting' (1962, para. 173 / p. 304). But again there is no connection with a technical mechanism of bondage such as Umāsvāti's *kaṣāya* doctrine.

the *ajīva* type. It would seem to refer to *pudgala* (matter) which can in some way aid, or be manipulated by the individual to bring about karmic influx. This substratum is divided into:

2 (kinds of) *nirvartanā* ('production' / 'performance'):
- i) *mūlaguṇa* - of body, speech, mind, inhalation, exhalation,
- ii) *uttaraguṇa* - making objects of wood, clay, etc., pictures and statues. (That is to say, the *mūlaguṇas* are what the body performs naturally, and the *uttaraguṇas* are what the body does by extension.)

4 (kinds of) *nikṣepa* ('placing' / 'putting down'):
- i) *apratyavekṣita* - 'without seeing'
- ii) *duṣpramārjita* - 'without cleansing of dust, etc.'
- iii) *sahasa* - 'hurriedly'
- iv) *anābhoga* - 'inattentively'/'putting something where it ought not to be put'.

2 (kinds of) *saṃyoga* ('combining' / 'mixing up'):
- i) *bhaktapāna* - 'food and drink'/'different foodstuffs'
- ii) *upakaraṇa* - 'mixing up things - implements, clothes, etc.'

3 (kinds of) *nisarga* ('movement'/ 'urging'/ 'operating'):
- i) *kāya* - 'by body'
- ii) *vacana* - 'by speech'
- iii) *manas* - 'by mind'

[Definitions taken from *Sarvārthasiddhi*.]

As Ohira has pointed out, the materials used in Ch. 6 of the *Tattvārtha Sūtra* are widely dispersed throughout the canonical texts.[59] And it would seem that in dividing the substratum (*adhikaraṇa)* of influx into two, *jīva* and *ajīva*, Umāsvāti is either drawing on two different canonical lists or, more likely, in making this division he is expanding his

[59] Ohira p. 61.

own *kaṣāya* doctrine in the first *adhikaraṇa* - that of *jīva* - and merely repeating the received (ascetic) *adhikaraṇa* of influx in the *ajīva* list. In other words, the division of the mechanism of bondage into two types of karma, that which causes bondage - which 'sticks' or adheres - and that which does not, is prepared for or justified by this division into two types of *adhikaraṇa* ; mere physical action of a mechanical kind, and motivated, impassioned action, are separated. Such a separation would not be necessary unless the soteriological consequences of there being two substrata of influx (i.e. two types of karma producing action) were perceived as different. Both can bind, but Umāsvāti, in attempting to combine the two, puts emphasis on the first: it becomes a question of behaviour *and* attitude, not just of behaviour.

This opens the way for the later commentators and their preoccupation with attitude. Furthermore, there is no logical reason why there should be influx of two types of karma - binding and non-binding - unless the *kaṣāya* doctrine is a later addition. For if the idea that it is only passionate action which binds had been there in the earliest form of the doctrine, there would have been no reason to posit a complex doctrine of 'stickiness', etc.: Jains would simply have been able to say that activity accompanied by passion causes influx of karma and other activity does not. (The original doctrine must have been that physical activity alone was the source of karma and thus binding.) It is clear, therefore, that there are two layers of doctrine here, and that the superimposition of one upon the other marks a change for which there are historical rather than logical (i.e. strictly doctrinal) reasons.

Returning to the *adhikaraṇa* of the *ajīva* type enumerated at *Tattvārtha Sūtra* 6:9 (10), it is probable that this list is based upon the original rules for ascetics in their wandering life. In fact all the categories are to do with *hiṃsā* caused by physical activity, and relate very closely to the 5 *samiti*. These are enumerated at *Tattvārtha Sūtra* 9:5, where they are listed as one category of the modes of behaviour which lead to *saṃvara*, the cessation of influx (*Tattvārtha Sūtra* 9:2).[60]

The 5 *samiti* are:

i) *īryā-samiti* - care (awareness) in walking,
ii) *bhāṣā-samiti* - care in speaking,
iii) *eṣaṇā-samiti* - care in accepting alms,
iv) *ādāna-nikṣepaṇa-samiti* - care in picking things up and in putting them down,
v) *utsarga-samiti* - care in performing excretory functions.[61]

Comparing this list with that of the four divisions of the *adhikaraṇa* of the *ajīva* type, given above, the following correspondences can be discerned:

1) *īryā-* and *bhāṣā-samiti* correspond to the 2 *nirvartanā*,
2) *eṣaṇā-samiti* corresponds to *saṃyoga*,
3) *ādāna-nikṣepana-samiti* corresponds to *nikṣepa,*
4) *utsarga-samiti* corresponds to *nisarga*.

That is to say, the 5 *samiti* are the antidotes to the 4 *adhikaraṇa* of the *ajīva* type: they advocate care in relation

---

60 It is worth noting that, according to Ohira p. 65, *saṃvara* is not defined in the canonical texts in the fashion expressed by Umāsvāti at *TS* 9:1 (as the stoppage of the inflow of karmic matter into the soul - *āsravanirodhaḥ saṃvaraḥ*). Nor do the sixfold *saṃvaradvāras* (*TS* 9:2) occur as a set category in the canon; rather, they were formulated by Umāsvāti. They are, nevertheless, predominantly physical in character. The first among them is *gupti*, defined at *TS* 9:4 as *samyagyoganigraho gupti* - 'restraint / prevention is proper control (*nigraha*) over *yoga*' (i.e. over the activities of body, speech and mind). Thus it is still restraint of activity which is seen as the pre-eminent means to release (as opposed to attaining a better re-birth), rather than restraint of 'passions' as such. Also note that *gupti* here, as restraint / control of the three *yogas*, would appear to have the meaning normally assigned to '*yoga*' in other schools.

61 Cf. Pāli *sati*, the 'mindfulness' or 'awareness' of early Buddhism. *Samiti* may be a backformation from this, therefore having the sense of 'awareness'.

to matter. Taking each of these in turn:

1) *īryā-samiti* and *bhāṣā-samiti* refer respectively to care in walking and care in speaking. The connection of these with the *ajīva-adhikaraṇa nirvartanā* ('performance'), which is divided into *mūlaguṇa* and *uttaraguṇa*, seems at first to be only partial. That is to say, the connection holds in so far as, if *mūlaguṇa* refers to what the body performs or does naturally, simply by being the body, and *uttaraguṇa* to what it does by extension, then *īryā* and *bhāṣā-samiti* correspond to the first two *mūlaguṇa*, the 'performance' of body and speech (i.e. one should take care in walking and speaking). This would leave the *mūlaguṇa* of mind, inhalation and exhalation, and the *uttaraguṇa* as later additions to, or elaborations of, the original doctrine, probably to meet with circumstances previously unforeseen (e.g. the manufacture of images, etc.). ('Mind' may well have been added simply because the formula 'body, speech, and mind' had become a cliché.)[62]

2) *eṣaṇā-samiti* refers to care in accepting alms, and clearly corresponds to the *ajīva adhikaraṇa saṃyoga*, although the latter has the extended sense of mixing up or (literally) contact with implements, clothes, etc. (*upakaraṇa*), as well as mixing up or contact with food and drink (*bhaktapāna*).

3) *ādāna-nikṣepana-samiti* corresponds to the *ajīva adhikaraṇa nikṣepaṇa*, again elaborated into four ways of putting things down carelessly.

4) *utsarga-samiti* is the rule of conduct which

---

62 Note that *mūlaguṇa* in this context should not be confused with the '8 basic restraints' prescribed for the Jaina layperson, also known as *mūlaguṇa*, viz. abstaining from partaking of meat, alcohol, honey, or any of five kinds of figs (see *JPP* p. 167). This definition of *mūlaguṇa* does not occur in the *TS*.

prescribes care in performing excretory functions. The *ajīva adhikaraṇa nisarga* is defined by the commentators as 'urging', 'movement', and 'operating'.[63] Thus, according to the *Sarvārthasiddhi*, 'Urging (behaviour) is of three kinds, urging the body, speech and mind to act'.[64] It should be noted, however, that this threefold division is not made by Umāsvāti himself, and that *nisarga* as well as *utsarga* can have the meaning 'evacuation of excrement'. This may indicate that Umāsvāti's commentators (and possibly Umāsvāti himself) had the *saṃvaradvāra gupti* in mind when they defined the *ajīva adhikaraṇa nisarga* in this way. *Gupti* is defined (at *Tattvārtha Sūtra* 9:4) as *samyagyoganigrahaḥ,* proper control (*nigraha*) over activity (*yoga*) - i.e. control over the activities of body, speech, and mind, which would be the antidote to urging the body, speech, and mind to act (the three kinds of *nisarga*).

The likelihood that *nisarga* originally referred to evacuation of excrement is strengthened by its incompatibility (as it is defined by the commentators) with the other *adhikaraṇa-ajīva*. For the presence of *manas*, regarded as denoting the operation of the mind of an individual, introduces the idea of intention, of internal 'action' into a list which refers to the physical manipulation of matter (*pudgala*).[65]

It is possible to conclude, therefore, that of Umāsvāti's categories *ajīva* and *jīva adhikaraṇa*, the former was derived from the original monastic rules concerned with preventing the influx of binding karma, since it is occupied

---

63 S.A. Jain p.174; J.L. Jaini (1920); Sukhlalji (*TS* 1974).

64 S.A. Jain's trans. p. 174 of *SS* on *TS* 6:9: *nisargas trividhaḥ - kāyanisargādhikaraṇaṃ vāg... mano...*, etc.

65 Such incompatibility is, of course, reduced if *yoga* is read in the sense suggested by Dixit (see above) - viz. as doing an act oneself, having it done through one's agent, or allowing it to be done by someone else; but that is not the way the commentators take it.

entirely with physical activity and the *hiṃsā* caused by it. In other words, the list of *ajīva-adhikaraṇa* is based on the canonical rules for those wandering ascetics whose primary concern was not with a particular attitude of mind, or intention, but with the avoidance of any physical action which might cause harm to any of the myriad *jīva*s by which they were surrounded. The latter (*jīva-adhikaraṇa*) is added by Umāsvāti to account for the proliferation of karmic positions that less than perfect ascetics, or lay people, can find themselves in.

2.5 *Parigraha: the householder and the kaṣāya doctrine*

In the developed *kaṣāya* doctrine (the one which is presented by Umāsvāti) what was once a single instrument of bondage (viz. violent or harming activity engendered by *lobha* and *parigraha*) has now become two: bondage is caused by passion (*kaṣāya*) and harming activity. It is no longer simply the case that passions, or *lobha*, etc., lead to violent activity, rather violent activity is now not even considered 'violent' *unless* it is accompanied by passion; and thus, without passion, it is no longer binding either. The notion, expressed in the earliest textual layers, that even accidental *hiṃsā* is binding, has been removed. How is this development, which is at the heart of the tension between later doctrine and practice, to be explained?

As has been shown, in the earliest texts *parigraha* or *lobha* is considered, along with violence (*ārambha*), to be the worst kind of behaviour, and such *parigraha* or 'greed' is inextricable from the life of the householder. Indeed, for the composers of monastic texts such as the *Dasaveyāliya Sutta*, *parigraha* is precisely what defines the state of being a householder. Thus, according to these sources, there is very little possibility other than a bad rebirth for a householder. The householder's state is one of *parigraha*, and thus of *ārambha*, simply because he is a householder;

only the monk or nun has the potential to cease from *parigraha* and *ārambha*, and thus attain *mokṣa*. The idea that acts involving the employment of human and animal labour were particularly sinful, and others less so, does not appear in the earliest doctrinal layer. There, all acts which harm *jīvas* are considered to be effectively binding. Indeed, the householder only puts in an appearance in these texts to act as a kind of lighthouse, warning the ascetic away from, or at least setting severe limits to, social contact. The householder's inevitable rebirth and suffering are pointed out, like wreckages, as a warning to those who come too close or are tempted to return to life in the world.

In later Jaina theory, however, the pious householder is considered to be on the same soteriological continuum as the monk: the former may take partial vows (*aṇuvrata*) which are seen as preparing him or her for the eventual assumption of the *mahāvrata* of the mendicant.[66] Thus while the *aṇuvrata* of *ahiṃsā*, which applies only to *trasa* beings, can never be soteriologically sufficient - it cannot lead in itself to liberation - it is nevertheless a step upwards on the ladder which leads to *mokṣa*; one can expect at least a better rebirth. Such a progression is never contemplated in the very earliest textual layers, where the idea of a 'pious' householder is not even admitted. Indeed, such a concept would be a contradiction in terms.

Moreover, according to later Jaina doctrine, *parigraha* is defined as *mūrcchā*,[67] 'infatuation' or the 'delusion of possession'.[68] In the *Sarvārthasiddhi* *mūrcchā* is glossed as 'not turning away from the aims of acquiring and keeping conscious and unconscious externals, such as cows, buffaloes, jewels, pearls, possessions, etc., and

---

66 See *JPP* p. 160ff.
67 *TS* 7:17.
68 *JPP* p. 177.

internal conditions, such as desire, etc.'.[69] The *Sarvārthasiddhi* goes on to say, delusion 'is the root of all imperfections. When someone has the idea "This is mine", the need to take care of it, etc., (also) arises. And from that violence necessarily follows'.[70] And as P.S. Jaini points out, the term *parigraha* is 'further made synonymous with the four passions (*kaṣāya*) and nine sentiments (*no-kaṣāya*) ...; these are known as the "internal possessions" and their renunciation (the avoidance of activities which generate them) constitutes the essence of the aparigrahavrata' (the fifth *aṇuvrata* of the layman according to later Jaina doctrine).[71] This kind of renunciation is, however, not considered possible until a person has detached himself from the 'external possessions' - land, houses, silver, gold, etc. So the layman expresses his seriousness about *aparigraha* by setting limits to what he may own (i.e. he gives himself less to be attached to and, at the same time, engenders an attitude of non-attachment towards what he already has).[72] (It is interesting to note, however, that, even at this relatively late doctrinal stage, the renunciation of passion is approached, not via a direct confrontation with the internal state, but through the renunciation of activities

---

[69] *bāhyānāṃ gomahiṣamaṇimuktāphalādīnāṃ cetanācetanānām ābhyantarāṇāṃ ca rāgādīnām upadhīnāṃ saṃrakṣaṇārjana-saṃskārādilakṣaṇāvyāvṛttir mūrcchā* - *SS* on *TS* 7:17.

[70] *tanmūlāḥ sarve doṣāḥ |*
mamedam iti hi sati saṃkalpe saṃrakṣaṇādayaḥ saṃjāyante |
tatra ca hiṃsā 'vaśyaṃbhāvinī | - *SS* on *TS* 7:17.

Cf. J.L. Jaini (1920) on *TS* 7:17: ...'worldly objects are said to be Parigraha because they are the external causes of internal attachment'.

[71] *JPP* p. 177; the *aṇuvrata aparigraha* is defined variously as 'non-possession', 'non-attachment', 'the delusion of possession', 'harbouring false notions of "this is mine"', etc. See discussion of *Das.* 8:37, p. 37ff., above, for the relation of *parigraha* and *kaṣāya*. *No-kaṣāya*, 'sentiments', are nine subsidiary passions, such as laughter, fear sexual cravings, etc. - see *JPP* p. 120 for a full list.

[72] See *JPP* p. 177.

which are thought to generate it.)

As P.S. Jaini puts it:

> By undertaking the aparigrahavrata, a Jaina layman systematically reduces his tendencies to fall into such passions; thus he protects his soul from increased karmic entanglement and lays the groundwork for complete nonattachment, the path of the mendicant.[73]

How does this change in attitude towards the householder relate to the development of the *kaṣāya* doctrine? The following hypothesis is offered.

In the early karma doctrine, only one train of events is necessary for karmic bondage: *parigraha* or *lobha* (including the other passions) causes *hiṃsā*, and *hiṃsā* causes bondage. (It should be noted that *parigraha* is by no means the *only* way in which *hiṃsā* can be brought about, but it is seen as being the major threat to the monk, and the one most difficult to counteract.) In the developed doctrine, presented by Umāsvāti, for bondage to take place (i.e. for karma to attach itself to the *jīva*) there have to be two separate occurrences: 1) there has to be *yoga* ('activity') which causes an influx of karmic matter, and 2) there has to be *kaṣāya* which causes that karmic matter to adhere to the *jīva*. Thus 'greed' (*lobha* or *parigraha*) - the passion subsuming all others in the earliest texts -, which was previously seen as being synonymous with a particular way of life (the householder's), becomes in the later doctrine (under the technical term '*kaṣāya*') an internal process or attitude. From being the defining characteristic of a particular way or condition *of* life, it comes to denote anattitude *towards* life; the emphasis is shifted from the external to the internal, from the social to the individual. In effect, renunciation is partially internalised.

---

[73] *JPP* p. 178.

In this way, what was once an anti-householder doctrine becomes one which accommodates and compromises with the householder's way of life. In other words, *parigraha* and *aparigraha* have been redefined as attitudes, inner states; therefore it is possible, at least in theory, to retain possessions without necessarily incurring bondage. With the right attitude (non-attachment), possessions do not necessarily lead to *hiṃsā* and bondage.

Nevertheless, Jaina monks and nuns, by definition non-householders, continue to concentrate on behaviour: their attitude to the external world is significant predominantly in so far as it governs the way in which they behave in that world. Thus, in practice, for the ascetic, attitude remains a contributory rather than a necessary factor in liberation or bondage, in the same way that *kaṣāya* was in the earliest doctrine. (But as with *kaṣāya*, that of course makes it is no less demanding of the most careful attention.)

It can be seen from this that the later doctrine, which accommodates the householder, is never completely integrated with the earlier one. And as we have shown, there are instances in the *Tattvārtha Sūtra* where the latter pushes through the surface of the former to bring about an apparent inconsistency. To take a relevant example, at *Tattvārtha Sūtra* 9:6 *śauca* (purity) is named as one of the constituents or types of that *dharma* which, in turn, is one of the causes of *saṃvara* (the stoppage of karmic influx). Commenting on this, the *Sarvārthasiddhi* specifically defines *śauca* as 'complete freedom from greed'.[74] As has been made clear above, greed (*parigraha / lobha*) was considered by the earliest surviving canonical sources as one of the two worst sins; moreover, it was considered to be the defining characteristic of the householder's way of life. It is greed which causes a person to undertake

---

74 *prakarṣaprāptalobhān nivṛttiḥ śaucam* - *SS* on *TS* 9:6.

harming activity. Thus absence of greed means the absence of harming activity and of the potential for it. It is this condition which is considered to be a state of purity, and by definition it is only the monk or nun who experiences this greed-free state. In other words, in the earliest texts greed is seen as *the* polluting, *hiṃsā*-initiating, bondage-causing vice. This connection is retained in the *Tattvārtha Sūtra*, where *lobha* is, by implication, synonymous with impurity, and freedom from greed is defined as *śauca*, although now the context has been internalised, in that the emphasis is placed on the stoppage of *kaṣāya*, the attitude which is seen as instrumental in bondage. However, it is clear that originally the distinction between 'pure' and 'impure' was an existential distinction between the life of the monk and the life of the householder. And this earlier distinction resurfaces in the *Sarvārthasiddhi* when *śauca* is defined as 'freedom from greed'.

There may also be a suggestion here of a polemical statement aimed at Brahmanical ideas of what constitutes purity and *dharma*. That is to say, the Jains are reinterpreting *śauca* in a manner which shows that *they* are the truly pure, and it is the brahmans who are succumbing to greed, the antithesis of purity, just when they claim to be most pure. In both cases, impurity leads to further karmic bondage; the difference arises over how purity is defined. Brahman sacrificers cause *hiṃsā*, therefore they are impure. *Hiṃsā* (= impurity) is generated by greed, i.e., greed for results from the sacrifice. It is sacrifice, the characteristic mark of the *śrauta* brahman, which makes the brahman impure in the Jaina's eyes. And from the Jaina ascetic's point of view, the brahman is doubly impure, for in order to be qualified to sacrifice he has to be a householder.

In short, the behaviour of Jaina ascetics continues to be conditioned by the earliest beliefs about the conditions under which bondage takes place. (This is, of course, progressively true of advanced lay behaviour, as it approaches, through the *pratimā*s, etc., the ascetic ideal.)[75] They remain, above all, concerned with the effects of physical activity. Thus, while from the ordinary householder's point of view there is a continuum between his *aṇuvrata*s and the *mahāvrata*s of the monk, from the monk's point of view there is still an absolute distinction. This basic incompatibility of the two ways of life underlies Umāsvāti's attempt in the *Tattvārtha Sūtra* to reconcile them.

---

[75] See *JPP* p. 186 for a full list if the eleven *pratimās*. Note especially: 8) *ārambhatyāga-pratimā*, the stage of abandonment of household activity, and 9) *parigrahatyāga-pratimā*, the stage of abandonment of acquisitiveness (by formally disposing of one's property).

3
Conclusions

Commenting on the juxtaposition of the archaic and the classical in Jaina doctrine - on the tradition's incompletely worked-out philosophy and its tendency to fantastic proliferation - Frauwallner concludes that all this is the result of fundamental adherence to the doctrines proclaimed by Mahāvīra.[1] Because the Jina is omniscient, his doctrines, once uttered, could not be changed or displaced, and that 'explains the many antique features which the system has preserved'.[2] There was no room for consistent developments in thought, or for 'the erection of a uniformly compact doctrinal edifice'.[3] In these circumstances, according to Frauwallner, it is not surprising that wherever the 'traditionally handed-down dogmatics showed a lacuna', fantasy was allowed to flourish without a check.[4] In short, Jaina thought after Mahāvīra was paralysed by the need to preserve the often archaic content of Mahāvīra's teaching in more sophisticated religious and philosophical circumstances.

There is evidently some truth in this analysis, but as it stands it remains an inadequate explanation because Frauwallner has divorced Jaina beliefs and doctrines from practice; he is concerned with Jainism as a 'philosophy' rather than as a religion. The two levels of doctrine regarding activity, the influx of karma and bondage, which are imposed upon each other and which fit so incompletely, are the result of two different historical processes - within Jainism and within Indian religion in general - which come together over a particular period. These two processes may, for short, be labelled 'Early Jainism' and 'Umāsvāti's

---

[1] Frauwallner (1973) Vol. II, p. 213.

[2] Ibid.

[3] Ibid.

[4] Ibid. p. 214.

Jainism'. By 'Early Jainism', is understood that exclusively ascetic, mendicant path to liberation which appeared at approximately the same time as other heterodox systems, notably Buddhism, partly as a reaction to Brahmanical religion, but, in Jainism's case, perhaps mostly as a refinement of an even earlier, archaic asceticism.[5] 'Umāsvāti's Jainism', on the other hand, belongs to a much wider social world, in the sense that it is an attempt to systematize, as far as possible, Jaina doctrine for the whole Jaina community, and perhaps most of all for a growing lay audience. That is to say, Umāsvāti is attempting to reconcile the social fact of an active lay following, and the need to preserve such a following, with a body of canonical texts, the oldest and most important components of which (containing perhaps the teachings of Mahāvīra himself) were directed specifically at ascetics who had renounced the householder's world precisely because, as the doctrines expounded in those texts make clear, there was no possibility whatsoever of obtaining liberation within it.

It is also significant that Umāsvāti is writing in Sanskrit. Thus he is not writing simply for the benefit of his own community, but also in order to dispute with outsiders, proponents of rival *darśana*s. In other words, for Jaina practice to be preserved and defended, its doctrinal superstructure has to be defended. Moreover, since Jaina renouncers keep moving, and are unlikely to know or learn Sanskrit, the very nature of Umāsvāti's enterprise suggests that it is concerned with problems in the wider society.

The whole history of Jaina doctrinal development is one of the struggle to prevent the clearly delineated but extremely demanding requirements of the ascetic's path coming into direct conflict with the life led by the Jaina lay-person, when the practice of both ascetic and laity is re-coded in doctrinal terms. It is precisely this conflict and the need to avoid it which leads, on the one hand, to the

---

[5]See Basham for some discussion of 'Jainism' before Mahāvīra; also R. Williams 1966, pp. 2-6.

proliferation of doctrines to do with karma and bondage, and, on the other, ensures that no complete systematization is possible.

As has been made clear, in the very earliest texts, where there is effectively no alternative to extreme asceticism other than a bad rebirth, there is no need for doctrine to be worked out in any great detail. From the ascetic point of view, which is the 'Jain' point of view at this stage (the earliest texts were composed by and for ascetics), the chance of a lay person attaining a heavenly rebirth is considered so remote as to be practically impossible. Proliferation of heavens and hells tends to occur only when a system becomes concerned with something more than simple liberation, i.e. when it acquires a lay doctrine. And only then do ideas like that of *śubha yoga* leading to *puṇya karma* become intelligible. (When the path to liberation is as demanding as the Jain one, ascetics too, of course, become interested in the higher *saṃsāric* worlds.)

Given the basic teachings of early Jainism on the multiplicity of *jīvas*, *ahiṃsā*, and the bondage of material karma, then the ascetic's path is theoretically very clear: he or she must give up all harming activity. Whether this in effect means all activity, or whether there is a distinction between activity of different kinds, is not clear from the earliest texts. It is probably taken for granted that in this context any action which harms *jīvas* is meant, and thus potentially, at the very least, any physical activity is harmful.

There is, therefore, a sense in which, beyond a few normative teachings of early Jainism, all doctrinal elaboration is aimed at a lay audience, both to justify their position as laity and to put them on the soteriological 'ladder'. This is reflected by the fact that doctrines concerning the internalization of significant action, which if carried to their logical conclusion might be thought to undermine, or even be fatal to ascetic practice, actually make no difference to the ways in which monks and nuns behave. They go on acting as though the overwhelmingly important thing is physical activity, or the lack of it, in the external world: attitude is only important in so far as it leads to certain kinds of behaviour.

The doctrinal content of the earliest canonical literature is simply intended to reinforce ascetic practice. The problem for Umāsvāti is to reduce the incompatibility of a purely ascetic 'doctrine' with the householder's life, without juxtaposing them in such a way that they are seen to be openly opposed. In other words, he has to systematize, but he has to do so incompletely or imperfectly.

It is this necessary incompleteness which gives rise to much of the problematic and poorly fitting terminology in the *Tattvārtha Sūtra*. Two different historical layers, reflected in two different kinds of behaviour, are imperfectly systematized in the one work by a process of partial internalization, and therefore of gradation, of the path to liberation. This is most evident when Umāsvāti takes earlier 'lists', or concepts, and attempts to deposit them without change in new categories. It is not surprising, therefore, that later commentators have struggled without success to integrate then fully, and that in the process original meanings have been obscured or lost. The problematic nature of some Jaina terminology thus arises out of the need to revise earlier ideas in, and for, a more sophisticated and complex religious milieu, while retaining that canonical authority which is expressed in the ideal of ascetic practice. In other words, such terminological problems stem from the extreme asceticism of early Jaina practice and its incompatibility with lay practice: the two positions are so antithetical that they cannot both be preserved and at the same time fully incorporated within the same system.

The extent to which Umāsvāti internalizes earlier doctrine, and the effect of this process on both lay and ascetic practice, requires some further discussion. According to classical Jaina theory, it is possible for a lay person to ascend by stages to the threshold of total asceticism, and then pass through mendicancy to liberation.

This is expressed theoretically by a soteriological gradation or ladder, whose rungs are the 14 *guṇasthāna*, the stages through which an individual passes on the way to *mokṣa*.[6] Most, although not all, of the component parts of the *guṇasthāna* doctrine are known to Umāsvāti, but they are not assembled into a *śreṇi* or 'ladder' by him; while various karmic states are described individually, they are not placed in a hierarchy.[7]

According to the developed theory, the aspirant gradually eliminates the passions, and it is only finally, in the instant prior to his death, that *yoga*, the last cause of bondage, comes to an end.[8] Thus the problem of action - of how not to jeopardize one's ultimate liberation while at the same time acting to a greater or lesser extent in the world - is overcome by making 'activity' as such (i.e. unmotivated, unimpelled activity, even down to the beating of the heart) a barrier to liberation only on the final rungs of the ladder, which are usually taken as meaning the last moments of life. (There are more immediate barriers to be overcome before that stage is reached.) One of the reasons theoreticians after Umāsvāti are able to shift *yoga* up the ladder in this way is because the *kaṣāya* doctrine makes the lower rungs the province of passions and their elimination. In other words, such a doctrine makes room for the theory of a graduated path of spiritual development, *culminating* in the elimination of all activity. This should be compared with the earliest, ascetic 'Jainism' - that of the Jaina monks - where the elimination of harming activity, the vow of total *ahiṃsā*, is regarded as the pre- or accompanying-condition of any spiritual development.

The stages of spiritual progress which lead the layman

---

6 For the full list, see *JPP* pp. 272-3.

7 See Ohira pp. 99-103. Also on the evolution of the *guṇasthāna* doctrine, see Dixit 1971, pp. 14-15. The doctrine as later developed is mentioned in the *Bhāṣya*, which, as we have seen, is probably later than the *TS* and not by Umāsvāti (p. 46-47, above); the *SS* on *TS* 9.1 has a complete list.

8 See *JPP* p. 273.

into the sixth *guṇasthāna*, which is the stage of taking the ascetic's vows (*mahāvrata*), are further subdivided into 11 *pratimā*.[9] In other words, certain kinds of behaviour and attitude will enable the aspirant to make some progress towards liberation, but these have to be superseded or improved upon as he moves up to the next 'rung'.

The theoretical stress on internal discipline as the chief means of ascending the ladder clearly reflects the difficulty of achieving a completely inactive state short of death (i.e. short of the ideal goal of ritual death by fasting, *sallekhanā*).[10] It is true that to achieve final liberation the complete cessation of first external activity and then all activity has to be achieved, but only at the very end of life. For the laity, therefore, *yoga* has been effectively down-graded as a force in bondage - or, to be accurate, 'up-graded' so far that it is only to be reckoned with at the top of the soteriological ladder. It seems that they scarcely have to worry about it.

For the ascetic, however, the emphasis of the earliest doctrine on the centrality of physical action *vis à vis* bondage, keeps its force. The partially internalized doctrine, where what counts most is intention, is at a lower level soteriologically than the physical and material concerns of the monk. What distinguishes the monk most clearly from the lay person in 'classical' Jainism, in terms of daily practice, is still the strength of the monk's vow (*vrata*) concerning *ahiṃsā*.[11] And the authority for this *mahāvrata* of *ahiṃsā* is derived predominantly from the earliest canonical texts (the *Āyāraṃga*, etc.), i.e. it is the original doctrine concerning non-violence, aimed exclusively at renunciants.

It should be remembered, however, that the canonical texts, which reflect the monks' view of the world, and the *Tattvārtha Sūtra,* which (as I argue) reflects a wider view,

---

[9] See *JPP* p. 186 for a full list; and R. Williams 1963, pp.172-181.

[10] On *sallekhanā*, see *JPP* pp. 227-223.

[11] See *JPP* p. 241.

co-exist. The latter does not replace the former. This reflects the way in which the two doctrines concerning bondage co-exist within the one religious system. There are two different authoritative references, depending upon whether one is a householder or a monk; but these only conflict when they are viewed together, theoretically; in practice, the perspective is always from within one or the other of these.

Nevertheless, even within the new soteriological gradation, it is only necessary to look at the vows (*vrata* - literally, 'restraints') which constitute even the lay *pratimā*, in order to see what is considered important in terms of practice, as opposed to theory. The emphasis of these is heavily ascetic, i.e. they involve above all the restriction of physical activity. In fact they constitute a progression towards the full asceticism of the monk or nun, carrying the *vratin* further and further away from ordinary householder existence.[12] So whatever the theoretical stress on internal discipline or dispassion, in terms of actual conduct there is no remission of physical asceticism; rather such conduct is *extended* into the lay sphere. The ladder is lowered from above, not erected from below. P.S. Jaini, commenting on the *Chedasūtras*, writes that they 'provide valuable insight into the numerous restrictions imposed upon itself by the [monastic] community, mainly in order to preserve its integrity in the face of increasing dependence upon the laity'.[13] I would add to this that another way to annul such a threat is for the ascetics to encourage the laity to become more like them, more ascetic. Whatever one's internal

---

[12] See *JPP* p. 187 for a list, and ibid. pp. 157-187 for a discussion of how these relate to the *pratimā*. Jaini relies here upon R. William's study of mediaeval *śrāvakācāra* texts, *Jaina Yoga* (1963) OUP. See also *TS* 7:19ff. for householder *vrata*; these have been identified by R. Williams 1963, p. 2-3, as essentially Digambara *vrata*, whereas the 'autocommentary' is markedly Śvetāmbara in tone (ibid. p. 2, fn. 1), providing further evidence that the *TS* and its *bhāṣya* are not by the same hand.

[13] *JPP* pp. 63-64.

state, the only way of confirming it or expressing it, either to oneself or to others, is through external conduct. (I shall return to this idea in my discussion of Kundakunda.)[14]

As P.S. Jaini remarks, 'even the clerics of many religions do not live so strict a life as these rules [of lay conduct] demand'.[15] Consequently, as he goes on to say:

> the partial vratas and the pratimās, while theoretically set down for all laymen, tend to constitute an ideal path followed only by a highly select few ... it is a rare individual who actually vows to accept the restraints or perform the holy activities described there.[16]

It is clear from this situation - one which only develops fully in the post-Umāsvāti period - that Umāsvāti's internalization of discipline, through his *kaṣāya* doctrine, does not or is not allowed to influence ascetic behaviour. In so far as the monk or advanced lay person takes on internalized doctrines, he does so in addition to his original *vrata*, not instead of the latter or as a version of them.

A further consideration which may be mentioned here - again, I shall return to it in my discussion of Kundakunda - is the 'ritualisation' of ascetic conduct. By this I mean the idea that if one follows the prescribed action to the letter, the result (in the Jaina case, liberation) is guaranteed. Correct thinking and correct feeling may be essential to the correctitude of a ritual, but the only way these can be monitored or expressed is through external behaviour. The *īryāpatha-sāmparāyika* division in the *Viyāhapannatti* apparently reflects at least a degree of such ritualisation. There the initial division between the two modes of *āsrava* / *karma* is not so much based upon the results of two modes of behaviour available to the same individual, as upon the institutional distinction between two modes of life,

---

14 See, for example, pp. 217-224, below.

15 *JPP* p. 188.

16 Ibid.

incorporating two roles (that of the lay-person and that of the monk) which are mutually exclusive and which, in soteriological terms, inevitably have different outcomes.

Umāsvāti's introduction of a technical *kaṣāya* doctine, linked to the *īryāpatha-sāmparāyika* distinction, would, however, seem at the very least to make room for a less mechanical and more attitude-dependent approach to ascetic conduct. For in theory, the *kaṣāya* doctrine bridges or blurs the institutional distinction between ascetic (*īryāpatha*) and lay or non-ascetic (*sāmparāyika*) activity, since greater or lesser degrees of bondage now depend on the degree of passion accompanying or motivating an action, not on who performs it. Indeed, taken to its logical conclusion the *kaṣāya* doctrine would seem to undercut the rationale for ascetic behaviour altogether. (Clearly, internalisation can only go so far before it threatens the whole basis of a monastic system grounded in severe physical restraint, and with it any specific 'Jaina' identity.)[17] But as we have remarked, it has no such effect, and it is probably not intended that it should have. What then is its purpose?

I suggest that the real importance of Umāsvāti's *kaṣāya* doctrine is for the ordinary lay person (i.e. the majority of the Jaina community), in that it provides a rationale for ordinary lay conduct. That is to say, once the principle that bondage is the ineluctable result of physical harm done to *jīvas* has been modified, and the principle that only actions motivated or actuated by passion are binding has been accepted, then it becomes possible for one to lead a good life, with good soteriological prospects, without necessarily abandoning one's position as a householder. Thus by controlling one's passions or attitude while performing a particular action, one can reduce or avoid the karmic effect associated with it. Or, to put it in the overlapping but not entirely integrated terminology, one can accrue *puṇya* as

---

[17] See Kundakunda sections below, *passim*, for a full discussion of this.

opposed to *pāpa karma*. In other words, when they are allied to internal control, one's actions in the world are not necessarily counter-productive. A householder's life can now be viewed positively: there is such a thing as a (relatively) good action. This is particularly significant with regard to *aparigraha*: an attitude of non-possession while living in the world is not necessarily a contradiction in terms, providing the emotions associated with possession of objects are controlled. (And it is interesting to note that the *Sarvārthasiddhi* on *Tattvārtha Sūtra* 7:19 refers to a 'psychical home' (*bhāvāgāram*) - home-focused thoughts (caused by conduct-deluding karmas), the abandonment of which constitutes true 'homelessness'.)

As we have seen, the *guṇasthāna* and *pratimā* ladders formalize in theoretical terms the idea of gradation in spiritual - in practice, increasingly ascetic - progress. The householder is now at least on the same ladder as the ascetic. Umāsvāti's *kaṣāya* doctrine supports this in a tangential way; but, potentially, it is of most significance for those on the very first rungs of that ladder, the majority of the Jaina community. Through it, their affective subscription to Jainism's distinctive ethical code (preserved by the ascetics and exemplified in their behaviour) is not disqualified by their status as householders. In other words, their identity as 'Jains' is given theoretical (effectively doctrinal) validation. Some of this Jaina majority will, of course, make progress up the *pratimā / guṇasthāna* ladder, and as they do so - as their lives become more ascetic - the greater will be the importance of external conduct and the less relevant internalization on its own.

It is possible to conclude, therefore, that the doctrines found in the *Tattvārtha Sūtra* concerning the mechanism of bondage and the significance of *yoga* are aimed at the Jaina community as a whole. From the fact that Jaina ascetics continue to behave in the manner enjoined in the earliest canonical literature, it is clear that Umāsvāti's incomplete systematization is not so much evidence of a compromise between lay and ascetic life - indeed, the ascetic cannot compromise in this respect without abrogating the whole import of the canonical doctrine of *ahiṃsā* - as evidence of the need to construct a common doctrinal framework in which both ways of life are justified without nullifying each other by too close a contact. (The ascetic's authoritative reference remains, of course, the canon and / or the tradition which is embodied in ascetic practice.)

It may be that this process goes hand in hand with the need for the Jaina community to live in concord with Brahmanical society as a whole, while retaining its individuality. The reaction against Brahmanism evidenced in the canonical texts is a reaction of ascetics against specific Brahmanical practices. But for the laity to survive, there was an increasing need to over-code Jaina behaviour and doctrine to present a more Brahmanical front, while at the same time preserving the true purport of Jaina teachings. The beginning of this process may perhaps be seen in the development of the *guṇasthāna* theory, which, in terms of its function, seems analogous to the orthodox *āśrama* doctrine. The culmination comes with Jinasena's attempts to integrate the Hindu *saṃskāras* into Jaina lay practice in his *Ādipurāṇa* (perhaps written to justify an already existing state of affairs).[18] But it is in Umāsvāti's *Tattvārtha Sūtra* that the first real attempt is made to present Jaina doctrine as an autonomous religious system which includes both monks and laity, rather than simply the teachings of a heterodox renouncer. It is here that one first has the sense of a community being addressed, rather than a collection of individual monks. And it is here too that Jainism can be seen consciously addressing outsiders. In other words, it now turns to face the wider Indian religious world which surrounds and threatens to infiltrate it.

With the works ascribed to Kundakunda we find Jainism somewhere near the centre of this terrain, subject to both internal and external pressures and developing social

---

[18] See *JPP* p. 291ff., and R. Williams 1963, pp. 274-275.

and philosophical strategies for dealing with them. And it is to these that I now turn.

PART III

KUNDAKUNDA: THE *PRAVACANASĀRA*

4

Kundakunda: content and context

4.1 *Kundakunda: primary sources and chronology*

In this and the following part I shall examine two of the major Prākrit works ascribed to the Digambara *ācārya* Kundakunda, the *Pravacanasāra* and the *Samayasāra*.

Giving even an approximately accurate date to Kundakunda presents formidable problems. The revered and influential position he holds within the Digambara tradition only adds to the difficulties. Traditionally, two dates are ascribed to Kundakunda: the middle of the third century C.E. (fl. 243 C.E.), and the first half of the first century C.E., the latter being the more popular. Upadhye shows that the traditional evidence for these dates is drawn largely from much later commentators and is totally inadequate.[1] Moreover, the idiosyncratic nature of some of Kundakunda's teaching in the context of the rest of the Jain tradition makes comparison with such texts as the *Tattvārtha Sūtra* unhelpful in this respect. And as we shall see, the nature of Kundakunda's texts is such - they are clearly compilations of older material held together by new philosophical and soteriological strategies - that it is difficult to remain confident that all or even any of them should be ascribed to a single author or redactor. Conversely, there are close enough thematic links between the *Pravacanasāra* and the *Samayasāra* to make it obvious that they originated in the same religious and philosophical milieu. They can, therefore, profitably be studied together.

The evidence for Kundakunda's date has been most

---

[1] Upadhye 1935, p. xff.

extensively reviewed by Upadhye in his introduction to the *Pravacanasāra*.[2] Here I shall confine myself to a brief summary of Upadhye's main arguments, and then offer some criticisms.

Upadhye remarks that Pūjyapāda, the earliest Digambara commentator on the *Tattvārtha Sūtra*, quotes (at *Sarvārthasiddhi* 2:10) five gāthās which are found in the same order in the *Bārasa-Aṇuvekkhā* (25-19), a work ascribed to Kundakunda. Pūjyapāda, however, 'does not say as to from what source he is quoting'.[3] Nevertheless, Upadhye thinks that their context and serial order indicate the genuineness of these quotations, i.e. Pūjyapāda is quoting from Kundakunda. If this is so then it would set a later limit to the age of Kundakunda since, according to Upadhye, Pūjyapāda lived earlier than the last quarter of the fifth century C.E.[4] Upadhye then reduces this upper limit by reference to the Merkara (Mercara) copper plates of śaka 388 (466 C.E.) which mention a Kundakundānvaya, giving the names of at least six *ācāryas* of that lineage.[5] This 'indicates that Kundakunda will have to be put at least a century, if not more, earlier than the date of the copper-plates' (i.e. c.350 C.E.).[6] Upadhye then assumes that the lineage of a saint does not begin immediately after his death, and so takes the date back a further 100 years.[7] Thus his later limit is now c.250 C.E. He concludes, however, 'I am inclined to believe, after this long survey of the available material, that Kundakunda's age lies *at the beginning of the Christian era*' (his italics).[8] In other words, he reverts to the traditional dating, albeit for

---

[2] Ibid. pp. x-xxiv.

[3] Ibid. p. xxi.

[4] Bronkhorst p. 161, says that he lived 'not long after 455 A.D.'; see above, p. 46.

[5] See Upadhye pp. xix - xxii, where he refers to *Epigraphia Carnatica I, Coorg Inscriptions No. 1.*, B.L. Rice, Madras, 1914.

[6] Upadhye p. xix.

[7] Ibid. p. xxii.

[8] Ibid.

different reasons to those traditionally advanced.[9]

In support of this, Upadhye offers some linguistic evidence, namely, that the Prākrit dialect used in the *Pravacanasāra*, for instance, seems to be earlier than that of the Prākrit portions of the *Nāṭyaśāstra* of Bharata (usually assigned to the beginning of the second century C.E., but, as Upadhye admits, the date is uncertain).[10] He also claims that not a single Apabhraṃśa form is traceable in the *Pravacanasāra*, possibly indicating a period when Prākrits had not yet developed Apabhraṃśa traces.[11] (He has already noted the strong influence of Sanskrit on the Prākrit dialect of the *Pravacanasāra* - dubbed 'Jaina Śauraseni' by Pischel: e.g. it retains intervocalic 'c' and even 'p' at times; *deśī* words are also conspicuously absent.)[12]

I see the following problems with Upadhye's arguments. First, the ascription of the *Bārasa-Aṇuvekkhā* to Kundakunda can itself only be made on traditional grounds. Furthermore, as Upadhye himself admits,[13] the text may be a compilation of traditional gāthās, and nothing in the content of the verses quoted by Pūjyapāda indicates that they are necessarily non-traditional material.[14] Consequently, we do not know that Pūjyapāda is quoting from Kundakunda. On these grounds, even the upper limit is uncertain.

Second, the Mercara copper plate inscription is now considered to be a forgery of the eighth or ninth century. Chatterjee describes these plates as 'definitely spurious'.[15]

---

[9] Cf. Keith's 1936 review (pp. 528-9) of Upadhye's edition of the *Pravacanasāra*. He concludes from Upadhye's own evidence that Kundakunda 'may be placed not later than the fourth century A.D.', but how much earlier than that is not clear.

[10] Upadhye p. xxiii.

[11] Ibid.

[12] See ibid. pp. cxx-cxxi, cxxiv.

[13] Ibid. p. xl.

[14] See *SS* on *TS* 2:10.

[15] Chatterjee p.234, referring to *Epigraphia Carnatica* (revised ed.) 1972, Vol. I, Introduction pp. xf.

He goes on to argue that even if this plate were a genuine copy of an older record, by assigning twenty-five years to each of the six monks named, the earliest, Guṇacandra, would not be before 325 C.E. So, on the basis of Pūjyapāda quoting from the *Bārasa-Aṇuvekkhā*, Chatterjee assigns Kundakunda to the fourth century C.E. He remarks, however, that 'the *anvaya* of Kundakunda appears only in the records of South India, which were inscribed after 900 A.D.'.[16]

Even if the Mercara copper plate were genuine, it only shows that there was an *ācārya* called Kundakunda, it does not indicate that the works we have that are ascribed to 'Kundakunda' are, either in toto or in part, necessarily by this particular teacher. Indeed, as Upadhye points out,[17] the only mention of Kundakunda's name in any of the works attributed to him is in the last gāthā of the *Bārasa-Aṇuvekkhā*, a verse which is not even found in some manuscripts.[18] Moreover, Amṛtacandra, his first extant commentator (c. tenth century C.E.) does not mention Kundakunda's name, and it is only with Jayasena (twelfth century C.E.) that a firm attribution is made.

Third, the linguistic evidence is highly approximate and largely depends upon unsure relative dating. It clearly needs much further research, but even then it would be unlikely to yield any chronological certainty.[19] Schubring, however, in his article 'Kundakunda echt und unecht',[20] compares the form and style of the *Aṭṭhapāhuḍa* collection of texts (which are attributed to Kundakunda) with the form and style of other texts, particularly the *Samayasāra*. By

---

[16] Chatterjee p. 325.

[17] Upadhye p. ii.

[18] See ibid. p. xl.

[19] See F.W. Thomas, intro. to Faddegon's trans. [Kundakunda (3)] 1935, p. xix. Thomas puts Kundakunda in the third or fourth century C.E.; cf. P.S. Jaini, *JPP* p. 79, who favours the second or third century. See also Frauwallner 1973, p. 183 - fourth century C.E.. Caillat 1987, p.508, dates Kundakunda to the first century C.E. without comment.

[20] Schubring 1957, pp. 537-574.

doing so, he shows that the *Aṭṭhapāhuḍa* texts are much younger. He concludes, therefore, that the *Aṭṭhapāhuḍa* should no longer be considered a product of the classical period of Digambara literature and should not be classified as a work by Kundakunda.[21] From their relative freedom from Apabhraṃśa forms, he takes works such as *Samayasāra*, *Pravacanasāra*, and *Pañcāstikāya* to belong to a genuine Kundakunda, whom, elsewhere, Schubring dates to the 2nd-3rd century C.E.[22]

None of this, however, brings us closer to a convincing date for the author(s) / redactor(s) of the *Pravacanasāra* and the *Samayasāra*. As Upadhye admits, 'we have to grope in darkness to settle the exact date of Kundakunda'.[23]

There is, however, some internal evidence as to the nature and chronology of these texts. E.H. Johnston in his study of early Sāṃkhya notes in passing that:

> Kundakunda's use of the terms *pariṇāma* and *paramāṇu* are more appropriate to a date in the neighbourhood of the third or fourth century A.D., and similarly in the *Samayasāra* .... 124, 127, and 356-361, he refers to the Sāṃkhya doctrine of the connection between soul and *prakṛti* in language that could hardly have been used at a much earlier date.[24]

My own research shows that the technical way in which the term *samaya* itself is used in the *Samayasāra* indicates a relatively late date (early fifth century or later) for that text.[25] Furthermore, the way in which Kundakunda uses the two truths doctrine (*vyavahāra-naya* and *niścaya-naya*) seems much closer to Śaṅkara's distinction than to the

---

21 Ibid. p. 574.

22 Schubring 1966, p. 36. Upadhye accepts the *Pāhuḍas* as genuine Kundakunda (see pp. xxvi-xxxvii), but Schubring convincingly dismisses this (1957, pp. 567-568).

23 Upadhye p. xix.

24 Johnston p. 14, fn. 1.

25 See below, p. 233ff.

Buddhist one. This alone might make one wonder how early parts of the *Samayasāra* can be dated. And a close examination reveals that this two truths doctrine is utilised in the *Samayasāra* in two different and ultimately conflicting ways - a clear enough indication that we are dealing with a composite text. In other words, *the text as we have it* has been subject to substantial modification and addition, probably as a result of non-Jaina philosophical influences.

This leaves as open questions the identity and date of the 'original' Kundakunda. But even if it were possible to answer these, it is unlikely that our understanding of the texts as we have them now would be significantly advanced. Moreover, my purpose here is to chart a particular development within Jaina thought and religion, and to define its practical limits. And for that project a cursory inspection of the *Pravacanasāra* and the *Samayasāra* shows that they are related within the same broad tradition, and so may be fruitfully examined in tandem regardless of specific authorship. Nevertheless, within that context, it is important to bear in mind the above problems and to assess each work, and even to some extent each gāthā, individually. As Upadhye admits, 'the compilatory character of Kundakunda's works nullifies the criterion whether a gāthā fits a particular context or not'.[26] He goes on to say that the available manuscripts are all accompanied by various commentaries and so are already 'under the bias' of particular commentators.[27] In this respect, I shall refer in particular to the first extant commentaries on the *Pravacanasāra* (the *Tattvadīpikā*) and the *Samayasāra* (the *Ātmakhyāti*), both by Amṛtacandra, who is tentatively dated by Upadhye to the end of the tenth century C.E.[28] I shall also occasionally refer to Jayasena's

---

[26] Upadhye p. l.

[27] Ibid. p. li.

[28] Ibid. pp. c-ci. Cf. R. Williams 1963, p. 24, and F.W. Thomas, intro. to Faddegon [Kundakunda (3)], p. xxiv, for other possibilities.

commentaries, which were probably written in the second half of the twelfth century C.E.[29] There is therefore a considerable time-lag between the texts and their first commentaries. This may not, however, be as great as has usually been thought.

In what follows, I shall for convenience refer to both the *Pravacanasāra* and the *Samayasāra* as the works of Kundakunda, while keeping the above reservations in mind.

4.2 *Upayoga*

At the heart of Kundakunda's soteriology in the *Pravacanasāra* is the doctrine of *upayoga* (Pk. *uvaoga*). I shall begin this section, therefore, with a brief examination of the way in which this term is used in texts prior to, or approximately contemporary with, those attributed to Kundakunda. I shall then look in detail at the ways in which the meaning of the term was modified and developed by Kundakunda in the *Pravacanasāra*.

i) Upayoga before Kundakunda

Among the earliest surviving texts there appears to be no direct reference to *upayoga* in the *Āyāraṃga*, the *Sūyagaḍaṃga*, or the *Dasaveyāliya Sutta*s. The term does appear, however, at *Uttarajjhayaṇa* XXVIII.10, where it is said that the characteristic of the *jīva* is manifestation (or application) through (or with) 'knowledge, perception, happiness and suffering'.[30] It is not clear whether *upayoga*, which can have the meanings 'application', 'manifestation',

---

[29] See Upadhye p. liv.

[30] *jīvo uvaogalakkhaṇo* |
ṇāṇeṇaṃ daṃsaṇeṇaṃ ca suheṇa ya duheṇa ya || *Utt.* XXVIII.10 ||
Jacobi translates this as 'The characteristic ... of the soul [is] the realisation (*upayoga*) of knowledge, faith, happiness and misery' - 1895, p. 153.
For the meaning of *daṃsaṇa (darśana)*, see p. 98, below. P.S. Jaini (*JPP* p. 97) defines *darśana* as 'insight ... into the nature of reality (along with faith in this view)'. Cf. *Pañc.* 115, quoted p. 187, below.

or 'employment', should be taken here in its full technical sense of 'application' or 'manifestation of consciousness'. The passage could mean that *ṇāṇa*, *daṃsaṇa,* etc., are particular types of *upayoga*, or that *upayoga* is one of a number of characteristics of the *jīva*; but in either case it need not mean 'consciousness' as such, although the assumption among commentators and translators is that it does.

In the following verse (*Uttarajjhayaṇa* XXVIII.11), which has a different classificatory system, it is clear that *uvaoga* (*upayoga*) is one among a number of characteristics of the *jīva*, and not yet the defining characteristic:

> The characteristics of the soul are knowledge, faith, conduct, austerities, energy and application (*uvaoga*).[31]

This verse (11) seems to be a mixture of the prescriptive and the descriptive. It is also worth noting that *daṃsaṇa* (*darśana*) can mean either 'faith' or 'perception', and although it is not clear which sense is being applied here, it is probable, since they imply each other, that it is being used in a non-exclusive way. Nevertheless, between them these two verses do contain in embryo all the elements of the later *upayoga* doctrine, although they are not yet - or not explicitly - arranged in a causal hierarchy. That is to say, they contain *upayoga*, *jñāna* and *darśana*, as well as *śubha* and *aśubha* (assuming that *sukha* and *duḥkha* result from *puṇya* and *pāpa* which, in the later doctrine of Kundakunda, are the products of *śubha*- and *aśubha*-*upayoga* respectively). Thus these verses clearly originate from a period before the *upayoga* doctrine was fully developed, despite the fact that as a whole Chapter XXVIII was a relatively late addition to the body of the

---

31 *ṇāṇaṃ ca daṃsaṇaṃ ceva carittaṃ ca tavo tahā* |
vīriyaṃ uvaogo ya eyaṃ jīvassa lakkhaṇaṃ || *Utt.* XXVIII.11 ||
Jacobi (ibid.) translates *uvaoga* here as 'realization (of its developments)'.

Uttarajjhayaṇa. This is borne out by the fact that the formal division of *upayoga* into *jñāna* and *darśana* has not yet been made here, although, as we shall see, that particular classification can be traced back at least as far as the *Pannavaṇā Sutta*.[32]

References to *upayoga* in the *Viyāhapannatti* (*Bhagavatī*) take us much closer to the classical doctrine. At *Viyāhapannatti* II.10a (147b) we read that the *guṇa* (essential property) of the *atthikāya* (fundamental entity) *jīva* makes possible *uvaoga* ('the spiritual function').[33] And at II.10c (149a) it is asserted that the 'characteristic (*lakkhaṇa*) of soul is the spiritual function (*uvaoga*)'. The soul by its own nature (*āya-bhāveṇaṃ*) possesses will (*vīriya*) 'which enables it to apply this spiritual function in the infinite number of possibilities (*pajjava*) of cognition - viz. in the domains of the five knowledges, the three non-knowledges and the three visions (*daṃsaṇa*) - thus revealing the true nature of soul (*jīva-bhāva*)'.[34]

At *Viyāhapannatti* XVIII.10e (760a) the brahman Somila asks Mahāvīra whether he is 'one or two ... imperishable (*akkhaya*), immutable (*avvaya*) and stationary (*avaṭṭhiya*) or has he different forms in past, present and future (*aṇega-bhūya-bhāva-bhaviya*)?' Mahāvīra replies that:

> He is all of these, since from the point of view of [the] essence [of his soul, *Abhay.*][35] (*davv'aṭṭhayāe*) he is one, from the point of view of knowledge and vision (*nāṇa-daṃsaṇ'aṭṭhayāe*) he is two; as to *paesas* [space-points] he is imperishable, immutable and stationary, but as to *uvaoga* he has different forms in past, present

---

[32] See Schubring 1962, para.82; and below.

[33] Deleu's 1970 trans. References are to his critical analysis.

[34] Deleu II.10c. Cf. XII.4.4a (608a): 'The characteristic of the fundamental entity (*atthi-kāya*) soul (*jīva*) is the spiritual function (*uvaoga-lakkh* ...) which reveals itself in the different knowledges etc., ref to II.10c.' For a description of these five knowledges, etc., see discussion of *Pañc*. 41, p. 101, below.

[35] I.e. according to Abhayadeva's Vṛtti on *Viy*.

and future.[36]

Here it is interesting to note that the form of *uvaoga*, as 'spiritual function', is something that changes; moreover, it is essentially something that the soul changes itself.[37]

Viyāhapannatti also uses the terms *aṇāgārôvautta* and *sāgārôvautta* to designate two types of *uvaoga*. Deleu, following Schubring's translation of *sāgāra*- and *aṇāgāra-uvaoga*,[38] renders these as 'faculty of abstract or indistinct imagination' and 'faculty of concrete or distinct imagination', respectively.[39] At *Viyāhapannatti* XXV.6.17 (899b) all classes of *niyaṇṭha* (monks) are said to have 'the formally distinct or the formally indistinct imagination (are *sāgārôvautta* or *aṇāgārôvautta*)'.[40] *Uvautta* is the Prākrit form of the Sanskrit *upayukta*, meaning 'employed' or 'applicable to'; similarly, *upayoga*, as we have seen, can have the meaning of 'application', 'manifestation', or 'employment' (of consciousness), and these are the translations I shall prefer.[41] Deleu's use of 'imagination' (see above) to translate the term seems eccentric. But at *Viyāhapannatti* V.4 (221b) he renders *uvautta* as 'attentive'; and at XVIII.8.3 (755a) he gives *sāgāra* as 'formally distinct' and *aṇāgāra* as 'formally indistinct'. The Prākrit term *āgāra* corresponds to the Sanskrit *ākāra*, 'form' or

---

36 Deleu 1970.

37 Note also that *jñāna* and *darśana* share the same context as *upayoga* here, but they are not linked as explicitly as in the *TS*, for instance. See below.

38 See Schubring 1962, para. 82.

39 See, for instance, *Viy*. VI.3.5 (257b), and XIX.8 (770b).

40 Deleu 1970. If *uvautta* corresponds to *uvaoga* then this can hardly be true of monks alone, since *uvaoga* is the characteristic of all *jīvas*; it is, however, possible to use *upayoga* in the more limited sense of 'understanding'- see p. 102, below.

41 Frauwallner (1953, pp. 258, 287) translates *upayoga* by *Betätigung*, 'work' or 'activity'; but perhaps 'activation' / 'actuation' - and so 'awareness' (P.S. Jaini 1980, p. 223) and 'active consciousness' (Tatia pp. 55-56) would be better.

'figure'; thus, taking *uvautta* as 'attentive', *sāgārôvautta* would be 'attentive to something with form', and *aṇāgārôvautta* 'attentive to something without form' (i.e. determinate or indeterminate cognition / manifestation of consciousness), corresponding to the two kinds of *upayoga*, *jñāna* and *darśana* ('knowing' and 'perceiving').[42]

P.S. Jaini, following the *Sarvārthasiddhi*, has summarised the classical *upayoga* doctrine concisely.[43] He states that the *jīva* has three main qualities (*guṇa*): *caitanya*, *sukha* and *vīrya* (consciousness, bliss and energy). Of these, consciousness is central, the distinguishing characteristic of the soul. Through the operation of this quality the soul can be the knower (*pramātṛ*), 'that which illuminates both objects and itself'. *Upayoga* is 'application of consciousness' (which Jaini refers to as 'cognition').[44] It is twofold, consisting of *darśana* (perception, first contact, or 'pure apprehension') and *jñāna* (comprehension of the details of what has been perceived).[45]

If we are looking for the origins of the technical use of *upayoga* to mean 'application of *consciousness*', it is worth noting that at *Pañcāstikāya* 41*1(42) and 41*2(43), for instance, *upayoga* is used in a somewhat different and apparently less embracing sense as a component part of *matijñāna* and *śrutajñāna* (the first two types of *jñāna* in the list of 5[8]), with the meaning of 'understanding of

---

42 For these see discussion of *TS*. 2:9 below.

43 *JPP* p. 104.

44 Cf. P.S. Jaini 1980, p. 223, where Jaini translates *upayoga* as 'awareness'. The purest *upayoga* (i.e. *kevalajñāna*) is connected with the *siddha*, and the impurest with the submicroscopic *nigoda*. Thus the degree to which one's *upayoga* is obscured by impurity exactly reflects one's place in the karmic hierarchy (ibid.). Also see Tatia, who translates *upayoga* as 'active consciousness' (pp. 55-6 and p. 55, n.5).

45 For controversies over whether these are two distinct *guṇas* of the soul or simply aspects of the one, see Tatia, pp. 70-80. And for further details of the standard use of *uvaoga* / *upayoga*, see Schubring 1962, paras. 71 and 82.

things' (i.e. 'application of knowledge'). Tatia comments that *upayoga* here means 'active consciousness', as opposed to *labdhi*, 'dormant consciousness':[46] 'soul is called *upayukta* or *upayogavān* when it is actually engaged in knowing something. Mere capacity for knowledge without actual knowledge is *labdhi*'.[47] Although not relevant to the present enquiry, further research on this particular distinction might well shed light on the beginnings of the technical use of *upayoga*.

Turning to the *Tattvārtha Sūtra*, we find that *upayoga* is again defined as the *lakṣaṇa*, the distinguishing characteristic of the *jīva*. So, in referring to the *jīva*, *Tattvārtha Sūtra*. 2.8 reads (in its entirety):

> Application of consciousness is the distinguishing characteristic (of the soul).[48]

In the next verse (*TS*. 2.9),[49] application of consciousness (*upayoga*) is said to be of two kinds (subdivided into eight and four kinds respectively). These two categories, according to the *Bhāṣya* and the *Sarvārthasiddhi*, are *jñāna* (knowledge) and *darśana* (perception); that is to say, application of consciousness with and without 'form'.[50]

Enlarging on this, the *Sarvārthasiddhi* remarks that:

> Apprehension of the mere object (the universal) is perception, and awareness of the particulars is knowledge. These occur in

---

46 Tatia p. 55.

47 Ibid. p. 56.

48 *Upayogo lakṣaṇam* [*TS* 2:8].

49 Schubring 1962, para. 82, traces this back to *Pannavaṇā* 29.

50 *upayogo dvividhaḥ sākāro anākāraś ca jñānopayogo darśanopayogaścety arthaḥ* [*Bhāṣya* on 2:9].

Cf. use in *Viy*. above. Note also the use of *sākāra* and *anākāra* at *Pravacanasāra* 2:102 to denote, respectively, the roles of the ascetic and the layperson. The two usages are clearly connected, in that while *jñāna* can be seen to be more characteristic of the ascetic, *darśana* is relatively predominant in the lay person.

succession [*darśana* and then *jñāna*] in ordinary mortals (non-omniscients), but simultaneously in those who have annihilated karmas.[51]

This accounts, in part, for the kevalin's omniscience. It also makes it clear that *upayoga*, when unobstructed by karmas, is instantaneous knowledge and perception (i.e. pure consciousness), the characteristic nature of all *jīvas* attained in *kevalajñāna*.

At *Tattvārtha Sūtra*. 2.8 we have seen that *upayoga* is a manifestation of what it is that differentiates the *jīva* from the non-*jīva* (*ajīva*) - its 'jivaness' or *svatattva*. In sūtra 2.1, however, Umāsvāti has described the *jīva*'s inherent nature (*svatattva*) in terms of *bhāvas* of five kinds, arising from the four types or conditions of karma plus the *jīva*'s natural or inherent *bhāva* (*pāriṇāmika bhāva*), independent of karmas. According to this sūtra, the five kinds of *bhāvas* ('dispositions' or 'states of the soul') are:[52]

1) *aupaśamika* - arising from subsidence of karmas (of the deluding kind),
2) *kṣāyika* - arising from destruction of karmas (of the four *ghātiya*, or destructive kinds),
3) *miśra* (*kṣāyopaśamika*) - arising from the destruction- cum-subsidence of karmas (of the destructive kind),
4) *audayika* - arising from the rise of karmas (the fruition of karmas),
5) *pariṇāmika* - that which undergoes modification, i.e. the inherent nature / capacity of the *jīva* (independent of karmas).

We have already seen that at *Viyāhapannatti* II.10c the

---

51 Trans. by S.A. Jain p. 56. of:
sākāraṃ jñānam anākāraṃ darśanam iti /
tac chadmastheṣu krameṇa vartate /
nirāvaraṇeṣu yugapat.

52 Following the *SS* on *TS* 2:1, which reads:
aupaśamikakṣāyikau bhāvau miśraś ca jīvasya svatattvam audayikapāriṇāmikau ca.

jīva-bhāva or 'true nature of soul' is said to be revealed through *upayoga*, which in turn applies itself through the five *jñāna*s, etc. What then is the connection between the five *bhāvas* (i.e. *bhāva* used in a technical sense) and *upayoga*?

Perhaps the clearest line to take is that followed by P.S. Jaini in *The Jaina Path of Purification*,[53] where he points out that in the standard Jaina doctrine of *anekānta* (manifold aspects) an existent (*sat*) is composed of three aspects: substance (*dravya*), quality (*guṇa*) and mode (*paryāya*) - a substance being a substratum (*āśraya*) for manifold *guṇa*s which, while free from qualities of their own, continuously undergo modifications (*pariṇāma*) while acquiring new modes (*paryāya* or *bhāva*) and losing old ones.[54] The point to note is that *bhāva* can be used as a synonym for *paryāya*. Applying this to the present case, we can see that consciousness (*cetanā* / *caitanya*) is a *guṇa* of the *dravya jīva*; *upayoga* is that consciousness manifested or applied in *jñāna* and *darśana*; the particular forms of *jñāna* (such as *matijñāna*, *kevalajñāna*, etc.[see below]) are thus *paryāyas* or *bhāvas* of the *guṇa jñāna* (which is really an aspect of the *guṇa cetanā)*. So the various kinds of *jñāna* , for example, are *bhāvas* or 'modifications' of the *jīva*, reflecting the karmic condition of the *jīva* at that time - which itself was brought about by previous *bhāvas*. For this reason, *bhāva* is sometimes translated as 'thought-activity' or 'psychological disposition', but for a Western reader this could be misleading unless it is clearly understood that *bhāva*, as a modification or particular form of *upayoga*, is no more attributable to *manas* (mind) than is *upayoga* itself. (*Tattvārtha Sūtra* 2.11 is specific that there are two kinds of *jīvas*, those with minds and those without; whereas *upayoga* characterises *all jīvas*.) 'Manifestation of consciousness' and 'thought activity' should therefore be

---

53 Op. cit. pp. 90-91.
54 See *TS*. 5:29, 30, 38.

taken in the sense of having consciousness (*cetanā*) as their base (*āśraya*). And as Kundakunda explains in his most orthodox work, the *Pañcāstikāya* [38, 39], *cetanā* is experienced by the three kinds of *jīvas* in different ways: one kind of *jīva* (in fixed organisms and plants) simply experiences the fruits of karmas (*kammāṇaṃ phalam ekko*), another kind (embodied beings, etc. - *ekko kajjaṃ*) experiences 'conative activity' as well, and another (the kevalin who is free from all physical and organic conditions) has 'pure and perfect knowledge' (*ṇāṇam adha ekko*).[55]

In short, *bhāvas* are modifications or particular forms of *upayoga*. Thus by comparing the list of *jñāna*s given in the *Tattvārtha Sūtra* with the five *bhāvas* (listed at *Tattvārtha Sūtra* 2.1) we can see the way in which the former are all essentially modes (*bhāvas*) of the *jñāna* component of *upayoga*.

The eight kinds of knowledge (sometimes divided into five right and three wrong) are as follows:

1) *matijñāna* - sensory
2) *śrutajñāna* - scriptural
3) *avadhijñāna* - clairvoyance
4) *manaḥ paryayajñāna* - telepathy
5) *kevalajñāna* - omniscience
6) *matyajñāna* - wrong sensory
7) *śrutyajñāna* - wrong scriptural
8) *vibhaṅgajñāna* - wrong clairvoyance.

Corresponding to the other component of *upayoga*, four kinds of *darśana* are usually listed with the *jñāna*s:

1) *cakṣurdarśana* - perception through the eyes
2) *acakṣurdarśana* - perception through the senses other than the eyes

---

[55] Following Chakravartinayanar [Kundakunda (2)].

3) *avadhidarśana* - clairvoyant perception
4) *kevaladarśana* - omniscient perception.[56]

This list sometimes occurs without either *kevalajñāna* or *kevaladarśana*;[57] that is because these two are not strictly speaking separate types of *jñāna* and *darśana* (*upayoga*) but the substrata of all the others - pure *jñāna* and *darśana* without the impediment of karmas. Similarly, *pariṇāmika bhāva* is not a *bhāva* or modification of the *jīva* as such, but the natural state of the *jīva* when it is free from karmic modification (i.e. from *bhāvas*).[58] To put this in terms of the classical karman doctrine,[59] *bhāvas* are states produced in the *jīva* by karmas. Thus five *bhāvas* are possible in the *jīva* 'which can manifest themselves simultaneously in a greater or smaller number'.[60] These basic five subdivide into a total of fifty-three possible states of the *jīva*, among which are the different kinds of *upayoga* (*jñāna* and *darśana*) and thus the eight *jñāna*s. The amount or fraction of *upayoga* - which, it should be remembered, is the necessary characteristic of a *jīva* and so cannot be totally absent - is different in different beings, depending upon the degree to which their inherent *kevalajñāna* (or *pariṇāmikabhāva*) is obscured by material *karman*. In other words, the five (fifty-three) *bhāvas* list all the

---

[56] See *TS* 1 for a detailed discussion of the kinds of *jñāna*; also see the *SS* on *TS* 2:9, and *Pañc.* 41 which repeats the list exactly.

[57] See, for instance, *TS* 2:5.

[58] In terms of Kundakunda's doctrine (see below), true *bhāvas* (1-4) must be modifications of either *śubha* or *aśubha upayoga*; *pariṇāmika* is free from karmas and thus identical to *kevala-* and *darśana-jñāna*, which comprise the state of *śuddha-upayoga*. As explained on p.103, *pariṇāmika* refers to the *jīva*'s natural or inherent *bhāva*, independent of *karman*. Or to put it the other way round, being the natural condition of the *jīva*, it is that state which is the substratum of, or has the *potential* to undergo, modification under the influence of *karman*; but for that very reason, it is in itself free from such modification.

[59] Schematised by Glasenapp p. 40ff.

[60] Glasenapp p. 40.

possible states of the *bound* soul (i.e. its karmic states). Distributed among these states are the *jñāna*s and *darśanas* which make up *upayoga*; that is to say, since the various *jñāna*s and *darśanas* (apart from *kevalajñāna* and *kevaladarśana*) are essentially *bhāvas*, they are ultimately products of karmic bondage.

Before leaving the subject of *bhāvas*, it is interesting to note that Kundakunda at his most orthodox (in the *Pañcāstikāya*) equates, in terms of their function, *bhāva* with *kaṣāya*, and that *bhāva* here plays the role that is taken by *upayoga* in the *Pravacanasāra*.[61] So *Pañcāstikāya* 147 (Upadhye's ed.; 154, SBJ edition) reads:

> Whatever arisen state (*bhāva*) the impassioned self creates, auspicious or inauspicious, that state becomes the bond through that various material *karman*.

And the following verse [*Pañcāstikāya* 148 (155)] continues:

> Physical combination (of karmic matter with the *jīva*) is caused by activity (*yoga*). Activity is of mind, speech and body. Bondage is caused by *bhāva*(s); *bhāva*(s) consist(s) of pleasure and attachment, aversion and delusion.

In other words, it is *yoga* which causes influx of material *karman*, and *śubha* and *aśubha bhāvas*, consisting of passions, which are instrumental in that *karman* adhering to the *jīva*. This is simply the standard, two stage *kaṣāya* doctrine of the *Tattvārtha Sūtra*, with the two components sometimes referred to as *dravyabandha* and *bhāvabandha* (the material and efficient causes of bondage). Thus, when *upayoga* is substituted for its equivalent, *bhāva*, it is clear that the *upayoga* doctrine performs precisely the same function in Kundakunda's soteriology as the *kaṣāya* doctrine in Umāsvāti's. This remains true while *upayoga* is

---

[61] For *bhāva* in the *Samayasāra*, see p. 267ff., below.

characterised merely as *śubha* and *aśubha*, i.e. while it refers exclusively to *saṃsāric* manifestations of consciousness. However, as will become clear, when the emphasis is switched from *saṃsāric* to *nirvāṇic*, from the impure to a pure state of consciousness, and the latter is viewed as a positive state (as opposed simply to the absence of *saṃsāric* states), Kundakunda's *upayoga* doctrine comes to provide a radically altered perspective on Jaina theory and practice - a possibility latent in the *kaṣāya* doctrine but not activated.

It is possible in this way, and with hindsight, to trace the development of the *upayoga* doctrine (or at least the stages in which it is presented) in Kundakunda's works. For purposes of simplification, we can point to the passages just quoted as examples of an 'earlier' strand of the doctrine,[62] before a *śuddha* / *aśuddha* distinction is introduced. Nevertheless, the material for the 'later doctrine' is already in place. The eight *jñāna*s and four *darśanas* (the component parts of *upayoga*) listed above (pp.105-6) can be divided, from a soteriological perspective, into more [6-8] (*aśubha*) or less [1-4] (*śubha*) 'negative' states (*darśana* [1-3] would be 'neutral'), counterbalanced by a 'positive' state (*kevalajñāna* and *kevaladarśana*). As remarked above, the latter is essentially freedom from karmic impediments, so it is not, strictly speaking, a manifestation or application of consciousness at all, rather it is the essence of the *jīva* unbound. Only *śubha* and *aśubha upayoga*s are *upayoga*s as such, since only they are the product of *bhāvas*, i.e. of karma-controlled states. The fact, already mentioned, that *kevalajñāna* and *kevaladarśana* are sometimes missing from the list of types of *upayoga*[63] probably reflects the realisation of this, as well as giving a strong indication that this doctrine was modified over a period of time and only

---

62 Cf. my comments below on *Pravacanasāra* 2:63.

63 See, for example, *TS* 2:5.

reached its 'final' form with Kundakunda.[64]

The consequences of seeing *kevalajñāna* and *kevaladarśana* combined - the latter being subsumed in the former - as a form of (pure) consciousness, as Kundakunda does in the *Pravacanasāra*, are extensive, as I shall make clear. Here I shall restrict myself to the comment that, if it is the quality of *consciousness* that is instrumental in bondage and freedom (and the role of *yoga* [activity] has, via the two tier system of the *Tattvārtha Sūtra* and its precursors, become largely irrelevant to the actual mechanism of bondage), then it is only a relatively small step to saying that material *karman*'s association with the *jīva* (i.e. bondage) is 'unreal'. For if the true nature of the soul is pure consciousness, then how can this be touched in reality by *karman*, which is material? And as will be seen, Kundakunda comes to assert that it is only from the *vyavahāra-naya* that the *jīva* is characterised by *bhāvas*, or *śubha* and *aśubha upayoga* (i.e. bondage through karmic matter); from the *niścaya* view, which in the *Samayasāra*, at least, he takes to be the 'real' view, the *jīva* has no connection with these. Soteriology thus becomes a matter of knowing and realising the true nature of the self, by means of *jñāna* and meditation. *Tapas*, on the other hand, has - at least in theory - been down-graded.[65] Emphasis is switched from an obsession with the minutiae of the karma theory, where potentially every action has soteriological repercussions and interaction with the material world is crucial, to ways of achieving soteriological autonomy and

---

64 Three stages are suggested:

1) *upayoga* is used in the strict sense of '*manifestation* of consciousness', so the state of the *kevalin* is not included among the *jñānas* and *darśanas*, the component parts of *upayoga*,
2) *kevalajñāna* and *kevaladarśana* are added to the list of *upayogas*,
3) *kevalajñāna* = *śuddhopayoga* = the self, consciousness in its 'original', pure state, which is not a manifestation or application at all.

65 For a general discussion of these strands in Indian religions, see Gombrich 1988, p. 44f.

by-passing the karmic world altogether through the realisation of its irrelevance, or even its unreality, in terms of the essential self. In the light of orthodox Jaina doctrine such a position - although perhaps logical given the premises on which the doctrine is founded - is, to say the least, startling, and will require considerable comment once the evidence has been considered.

To return to the present argument, we have seen that *upayoga* is the term used to designate 'application of consciousness', and that this is considered the defining characteristic of the *jīva*. However, so far *upayoga* has not been - and is not in standard expositions of Jaina doctrine which follow the *Tattvārtha Sūtra* (including most secondary sources in Western languages) - directly designated as the instrument by which the soul causes itself to be bound. Given that Umāsvāti in the *Tattvārtha Sūtra* identifies *kaṣāyas* (passions) as the efficient cause of bondage through karma, and that *kaṣāyas* need some kind of initial consciousness to engender them, then it might be inferred from the doctrines of the *Tattvārtha Sūtra* that ultimately *upayoga* is 'responsible' for bondage.[66] This is still some way from saying that it is the quality of consciousness alone which is directly instrumental on every count in binding and freeing individual *jīvas*. This in turn is equivalent to saying that the soul is totally responsible for and in control of its own bondage or freedom, given that *upayoga* is *the* characteristic of *jīvas*. To say so is not to maintain that particular states of consciousness cannot be, and are not, accounted for in terms of greater or lesser degrees of karmic obstruction, but that the cause of that obstruction comes to be seen in terms of the new central 'metaphor', i.e. consciousness itself, rather than in terms of particular physical activities and their consequences. And when pure consciousness is identified with an 'original',

---

[66] Umāsvāti himself does not link the two, although the connection is evident from, for example, the way in which *bhāva* is used in the same context in the *Pañcāstikāya* (see above).

pure self, this inevitably comes to undermine a theory of bondage based upon material karma. In other words, when ignorance (*ajñāna / avidyā*) of the true nature of the self becomes the overriding factor in bondage, material *karman* itself starts to lose reality.

ii) Upayoga according to the Pravacanasāra

Although what I shall call Kundakunda's '*upayoga* doctrine' is used repeatedly in the *Pravacanasāra* to explain the mechanics of bondage and liberation, there is no one group of gāthās in which it is systematically explained or justified in philosophical or doctrinal terms. On the contrary, it is presented as though it were a commonly accepted doctrine in need of little direct explanation. In this it demonstrates its compatibility with the nature of the text in which it occurs, since the latter has more the appearance of a mosaic of 'traditional', or earlier material, arranged on a roughly thematic basis, rather than something composed as a unity. However, as far as I know, the *upayoga* doctrine does not appear in this form in any recorded source prior to Kundakunda. Indeed, commentators frequently remark upon the peculiarity, or uniqueness of Kundakunda in this respect.[67] For all hermeneutic purposes, therefore, he must be taken as the originator of this particular form of the *upayoga* doctrine.

The purpose of this compilation, at least in Books 1 and 2, is to instruct advanced mendicants (*śramaṇas*) in the discipline which leads to self-knowledge and final liberation. Book 3, insofar as it is directed at all, seems to have a different audience in mind, namely, those just setting out on the *śramaṇas'* path and advanced lay people. As I shall show, taken in the context of the *upayoga* doctrine of the first two books, there is, in terms of soteriology, something concessionary, and even

---

[67] See, for instance, Tatia, p. 74.

contradictory, about Book 3; and this presents valuable evidence about the ways and extent to which the 'worldly' concerns of the laity were accommodated in the pattern of a largely 'internalised' ascetic soteriology.

Given the unsystematic nature of the *Pravacanasāra*, it is useful at the outset to give a schematic, if somewhat simplified version of the doctrine I shall go on to examine in greater detail in context. According to Kundakunda, *upayoga*, composed of *jñāna* and *darśana*, is the 'self' of the self, the *ātman* of the *ātman*. It appears in two forms, as *śuddha* or pure *upayoga*, and as *aśuddha* or impure *upayoga*. *Aśuddhopayoga* is further divided into *śubha* (auspicious) and *aśubha* (inauspicious) *upayoga*. *Śuddhopayoga* is the characteristic of liberated and liberating states of consciousness; *aśuddhopayoga* is the characteristic of bound and binding states of consciousness. *Śuddhopayoga*, the soteriological ideal, is the condition achieved or aspired to by the most advanced ascetics (i.e. the most practised in terms of inner discipline). *Aśuddhopayoga* is the condition of the majority (i.e. of ascetics short of the ideal, and of the laity). There is, however, a gradation in the quality of bondage in this latter condition, so that ascetics and advanced lay people have, or should aspire to bring about through particular kinds of behaviour, *upayoga* that is more *śubha* than *aśubha*. (At least, according to some gāthās they should aspire to do so; as we shall see, it depends upon which audience is being addressed.)

Upayoga is thus both instrumental in and typical of certain states of consciousness which are directly linked to both soteriological status and social role. Most importantly, it is seen to be directly and solely instrumental in bondage, something which differentiates its appearance in Kundakunda's works significantly from its use elsewhere (outlined above). In schematic form the doctrine may be presented as follows:

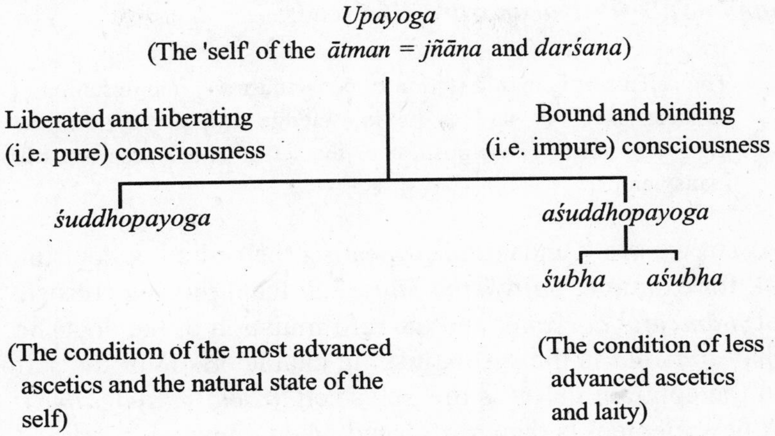

Bearing in mind Upadhye's warning that *upayoga* is 'a very mobile term, whose shade of meaning slightly changes according to the context',[68] I shall deal first with the general features of *upayoga* as described in the *Pravacanasāra*, and then, in the next chapter, with its specific implications for the mechanisms of bondage and liberation.

At *Pravacanasāra* 2.35, the substance *jīva* (*davvaṃ jīvaṃ*) is described as *cedaṇovajogamao*, i.e. as consisting of the manifestation of consciousness;[69] and according to Amṛtacandra's commentary on the *Pravacanasāra*, the *Tattvadīpikā*, this is the distinguishing characteristic (*viśeṣa-lakṣaṇa*) of the *jīva*. The Commentary adds that *upayoga* is a 'modification', or 'transformation' (*pariṇāma*) of the *jīva*, which has the form of a function or mode of being of the substance (*dravya-vṛtti-rūpa*).

This is consistent with texts such as *Tattvārtha Sūtra*

---

[68] Upadhye, Index, p. 36.

[69] Upadhye takes it as a *dvandva* compound: the *jīva* is 'constituted of sentiency and manifestation of consciousness'.

2.8 (see above), as is the remark that the *guṇa* (the quality - i.e. unique quality) of the *ātman* is *upayoga* (*guṇovaoga tti appaṇo*).[70] *Pravacanasāra* 2.63 reads:

> The self's self is manifestation of consciousness; manifestation of consciousness is said to be knowledge and perception; the manifestation of consciousness of the self is either auspicious or inauspicious.

Again we see Kundakunda repeating the orthodox doctrine of, for example, *Tattvārtha Sūtra* 2.9, that *upayoga* consists of *jñāna* and *darśana*, and the reformulation of the doctrine that *upayoga* is the distinguishing characteristic of the self in the epigram that it is the 'self's self' (*ātmā upayogātmā*). A new element is then introduced when *upayoga* is defined as being either *śubha* or *aśubha* ('auspicious' or 'inauspicious'). However, no mention is made of *śuddhopayoga* here. In the light of the full *upayoga* doctrine, where *śubha* and *aśubha* are both classified as *aśuddha*, this requires some comment.

Amṛtacandra in his commentary on the gāthā (2:63) ignores this omission of *śuddhopayoga* and takes the standard line that *upayoga* is divided into two, pure and impure,[71] and that of these two, while the pure is free from attachment (*niruparāga*), the impure has it (*soparāga*). The latter is of two kinds, *śubha* and *aśubha*, corresponding to the twofold nature of attachment, which takes the form of virtue (*viśuddhi*) or affliction (*saṃkleśa*). In the context of the *Pravacanasāra* as a whole, and of the next gāthā in particular, this expansion is quite natural. However, taken in isolation, *Pravacanasāra* 2.63 presents a clue as to the origins of 'Kundakunda's' *upayoga* doctrine. I would suggest that this gāthā reflects, or is part of, an earlier

---

[70] *Pravac.* 2:42.

[71] *upayogo dvedhā viśiṣyate śuddhāśuddhatvena* - *TD* on 2:63.

strand of doctrine, one which arose out of or was developed to accommodate lay aspirations, and that the division of *upayoga* into *śubha* and *aśubha* was one of the tools of this development. In brief, beneath the karmic net which characterises life-in-the-world, such a doctrine makes for a limited or impermanent hierarchy of goals and rewards, measured by accumulated amounts of merit and demerit (*puṇya* and *pāpa*) which are associated with particular types of consciousness (*śubha* and *aśubha*) (an association which will be examined in more detail when I come to consider the precise mechanism of bondage). For the *śramaṇa,* however, whose ideal goal is total liberation from the karmic net, and thus from rebirth, consciousness directed into the world is at best a potentially dangerous irrelevance. *Śubha* and *aśubha puṇya* and *pāpa*, are equally binding for the ascetic, whose aim is to stop all 'action' (the instrument of *karman*), even the action of consciousness insofar as it is manifested or directed. Such a reading is borne out by the fact that *śuddhopayoga*, when it comes to be posited in the full doctrine as the consciousness of pure ascetics, is (as one would always expect from a pollution-free state) viewed in negative terms, i.e. the term designates the absence of *aśuddhopayoga*. As Upadhye puts it, *śuddhopayoga* 'is not a positive spiritual something, but only immunity from the remaining two *upayoga*s', *śubha* and *aśubha*, and '*upayoga*s are manifested by the soul because of its being associated with karmic matter'.[72] In other words, *śuddhopayoga* characterises the soul as it is in itself, free of karmic accretion. This seems to be the state which is intimated but not named or given any technical designation at *Pravacanasāra* 2.64:

---

[72] Upadhye p. lxxiii.

> If the application of consciousness is auspicious the soul accumulates merit; or if inauspicious, demerit; when there is neither (*śubha* nor *aśubha*) there is no accumulation.

Despite Amṛtacandra's commentary and Upadhye's remarks to the contrary,[73] *upayoga* as a technical term seems to apply here only to *śubha* and *aśubha*. Nothing is said about a condition totally free of *karman*; it is merely stated that in the absence of *śubha*- and *aśubha-upayoga* there is no (further) accumulation. Nevertheless, it is quite natural to infer from this a kind of neutral or non-applied state of consciousness. And one may guess that when Jaina scholastics came to consider this doctrine of *śubha*- and *aśubha-upayoga* logically, they were led to posit a further category - *śuddhopayoga* - which was characteristic of developed *śramaṇas*. Technically, it would seem that such a pure state of consciousness is not *upayoga* at all; i.e. it is not a manifestation or application of consciousness but pure consciousness itself, the *pariṇāmika bhāva* (of *Tattvārtha Sūtra* 2.1) in which the *jīva* 'experiences' *kevalajñāna*. Thus, theoretically, it should make no difference to the behaviour of ascetics, since there is nothing additional which they must do in order to achieve it; i.e. they must continue as always to avoid the accumulation of new *karman* and to burn off the residue of 'old' *karman*. However, the fact that the instruments of bondage for lay people (*śubha*- and *aśubha-upayoga*) are seen as internal - states of consciousness rather than physical actions - means that any logical development of the doctrine will be in terms of 'internal' states rather than external behaviour. And this tendency was no doubt aided by the fact that, by the time it was developed logically, bondage for ascetics was already conceived of as predominantly the result of internal attitudes or 'passions' (as in the *kaṣāya* doctrine,

---

[73] Upadhye p. lxxii.

classically formulated in the *Tattvārtha Sūtra*).

That the *upayoga* doctrine represents the culmination and logical end of a lengthy process of 'internalisation' regarding the mechanisms of bondage and liberation, I shall argue at greater length below. Here, I wish to point out that although, technically, *śuddhopayoga* is the absence of something and not a thing or condition to be attained as such, and that theoretically its articulation should make no difference to the behaviour of *śramaṇas*, in practice it quickly begins to be conceived of in a positive way. And once it becomes something to be achieved, then ways other than simple avoidance of *aśuddhopayoga* can be prescribed for achieving it. Moreover, its 'internal' or psychological nature, is bound to be reflected in the methods enjoined for its attainment. Thus in the *Pravacanasāra* the development of knowledge (*jñāna*) of the true nature of the self (its essential purity), and its realisation through meditation, come to be seen as the quintessential soteriological activities of the *śramaṇa*. The radical implications of this, both for the institution of the renouncer and for ascetic behaviour as previously prescribed, and the reasons why such implications were tempered or largely avoided in practice, will be discussed below as the appropriate passages from the *Pravacanasāra* are examined in detail.

A full statement of the *upayoga* doctrine first appears in the *Pravacanasāra* at 1.9:

> When the *jīva*, whose nature is (subject to) modification, modifies (itself) through auspicious or inauspicious (states of consciousness), it becomes auspicious or inauspicious, then through the pure it becomes pure.

According to this gāthā, the *jīva* modifies itself (i.e. its soteriological state) through the development of three different states of consciousness, viz. auspicious (*śubha*), inauspicious (*aśubha*), and pure (*śuddha*), and it becomes these states to the degree that its consciousness is them. That is to say, according to this view the *jīva* is not essentially different from its modification (*pariṇāma*). So, as the *Tattvadīpikā* (on *Pravacanasāra* 1.9) remarks, when the *ātman* (= *jīva*) modifies itself through the *bhāva* of *śubha* or *aśubha rāga* (passion or attachment), having modification (*pariṇāma*) for its *svabhāva*, it becomes *śubha* or *aśubha*, like a crystal modified by the colour of a red (*rāga*) contiguous object. Similarly, when it modifies itself through a pure, passionless state,[74] it becomes *śuddha*, like a crystal modified by a pure colour (in effect, an unmodified crystal).

What then are the (soteriological) conditions or goals connected with these states or modifications of consciousness? At *Pravacanasāra* 1.11 we read:

> When the self which has modified itself through *dharma* is joined to pure consciousness (*saṃpayoga*), it attains the bliss of liberation (*ṇivvāṇa*), or if joined to auspicious (consciousness) it attains heavenly bliss.

Two stages seem to be implied here. First, it is necessary to modify oneself through *dharma*. *Dharma* has been defined (at *Pravacanasāra* 1.7) as 'conduct' (*cāritra*), which could hardly be argued with from the orthodox Jaina point of view; however, in the same gāthā, *dharma* is further defined as *sama* (*śama*), equanimity, and *sama* as the *pariṇāma* of the *ātman* in which it is free from the disturbance of *moha* (delusion).[75] *Dharma* is thus not so much linked with *cāritra* in the sense of physical activity in the world, as with a particular state of mind, *sama* (Sk. *śama*, 'tranquillity', 'absence of passion'), connected here

---

[74] *śuddhenārāgabhāvena* - *TD* on *Pravac.* 1:9.

[75] *mohakkhohavihīṇo* - *Pravac.* 1.7 (= Sk. *mohakṣobhavihīnaḥ*).

specifically with the absence of *moha*, and probably attained through some form of preliminary meditation or 'calming'.[76] The second stage involves the development of *śuddha* or *śubha* states of consciousness, one resulting in final liberation (*nirvāṇa*), the other in rebirth in a heavenly world. This at least is the sense if we take *saṃpayoga* as a synonym for *uvaoga*, as the context would suggest. This is what the commentary (*Tattvadīpikā*) does, in the process warning against the (heavenly) bondage attendant upon *śubhopayoga* and enjoining *śuddhopayoga* instead.

The following gāthā (1.12) lists the inevitable (de)gradations of the *ātman* through the rise of the inauspicious manifestation of consciousness. This is contrasted (at 1.13) with the 'happiness' (*suham / sukham*) of those who have attained *śuddhopayoga*, providing the first unambiguous reference in the text (as opposed to the commentary) to the technical term *śuddhopayoga*.

In the light of what follows, the description (at 1.14) of the *śramaṇa* whose *upayoga* is *śuddha* as one who has understood well the *padārtha*s (i.e. the nine *tattva*s) and the *sūtra*s, who is endowed with self-control (*saṃyama*) and *tapas*, who is free from desire (*vigatarāga*), and to whom *sukha* and *duḥkha* are alike, seems more like the attempted elision of a received 'external' tradition with a more recently formulated 'internal' one than a description of the ideal embodiment of *śuddhopayoga* as such.

Gāthā 1.15 emphasises the autonomy of the *ātman* whose *upayoga* is pure: it becomes itself the self[77] because it is free from all forms of destructive *karman*.[78] Having reached this state, it is omniscient and known as self-existent (*sayaṃbhu / svayambhū*) (1.16). The point to note

---

[76] For comments on Jaina meditation, see p. 185ff., below.

[77] *bhūdo sayam evādā* - *Pravac.* 1.15 (= *bhūtaḥ svayam evātmā*).

[78] See *JPP* p. 115ff.

here is that this journey to omniscience, to total purity, is seen as the recovery or realisation of the 'real' or 'true' self, i.e. of its essentially unbound nature.[79]

Svayambhū (self-existent) is a resonant term in Indian religious thought, and it is probably not coincidental that the text here uses an expression with a decidedly monistic and Vedāntic ring to it, one which is used in various contexts as an epithet for the highest principle.[80]

Returning to the condition of those who are still characterised by *aśuddhopayoga*, we read at 1.46 that:

> There would be no *saṃsāra* for any embodied *jīva* if the *ātman* by itself, through its own nature, did not become auspicious or inauspicious.[81]

In other words, bondage - life in *saṃsāra*- is the direct result of particular states of consciousness which are self-generated. Thus the *ātman* does not find itself bound, its condition in the world is not existentially 'given'; it has bound itself. As the commentary (*Tattvadīpikā*) puts it:

---

[79] That it has this meaning, despite the standard Jaina doctrine that the self has been bound in matter from beginningless time (see *JPP* p. 107), will be made clear below. As the commentary (*TD*) on this gāthā (1:16) remarks, from the *niścaya* point of view - i.e. the determined or higher, as opposed to the conventional (*vyavahāra*) view (see p. 126, fn. 5, below) - there is no causal or instrumental relation between the self and anything else, viz. the *ajīva* category, including material *karman* (*na niścayataḥ pareṇa sahātmanaḥ kārakatvasambandho 'sti*).

[80] See, for example, *Bṛhadāranyaka Upaniṣad* 2.6.3.: *brahma svayambhū brahmaṇe namaḥ*. I shall have much more to say about the condition of the *śramaṇa* whose *upayoga* is *śuddha* in the sections on the mechanisms of bondage and liberation.

[81] It should not be thought that I am taking these gāthās out of context. Gāthā 1:46 provides a good example of the disjointed nature of parts of the *Pravacanasāra*, for it is sandwiched between a gāthā on the activities called *kṣāyikī* (due to the destruction of karmas) and one on the knowledge called *kṣāyika* (produced after the destruction of karmas).

If the *ātman* itself is not transformed exclusively by its own nature, consisting of auspicious and inauspicious states, then it remains with its own pure state, without division, in every way and forever.[82]

This is strikingly at odds with the standard Jaina doctrine, summarised by P.S. Jaini as follows: the soul's 'involvement with the material universe ... has had no beginning, and it is likely to continue almost indefinitely'; furthermore, the Jaina 'believes it is incorrect to imagine that the soul was once pure but later became defiled. It has always been impure, just as a seam of gold has "always" been imbedded in the rock where it is found'.[83] Gāthā 1.46 implies a different view - that the natural or 'original' condition of the soul is unbound. In other words, Kundakunda denies that it is an ontological given that the soul is entrapped in matter from beginningless time, without initial cause; instead, he states that the cause of bondage (being in the state of *saṃsāra*) is the soul's developing by itself into *śubha* and *aśubha* states. And once an original cause for bondage is posited, it is possible to go beyond that and describe the state *before* bondage, and this becomes the original or natural condition of the soul, i.e. the state from which each individual *jīva* has started and to which it aspires to 'return' - in this case *śuddhopayoga*. Furthermore, if from the individual's point

---

82 *yadi khalv ekāntena śubhāśubhabhāvasvabhāvena svayam ātmā na pariṇamate tadā sarvadaiva sarvathā nirvighātena śuddhasvabhāvenaivāvatiṣṭhate* - *TD.* on *Pravac.* 1.46.

As we shall see, in the *Samayasāra* Kundakunda actually affirms this view: from the *niścaya* standpoint, the soul is, in every way and forever, in its own pure state. That *naya* is clearly not the one taken here - i.e. the soul does in some real sense transform itself - however, some important doctrinal modifications (noted below), make this gāthā one signpost on the road to such a position.

83 *JPP* p. 107.

of view *saṃsāra* is self-generated by the *ātman* through its manifestations of consciousness, this not only implies that the *ātman* is prior to *saṃsāra* but also that it 'creates' *saṃsāra* through its own states of consciousness (i.e. 'creates' it in the only significant sense - for itself). Taken in this way, *saṃsāra* would thus be the creation of impure or 'false' states of consciousness. Given the essential purity of the soul, however, this false consciousness can only take one form, namely, delusion regarding the *ātman*'s true nature. This is indeed the case in the *Pravacanasāra*, where *moha* comes to be seen as the chief agent in bondage, and is directly linked to *aśuddhopayoga* (*śubha-* and *aśubha-upayoga*).[84] This, as will be made clear, has radical implications for the prescribed methods of liberation, entailing release through inner transformation of consciousness and knowledge (*gnosis*). But before considering these, I shall now discuss the mechanism of bondage as portrayed in the *Pravacanasāra* in greater detail.[85]

---

[84] For a full discussion of this, see p. 124ff., below.

[85] Whether it is possible logically to hold a view that the world - *saṃsāra* - is a product of false consciousness, and that false consciousness is produced by various obscuring karmas which are themselves the material constituents of *saṃsāra*, is not a problem directly confronted in these texts. However, the implication of Kundakunda's *niścaya* view is that false consciousness is entirely self-generated and thus really has nothing to do with *karman* at all. The *vyavahāra* view, of course, is different; and that is enough, according to the orthodox Jaina philosophical position, to neutralise the difficulty. For a historian, however, the fact that contradiction is built into the system explains nothing; rather it is necessary to explain why such a system, with its deliberate imperviousness to argument, should have been erected in the first place. Kundakunda's 'logical' (*niścaya*) view, by demonstrating the position Jaina scholastics would have found themselves in without the safety-curtain of the various *nayas*, helps us to formulate such an explanation. For, as we shall see when we examine the *Samayasāra*, he remained largely true to the logic of his own argument by employing the *niścaya* / *vyavahāra* distinction in a

---

non-'contradictory', and thus, according to his critics within Jainism, one-sided and heretical way.

5

The mechanism of bondage according to the *Pravacanasāra*

5.1 *The mechanism of bondage*

The principal passages dealing with the mechanism of bondage in the *Pravacanasāra* are clustered in a group in Book 2 (c. gāthās 2.77-2.97). The pivotal gāthā here is *Pravacanasāra* 2.81, where the question is asked, how is it possible for the non-material *ātman* to be bound by material *karman*. The text in full reads:

> The embodied (*mūrta*, i.e. material objects), having qualities such as *rūpa*, etc., is bound by mutual touching; the *ātman* is quite different from [the opposite of] that, so how can material *karman* be bound to it?

In many ways this is a crucial question for Jaina dogmatics, and no less so for Kundakunda. It was one which was probably quickly identified by opponents in rival *darśanas* as a weak point in the Jaina argument; and as we shall see, it may well have been Kundakunda's attempt to solve this specific problem, although perhaps more for 'internal' than 'external' reasons, which first put him on the path that ends in the apparently heterodox views of the *Samayasāra*.

To understand the importance of the problem we must look at the way the argument is developed in the *Pravacanasāra* in some detail. At 2.77 it is said that molecules (*khaṃdha* / *skandha*), 'capable of becoming *karman*', coming into 'contact' with, or 'attaining to' a transformation of the *jīva*, develop into the state of *karman* (*kammabhāva*); but it is not by the *jīva* that those *skandha* are transformed. In other words, it is neither the *jīva* nor the *skandha* which is directly instrumental in the 'creation' of *karman* (and thus bondage), but the meeting of the two, i.e. of the *jīva*'s condition, or mode at the time, with the molecules (*pudgala-skandhas*). However, as the commentary (*Tattvadīpikā*) makes clear, it is the *skandhas* which have the potential to transform into the *karman* state (*karmabhāva*), even without the *jīva* side of the equation. So the soul (*puruṣa*) is not the agent of the *karman*-state of material masses (*pudgalapiṇḍa*).[1] Thus the creation of karmic bondage is defined here as the transformation of material molecules by 'contact' with the modifications of a *jīva*, with 'contact' and transformation, and not the *jīva*, being the instrumental factors as such. Clearly, the particular modification of the *jīva* also plays a crucial role, one we shall consider later, although it is not emphasised here.[2] It is this material, transformed into *karman*, which goes to make up the various bodies the *jīva* is bound into in its various births.[3] However, as the commentary reminds us, the *jīva*, since it is not material, cannot be - and therefore should not be identified with - any of these bodies.[4]

The soul's characteristics are then enumerated:

> Know that the *jīva*, whose quality is consciousness (*cetanā*), is without taste, without form ('colour'), without odour; it is unmanifest (i.e. cannot be touched), without sound, beyond the range of a distinguishing or characteristic mark, and without describable configuration. [*Pravacanasāra* 2:80]

This is clearly a description of the *jīva* in its unbound or pure state (i.e. in Kundakunda's terms it is the *niścaya* view

---

[1] *na pudgalapiṇḍānāṃ karmatvakartā puruṣo 'sti - TD* on *Pravac.* 2:77.

[2] What is meant by 'contact' in these circumstances, and thus the reason for its being placed between inverted commas, will be clarified below.

[3] *Pravac.* 2:78.

[4] *TD* on 2:79.

of the *jīva*).[5] Nevertheless, there is something odd about such a gāthā in a Jaina context. Why, for instance, is the *jīva* said to have no definable structure or configuration, when standard Jaina doctrine is that it has the shape of its current or, if released, final body?[6]

I shall have more to say about this later, but it is unlikely that it is simply a coincidence that the characterisation of the pure *jīva* given above could be just as well a description of the Vedāntic *ātman-brahman*, even down to the fact that it has *cetanā* as its quality (*guṇa*). In this respect it is interesting to compare Kundakunda's characterisation with that given in, for instance, Nemicandra's *Dravya-saṃgraha*, a tenth century Digambara work referring back to the *Ṣaṭkhaṇḍāgama* and

---

5 Matilal points out that Kundakunda's dual classification (*vyavahāra-* and *niścaya-naya*) 'has no direct connection with the usual seven standpoints of the Jainas, but corresponds to the ... distinction of two levels of truth in Mādhyamika Buddhism' or the same distinction made in Śaṅkara's school of Advaita Vedānta. This view, which is peculiar to Kundakunda and those following him, describes the soul from the *niścaya* standpoint 'as independent, self-existent and uncontaminated by matter. This is the truth in the ultimate sense, a goal to be arrived at the final stage (sic.)'. But the *vyavahāra* standpoint 'describes the soul as one that is involved in karma as well as in the birth and re-birth cycle (*saṃsāra*)' (1981, p. 43).

I shall discuss this distinction and the ways in which Kundakunda uses it at length when I deal with the *Samayasāra* - see p. 239ff., below.

6 *Saṃsthāna* is the term used, for example, at *TS*. 8.11 to denote the figure of the body. There are, however, other instances of this kind of description; thus in a passage in the *Āyāraṃga-sutta* the liberated self is held to be indescribable: *arūvī sattā, apayassa payaṃ ṇatthi* - 'its essence is without form; there is no mark for what is without mark' (quoted by P.S. Jaini, *JPP* p. 271, fn. 41., who translates, 'there is no condition of the unconditioned').

On the dimensions of the *jīva*, see *JPP* pp. 58ff., 102, 269. As P.S. Jaini remarks, it is only the Jainas who posit a soul that is at the same time 'nonmaterial and yet subject to contraction and expansion when in its mundane state' and is therefore 'of the same dimension as its body (*sva-deha-parimāṇa*)' [*JPP* p. 58]. So this is part of the same problem as that raised at *Pravac*. 2:81.

the *Kaṣāyaprābhṛta,* the only works designated canonical by the Digambaras. There, a kind of composite view of the soul is given which includes the characteristic of its being the size of its body; and when the *niścaya* view is raised it simply designates the soul as that which has *cetanā*:

> It (the soul) is (1) *jīva* (that which lives); (2) possessed of *upayoga* ...; (3) *amūrta* (immaterial); (4) *kartā* (the doer of all actions); (5) *sva-deha-parimāṇa* (of the size of its body, which it completely fills); (6) *bhoktā* (enjoyer of the fruits of actions); (7) *saṃsāra-stha* (located in the cycle of death and rebirth); (8) *siddha* (in its perfect condition a siddha); (9) *ūrdhvagati* (of an upward tendency). That which in the three times has four *prāṇas*, viz. senses, power, vitality, and respiration, is conventionally soul; but from the essential point of view that which has consciousness is soul.[7]

The term '*niścaya*' is used here merely to designate the focused or narrow view of the essential characteristic of the soul; and unlike the *niścaya* view given at *Pravacanasāra* 2.80, it does not contradict the *vyavahāra*, or conventional Jaina view. That the *niścaya-naya* of the *Pravacanasāra* is apparently irreconcilable to the conventional *naya* does not, of course, disqualify either according to Jaina 'logic'; however, I shall have more to say about this when I discuss the possible reasons for the development of the *naya* doctrine and Kundakunda's unconventional, not to say 'heretical' reading of it, below.

---

7 *jīvo uvaogamao amutti kattā sadehaparimāṇo* |
bhottā saṃsārattho siddho so vissasoḍḍhagaī || 2 ||
tikkāle cadu pāṇā iṃdiyabalamāu āṇapāṇo ya |
vavahārā so jīvo ṇicchayaṇayado du cedaṇā jassa || 3 ||
Nemicandra's *Dravya-saṃgraha*, quoted by J.L. Jaini 1940, p.83; his translation with alterations.

I am unable to translate *vissasa*, but it is probably connected with (Sanskrit) *viṣvañc*, 'going in all directions'. That is to say, the soul, depending upon its karmic condition, is capable of going in any direction on the death of the body, although its inherent tendency is upward. It may be that *vissasa* is a corrupt reading.

Returning to the *Pravacanasāra*, we come again to the crucial question (at 2.81), how can the immaterial soul be bound by material *karman*? The fact that this question is being asked at all is highly revealing of the shift in doctrinal emphasis, one which, as we shall see, entails or accompanies a shift in practice. For according to standard Jaina doctrine there is no need to make such a query, since it is an existential fact - a 'given' - that the *jīva* has been entrapped in matter from beginningless time. As we have noted above, and as P.S. Jaini points out, the Jaina envisions his soul's 'involvement with the material universe' as having had no beginning. Furthermore, he 'believes it incorrect to imagine that the soul was once pure but later became defiled. It has always been impure ... '.[8] Thus, the received doctrine points to a question which is more practical than theoretical, viz. how can what is impure be made pure?

If, however, you try to account for the fact that the *jīva* is, or appears to be bound, first you must assume some primal or 'original' state in which it is *not* bound, and then attempt to show what is demanded by this particular question (*Pravacanasāra* 2.81), namely, how is it that the pure can become, or appear to be, impure? This is easy enough to answer when the two have the same ontological basis (a white sheet can be covered in mud), but when they have no such common ground, one being material and the other not, then a logically satisfactory answer such as might silence an opponent is going to be much harder to formulate. As the *Tattvadīpikā* (on 2.81) puts it: with embodied, material substances (*mūrtayor ... pudgalayor*) which have *rūpa*, etc., mutual bondage due to particular touch (i.e. to the state of being smooth or rough / sticky or dry [*snigdha* or *rūkṣa*]) is recognised;[9] but how can the *ātman*, being incorporeal (*amūrta*), and so without

8 *JPP* p. 107.

9 *snigdha-rūkṣatva-sparśaviśeṣād-anyonyabandho 'vadhāryate* - *TD* on 2:81.

particular contact or touch, stickiness or dryness, be connected with material *karman* (*karmapudgala*) which has those qualities?

To see how Kundakunda (and Amṛtacandra) attempt to answer this question, we must look in detail at the gāthās following *Pravacanasāra* 2.81.[10]

At 2.82, we are told that although the *jīva* is without *rūpa*, etc. (as enumerated at 2.81), itself, nevertheless, it sees and knows (*pecchadi jāṇādi*) substances (*dravya*) which have *rūpa*, etc., and that the mechanism of bondage is analagous to this. Thus the *jīva*, which consists of *upayoga*, having attained to various objects (of the senses), is infatuated, attached or averse, and so it is combined with them.[11]

The *Tattvadīpikā* (on 2.83) explains that the *ātman*, composed of *upayoga*, meeting with various distinct forms / objects, betakes itself (*samupaiti; sam-upa- √i*) to *moha*, *rāga*, or *dveṣa*. And because the innate nature of the *ātman* (*ātmasvabhāva*) is 'coloured' (*uparakta*) by *moha*, etc., which are conditioned or modified by the 'other' (*parapratyaya*) (i.e. the *ajīva*, the 'various objects'), like a crystal gem whose nature is coloured by the objects close to it, so the *ātman* becomes itself 'bondage' (*bandha*) because it is paired with their natures (*tadbhāvadvitīyatvāt*).

The gist of this seems to be that passions are generated in the *ātman* by proximity to objects, that such passions are modifications of the *upayoga* which characterises the *ātman*, and that this is what constitutes bondage. In other words, the *ātman* binds itself through its own *upayoga*.

On the one hand, this gāthā and its commentary seem to be harking back to earlier ideas about the soul being

---

10 Since there is a good deal of repetition in these verses, in what follows I shall rely more on summary than direct quotation; the relevant gāthās are *Pravac.* 2:81-2:97.

11 *Pravac.* 2:83. There is some ambiguity here over whether *tehiṃ* refers to the sense-objects or to the passional states; Upadhye translates it as referring to the latter, although it amounts to the same thing.

'coloured' (the *leśyā* doctrine) which strongly suggest that the soul was once viewed in material terms, while on the other hand, the very idea of bondage seems to have been lifted out of the sphere of *material karman* altogether: the soul now binds itself through modification of its manifestation of consciousness.[12] Such modifications are said to be brought about by contact with or proximity to material objects; yet the *mechanism* of this is not explained; at the level of contact the problematical gap between the material and the immaterial remains. However, it looks very much as though bondage has in effect been dematerialised. For if it is the particular manifestation of the immaterial soul's own consciousness which is instrumental in bondage, what place is there for the original *karman* theory?[13] The only answer is that it is the particular *upayoga* which 'causes' the karmic particles to adhere to the *jīva* (i.e. *upayoga* has the same role as *kaṣāya* does in the classical theory), but this only returns us to the original problem: how can what is immaterial - a state of consciousness characterising an immaterial soul - be instrumental in its own bondage by matter? A close reading of Kundakunda and Amṛtacandra suggests that they were aware of these problems. In particular, the epistemological divide between the *vyavahāra* and the *niścaya* views, with Kundakunda's peculiar interpretation of this division (which becomes so evident in the *Samayasāra*), provide them with a possible route out of this impasse. But as we shall see later, this way offers such a threat to the whole tradition of Jaina doctrine and practice that, with the exception of the *Samayasāra*, it cannot be

---

[12] On *leśyā* see, for instance, *Utt*. XXXIV and Jacobi's footnote on *Utt*. XXXIV.1 (1895, p. 196) which quotes the same metaphor of the crystal (*sphaṭika*) from the *Avacūri* with regard to the *leśyā*'s influence on the soul. See also Schubring (1962) para. 97-98.

[13] Although, as we shall see below, Kundakunda and Amṛtacandra are reluctant to admit this: according to the *niścaya* view, *jīva* is the instrumental cause of material *karman*, and the material cause of its own modifications.

openly entered into or allowed to go beyond implication.

Pravacanasāra 2.84 confirms that it is by the (internal) state or attitude (*bhāva*) with which the *jīva* sees and knows objects that it is stained (*rajjadi*), and it is this state which is instrumental in bondage. According to the commentary (*Tattvadīpikā*), this *bhāvabandha* corresponds to, or represents, *snigdha* and *rūkṣa*, i.e. it takes the place of the material instruments of bondage. Thus *dravyabandha* is controlled or modified by *bhāvabandha*.[14] To put it simply, *bhāva* is what counts in bondage, *dravya* cannot be bound without it.[15]

At *Pravacanasāra* 2.85 it is reiterated that whereas bondage between material atoms takes place through touching (*sparśa*), bondage of the *jīva* takes place through passion (*rāga*, literally, the act of colouring); moreover, *pudgala* and *jīva* are said to be bound together by 'mutual interpenetration' (*aṇṇoṇṇassavagāho*). As the next gāthā (2.86) makes clear, this last part refers to the standard Jaina doctrine that *pudgala* and *jīva* / *ātman* do not touch in bondage but occupy the same space:

> The self has space-points; material bodies enter into those space-points. They remain there as fit; they go [or] they are bound.

This takes us to the heart of the problem, succinctly diagnosed by P.S. Jaini when he explains that:

> Jainas view the soul's involvement with karma as merely an "association" (*ekakṣetrāvagāha*, literally, occupying the same locus); there is said to be no actual *contact* between them, since this would imply a soul which was, like karma, material by nature. Just how a non-material thing can in any way interact with a material one is not well clarified. The texts simply suggest that we can *infer* such an association from our own "experience" of

---

[14] *atha punas tenaiva paudgalikaṃ karma badhyata eva, ity eṣa bhāvabandhapratyayo dravyabandhaḥ* - *TD* on *Pravac.* 2:84.

[15] Cf. *TD* introducing 2:87, below.

> bondage, just as we infer the association of an immaterial consciousness and a material object from the experience of perception.

He then refers to the passage from the *Pravacanasāra* and the *Tattvadīpikā* (2.82) which we have noticed above.[16]

The attempts of the *Tattvadīpikā* to explain the fact of bondage, given these conditions, merely circle the conundrum without engaging it (and it is difficult to imagine what solution could be offered to a problem expressed in such terms). Thus the *Tattvadīpikā* on *Pravacanasāra* 2.86 'explains' that the *ātman* has innumerable space-points (*pradeśa*), equal to those of the inhabited universe (*lokākāśa*);[17] within those *pradeśa*s the soul vibrates, depending on the 'atom groups' (*vargaṇā*) of body, speech and mind. Karmic material, having a similar vibration (*parispanda*), enters the *pradeśa*s and remains there. Then, if the soul is in a state (*bhāva*) of *moha*, *rāga* and *dvesa*, it is also bound. (In addition to the problem of how a *bhāva* brings about material bondage, here there is also the question of how material atoms can 'cause' the immaterial soul to vibrate.) The *Tattvadīpikā* on *Pravacanasāra* 2.85 claims that the modifications (*paryāyas*) of *rāga*, *moha* and *dveṣa* are limiting adjuncts (*upādhikas*) in relation to the *jīva*, and that their oneness with the *jīva* constitutes bondage. Moreover, the bondage (interpenetration) of *jīva* and *karmapudgala* is merely the occasion (*nimitta*) of their mutual modifications, i.e. they modify themselves, not each other.[18] Quite how this process is set off is again not explained.

The commentary (*Tattvadīpikā*) on *Pravacanasāra* 2.82 related this directly to the *upayoga* doctrine, explaining

---

16 *JPP* pp. 113-114.

17 On this, see *JPP* p. 102.

18 *jīvakarmapudgalayoḥ parasparapariṇāmanimittamātratvena viśiṣṭataraḥ parasparam-avagāhaḥ sa tadubhayabandhaḥ* - *TD* on *Pravac.* 2:85.

that, although the self, because it lacks touch due to its absence of *rūpa*, has no union with *karmapudgala*, the *vyavahāra* view of bondage by *karmapudgala* is 'proved' (*sādhaka*) by the union with states of *rāga*, *dveṣa*, etc., 'based upon a manifestation of consciousness conditioned by *karmapudgala* existing in the state of being immmersed in the same space [as that occupied by the self]'.[19] In other words, *karmapudgala*, occupying the same *pradeśa*s as the *jīva*, brings about (*śubha* or *aśubha*) *upayoga* (*rāga*, *dveṣa* and *moha*), which is instrumental in bondage. Thus, according to the *vyavahāra* view, it is still material *karman*, or *dravyabandha*, which 'causes' *bhāvabandha* (particular manifestations of consciousness); so it is *karmapudgala* which is ultimately responsible for bondage. The *niścaya* view here, on the other hand, is that it is *bhāvabandha* (*upayoga*, etc.) which is the cause of *dravyabandha* and thus the initiating cause of bondage. That is to say, it is the self-transformation of the *jīva* into states of *upayoga* characterised by *rāga*, etc., which 'sets off' the transformation of *karmapudgala* and brings about bondage. (I shall have more to say about this below.) This *niścaya* view is given in the *Tattvadīpikā* at 2.86, and again in the introduction by Amṛtacandra to the next gāthā (2.87).[20] The actual text (*Pravacanasāra* 2.87) is less technical but quite clear:

> The impassioned self binds *karman*, the self free from passion is freed from *karman*: this is the summary statement of the bondage of souls - know this in reality.

The *Tattvadīpikā* comments that the *jīva* free from *rāga*

---

[19] *ātmano nirūpatvena sparśaśūnyatvān na karmapudgalaiḥ sahāsti saṃbandaḥ, ekāvagāhabhāvāvasthitakarmapudgala-nimittopayogādhirūḍharāgadveṣādibhāvasaṃbandhaḥ karmapudgala-bandhavyavahārasādhakas tv asty eva* - *TD* on *Pravac*. 2:82.

[20] *dravyabandhasya bhāvabandho hetuḥ* - *TD* on 2.86. *atha dravyabandhahetutvena rāgapariṇāmamātrasya bhāvabandhasya niścayabandhatvaṃ sādhayati* - *TD* intro. to 2.87.

not only fails to bind fresh (*abhinava*) *karman*, but it also rids itself of old *karman*, and so liberates itself (i.e. absence of *rāga* functions as both *saṃvara* and *nirjarā*). It is clearly, therefore, modification into attachment (*rāgapari ṇāma*) which is the 'real' bondage (that is to say, according to this view, it is the prime or ultimate cause of bondage).

What precisely is being claimed here, and what are we supposed to understand by the use of *vyavahāra* and *niścaya* in this context? In an attempt to clarify this, I shall construct a theoretical model to test against the text. And it is worth remembering that, freed from the commentary, this section of the *Pravacanasāra* has all the appearance in its present form of being a compilation of gāthās on bondage, and so may represent different layers of doctrine.

First, it should be noted that *Pravacanasāra* 2.97, which draws the line under this section on bondage, says that this description of the bondage of the *jīva* has been preached by Arahants for *yati*s (ascetics) from the *niścaya* point of view, whereas another point of view, the *vyavahāra* one, is preached for others (i.e. the laity). In other words, this is a teaching aimed specifically at *śramaṇa*s.

The *vyavahāra* view, which is not preached here, is, as we have seen, outlined in the commentary (*Tattvadīpikā*) on 2.82. It amounts to this: *dravyabandha* (*karmapudgala*) is the cause of bondage, for it is *karmapudgala*, through occupying the same *pradeśas* as the *jīva*, which brings about the modification of consciousness (*upayoga*) into *rāga*, *dveṣa* and *moha* (*śubha* and *aśubha*),[21] which in turn is the cause of further bondage (i.e. it 'sets off' the binding of further *karman*).

The *niścaya* view is that it is *bhāvabandha* (*śubha-* and *aśubha-upayoga*) which is the cause of bondage, since, although *karmapudgala* occupies the same *pradeśa*s as the *jīva*, there is no contact (*sparśa*) between the two. Rather, their contiguity 'sets off' in the *jīva* self-transformations into

---

21 See *Pravac.* 2:88.

states of *upayoga*, characterised by *rāga*, *dveṣa* and *moha*, and these alone cause *karman* to bind the *jīva*.[22] (What is meant by '*karman*' in this case will be discussed below.)

The content of these two views can be combined or reconciled in a circular model, in function not unlike the *paṭicca-samuppāda* of the Buddhists. That is to say, *karman* causes transformation of consciousness, causing (new) *karman* to be bound, causing (further) transformation of consciousness, causing (new) *karman* to be bound, etc. The *vyavahāra* and the *niścaya* views both turn this circle into a chain. The difference between them is that, from the *vyavahāra* perspective, *karmapudgala* is the initiate cause of bondage (although strictly speaking *dravyakarman* is beginningless, corresponding to the standard Jaina view of the predicament of the *jīva* in *saṃsāra*, that it has always been bound), while, from the *niścaya* perspective, it is *upayoga* which is the initiate cause.[23]

The *vyavahāra* view is spelt out at *Pravacanasāra* 2.29:

> The soul, tainted by *karman*, attains to a modification which is connected with *karman*; thus *karman* adheres; therefore *karman* is a modification (of the soul).[24]

The *Tattvadīpikā* on this gāthā explains that the modification (*pariṇāma*) of the *ātman* is the cause of material *karman* adhering (*dravyakarmaśleṣahetuḥ*), and the cause of this *pariṇāma* is itself *dravyakarman*. This is not, however, the 'fault' (*doṣa*) of 'mutual dependence' (*itaretarāśraya*) because the *ātman*, which is bound by beginningless *dravyakarman*, employs as its cause the prior *dravyakarman*.[25] And because new and old material

---

22 See *Pravac.* 2:87.

23 The precise meaning of *karman* in the *niścaya* chain will be discussed below.

24 Upadhye adds, 'developed by passions etc.'.

25 *anādiprasiddhadravyakarmābhisaṃbaddhasyātmanaḥ prāktanadravyakarmaṇas tatra hetutvenopādānāt* - *TD* on

karman are effect and cause, then the modification of the self is *dravyakarman*, and the *ātman*, because it is the agent of its own modification, is figuratively (also) the agent of *dravyakarman*.[26] Here the emphasis clearly falls on material *karman* as the 'real' or 'first' cause of bondage, i.e. the cause which one must concentrate on removing to achieve liberation.[27]

The standard explanation of these two views is given in the *Tattvadīpikā* on *Pravacanasāra* 2.97, where it is claimed that both are correct, since the *dravya jīva* is thought of as both pure and impure.[28] For according to the standard *nayas* doctrine,[29] these are two ways of expressing the same thing - from the point of view of substance (*dravyārthika*) and from the point of view of modification or mode (*paryāyārthika*). So from the former the *jīva* is pure, from the latter it is impure. Here, according to the *Tattvadīpikā* on 2.97, the purity of the *jīva* is emphasised because it is the most 'effective' or 'conclusive' (*sādhakatama*). In other words, as a pedagogic principle, either the purity or impurity of the *jīva* is stressed, depending upon which audience is being addressed. To use a Buddhist term again, this might be seen as a 'skilful means' to engender the type of behaviour most required at a particular rung on the soteriological ladder. However, from a logical point of view (i.e. the point of view required in debate) this brings us no closer to answering the question raised at *Pravacanasāra* 2.81, namely, how can the immaterial soul be bound by, or bind, material *karman*? Nor does it answer the variant on that question, raised here

---

Pravac. 2:29.

[26] *tathātma cātmapariṇāmakartṛtvād dravyakarmakartāpy upacārāt* - ibid.

[27] Cf. the *niścaya* view at *Pravac.* 2:30, where the *jīva* is said *not* to be the agent of material *karman*; rather its action in transforming itself is viewed as *karman*, therefore it binds itself.

[28] *ubhāv apy etau staḥ śuddhāsuddhatvenobhayathā dravyasya pratīyamānatvāt* - *TD* on *Pravac.* 2:97.

[29] See, for instance, J.L. Jaini 1940, p. 116.

by the *niścaya* view: how can what is essentially pure transform itself into something impure? To say that at the same time it is and is not bound by material *karman*, depending on one's point of view, is to side-step the question.

To be clear about this, the *naya* view is not the tautological one that, from the standpoint of the liberated *jīva*, there is no bondage by material *karman*, while, from that of the unliberated soul, there is. Rather, it is saying that *at one and the same time* the *jīva* is bound and not bound by *karmapudgala*, depending on one's point of view. This is in many ways a risky concession; to say that there is a viewpoint from which the *jīva* is unaffected by material *karman*, here and now in *saṃsāra*, even if the purpose of such a statement is primarily prescriptive and is not supposed to be a complete view, is to open a vista upon a potentially very different soteriological route. It is this path, as we shall see, that Kundakunda takes in the *Samayasāra* through his use of a *vyavahāra* / *niścaya* distinction which has more in common with Mādhyamika Buddhism and even more with Advaita Vedānta than with the Jaina philosophy of Anekāntavāda. Here, we can come closer to understanding the origins of that departure by examining further the implicit tendency of this section of the *Pravacanasāra* on the mechanism of bondage.

As we have seen, the *niścaya-naya* is one attempt to break out of the logical impasse created by the material bondage of a non-material soul. It suggests that, at some level, the soul binds itself, which, if it is non-material, would seem to be the only intelligible explanation for the fact of bondage. (Although this, of course, raises other theoretical problems.) However, Jainism as a religion, as opposed to a philosophy, needs at the same time to keep the connection with material *karman*, which is the basis of all its ethical and ascetic practices. This connection is provided by the *vyavahāra-naya*. As an ungenerous opponent might remark, the *naya* doctrine seems like a Jaina attempt both to have their material *karman* and to destroy it. It might be objected here that *karman*, although not an initiating cause, is still an essential component in the mechanism or chain of bondage according to the *niścaya* view. To see whether this is really the case, we must make a closer examination of the relevant gāthāṣ in the *Pravacanasāra*.

As we know, the *niścaya* view is that when the soul is attached or impassioned (*ratta*) it binds *karman*, and that when it is free from *rāga* it is free from *karma*s (*Pravacanasāra* 2.87). Expanding on this, the next gāthā (2.88) states that bondage comes from modification, which consists of attachment (*rāga*), aversion (*dosa*), and infatuation or delusion (*moha*).[30] Delusion and aversion are inauspicious, attachment is either auspicious or inauspicious (depending upon whether it takes the form of purification (*viśuddhi*) or defilement (*saṃkleśa*) [*Tattvadīpikā*]). *Pravacanasāra* 2.89 continues:

> It is said among ignorant people (*aṇṇesu*) that the *śubha* modification is merit (*puṇya*), the *aśubha* is demerit (*pāpa*). The modification that does not result in anything else is, according to the Jain religion, the cause of the destruction of *duḥkha*.

In other words, while *aśuddhopayoga* is the cause of *puṇya* and *pāpa*, the cultivation of *śuddhopayoga* leads to liberation.[31]

Next (at 2.90), it is affirmed that the *jīva* is essentially different from its embodiments in the six classes of living beings, whether immobile (*sthāvara*) or mobile (*trasa*). For as the *Tattvadīpikā* puts it, among these six classes of embodied *jīva*s, there are other substances (viz. *pudgala*, etc.), whereas the *ātman* is its own substance.[32]

---

[30] Cf. *Pravac.* 1.84.

[31] Compare this with 2:64 (quoted above), which is probably the gāthā which 2:89 refers back to, where it is clearly stated that it is *upayoga* which accumulates karmic residue (merit and demerit).

[32] *atra ṣaḍjīvanikāyātmanaḥ paradravyam eka evātmā sva-*

We now come to a crucial gāthā [2.91]:

> Who does not know thus the *paramātman*, encountered in their own natures, conceives through delusion the idea 'I am (this), this is mine'.

This gāthā has a number of ambiguities; for instance, *paramappāṇaṃ* apparently refers to the *Paramātman* - a neo-Vedāntic term possibly used by Kundakunda at 2.102 (see below), and frequently employed in the *Tattvadīpikā*, especially on Book 1 - rather than to the *ajīva* and the *jīva* (which is the way Upadhye takes it). However, the general meaning is clear: whoever does not know the essential nature of the *ātman* - its difference from its embodiments - comes to have the delusive idea that what is in reality not himself - the *ajīva* or *para* - *is* himself; he confuses two totally separate categories. This cognitive or epistemological confusion about the true nature of the self is, as we have seen (2.88), a self-transformation of the *jīva* (*aśubhopayoga*), said to have been 'set off' by contiguity with material *karman*, although the mechanism of the latter cannot be explained (and, as I shall suggest, is not really needed according to the logic of the internalised system).

In short, delusion (*moha*) is at the beginning of the causal chain of bondage; for if the soul is not really connected with *ajīva* (including *karman*) then only *moha* can 'persuade' it to think that it is. However, *moha* itself, in the standard explanation, is a result of material *karman*. If this is how Kundakunda views *moha* - i.e. if material *karman* is still playing an instrumental or catalytic role in bondage because of the inexplicable reaction of the *jīva* to its contiguity - then one would expect freedom from *moha*, etc., and thus from bondage, to result from the destruction or obstruction of material *karman*. However, according to the *Pravacanasāra*, it is *meditation* on the fact of the

---

dravyam - *TD* on 2:90. Note the typically Vedāntic distinction here between *jīva*, embodied soul, and *ātman*, pure or essential soul.

complete separateness of the pure self, and thus the realisation of that fact, which brings about freedom from *moha*, and liberation; nothing is said about material *karman*, all is internal. To illustrate this point, it is necessary to trespass a little on themes I shall consider in their full context and at greater length in a later section, 'The mechanism of liberation'.

There is a clear connection between the description of the *jīva* subject to *moha* at *Pravacanasāra* 2.91 and gāthās 2.98 and 2.99. *Pravacanasāra* 2.98 reads:

> He who does not abandon the idea of 'mine' with regard to body and possessions - (thinking) 'I am (this), this is mine' - gives up the state of being a *śramaṇa* and becomes one who has resorted to the wrong road.

And 2.99 provides the antithesis to this, i.e. it describes the attitude of the *śramaṇa*:

> He who meditates in concentration, thinking 'I am not others' and they are not mine; I am one (with) knowledge', comes to be a meditator on the (pure) self.

At *Pravacanasāra* 2.100, the self, which in meditation 'I' know to be myself, is described as being constituted of *jñāna* and *darśana*, an object beyond the senses, eternal (*dhuva*), unmoving (*acala*), without support (i.e. independent) (*aṇālamba*), and pure (*suddha*). Bodies, possessions, happiness, suffering, enemies and friends are not the 'eternal associates of the soul' (*jīvassa ṇa saṃti dhuvā*);[33] the self whose self is *upayoga* is eternal (*dhuvovaogappago appā*), i.e. the pure self (2.101). Knowing this (its true identity), the pure self meditates on the highest self (the *paramātman*) / the self and the other (the non-self),[34] with formed or formless thought, and so

---

[33] Upadhye's trans., p. 23.

[34] *TD* translates as *paramātman*, the Prākrit text prints *paraṃ*

destroys the evil (literally, 'very difficult') knot of *moha* (*khavedi so mohaduggaṃṭhiṃ*) [2.102]. And he who has overcome this knot of delusion, having destroyed *rāga* and *dveṣa* (which, as the *Tattvadīpikā* points out, have *moha* as their root), being indifferent to pleasure and suffering, attains to undecaying happiness (*sokkhaṃ akkhayaṃ*), i.e. liberation (2.103).

This whole passage is, of course, redolent of Vedānta. Here, I simply want to point out that liberation is seen to be attained not by the destruction of that *karman* which (very tenuously) has been said to bring about *moha*, but by the destruction of *moha* itself through meditation on the essential purity and complete separateness of the soul. In other words, it is lack of knowledge of the true nature of the self which really *constitutes moha*; consequently, it is the knowledge (gnosis) and realisation of the self's true nature which banishes *moha* (*aśuddhopayoga*) and, by revealing and realising the inherent purity of the soul, accomplishes liberation. The role of material *karman* in this mechanism of bondage and liberation has thus for all significant purposes been forgotten. And it can be forgotten because the logic of the system no longer requires it. I refer to 'material' *karman* because its function has actually been taken over by immaterial *aśuddhopayoga* / *moha*, caused, in the *niścaya* view, by the *jīva*'s self-transformation. As the *Tattvadīpikā* on *Pravacanasāra* 2.91 puts it:

> Therefore the instrumental cause of the soul's connection with other substance is merely the absence of an accurate distinction between what is self and what is other.[35]

In other words, given that the cause of the *jīva*'s connection with other substance is the delusion that the soul

---

appagaṃ, two separate words, but how this is translated makes no difference to the present argument.

[35] *ato jīvasya paradravyapravṛttinimittaṃ svaraparaparicchedā-bhāvamātram eva* - *TD* on *Pravac.* 2:91.

is involved with the non-soul (including material *karman*), then the implication is that, since in reality the *jīva* has no connection with anything material, it cannot in reality be bound by *karman*. To believe otherwise amounts to *moha*, and it is this which is the 'fact' of the soul's bondage. Consequently, the *belief* that material *karman* can bind the non-material soul takes over *karmapudgala*'s binding (i.e. its only) function, and Kundakunda has, in effect, internalised or dematerialised *karman*; bondage is now a matter of delusion, a false attitude manifested in a feeling of possessiveness with regard to the material (everything that is *ajīva*).[36]

The emphasis on *moha*, defined as the delusion that the self and the 'other' have any connection with or influence on each other, renders any 'two-cause' system of bondage - whatever the material and instrumental causes - effectively redundant. For how can something which does not and cannot *really* have any connection with what it is supposed in part to act upon be cited as a cause, material or otherwise? Furthermore, since it is the self's contact with *paradravya*, including material *karman*, that is a delusion, then it is *paradravya* / material *karman* that becomes, from the soteriological perspective, an irrelevance: in the characterisation of the *Tattvadīpikā* on *Pravacanasāra* 2.101, 'unreal' (*asat*).[37] In short, the stress on *moha* points to a solution to the problem of bondage beyond that attempted through the standard use of the *vyavahāra* / *niścaya* distinction. (The way in which *moha* arises, whether it is self-generated and how, or whether it is, like the Vedāntic *avidyā*, inexplicable, is not dealt with in this text; and for practical purposes it is probably considered

---

[36] In this context, we may recall gāthā 1.46 (quoted p. 121, above): 'There would be no *saṃsāra* for any embodied *jīva* if the *ātman* itself, through its own nature, did not become auspicious or inauspicious.' Again this puts the 'blame' for bondage squarely on the *ātman* itself; the process is self-contained and internal.

[37] For comments on this, see below.

irrelevant.)

In this way, Kundakunda has silently rid himself of an embarrassment, since, to make *logical* sense of bondage when *karman* and the *jīva* belong to two ontologically different categories (the material and the immaterial), he had two options: either to make the *jīva* material (and so revert to what may have been the very origins of Jaina doctrine) or to make *karman* immaterial. That he has, in effect, chosen the latter is borne out by evidence from both the *Pravacanasāra* itself and the *Tattvadīpikā*. Thus the *Tattvadīpikā* on *Pravacanasāra* 2.97,[38] when it gives the *niścaya* view, actually refers to *karman* as though it were non-material: '*karman* of / for the *ātman* is modification into attachment'; 'it is duality of merit and demerit'.[39] In other words, *karman* - what binds - is, from this perspective, not something material (*pudgala*), but the modification of the immaterial self into states of consciousness (*śubha-* and *aśubha-upayoga*) such as *rāga* , which are meritorious or demeritorious. It is because the *ātman* is the agent (*kartā*), as it is also the appropriator (*upādātā*) and relinquisher (*hātā*), of modification into attachment, etc., that the latter is seen as its *karman*.[40] This is stated explicitly by Kundakunda at *Pravacanasāra* 2.30, where it is said that:

> The self itself is modification, and such modification is held to be action which consists of *jīva*; action is known as *karman*, therefore the self is not the agent (of material *karman*).

The *Tattvadīpikā* explains that, from the higher view, the *ātman* is the agent of that *bhāva-karman* which is in essence the modification of the self, but it is not the agent of *dravya-karman* which is in essence a modification of

---

[38] Cf. *Pravac*. 2:29-30 and *TD*.

[39] *rāgapariṇāma evātmanaḥ karma, sa eva puṇyapāpadvaitam* - *TD* on *Pravac*. 2:97.

[40] *rāgādipariṇāmasyaivātmā kartā TD* on *Pravac*. 2:97.

matter.[41] Similarly, at *Pravacanasāra* 2.92, it is affirmed that while the soul is the agent of its own nature it is not the agent of all those states composed of material substances. Thus, as the *Tattvadīpikā* points out, the *karman* of the soul (taken here in the sense of action done by the soul, but therefore also its karmic matter, what binds it) is its own modification (*svapariṇāma*). The soul does not bring about states of matter - it is not their agent - so they cannot be its *karman*. For the self, therefore, *karman* is not modification of matter.[42] And *Pravacanasāra* 2.93 continues with the statement that, although at all times it exists in the middle of matter, the *jīva* neither grasps, releases, nor brings about material karmas.

These two gāthās (2.92-93)[43] therefore offer a flat contradiction to the view (outlined above) that the soul is the instrumental cause of *karman*, and vice versa. That is to say, it contradicts the doctrines contained in Kundakunda's own *niścaya* / *vyavahāra* distinction. Dixit, who also notices this, identifies the 'thesis' put forward in these gāthās as Kundakunda's 'transition-point in his journey away from the traditional stand-point and towards the stand-point of the Samayasāra'.[44] Given the apparently disparate nature of much of the *Pravacanasāra*, this is probably too specific an attribution; nevertheless, the tendency is clear.

Despite the views given at 2.92-93, the next three

---

[41] *tatas tasya paramārthād ātmā ātmapariṇāmātmakasya bhāva-karmaṇa eva kartā, na tu pudgalapariṇāmātmakasya dravyakarmaṇaḥ* - *TD* on *Pravac.* 2:30.
The *vyavahāra* view is that it is modification of matter which is *karman* for the *ātman* (*pudgalapariṇāmātmanaḥ karma*, *TD* on *Pravac.* 2:97), and that the *ātman* is the agent, appropriator and relinquisher of the modification of matter (*pudgalapariṇāmasyātmā kartā*, *TD* on *Pravac.* 2:99; Cf. 2:29 and *TD*, quoted above).

[42] *evam ātmanaḥ pudgalapariṇāmo na karma* - *TD* on *Pravac.* 2:92.

[43] Cf. *Pravac.* 2:68-70.

[44] Dixit 1971, p. 134.

gāthās (2.94-96) reiterate that sometimes and somehow (either because its space-points are stained by *moha*, *rāga* and *dveṣa* [2.96], or because its association with *rāga* and *dveṣa* brings about a self-modification into *śubha* and *aśubha* (*-upayoga*) [2.95]), it is clung to by karmic dust. As we have already seen, there is no satisfactory explanation of this conjunction, and the *Tattvadīpikā* on these passages comes no closer to providing one. For it states that the self, being its own agent, modifies itself, and the modifications of everything not self are only the occasioning causes of self-modification. How these modifications which are not self cause self-modification when the two have no contact is not explained. It is simply claimed that matter treats the soul's self-modification as an efficient cause to modify itself into *karman*,[45] and that this *karman* then enters the self through the latter's (vibratory) activity.[46] (The perfunctory introduction of *yoga* here seems to be a sudden recourse to an earlier strand of doctrine.) Similarly, the soul treats matter as an efficient cause (*nimitta*) to transform itself into various states of consciousness.[47] How this transformation takes place and how *karman* is actually *bound* remain unexplained features of this circular doctrine in which matter uses its proximity to the self-modifications of the soul to transform itself, and the soul uses its proximity to the self-modifications of matter to do likewise.

If I have laboured these problems, it is simply to make the point that it is the very attempt to preserve the soul's immaterial autonomy, and yet at the same time explain the fact of its bondage, which opens the door to a radically different emphasis in the theory of bondage and liberation. For it is precisely this struggle which gives rise to a perspective from which *karman* can - at least in some lights

---

[45] *tasya svapariṇāmaṃ nimittamātrīkṛtya* - *TD* on 2:94.

[46] *yogadvāreṇa*, *TD* on *Pravac.* 2:95.

[47] See *TD* on 2:97, and *JPP* p. 117ff.

- be viewed as immaterial.[48] By stressing the *niścaya* view and the role of *moha* in the key passages on bondage in the *Pravacanasāra*, Kundakunda implicitly acknowledges the importance of a 'dematerialised' instrument of bondage for the development of his soteriology (a soteriology which, as we shall see, is taken to its logical conclusion in the *Samayasāra*). In this context, '*karman*' as employed at *Pravacanasāra* 2.87 - 'Know this to be the *niścaya* description of the bondage of souls: the impassioned self binds *karman*, the self free from passion is free from karmas' - may therefore be taken to mean not material *karman* but the '*ātman*'s *karman*', i.e. the *jīva*'s own manifestation of consciousness, (*aśuddha*-) *upayoga*.[49]

Again looking forward to the *Samayasāra*, and taking the *niścaya* view in the strictest sense of there being no contact at all between the omniscient (i.e. liberated) soul and matter, we read at *Pravacanasāra* 1.52 that:

> Although knowing those objects, the soul does not transform itself ('under their influence' - Upadhye), does not grasp them, nor is it born among them; thus it is recognised as being without bondage.[50]

This gāthā describes the condition of the liberated or omniscient soul. However, as will become clear, in the *Samayasāra*, Kundakunda comes to view this kind of statement as the *exclusive* truth about the soul. In other words, it is not and has never been *really* bound, but has

---

48 See above, comments on *Pravac.* and *TD* 2:92, 2:97.

49 It should be noted that this reading also takes us closer to the way in which the *naya* doctrine is frequently used in the *Samayasāra*: there, the *niścaya* view is that the *jīva* has nothing whatsoever to do with *paradravya*, and both the elements - *niścaya* and *vyavahāra* - of the doctrine as it was introduced in the *Pravacanasāra* now fall into the *vyavahāra* camp.

50 Cf. *Pravac.* 1.32: 'The omniscient lord neither grasps, nor releases, nor transforms the other; he sees everything and knows everything completely.'

only been thought to be so through the supposition of an, in reality, non-existent relationship between *jīva* and *ajīva*.[51] The corollary of this view - that the *jīva* binds itself through false consciousness or *moha* - is that it can liberate itself by attaining true or pure consciousness via meditational techniques which lead to the realisation of that fact. Since this false consciousness takes the form of a delusion that the self is in some way connected to the material world, when in fact it is intrinsically and always pure, then it is only a short step to the conclusion that the world of matter, and especially material *karman*, is less 'real' than the soul, and even totally *un*real. By the same token, it is possible to conclude that the soul was never really bound but only thought to be so. And these are in fact very close to positions taken by Kundakunda in the *Samayasāra*, although, as we have seen, there are also gāthās in the *Pravacanasāra* where they are strongly suggested, for instance, at 2.101.

It is worth looking briefly at Amṛtacandra's commentary on this last passage (*Pravacanasāra* 2.101) as an example of the direction Jaina theory can take once *karman* has been effectively dematerialised. (And it is probable that the commentator uses his knowledge of the *Samayasāra* to provide himself with an interpretative framework here.) The text reads:

> Bodies, goods, pleasures and sufferings, enemies and friends are not eternal for the soul (*jīva*). Eternal is the self (*ātman*) that consists of *upayoga*.

---

[51] The ontological status of *saṃsāra* vis à vis the *kevalin*'s omniscience cannot be entered into here; nor can there be consideration of what it can mean to 'know' something without having any relationship with it. However, the gist seems to be that the *kevalin* is in some sense co-extensive with *saṃsāra* - even the 'creator' of it - and so, in effect, the object of the *kevalin*'s knowledge is itself alone, the self and what it knows being synonymous. See especially Book 1 of the *Pravacanasāra*, 1:23-1:36 (discussed below).

The *Tattvadīpikā* on this begins as follows:

> For nothing is eternal for the self which is other [than the self] and which is, since any such thing is not distinct from other substances and is indeed separated from its qualities as it undergoes the influence of other substances, the basis of impurity. [It cannot be eternal] because being unreal-and-caused (*asaddhetumattvena*) it must have a beginning and an end in time, and because it is not self-established (*parataḥ siddhatvāt*).[52]

The introduction of the term *asat*, the 'non-existent' or 'unreal', to describe everything that is other than the self (i.e. everything that is *paradravya* or a*jīva*, including material *karman*) is radical, and yet, given the fact that the instrument of bondage has been internalised and the self established as absolutely different from and untouched by the 'other', not unpredictable. In other words, for soteriological purposes (and perhaps ontologically too) *saṃsāra*, made up of matter, including material *karman*, may be treated as irrelevant. (And we may also note here that *karman* and bondage by *karman*, being non-eternal, are, in contrast to orthodox Jaina doctrine, assumed to have a beginning.)

Soteriological interest is now focused entirely upon the realisation of the eternally pure *ātman*, which is the one way of destroying the bondage of *moha*. As the next gāthā (*Pravacanasāra* 2.102) puts it:

> He who, knowing this, meditates with purified self on the *paramātman* [or 'the self and the other'], with formed or formless 'thought', destroys the tight knot of delusion.

---

[52] *ātmano hi paradravyāvibhāgena paradravyoparajyamāna-svadharmavibhāgena cāśuddhatvanibandhanaṃ na kiṃcanāpy anyad asaddhetumattvenādyantatvāt parataḥ siddhatvāc ca dhruvam asti* - *TD* on *Pravac*. 2:101.

I owe the translation to Alexis Sanderson's interpretation of this passage and the *TD*. on *Pravac*. 2:100.

Since the effects of dematerialising *karman* and of seeing the soul as eternally pure are so far-reaching, it is little wonder that the Jainas struggled, by means of the *naya* doctrine, to preserve at some level the orthodox views that *karman* is material and that the soul has always been bound by it. For, liberated by this same *naya* distinction, Kundakunda is veering not just towards the heterodox, but towards the heretical; his doctrines entail not only a change in Jaina theory or 'philosophy', but, more importantly, they imply wide-ranging changes in Jaina practice, and so pose a threat to the whole social structure of Jainism as an independent Indian religion.

5 .2 *Moha*

Before examining Kundakunda's mechanism of liberation in detail, it is useful to say something more about the role of what, according to parts of the *Pravacanasāra*, has become the effective instrument of bondage: namely, *moha* and its attendant 'passions'.

The classical position, outlined at *Tattvārtha Sūtra* 8:9, is that there are 28 kinds of deluding (*mohanīya*) karmas. Without enumerating all the subtypes, the basic division here is between 'perception-deluding' (*darśana-mohanīya*) karmas and 'conduct-deluding' (*cāritra-mohanīya*) karmas. That is to say, *mohanīya* karmas produce *moha* or *avidyā* by deluding the *jīva* with regard to its belief and its conduct; or as P S. Jaini puts it, *mohanīya-karman* is *karman* 'that prevents the true perception of reality and the purity of the soul'.[53] In simplified diagrammatic form the division appears as follows:[54]

---

53 *JPP* p. 346 (Glossary); see also ibid. p. 131.

54 For a full enumeration, see *SS* on *TS* 8:9; Glasenapp pp. 8-11; *JPP* pp. 118-121.

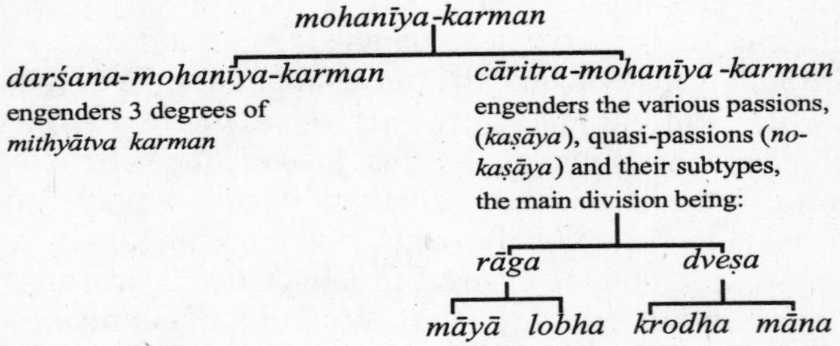

Jaini identifies these 'producers of delusion' as being at the heart of bondage, generating defilement which is characterised by confusion and desire and so causing the soul to become 'confused and desirous' [55] Thus, at one level, *darśana-mohanīya* and *mithyātva karman* clearly operate with regard to Jaina religious belief in general, and are explained as such. However, the same terms also carry a more specific weight. Tatia summarises this when he writes that in Jainism,

> the term *mithyātva* (perversity) is generally used to denote the idea of *avidyā*. The terms *mithyādarśana* or *mithyādṛṣṭi* (wrong view), *darśanamoha* (delusion of vision), *moha* (delusion) etc. are also used in the same sense.

He goes on to say that the function of *darśanamoha* is to delude the soul and misguide it; under such influence the *jīva* accepts, among other things, the *ajīva* as the *jīva*.[56] (Such a use of *mithyādarśana* can be found, for instance, at *Tattvārtha Sūtra* 8:1, *Bhāṣya* and *Sarvārthasiddhi*.)[57]

---

[55] *JPP* p. 117.

[56] Tatia p. 144.

[57] It should be remembered that Jaina philosophy uses the term *darśana* to denote both 'doctrine' or 'belief' and 'undifferentiated

Thus, as P S. Jaini puts it, the *mithyātva* state, engendered by *darśana-mohanīya-karman*, is manifested as a 'fundamental tendency to see things other than as they really are'.[58]

Cāritra-mohanīya-karman generates the various passions (*kaṣāya*), and these two forms of *mohanīya-karman* combine to produce a 'condition of spiritual stupefaction' or defilement. [59] In this state the soul is open to the influence of other types of *karman*, affecting its remaining qualities and, indeed, generating its state of embodiment.[60] Thus *mohanīya-karman* is of central importance to the classical theory of bondage; and although, as Jaini points out, it cannot be given first place in a beginningless cycle, it is impossible to eliminate other karmic influences 'as long as deluding factors remain'.[61]

However, although the importance of *mohanīya-karman* can hardly be denied in the classical theory, I should like to stress that it is the second term in the compound, '*karman*', upon which the emphasis falls in terms of achieving liberation from such bondage. It is the fact that it is caused by deluding-(material)-***karman*** that is of crucial significance, not the delusion itself, which is simply the particular form that *karman* takes. This becomes clearer if we look at the question of *cāritra-*

---

cognition' or 'perception' - see Glasenapp pp. 6-8.

[58] *JPP* p. 118.

[59] Ibid. p. 119.

[60] Ibid. pp. 120-121.

[61] Ibid. In this respect, *mohanīya-karman* has exactly analogous status to that held by *avijjā* ('ignorance' and a synonym for *moha*) in the Buddhist formula of Dependent Origination (*paṭicca-samuppāda*): *avijjā* stands first in the latter because it is the 'primary root of all evil and suffering in the world' [*Buddhist Dictionary* p. 31], and whereas it cannot be viewed as the 'causeless cause' of the world [*Visuddhi Magga* XVII, 36f., quoted in ibid.], it is, figuratively speaking, a root-cause. In particular, it is the root-cause of *lobha* / *rāga* and *dosa*, 'consequently all unwholesome states of mind are inseparably bound up with it' [ibid. p. 32]. Cf. the identical Jaina view given by the *TD* on *Pravac.* 2:103.

mohanīya-karman in slightly more detail, and thereby also remind ourselves of the essentials of Umāsvāti's *kaṣāya* doctrine.

In the classical theory, passion (*kaṣāya*) is said to be generated by destructive karmas of the conduct-deluding (*cāritra-mohanīya*) kind. Passion is two-fold, consisting of aversion (*dveṣa*) and attachment (*rāga*); 'the former is always divided into anger (*krodha*) and pride (*māna*) and the latter into deceitful manipulation (*māyā*) and greed (*lobha*)'.[62] It is the passions which produce *pramāda* ('carelessness') and thus *hiṃsā*, i.e. the latter is the product of volitional activity motivated by passion.[63] Thus *kaṣāya*, in effect, underlies all bondage: *yoga* attracts karmic matter to the *jīva* in the first place, deciding its type and quantity, while *kaṣāya* causes it to adhere, deciding its duration and intensity (*Tattvārtha Sūtra* 8:2-3). Passion is therefore necessary for bondage to take place. As we have seen,[64] *parigraha* (attachment to possessions) has the same nexus of associations as *kaṣāya* in general and *rāga* / *lobha* in particular. And at *Tattvārtha Sūtra* 7:17 *parigraha* is defined as *mūrcchā* ('infatuation' or 'delusion'), i.e. the delusion that something can be 'mine', as the *Sarvārthasiddhi* makes clear. Although, according to the *Sarvārthasiddhi*, infatuation or attachment (*parigraha*) 'is at the root of all evils' [65] - i e. it leads to *hiṃsā*, etc. - passion, nevertheless, has the controlling hand, and remains instrumental. To quote the same source, 'so the passionless person possessed of right faith, knowledge and conduct is free from delusion (*moha*). Hence there is no infatuation in his case'.[66] So even when the term '*moha*' is used in the

---

62 *JPP* p. 119; see *TS* 6:5 (6), cf. 8:1.

63 See above, pp. 54-55.

64 See above, p. 31ff.

65 *tanmūlāḥ sarve doṣāḥ* - *SS* on *TS* 7:17.

66 *tato jñānadarśanacāritravato 'pramattasya mohābhāvān na mūrcchā 'stīti niṣparigrahatvaṃ siddham* - ibid., trans. by S.A. Jain p. 199.

Sarvārthasiddhi, it designates something more affective than cognitive in character, contrasting with its employment in Kundakunda as something essentially cognitive.

The consequence of viewing *kaṣāya* as the instrumental cause in bondage is that the mechanism of liberation in the *Tattvārtha Sūtra* is directed towards the individual ridding himself of such passions, and thus both stopping the influx of, as well as shedding, the karmas which are caused to be bound by passions. *Tapas* (austerity) 'effects both (stoppage and dissociation) and ... is the chief cause of stoppage of influx'.[67]

Tapas is divided into 'external' and 'internal' austerities (see *Tattvārtha Sūtra* 9:19-20). Both categories are predominantly physical in character, although meditation (*dhyāna*) is included as the last of the internal austerities. Such meditation, however, is defined at *Tattvārtha Sūtra* 9:27 as 'concentration of thought on one particular object'.[68] It is not designed to engender *gnosis* or realisation of the true nature of self - in contrast to what we find in Kundakunda, where it is effectively *moha*, and not *kaṣāya* as such, which is seen as the root cause of bondage (see above).

In the *Tattvārtha Sūtra*, therefore, the instrumental causes of bondage are basically twofold (or, as subdivided, fourfold): *rāga* and *dveṣa* (*māyā* and *lobha*, *krodha* and *māna*). In the *Pravacanasāra*, however, *rāga* is used - perhaps in a more general sense - to denote 'passion' or 'attachment', and is usually part of a threefold division of the causes of bondage, completed by *dveṣa* and *moha*. *Rāga* and *dveṣa* are self-evidently a pair, or two sides of the same emotion; the employment of one towards one 'thing' entails the employment of the other towards another 'thing'.

---

[67] *ubhayasādhanatva ... saṃvaraṃ prati prādhānya* - *SS* on *TS* 9:3, trans. S.A. Jain p. 242.

[68] *ekāgracintānirodha* - *TS* 9:27 trans. S.A. Jain, p. 266.

And as we have seen,[69] when *rāga* is associated specifically with *parigraha*, and *dveṣa* with *ārambha*, then the former leads to or causes the latter. In the *Pravacanasāra* and *Tattvadīpikā*, *moha*, the newly introduced third element, is seen as being the root-cause of the other two.[70]

Why does Kundakunda add *moha* to the standard twofold *kaṣāya* doctrine? There are probably two related reasons: his dematerialisation of the cause of bondage (*karman*) (outlined above), and the influence of the standard Buddhist triad of karmically unwholesome roots (*mūla*), viz. greed (*lobha* = *rāga* = *taṇhā*), hate (*dosa*), and delusion (*moha*). It hardly needs pointing out that in a system where the *jīva* 'really' has no connection with matter, and where karmic bondage is seen as being essentially cognitive in nature, delusion or its synonym, 'ignorance', is likely to be suggested as the root cause of that bondage. In other words, even without the Buddhist model, some such grouping of *rāga* and *dveṣa* with *moha* was likely to have suggested itself to Kundakunda, given his stress on the total separation of soul and matter and his movement towards an immaterial *karman*. *Moha* thus has a similar role in Kundakunda's teaching to *avidyā* in Śaṅkara's Advaita Vedānta and *avijjā* / *moha* in the Pāli Canon.

In the *Pravacanasāra*, therefore, we are presented with what appears to be a less complex formulation than that given in the *Tattvārtha Sūtra*: *moha* is added to *rāga* and *dveṣa* and the three together constitute or give rise to *aśuddhopayoga*, and are thus responsible for bondage. However, Kundakunda's formula is clearly a refinement of the classical position in terms of his *upayoga* doctrine, and should not be supposed to predate it. His position appears to be less complex because the prolix categorisations of the

---

69 See above, Part I *passim*.

70 See above, pp. 141-142. As in the *TS* it is simply *mohanīya-karman* which is the generating cause of *rāga* and *dveṣa*.

underlying material *karman* theory have been pushed into the background or 'forgotten'. In other words, there are few indicators that every time one sees '*moha*' one should understand 'material *mohanīya-karman*'; on the contrary, *moha* as used by Kundakunda has clear non-material associations, and in this respect the fact that the Jaina's formulation reproduces the Buddhist triad of 'unwholesome roots' must be the result of sympathy rather than the attempt to 'colonise' a rival doctrine through re-definition. Some of the coincidences between the two formulations have been outlined above. But in summary I would suggest that Kundakunda's employment of '*moha* / *avidyā*' is closer to the Buddhist use of the term, with its cognitive and volitional associations, than it is to the material *mohanīya-karman* of standard Jaina doctrine, with its ramifications for ascetic practice (i.e. its requirement of extreme forms of *tapas*).[71]

The fact that Kundakunda uses *mohanīya-karman* as a category at least once in the *Pravacanasāra*,[72] but prefers to concentrate on the less obviously material *moha*, shows both his awareness of traditional doctrine and where he chooses to lay his emphasis. Faddegon, commenting on the use of *duṭṭho* / *duṣṭa* (glossed by the *Tattvadīpikā* as *moha*) at *Pravacanasāra* 1:43, remarks that *moha*, *rāga*, and *dosa* / *dveṣa* together form *mohanīya-karman*, and contrasts this triple division with 'the more intricate classification of *mohanīya-karman*' in the classical position (see, for example *Tattvārtha Sūtra* 8:9).[73] While not wishing to

---

[71] It should be noted that in Jayasena's recension of the *Pravacanasāra* there is an extra gāthā at 3:26b where the four passions are referred to in a perfectly orthodox, i.e. classical, sense. This is an exceptional case, and it is perhaps significant that it occurs in Chapter 3, which appears to be only loosely related to the first two chapters and may well have been compiled for a different purpose.

[72] At 1:15 and *TD*; cf. 1:19 and 1:43.

[73] Faddegon [Kundakunda (3)] p. 27, fn. 1. The full text of *Pravac.* 1:43 reads: 'The great Jinas say that portions of karmas are necessarily operating (and giving their fruit); he, who is infatuated with,

deny that Kundakunda's idea of *moha* ultimately derives from and sometimes reverts to the classical position, I would point to its role in a new formulation, its association with the *upayoga* doctrine, and especially its connection with realisation (*jñāna*) and not *tapas*, as indicators that the emphasis in the *Pravacanasāra* is on an effectively dematerialised instrument of bondage. The complexity of the orthodox classification of (physical) *mohanīya-karman* has thus been largely by-passed simply because an understanding of it is essentially irrelevant to the proposed means of liberation (*jñāna* through *dhyāna*); whereas, for reasons outlined above, the orthodox classification points towards *saṃvara* and *nirjarā* through *tapas* as the means to liberation.

5.3 *Hiṃsā in the Pravacanasāra*

i) The role of hiṃsā in the Pravacanasāra

With the stress on *moha*, its corollaries (*avidyā* and *aśuddhopayoga*) and antidotes (*jñāna* through meditation on the essential purity of the self, and *śuddhopayoga*) the characteristic Jaina procupation with the ethical imperative of *ahiṃsā* would appear, in the *Pravacanasāra*, to have been moved to the periphery of soteriological concern. How then does Kundakunda view *hiṃsā*, and what, according to him, is the relation of the latter to, for instance, *moha*?

In Book 3 of the *Pravacanasāra* we find a group of gāthās dealing with *hiṃsā* which, taken without the commentary, seem to have only a tenuous connection with the kind of doctrines expounded in the first two books. These verses certainly look more traditional and more orthodox; they are closer in feeling to the *Tattvārtha Sūtra* than to the *Samayasāra*. Nevertheless, they merit more

---

or shows attachment or aversion towards them, necessarily incurs bondage.'

detailed examination, for they provide some indicators of major changes in Jaina religious practice, and help to clarify the even greater changes implicit in Kundakunda's less orthodox doctrines.

At *Pravacanasāra* 3:16 *hiṃsā* is defined (in Upadhye's translation) as follows:

> Careless activities of a monk when sleeping, sitting, standing and walking, are always known as continuous harm unto living beings.

This would seem to be the most natural rendering, i.e. *hiṃsā* is harm to living beings as a result of careless physical actions on the part of the monk. *Prima facie,* this is a purely orthodox doctrine such as might be found in the *Dasaveyāliya Sutta*. Amṛtacandra, however, interprets it in the *Tattvadīpikā* in terms of Kundakunda's *upayoga* doctrine, an interpretation reflected in Faddegon's translation: 'Heedless action in lying, sitting, standing, going, etc., is considered to be at all times continual hurt (*hiṃsā*) to the *śramaṇa*-state'.

Thus Amṛtacandra (and Faddegon) take the Prākrit *samaṇassa* to be equivalent to the Sanskrit *śrāmaṇyasya*, rather than *śramaṇasya*, i.e. they add the suffix *-ya-* to *śramaṇa* and so turn it into an abstract meaning '*śramaṇa*-state'.[74] There seems to be no linguistic justification for this, but, as we shall see, it is resonant in terms of doctrinal change. (And although the original Prākrit gāthā may not be by Kundakunda, the interpretation given in the commentary demonstrates the kind of practice his *upayoga* doctrine implies, and is thus highly relevant to the present enquiry.) The *Tattvadīpikā* is worth quoting in full here. Amṛtacandra's introduction to the Prākrit gāthā tells us that this is a definition of what constitutes *cheda* - 'infringement' or, more specifically, an offence against the monastic rules. The commentary proper states:

---

[74] Cf. *Pravac.* 2:98 where *sāmaṇṇaṃ* = *śrāmaṇyam*.

For negligence is impure manifestation of consciousness because of the destruction, the injuring, of that *śramaṇa*-state whose form is pure manifestation of consciousness. And so (negligence) itself is *hiṃsā*. Therefore, the *śramaṇa*'s careless activity with regard to sleeping, sitting, standing and walking, etc., which is inherently connected with impure manifestation of consciousness, is always *hiṃsā* for him, a continuous force (lit. flowing continuously) at all times, which is another disadvantage consisting of infringement.[75]

Interpreting this, we may say that the monk 'hurts' himself - i.e. binds himself - through *aśuddhopayoga* of which *cheda* is the external sign. For since the ideal *śramaṇa*-state has the form of *śuddhopayoga*, then *aśuddhopayoga* is, in the first place, *hiṃsā* to the *śramaṇa* who aspires to that state, and, in the second, it necessarily entails (physical) *cheda*. That is to say, offence against the monastic rules *presupposes aśuddhopayoga*. So the original or initiating cause of *hiṃsā*, and thus of bondage, is internalised: the emphasis is on *aśuddhopayoga*, not on external *cheda* as such. Moreover, *hiṃsā* has been (re-) defined as an offence against the *śramaṇa*-state, i.e. an offence against the monastic rules (= *cheda*), and thus as harm to the self because of the *aśuddhopayoga* that is necessarily at the root of such neglect, rather than harm caused to other living beings as such. So it becomes apparent that it is now the *role* of the *śramaṇa* which is all important; obedience to the prescribed actions not only leads automatically to the goal, but, more importantly, it does so only because - as that very obedience indicates (externally) - internal purity (*śuddhopayoga*) has been maintained, for there can be no adherence to the monastic rules without such purity. Consequently, both monastic

---

[75] *aśuddhopayogo hi chedaḥ śuddhopayogarūpasya śrāmaṇyasya chedanāt tasya hiṃsanāt sa eva ca hiṃsā | ataḥ śramaṇasyāśuddhopayogāvinābhāvinī śayanāsanasthānacaṅkramaṇādiṣv aprayatā yā caryā sā khalu tasya sarvakālam eva saṃtānavāhinī chedānarthāntarabhūtā hiṃsaiva || TD* on *Pravac.* 3:16.

behaviour and *ahiṃsā* may be said to have been ritualised in the sense that it is now the mechanical performance of the prescribed action itself that counts, or is indicative, not the ahiṃsic *content* of the action.[76] What is significant is the harm caused to oneself through *aśuddhopayoga* rather than any harm that might be caused to others, although this entails no particular change in practice since the monastic rules, adherence to which is now the expression of inner-purity, were originally formulated to prevent harm to others. (That is to say, while originally it was harm to others that caused harm (= bondage) to the self, it is now *aśuddhopayoga*, a state of consciousness, whose external expression is *cheda*, offence against the monastic rules, that does so.)

In other words, obedience to the rules leads automatically to the goal, but only in the sense that such obedience refers back to, or is a necessary consequence of, an internal state of *śuddhopayoga*, which is what really counts for salvation. Thus total externalisation (the ritualisation of *ahiṃsā*) and total internalisation meet: one implies, or is a reflex of, the other. And although, theoretically, it is the internal (*śuddhopayoga*), as the agent of the external (monastic practice), which is really instrumental in binding and liberating, in terms of the visible - of external practice - it is simple adherence to the letter of the law which is seen to bring about liberation. But, again, it is internalisation of *hiṃsā* that allows it to do so.

As we have seen, it is the commentary and not Kundakunda's text (3:16) which engendered the above analysis. However, the following gāthā is more directly relevant to at least part of that interpretation:

> Whether the being dies or lives, injury is certain for the man who is unrestrained; there is no bondage simply by injury (i.e. 'by mere

---

[76] On my use of the term 'ritualisation' (the meaning is close to routinisation or formalisation), see above p. 86.

physical harm' - Upadhye) for the man who regulates himself according to the rules of conduct.

This gāthā has already been discussed above,[77] since it was quoted without attribution by Pūjyapāda (Devanandin) in the *Sarvārthasiddhi* on *Tattvārtha Sūtra* 7:13. It is possible that Pūjyapāda was referring directly to this gāthā from the *Pravacanasāra* (as the Jaina Granthamālā edition of the *Sarvārthasiddhi* claims), but it is more likely that both 'authors' quote from some earlier, unidentified, (possibly) canonical source. And in any case, as we have already noticed, this part of the *Pravacanasāra* shows every sign of having been compiled from other sources rather than composed by Kundakunda himself.[78]

For the purposes of the present enquiry, the important thing is to examine the way this section is brought into line by the commentary with the doctrines propagated by Kundakunda in Books 1 and 2 of the *Pravacanasāra*. In this context, therefore, gāthā 3:17 means that as long as the *śramaṇa* retains his internal purity, reflected externally in his adherence to the letter of the monastic rules, then he cannot do *hiṃsā* or be subject to its effects (i.e. be bound), even if physical harm is caused. (Note the intentional ambiguity of *hiṃsā*: it is injury done to others and therefore also to oneself.) In other words, outside the parameters set by the monastic code - which is the external reflection of internal purity - physical action and its consequences are irrelevant; it has no karmic and, therefore, no soteriological significance.

Amṛtacandra introduces this gāthā (3:17) with the claim that in it Kundakunda teaches two kinds of *cheda*, *antaraṅga* (internal) and *bahiraṅga* (external). He defines them as follows: 'Impure *upayoga* is internal infringement,

---

[77] See above, p. 53ff.

[78] Upadhye (p. liiiff.) comments that this verse has 'a traditional appearance, and [it] might be traced to a tract of literature which was once the common property of Digambaras and Śvetāmbaras'.

the taking of another('s) life is external'.[79] Whether it happens that another being's life is taken or not, the fact of 'careless conduct' (*aprayatācāra*) proves *aśuddhopayoga* (i.e. the external is a sign of the internal state), and so the existence of *hiṃsā* for that impure consciousness is certain.[80] (Read with 3:16 above, one may also understand from this that *aśuddhopayoga* causes *hiṃsā* to the self.) Conversely, 'careful conduct' (*prayatācāra*) proves the non-existence (*asadbhāvasya*) of *aśuddhopayoga* (internally); so *hiṃsā* does not occur for that consciousness, as is shown by the fact that there is no bondage (for that pure consciousness) even as the result of taking another's life.[81] Therefore, Amṛtacandra concludes, internal *cheda* is more powerful or important (*balīyaḥ*) than external. 'Nevertheless, external infringement should be admitted simply because it provides a place (or "seat") for internal infringement'.[82] In other words, external *cheda* is merely a sign of, or an emblem for, an internal state; the latter manifests itself in the former.

This is repeated and amplified in the *Tattvadīpikā* on 3:18. The gāthā reads:

> A Śramaṇa of careless conduct is called a murderer of the six (classes of) embodied beings; if he carefully practises (his course of conduct) he is forever uncontaminated like the lotus on water.[83]

Again it is the performance to the letter of the monastic rules which is crucial here. To this ritualisation the *Tattvadīpikā* adds the internalisation which may also be

---

79 Trans. after Faddegon [Kundakunda (3)] of *aśuddhopayoga 'ntaraṅgachedaḥ paraprāṇavyaparopo bahiraṅgaḥ*.

80 *suniścitahiṃsābhāvaprasiddheḥ* - *TD* on *Pravac*. 3:17.

81 *paraprāṇavyaparopasadbhāve 'pi bandhāprasiddhyā* - ibid.

82 *evam apy antaraṅgachedāyatanamātratvād bahiraṅgachedo 'bhyupagamyetaiva* - ibid.

83 Upadhye's trans. The six classes of living beings are the five *sthāvara* and the one *trasa*, i.e. the 'immobile' and the 'mobile'.

latent in Kundakunda's gāthā. Carefulness is something interior, an attitude; conversely, it is *aśuddhopayoga* which is at the root of all external 'carelessness' and the initiating cause of bondage. That is to say, it is *aśuddhopayoga*, the cause of the violence, which entails bondage; *hiṃsā* in itself is karmically neutral. Amṛtacandra works hard to stitch all this together:

> Since the existence of impure manifestation of consciousness, proved by careless behaviour, which does not occur without it, is hurtful since it is established that bondage is caused by the destruction of the lives of the six kinds of bodies; and since the absence of impure manifestation of consciousness proved by careful behaviour, which occurs when it is absent, is not hurtful; and because of the absence of even a small amount of bondage caused by the 'other' (viz. the *ajīva*), so that it is established that it is free from impurity, like a lotus lapped by water; therefore it is concluded that internal infringement, which has the form of impure manifestation of consciousness, should be prevented by all means by which external infringement, in the form of taking another life, which merely provides the occasion for that (internal infringement), is a fortiori prevented.[84]

Superimposed in this one gāthā and its commentary there may be as many as three layers of doctrine: 1) an archaic *hiṃsā* doctrine where any - even accidental - harm is binding, 2) a ritualised doctrine, where what counts is

---

[84] Trans. after Faddegon [Kundakunda (3)] p. 164, of *TD* on *Pravac.* 3:18:
yatas tadavinābhāvinā aprayatācāratvenaprasiddhyad aśuddhopayogasadbhāvaḥ ṣaṭkāyaprāṇavyaparopapratyayabandhaprasiddhyā hiṃsaka eva syāt | yataś ca tadvinābhāvinā prayatācāratvena prasiddhyad aāuddhopayogāsadbhāvaḥ parapratyaya bandhaleśasyāpy abhāvāj jaladurlalitaṃ kamalam iva nirupalepatva prasiddher ahiṃsaka eva syāt | tatastaistaiḥ sarvaiḥ prakārair aśuddhopayogarūpo 'ntaraṅgacchedaḥ pratiṣedhyo yairyais tadāyatanamātrabhūtaḥ paraprāṇavyaparoparūpo bahiraṅgacchedo dūrād eva pratiṣiddhaḥ syāt ||

that the *śramaṇa* should perform his prescribed role to the letter, and 3) an internalised *hiṃsā* doctrine, linked to Kundakunda's *upayoga* theory, whereby the external is merely a reflex of the internal state, and it is the latter which carries the soteriological weight.

In other words, the physical model of the killing of the six classes of embodied beings is retained, but the original doctrine is now interpreted in terms of 1) ritualised action, and 2) internalised doctrine. Perhaps that is why the gāthā says *vadhakaro tti mado*, 'he is *regarded as* a murderer', i.e. this is just a way of talking about the person who is internally careless (which is what really counts), using the old imagery, the old physical connection of carelessness and *jīva*s, in a new context. (Here, as elsewhere, ritualisation and internalisation complement each other.)

To expand on this, originally the five *samiti* can only have been formulated as rules for the avoidance of *hiṃsā* to the various kinds of *jīvas*.[85] The emphasis of the discipline is to avoid doing harm because such harm would automatically cause one to be bound by a new influx of *karman*. Yet here the discipline of *samiti* has been ritualised; it is adherence to the letter of monastic discipline that is crucial; if a monk follows the rules then, even if he does harm 'accidentally' - which would count as 'carelessness' in the original reading -, he is not bound by *karman*. Emphasis is switched from the *results* of actions to the actions themselves, and thus to the underlying attitude or volition accompanying them. This combination of ritualisation and internalisation disposes of the worry that even someone who is careful and observes the five *samiti* can be open to 'accident'. In other words, it removes the fortuitous from monastic life, for now it is attitude, externalised in particular ritualised actions, that really counts. Yet, once that shift of emphasis has been made, the doctrine that *hiṃsā* to *jīvas* (including *nigoda*) is what causes karmic bondage is undermined, for gāthās such as

---

85 See Part I, above.

Pravacanasāra 3:17 claim that 'unintentional' *hiṃsā* - or *hiṃsā* occurring after a certain degree of carefulness, encapsulated in the rules for ascetics, has been observed - does not bind. And if there is one case where *hiṃsā* does not bind, then the logic of the system is cracked and has to be reassembled. For now it is something mechanical, a rule, that decides whether *karman* is bound or not, not actual *hiṃsā*; at the same time, *hiṃsā* is internalised and redefined to mean an *attitude* of carelessness, externalised in offences against the monastic rules. (To borrow a term from T.S. Eliot and the critical vocabulary of English studies, it might be said that offence against the rules is the 'objective correlative' of the subjective state or attitude.) Consequently, the karmic quality of an act is, in effect, decided, as in the Buddhist case, by the intention and attention - the internal state - which accompanies it, not by the act itself or what it results in. However, since that internal state is reflected or externalised so closely in the external rule, there is little visible alteration in behaviour. In this respect, the particular rationales that the Buddhists and the Jainas give for their differing external practices are each a mirror-image, or reversal, of the other. For the Buddhists, the purpose of rules of conduct (*vinaya*) is to help the monk to cultivate certain inner states which are instrumental in liberation. For the Jainas (as represented by Amṛtacandra), however, the inner state has precedence over and conditions the outer: perfect conduct is not so much a means to the end as a reflection of the already internally-achieved end. In other words, for the latter, the rationale for external practice is not so much soteriological as social - a public demonstration of inner purity.

And in practice, this kind of public performance became important for Buddhism too. As Richard Gombrich points out, according to the view of ethics found in the Vinaya and commentarial literature (which was, of course, formulated with the Saṅgha in mind), *sīla* (morality) is 'the monk's successful role performance. It makes clear to society he is being a good and proper monk'.[86] This external decorum was the response to 'an overwhelming demand for empirical evidence of a monk's internal state'.[87] Thus the monk's moral habit, which is primarily an internal state, becomes 'instantly recognizable by a pattern of behaviour'.[88]

Such an explanation for the function of external practice is, of course, highly theoretical, since to achieve the optimum inner purity it is necessary to become an ascetic, and the only way to become an ascetic is to adopt the ascetic's vows. It is clear, therefore, that in practice the external must precede the internal. (The rationale works both ways: since the ascetic cannot follow his course of discipline without the necessary inner purity, the very fact that he *is* following it demonstrates to himself and others that he does have the requisite inner resources.) Nevertheless, the need for this type of theoretical justification of ascetic discipline demonstrates the extent to which the level of internalisation reached by Kundakunda and consolidated by his commentators offers a serious threat to standard Jaina practice. In other words, although the rationale for continuing ascetic practice may be weak, it is recognised that there does have to be some kind of rationale, otherwise the very complex of behaviour which provides the Jainas with their social and religious identity is made redundant. Thus, from this perspective, the real tasks of the post-canonical writers and scholastics are seen to be, on the one hand, the acknowledgement of the practical limits of 'carefulness' and, on the other, the need to rein in the logic of internalisation before it bolts and leaves behind any necessity for external practice, thus discarding the social identity such practice carries with it. As we have seen, a central element in this struggle to reinterpret ancient ascetic practices in doctrinal terms which are compatible with new social circumstances is the redefinition of what

---

86 Gombrich 1984, p. 100.

87 Ibid.

88 Ibid.

counts as *hiṃsā*, in the sense of 'bondage-causing *hiṃsā*'. For the whole of ascetic discipline is built on the theory that there are ubiquitous *jīva*s, that harm done to them constitutes *hiṃsā*, and that *hiṃsā* binds *karman*. In this context, the only way of setting practical limits to what counts as *hiṃsā* (i.e. to 'carelessness') - that is, the only way to alleviate the formidable difficulties of ascetic practice and thereby give hope of liberation (or at least a better rebirth) to those who are not advanced ascetics - is to internalise it. Only after such a process is it possible to 'return', as it were, to the external world with a modified (i.e. ritualised) form of ascetic practice - limited to literal adherence to the monastic code - which can be defended doctrinally.

This combination of mental discipline and adherence to the letter of particular physical *vrata* (whether monastic or lay) may be considered, at least in one respect, less taxing than the ancient, blanket adherence to physical *ahiṃsā*, and also, perhaps, easier to practise from within, or on the fringes of, society. For, when external behaviour becomes formalised, chance is removed from Jaina soteriology. The external world becomes less threatening, and life less contingent for the ascetic, who is now in more or less total control of his progress to liberation. This movement towards absolute personal control was probably inevitable, given that the world portrayed in the earliest canonical texts was a risk-saturated environment, even for the ascetic. The early 'canonical' *śramaṇa* is under constant threat from other people and from the physical world: they threaten him not just to the extent that he threatens them, but he is also constantly at risk from the fortuitous and the accidental.[89] (That is to say, he is under constant threat of being forced into, or finding himself by circumstances beyond his control, in a position where *ahiṃsā* is inevitable; and so he is under continual threat of further bondage.)

Such 'accidents' could, of course, be rationalised in

---

[89] See, for instance, the *Āyāraṃga* and *Das.aveyāliya Suttas*.

terms of karma theory, as the karmic fruits of some previous action. That kind of explanation, however, does not solve the problem of control. The ascetic develops self-discipline precisely in order to have absolute control over his karmic destiny; and absolute control is only possible in isolation from the contingent, material world. Consequently, the earliest Jaina discipline demanded almost superhuman control and concentration, a fact which must have severely limited the number of recruits. To survive, even as a *śramaṇa* movement, it must sooner or later have been necessary, among other things, for Jainism to hold out the prospect of a sure path towards release, free from chance and accident, the equivalent of the Buddhist *bhikkhu*'s being 'an island to himself'.[90]

Kundakunda is at the logical end of this movement towards ever-increasing autonomy. In contrast to the position of the early 'canonical' *śramaṇa*, the greatest threat to Kundakunda's ascetic comes from within himself. Essentially, this threat amounts to ignorance of his own nature. Once that ignorance is dispelled, then the rest (i.e. proper external action) falls into place. If you have realised your true nature, then karmic bondage is impossible: whatever you do is *hiṃsā*-free because it is the purified, knowing self that is doing it. No accident is possible where everything is *jñāna* - defined by Kundakunda as 'self' (*Pravacanasāra* 2:67, etc.). To put it another way, there is no longer any real interaction between the ascetic and the world of matter, since the latter can have no real effect on the former as long as his attitude is correct. The contingency which characterises ordinary life is blocked out, and the ascetic remains safe inside his own consciousness, his own *upayoga*. *Upayoga* is the fail-safe mechanism which ensures that the ascetic's salvation is in his own hands, and through it he becomes autonomous.

This divorce of the *śramaṇa* from the world of matter

---

90 See *Dīgha-Nikāya* II (*Mahāparinibbāna-Sutta*), quoted by Rahula p. 60.

goes in tandem with a doctrine such as Kundakunda's (in the *Samayasāra* and parts of the *Pravacanasāra*), which points towards the unreality of all except the pure soul. The *śramaṇa*'s internal state has thus become its own universe, hermetic, and for all practical purposes, idealist. He no longer struggles with the world of matter, but with himself, alone. At least, from the point of view of personal soteriology, this is probably the position in which Kundakunda and his followers would like to find themselves. However, since purity of attitude is impossible to demonstrate except through purity of action, in a social situation ascetic behaviour is the only indication of a holy life: monks and nuns remain exemplars in their behaviour. Such behaviour, therefore, is a means of mutually maintained social regulation: the ascetics do what the laity expect them to do, while in return, the laity remain faithful and support them while maintaining their own lower-grade but related practice.

ii) Hiṃsā, moha, and upadhi

In Jayasena's recension of the *Pravacanasāra*, gāthā 3:17 is followed by two extra gāthās not contained in Amṛtacandra's version (3:17b and 3:17c). The fact that these two (as well as 3:17) are quoted (with minor linguistic differences) in the same part of the *Sarvārthasiddhi* (on *Tattvārtha Sūtra* 7:13) lends weight to Upadhye's suggestion that we are dealing here with verses that form a group in some other source.[91] The gāthās read:

> When the foot of an ascetic who observes the *īryā-samiti* (i.e. who is careful in his walking according to the rule) has been raised for going out, should a minute creature (*kuliṃgaṃ*),[92] coming in contact with that, be hurt or killed, it is taught in the scripture that he is not liable even for the slightest bondage as a consequence of that; (the case is similar to the statement:) it is infatuation alone

---

91 See note 78, above.

92 *Kuliṃgaṃ* is glossed by Jayasena as *sūkṣma-jaṇtuḥ*.

that is called possession on the authority of the spiritual lore. [*Pravacanasāra* 3:17b & 3:17c][93]

In terms of doctrine these gāthās are probably closer to the *Tattvārtha Sūtra*, and its concern with *kaṣāya*, than to Kundakunda's *upayoga* doctrine; i.e. *prima facie*, internalisation of *hiṃsā* takes a different theoretical channel here. However, the redefinition of *hiṃsā* by the collation of the elements of the first and the fifth *mahāvrata*s (*ahiṃsā* and *aparigraha*),[94] and the further equation of *parigraha* and *mūrcchā*, brings us back to *moha* as the agent of bondage. Thus it is infatuation (*mūrcchā* / *moha*), stemming from a mistake about the *jīva*'s relationship to matter, which causes adherence to physical objects (*parigraha*), and so physical or 'external' *hiṃsā*. 'Internal' *hiṃsā*, harm to oneself, is the mental state of 'infatuation', external harm merely the indicator of that internal state, and

---

[93] Cf. Upadhye's trans. On *īriyāsamida*, Sk. *īriyāsamiti*, see *TS* 9:5 and *SS*; J.L. Jaini 1940, p.134; Schubring 1962, para. 173. Faddegon [Kundakunda (3), p. 201] gives the second half-verse of 3:17c a very different translation, viz. '... just as acceptance of swooning also is regarded according (as it is due) to (concentration) on the self'. That is to say, swooning, and thus causing *hiṃsā* by falling, has no binding effect when it is the result of meditation practice. However, although it is possible for *mucchāpariggaho* (Sanskrit: *mūrcchāparigraha*) to mean 'acceptance of swooning', in this context the interpretation seems strained. Given the close association of *mūrcchā* and *parigraha* in Jaina theory (see *TS* 7:17 and *SS*, where they are defined as equivalent), Upadhye's reading appears to be the correct one here. Moreover, the stress in these gāthās is clearly upon what Upadhye calls the 'mental condition', referring to which, his translation contains a footnote that is worth quoting in full:

'*Hiṃsā* is not merely *prāṇa-vyaparopaṇ*a, but *pramatta-yogāt prāṇa-vyaparopaṇam* (TS. VII, 13). It is passions, negligent and careless channels of activities etc., that matter most; it is the mental condition, rather than the visible act, that is of utmost importance. For instance, *parigraha* does not so much consist in having physical contact with external objects as being infatuated with them' [Upadhye fn. 1, p. 26 on 3:17*1-2].

[94] See above.

it is the latter which is really instrumental in terms of binding and liberating the *jīva*.

This is part of the same pattern of theory as *Pravacanasāra* 2:24, which remarks that 'there is no action without fruit, although the highest *dharma* is without fruit'.[95] The *Tattvadīpikā* reads this in terms of 'mental' action, the action of one who thinks (*cetana*), and such action is defined as a modification (*pariṇāma*) of consciousness (*caitanya*). However, this modification is only (karmically) fruitful (i.e. binding) for the *ātman* connected with 'delusion' (*mohasaṃvalita*; √*val*(I) + *sam*). When the connection of the soul with *mŏha* disappears, the action is without fruit, so there is no further rebirth. And it is this fruitless (i.e. *moha*-less) mental action which Amṛtacandra defines as the *parama-dharma*, 'the highest *dharma*'. This may be compared with *Pravacanasāra* 2:58, where it is the idea of 'mine' (*mamattaṃ*) with regard to external objects, especially the body, which is the cause of rebirth. (According to the *Tattvadīpikā*, this idea is the 'interior cause' of rebirth, a manifestation of attachment [*uparaktatva*].) Taking these two together, it is clear that it is the 'delusion of possession' - the idea that the *jīva* can have a real connection with anything *ajīva* - that is the real cause of rebirth. In other words, *hiṃsā*, the binding instrument, has effectively been internalised to *moha*, which, in turn, is a manifestation of, or equivalent to, 'false consciousness' or *aśuddhopayoga*.

Pravacanasāra 3:19 and commentary assemble a further set of equivalences around the concept of *hiṃsā* which point to *aśuddhopayoga* as the significant cause of bondage. Gāthā 3:19 reads:

> There is or there is not bondage, when a being dies in the course of physical activities; bondage is certain from attachment to

---

95 *kiriyā hi ṇatthi aphalā dhammo jadi ṇipphalo paramo - Pravac.* 2:24.

possessions, therefore ascetics should give up everything.[96]

Upadhye renders *uvadhi* (Sk. *upadhi*) as 'attachment to paraphernalia', although he has already used 'paraphernalia' (i.e. physical possessions) to translate the term *pariggaho* / *parigraha* at *Pravacanasāra* 3:15. At 3:19 he follows Jayasena, who, in the *Tātparya-vṛtti*, paraphrases *upadhi* by *parigraha*.[97]

Faddegon, in a footnote on 3:15, remarks that:

> *Tyāga* is renunciation of all wordly concerns (*parigraha*), i.e. of possessions; *vyutsarga* is abandonment of all that may become seductive (*upadhi*), specially that which is required for the welfare of the body. Thus *tyāga* and *vyutsarga*, *parigraha* and *upadhi* are nearly identical.[98]

However, in common with a number of other technical terms, such as *cheda*, *hiṃsā*, etc., *upadhi* can be shown to have two facets or areas of reference, one facing or referring to the external, physical world, and the other referring to an internal state or attitude. The earlier, technical sense (which is probably the one used at *Pravacanasāra* 3:15)[99] is found, for instance, at *Uttarajjhayaṇa* 29:34, where 'the renunciation of articles of use' (*upadhi-pratyākhyāna*) is prescribed.[100] The later internalisation of *upadhi* is evident in gāthās such as *Pravacanasāra* 3:19 (particularly when taken in conjunction with the next gāthā, 3:20), a phenomenon spelt

---

[96] Based on Upadhye's translation.

[97] As Faddegon [Kundakunda (3)] points out, p. 164, fn. 2. *TV* on *Pravac.* 3:19 reads: *atha bahiraṅgajīvaghāte bandho bhavati na bhavati vā parigrahe sati niyamena bhavitīti pratipādyati.*

[98] Ibid. p. 162, fn. 2.

[99] Cf. *Pravac.* 3:23, where it has the same meaning.

[100] Jacobi translates: 'By renouncing articles of use (except such as are obligatory - the broom etc.) he obtains successful study; without articles of use he becomes exempt from desires, and does not suffer misery' (1895, p. 167).

out in detail in the *Tattvadīpikā*, where the connection of *upadhi* and *aśuddhopayoga* is made explicit.

In his introduction to *Pravacanasāra* 3:19 Amṛtacandra states that, 'Now he (i.e. Kundakunda) teaches that similarly attachment to possessions (*upadhi*), since it is unequivocally an internal infringement, should be prevented.'[101] He goes on to explain in the commentary proper that,

> Whereas in the taking of another being's life through a bodily action the degree of infringement is held to be indeterminate (*chedatvam-anaikāntika*), - because its character as bondage is variable according to the presence or absence of impure manifestation of consciousness (*aśuddhopayogasadbhāvāsad-bhāva*), - with attachment to possessions (*upadhi*) the case is different. Its degree of infringement is unequivocal, because its character as bondage is unequivocal owing to the unequivocal presence of impure manifestation of consciousness, which is proved by its non-occurrence without that same (*tasya sarvarthā tadvinābhāvitvaprasiddhyad aikāntikāśuddhopayogasadbhāvasy-aikāntikabandhatvena chedatvam aikāntikam eva*).[102]

In other words, whereas the taking of life is not necessarily binding because it is not necessarily connected to *aśuddhopayoga*, *upadhi* is always binding because it is necessarily accompanied by *aśuddhopayoga*. The *Tattvadīpikā* goes on to say *arhats* and *paramāḥ śramaṇāḥ* (supreme *śramaṇa*s) have entirely rejected *upadhi*, and so it should be rejected by others too because, like 'internal negligence', it does not occur without *aśuddhopayoga*.[103]

In the *Tattvadīpikā* on the following gāthā (3:20),

---

[101] Trans. after Faddegon [Kundakunda (3)] p. 164 of: *athaikāntikāntaraṅgacchedatvād upadhis tadvat pratiṣedhya ity upadiśati*. Faddegon renders *upadhi* as 'appropriation'.

[102] *TD* on *Pravac.* 3:19, trans. after Faddegon.

[103] *ata eva cāparair apy antaraṅgacchedavat tad-anāntarīyakatvāt prāg eva sarva evopadhiḥ pratiṣedhyaḥ* - ibid.

Amṛtacandra claims that Kundakunda teaches that the purpose of rejecting *upadhi* is in fact to reject internal *cheda*. Moreover, since internal *cheda* is no different from *aśuddhopayoga*, then *upadhi* is another name for *aśuddhopayoga*; so it is really the latter, an impure state of consciousness, which is the instrument of bondage.[104]

The gāthā (3:20) commented on here reads:

> If there is no renunciation (absolutely) free from (any) expectation, the monk cannot have the purification of mind; how can he effect the destruction of karma, when he is impure in mind?[105]

In other words, purity of mind and renunciation of worldly-objects through an attitude of indifference are one and the same thing. For, if *ṇiravekkho / nirapekṣa* is taken to be the form of *cāgo / tyāga*, then the emphasis falls, not upon physical renunciation, but upon an *attitude* of indifference, an attitude which is the same thing as purity of mind. For the monk who does not have this purity of mind, how, it is asked in the next gāthā (3:21), can he be free from *mucchā / mūrcchā, āraṃbha / ārambha,* and *asaṃjama / asaṃyama* (delusion, physical harm from worldly activities, and lack of control), and how, being attached to *paradravya* ('other substance'), i.e. the external world, the *ajīva*, can he ever realise (lit. gain) himself?[106] And, consequently, in the *Tattvadīpikā*, *upadhi* is named as

---

104 *tato 'suddhopayogasyāntaraṅgachedasya pratiṣedhaṃ prayojanam apekṣyopadher vidhīyamānaḥ pratiṣedho 'ntaraṅga-chedapratiṣedha eva syāt* - *TD* on *Pravac.* 3:20.

105 Upadhye's trans.; *niravekkha / nirapekṣa* = 'indifferent to worldly objects'; *āsaya / āśaya* = 'heart', 'mind', 'resting-place'. The construction is odd here. The sense seems to require *nirūvekkhe cāge*, locative absolute. Faddegon's rendering of Prākrit *āsaya* as Sanskrit *āsrava*, rather than *āśaya* [p.165], makes no real sense: *āsrava* is by definition impure or, at best, neutral, whereas, in the context, *āśaya* is perfectly intelligible.

106 *tadha paradavvammi rado kadham appāṇaṃ pasādhayadi* - *Pravac.* 3:21.

the root cause of all these (*mūrcchā*, etc., and the attachment to *paradravya* which obstructs attainment of the *śuddhātman*).[107]

From the above we can see that a number of technical terms have been strung, as it were, into a necklace of equivalences, with the process of internalisation as the string which holds them together. Thus *upadhi* is equated with *parigraha*, *mūrcchā* / *moha*, *ārambha* / *hiṃsā*, and *antaraṅgaccheda* (= internal *hiṃsā*), and all these with *aśuddhopayoga*. Physical *hiṃsā* in itself is neutral in terms of bondage, but the underlying attitude is decisive: if renunciation is incomplete, if there is attachment, then consciousness is impure, and vice-versa. In other words, *parigraha*, in the form of *upadhi*, is *hiṃsā* internalised, i.e. it is *aśuddhopayoga*.

Because *upadhi* is characterised by the *Tattvadīpikā* as an unequivocally *internal* infringement,[108] an instructive comparison can be made with the use of the same term in the *Tattvārtha Sūtra* and the *Sarvārthasiddhi*. There, at *Tattvārtha Sūtra* 9:26, *upadhi* is characterised as being of two kinds, external and internal (*bāhyābhyantaropadhyoḥ*). The *Sarvārthasiddhi* comments that *vyutsarga* means *tyāga*, and that it is twofold, the giving up of external objects of attachment and the giving up of internal attachments.[109] External attachments are characterised as house, wealth, cereals, etc. (*vāstu-dhana-dhānyādi*), which are not appropriated (*anupāttam*, root *dā*). Internal attachments are the passions, which are natural to, or 'the dispositions of' [110] the self.[111]

---

107 For the minimal exceptions to the rejection of *upadhi* in the technical sense of 'physical possessions' - 'possessions' which are karmically neutral because the attitude or manifestation of consciousness accompanying them is pure - see *Pravac.* and *TD* 3:22-3:26.

108 Introduction to *Pravac.* 3:19, see above.

109 *bāhyopadhityāgo 'bhyantaropadhityāgaś ca* - *SS* on *TS* 9:26.

110 S.A. Jain's trans., p. 266.

111 *krodhādir ātmabhāvo 'bhyantaropadhiḥ* - *SS* on *TS* 9:26. The

Here, the term *upadhi* has the external sense of being connected with possessions, similar to the meaning employed at, for instance, *Pravacanasāra*, 3:15. It also has the internal sense of attachment to the body and being under the control of the passions. As the *Sarvārthasiddhi* explains, renouncing attachment for the body has a technical sense here, of limited or unlimited periods of *vyutsarga*, which is not significant for the present discussion. The renunciation of passions, however, is clearly linked to Umāsvāti's *kaṣāya* doctrine.

Comparing this with the other uses of *upadhi* discussed above, it is clear that, from its original meaning of physical articles of use,[112] the sense has been, to a greater or lesser degree, internalised and the meaning extended by both Umāsvāti and Kundakunda, but in different ways in accordance with their own explanations of the mechanism of bondage. Thus, in Umāsvāti's case, the internalisation is partial, and tied to the *kaṣāya* doctrine, *kaṣāya* being instrumental in bondage. In Kundakunda (and Amṛtacandra's) case, *upadhi* has been fully internalised - it is 'unequivocally an internal infringement' [113] - through being tied to the *upayoga* doctrine, in which *aśuddhopayoga*, a state of consciousness, is instrumental in bondage.[114]

Bhāṣya states that, 'external *upadhi* has 12 forms, internal *upadhi* is to do with (attachment for) the body and for passions' (*abhyantaraḥ śarīrasya kaṣāyāṇaṃ ca*).

112 See *Utt.* 29:34, quoted p. 171, above.

113 *TD* on 3:19, intro.

114 At *Pravac.* 3:73, there is an obscure reference to 'external and internal(?) *upadhi*' (*uvahiṃ bahitthamajjhatthaṃ*). Upadhye takes *ajjhattha* as *adhyātma*; Faddegon, following the *TD*, divides differently - *madhyastha*. However, this gāthā belongs to the last five of the *Pravacanasāra*, which are a self-contained group and may be a further addition to the text. In any case, the *TD* is unambiguous in describing *upadhi* as 'unequivocally an internal infringement'.

iii) Hiṃsā and 'compassion'

Kundakunda's internalisation and assimilation of *hiṃsā* and its equivalents to *aśuddhopayoga* has consequences for the whole nexus of Jaina doctrine, consequences which are illustrated throughout this part of my work. Here, by way of concluding this section, I shall point to one specific doctrinal implication, interesting both in itself and because it illustrates the distance Kundakunda has travelled from some of the positions advocated in the earliest extant texts.

As we have seen (at 3:20, above), it is purity of mind, characterised by an attitude of indifference towards all possessions, that distinguishes the true monk. The action of such a *śramaṇa* is free from delusion (*moha*) and so does not incur bondage (see *Pravacanasāra* 2:24-30); moreover, such action coincides exactly with the monastic rules. Mental disturbance both engenders and is engendered by *hiṃsā* / *parigraha*, but it is the mental component, the underlying attitude, which is karmically significant, not the harming act itself. This is illustrated by *Pravacanasāra* 3:20c (an obviously anti-Śvetāmbara gāthā, only present in Jayasena's recension), which reads:

> If he accepts a piece of clothing, gourd-bowl and anything else, necessarily there is involved harm unto living beings, and there is disturbance in his mind.[115]

This gāthā can be interpreted in two ways, both of which, in the context, are probably intended: first, it is implied that the taking of life causes a disturbance in the mind of the *śramaṇa*, and that it is that disturbance which is to be avoided rather than the taking of life per se, which is karmically neutral (see above). Second, and conversely, the very act of violence reflects an already existing mental

---

[115] Upadhye's trans. *Vikkheva* (see text) = Sk. *vikṣepa*, 'distraction', 'inattention'. See *JPP* pp. 38-41 on the major differences between Digambaras and Śvetāmbaras in matters of clothing, alms-bowls, etc.

disturbance which is the root cause of the physical act. Either way, it is the internal attitude which is significant: the purity (calmness) or impurity (disturbance) of mind. In other words, the basic strategy for (correct) conduct, as prescribed in early Jaina doctrine, has been retained but internalised: physical inactivity, the antidote to external *hiṃsā*, has been internalised to mental 'inactivity', i.e. to the attainment and maintenance of an inactive, and therefore pure, consciousness. Not even compassion must disturb this uncompromising stasis. On the contrary, since feeling clouds consciousness, compassion falls into the camp of *aśuddhopayoga*. One does not refrain from *hiṃsā* because it is compassionate to do so, one refrains because the practice of *hiṃsā* indicates internal impurity, i.e. impure *upayoga* which binds. Thus *ahiṃsā* achieved as the result of a feeling of compassion is, by definition, not fully *ahiṃsā* and cannot be fully liberating, although, in saṃsāric terms, it is relatively virtuous.

Kundakunda's position on compassion is made clear at *Pravacanasāra* 2:65, where he describes it as one of the constituents or prerequisites of *śubhopayoga* (which, we should remember, is ultimately a form of *aśuddhopayoga*):

> He, who recognises the great Jinas, attends on Siddhas as well as saints and is compassionate towards living beings, has an auspicious resultant of consciousness.[116]

Here the term used for 'compassion' is *aṇukaṃpā*.[117] This occasionally occurs in the early Śvetāmbara canon, for instance, at *Āyāraṃga* 2.15.4, where Indra is described as 'the compassionate god' (*anukaṃpaṃteṇaṃ deveṇaṃ*).[118] At *Āyāraṃga* 2.2.1.8, the compassion (*kaluṇa* = *karuṇā*) of householders towards ill monks or nuns is described as

---

[116] Upadhye's translation.

[117] 'Compassion' / 'mercy' / 'pity' - *Ardha-māgadhī koṣa*; cf. below, where the same term is used in the *TS*.

[118] See Pischel, para. 397.

resulting in himsic activities, such as attention to their bodies, washing, the lighting of fires, etc. This idea, that compassion is essentially a lay virtue, something to be excluded from the world-view of the *śramaṇa*s, persists in later Jaina theory. However, in the earliest parts of the canon there also occurs a different attitude towards the affective in general and compassion in particular. At *Āyāraṃga* 1.5.5.4 (*Suttāgame* 320), for instance, we are presented with a version of the 'Golden Rule' in which the *śramaṇa* is urged to practise *ahiṃsā* out of empathy (and thus compassion) for the suffering of others:

> As it would be to you, so it is with him whom you intend to kill. As it would be to you, so it is with him whom you intend to tyrannise over. As it would be to you, so it is with him whom you intend to torment. In the same way (it is with him) whom you intend to punish, and to drive away. The upright man who lives up to these sentiments, does therefore neither kill nor cause others to kill (living beings) ...[119]

Similarly, at *Āyāraṃga* 1.4.2.6 (*Suttāgame* 242) the suffering of others is proved by inference from personal suffering:

> First the persuasion of everyone should be ascertained, and then we will ask them severally: Is pain pleasant to you, or unpleasant? If they give the right answer, reply: For all sorts of living beings pain is unpleasant, disagreeable and greatly feared. Thus I say.[120]

---

[119] Based on Jacobi's trans., 1884, p. 50 of:
tumaṃ si nāma sa cceva jaṃ haṃtavvaṃ ti mannasi; tumaṃ si nāma sa cceva jaṃ ajjāveyavvaṃ ti mannasi; tumaṃ si nāma sa cceva jaṃ paritāveyavvaṃ ti mannasi; evam (taṃ ceva) jaṃ parighittavvaṃ ti mannasi; (evam taṃ ceva) jaṃ uddaveyavvaṃ ti mannasi; aṃjū c' eyapaḍibuddhajīvī tamhā ṇa haṃtā ṇa vighāyae - *Suttāgame* 320.

[120] Based on Jacobi's trans., 1884, p. 39, of:
puvvaṃ nikāyasamayaṃ patteyaṃ patteyaṃ pucchissāmo: haṃ bho pavādiyā kiṃ bhe sāyaṃ dukkhaṃ, udāhu asāyaṃ? samiyā paḍivanne yāvi evaṃ būyā: savvesiṃ pāṇāṇaṃ savvesiṃ bhūyāṇaṃ savvesiṃ

In other words, appeal is made to one's own experience, extended to others through feelings of empathy and compassion, as a reason for practising *ahiṃsā*. Here, we are probably close to the original rationale for the Jaina emphasis on *ahiṃsā*, whereas, in the later formulations, once behaviour has been formalised in a particular set of doctrinal rules, the dominating reason for *ahiṃsā* is that such practice is the only way to avoid karmic bondage; or, as in Kundakunda's reformulated doctrine, it is the reflex of an already-achieved state of internal purity which is, by definition, non-binding.

This later view is evident in the *Pravacanasāra* at, for instance, 1:85, which, in Upadhye's translation, reads:

> False perception of things, absence of kindness towards sub-human and human beings and indulging with objects of pleasure - these are the characteristics of delusion or infatuation.

However, in the light of *Pravacanasāra* 2:65 (above), I prefer to follow Faddegon here and take *karuṇābhāvo* as meaning 'the feeling of compassion towards animals and men' (i.e. *karuṇā-bhāva*, rather than *karuṇā-ābhava*).[121] This, indeed, is the interpretation that Amṛtacandra gives in the *Tattvadīpikā*. There, it is said that a component part of the 3 'stages' of *moha* is 'a feeling of compassion towards animals and men, who are simply worthy of respect'.[122] In other words, the *Tattvadīpikā* attempts to fit *karuṇābhāvo* into the triad, or three stages (*tribhūmika*), of *moha* (in the widest sense):[123] viz. 1) false perception and *karuṇā*

---

jīvāṇaṃ savvesiṃ sattāṇaṃ asāyaṃ apariṇivvāṇaṃ mahabbhayaṃ dukkhaṃ ti bemi - *Suttāgame* 242; cf. *Āy.* 1,6,5,4; 1,7,1,5; 1,7,3,2; *Sūy.* 1,7,2.

121 Faddegon [Kundakunda (3)] p. 53.

122 *tiryagmanuṣyeṣu prekṣārheṣvapi kāruṇyabuddhyā* - *TD* on *Pravac.*1:85.

123 See *Pravac.* 1:83-84 and *TD*.

correspond to *moha* (in the limited sense), 2) and 3) inclination towards / indulging with objects corresponds to *rāga* and *dveṣa*.

This does seem a little strained as it stands, for why should *karuṇā* be selected as one of two typical examples of *moha*? It may, therefore, be the case that in 1:85 we have a different 'definition' of *moha*, congruent with, but unrelated to, the *tribhūmika* division, which may have been unknown to the author of this gāthā in its developed technical sense. There is also the possibility here that Amrtacandra, or both Amṛtacandra and Kundakunda, are consciously using the fact that *karuṇā* plays such an important role in Mahāyāna Buddhism. That is to say, by including it within the circle of *moha*, *rāga*, and *dveṣa*, they are denying the idea that ultimately there can be such a thing as 'detached compassion', compatible with wisdom and liberation; in the final analysis, *karuṇā* is *aśuddha*. Such an interpretation may be supported by the apparent Jaina preference for *aṇukaṃpā*, rather than *karuṇā*, as the term for 'compassion'. In other words, it is possible that, at least when first employed by the Jains, *karuṇā* was chosen when some special shade of meaning was required.[124]

To take the contrast a little further, Rahula remarks that, according to Buddhist ethics, 'for a man to be perfect there are two qualities that he should develop equally: compassion (*karuṇā*) on the one side, and wisdom (*paññā*) on the other'.[125] Compassion represents 'the qualities of the heart', such as love, charity, kindness and tolerance, while wisdom represents 'the qualities of the mind'. Thus, in the ideal Buddhist way of life, wisdom and compassion - the cognitive and the affective - 'are inseparably linked

---

[124] It should, however, be noted that the Pāli Canon also uses *aṇukampā* in the sense of 'compassion'. For instance, it is said that the Buddha gave his teaching 'for the good of the many, for the happiness of the many, out of compassion for the world' (*bahujanahitāya bahujanasukhāya lokānukampāya*, quoted by Rahula p. 46).

[125] Rahula p. 46.

together',[126] for true wisdom is endowed with 'thoughts of selfless detachment, love and non-violence'.[127]

The Jains, by way of contrast, aim for a state in which the affective can be discarded altogether; for ultimately liberation is only to be attained from a condition founded in indifference to everything not self. This is made explicit at *Pravacanasāra* 2:67, which reads:

> Free from inauspicious manifestation of consciousness, not joined to auspicious (manifestation of consciousness) towards other substance, let me be indifferent; I meditate on the self whose essence ('self') is knowledge.

Since, as we have already noted at 2:65 (above), compassion (*aṇukampā*) directed towards other beings is a manifestation of *śubhopayoga*, then it is clear that compassion can have no part in this meditation practice, the aim of which is to destroy all connection with *paradravya*, a connection which in itself constitutes bondage.[128]

In other words, as one approaches the top of the ladder to salvation, one develops, on the one hand, an attitude of indifference, a kind of psychological stasis with regard to everything not self, and on the other, an intense concentration on, or realisation of, the inner 'knowledge' which constitutes the *ātman* alone. This isolation of the self from other selves, and from the world in general, mirrors, and eventually becomes, the isolation of the *jīva* that has attained *kevala-jñāna* at the apex of the universe.

Before leaving the subject of compassion, we should note that Kundakunda's categorisation of it as falling under

---

126 Ibid.

127 Ibid. p. 49. Rahula is, perhaps, sandpapering the joints here: such pairings are not unproblematical even for the Buddhists. For the tension between 'love' and 'self-restraint', see Gombrich 1971, pp. 320-6.

128 *eṣa me paradravyasaṃyogakāraṇavināśābhyāsah*, 'This is my practice of the destruction of the causes of conjunction with other substance.' - *TD* on *Prāvac.* 2:67.

śubha- but *aśuddhopayoga* has its analogue in Umāsvāti's *Tattvārtha Sūtra*, where it is placed among the *sātā*, i.e. pleasure-causing, category of the *vedanīya* (feeling-producing) karmas. *Tattvārtha Sūtra* 6:12 reads:

> Compassion towards living beings [in general] and the devout [in particular], charity, asceticism with attachment etc., concentration, equanimity, purity [= freedom from greed] - these lead to the influx of karmas that cause pleasant feeling.[129]

The *Sarvārthasiddhi* comments: 'Compassion is the thinking in sympathy of one whose mind is moistened by favour for the suffering of others as it were one's own'.[130]

As has been noted above, the *vedanīya-karma*s are a subtype of *aghātiyā karmas*, whose function is to generate embodiment. Thus, although compassion may be viewed positively in terms of worldly experience and as leading to worldly happiness, ultimately it too must be abandoned in the quest for liberation, since it is responsible for the adhesion of some kind of *karman* and so contributes to bondage, albeit in a tenuous way (i.e. at a relatively high rung of the soteriological ladder).[131]

The ritualisation of (external) *ahiṃsā*, in so far as it becomes a matter of following the rules to the letter with an attitude of non-attachment, can only further weaken the force of compassion as an agent in bringing about non-

---

129 Trans. after S.A. Jain p. 178 of: *bhūtavratyanukampādānasarāgasaṃyamādi yogaḥ kṣāntiḥ śaucam iti sadvedyasya* - *TS* 6:12.

130 *anugrahārdrīkṛtacetasaḥ parapīḍām ātmasthām iva kurvato 'nukampanam anukampā* - *SS* on *TS* 6:12.

131 But compare this with *TS* 7:11 and *SS*, where it is said of compassion (*kāruṇya*) - i.e. 'the disposition to render assistance to the afflicted' (*dīnānugrahabhāvaḥ*) [S.A. Jain's trans. of *SS* p. 195] - that it characterises the conduct of those who are able to practise non-violence and other vows to perfection' (*evam bhāvayataḥ pūrṇānyahiṃsādīni vratāni bhavanti* - *SS*). Cf. *Pañc.* 144 (SBJ ed.) on active compassion. Once more, there are clearly two layers of doctrine here.

violence and liberation. Feeling with regard to other beings is at best irrelevant in these circumstances. At worst, it agitates and clouds consciousness; thus, once *hiṃsā* has been internalised as the harm one does to oneself through *aśuddhopayoga*, i.e. through affective activity of consciousness, compassion, although undoubtedly a lay virtue, becomes just one more means of tying the ascetic to *saṃsāra*. That is to say, compassion is consciousness directed towards the external world, towards *paradravya*. Against this there is the antidote of mental stasis or indifference, the purely cognitive, but, especially in Kundakunda, there is also consciousness directed 'inwards', at the *ātman*: i.e. the means becomes not just non-action (mental and physical) but insight into and realisation of the nature of the *ātman* itself, of its essential isolation from everything else. And it is to this, Kundakunda's mechanism of liberation, that attention must now be turned.[132]

---

[132]The fact that logically liberation requires the cessation of all activity and, in the case of extreme internalisation, an undisturbed, pure consciousness, has not always been tempered in Jaina practice by what P.S. Jaini calls 'a real and active concern with the prevention and alleviation of suffering' [*JPP* p. 313]; nor has the spirit of *anekāntavāda* always informed and restrained behaviour based on such doctrines. Jaini cites the case of an 18th C. Sthānakavāsi monk [the Sthānakavāsis are themselves an offshoot of the Śvetāmbaras], Bhīkhanji, who established a sect, the Terāpantha, 'based on the doctrine of total non-assistance to any living being (except mendicants)' [*JPP* p. 313]. The theoretical basis for this is that, by aiding or 'saving' other creatures, you become responsible for their future violence; moreover, '"helpful" behavior almost always involved some interest in the result, hence brought an increase in karmic attachments' [*JPP* p. 314 fn. 63]. This proved unacceptable to the Jaina community at large, and ensured the isolation of the small group of Terāpantha mendicants. However, as Jaini puts it, Bhīkhanji exploited 'the doctrinal split inherent in any community that preaches the ideals of total renunciation and *mokṣa*, on the one hand, and the value of compassionate and charitable behavior (leading to heaven) on the other' [ibid.]. In some ways, the position Kundakunda advocates for those who aspire to liberation foreshadows Bhīkhanji's: compassion too, whether actuated in behaviour, or as an attitude of mind, keeps one in bondage and prevents spiritual progress

beyond a certain level of attainment. The reaction to the Terāpantha also highlights the readily perceived threat posed to Jaina social identity by such 'isolationism'. In Bhīkhanji's case, it is the ethical norm of the lay community which is threatened; in Kundakunda's, internalisation also jeopardises ascetic practice, and thereby the entire structure of Jaina religious and social identity.

6

The mechanism of liberation according to the *Pravacanasāra*

6.1 *Cāritra*

It is a commonplace of Jaina doctrine that liberation (*mokṣa*) cannot be achieved through *samyag-jñāna* - 'right knowledge' (and *samyag-darśana,* 'right faith') - alone: *samyak-cāritra* - 'right conduct', the third 'jewel' of the triad, is also required. As the very first sūtra of the *Tattvārtha Sūtra* puts it: *samyagdarśanajñānacāritrāṇi mokṣamārgaḥ:* 'Right faith, right knowledge, and right conduct are the path to liberation'. (Or to invert the formulation, the condition of bondage is threefold, consisting of *mithyā*-(wrong)-*darśana*, *mithyā-jñāna*, and *mithyā-cāritra*.)[1] These three together constitute a single path to liberation.[2] Right conduct, moreover, is defined (by the *Sarvārthasiddhi* on *Tattvārtha Sūtra* 1.1) as 'the cessation of activity leading to the taking in of karmas'.[3] Consequently, as Tatia explains, the attainment of perfect knowledge does not result in immediate liberation, since the latter requires perfect conduct too, and that is only attained when *all* activity (*yoga*) ceases (i.e. in the last moment before death).[4]

Prima facie, this would seem to act as a check on any tendency, such as Kundakunda's emphasis on *jñāna*, to undermine the rationale of physical, external discipline through the internalisation of practice. However, this only

---

[1] See Tatia p. 151.

[2] See *SS* on *TS* 1.1: *mārga iti caikavacananirdeśaḥ samastasya mārgabhāvajñāpanārthaḥ* - 'The singular "path" is used in order to indicate that all the three together constitute the path to liberation'.

[3] S.A. Jain's trans., p. 3, of *karmādānanimittakriyoparamaḥ.*

[4] Tatia p. 153.

holds good as long as *cāritra* itself is seen predominantly in terms of restraint from external, physical action; Kundakunda, however, makes it clear at the beginning of the *Pravacanasāra* that for him *cāritra* too is essentially something internal, a matter of attitude. In this work, as will become evident, *cāritra* is intimately linked to the attainment of *jñāna* through *dhyāna*, rather than to the practice of external *tapas*. Thus, for Kundakunda, *samyak-cāritra* becomes merely an augmentation to, or instrument of, *samyag-jñāna*, whereas the classical view is that it is *samyag-jñāna* which results in *samyak-cāritra*, and that it is the latter which is soteriologically crucial.[5]

Evidence of this internalisation is provided at the beginning of the *Pravacanasāra*. There, in gāthā 1:6, it is stated that the *jīva* attains *nirvāṇa* by conduct (*cāritra*) which has as its most important component perception and knowledge (*darśana* and *jñāna*).[6] Such conduct, as the *Tattvadīpikā* explains, is that which is free from attachment (*vītarāga*). However, in the next gāthā, *cāritra* is given a more precise definition:

> Conduct is indeed *dharma*; *dharma* is defined as equanimity [*śama*]; for equanimity is a modification of the self which is free from delusion and disturbance (or 'the disturbance of delusion'). [*Pravacanasāra* 1:7]

That is to say, ideal conduct is an *attitude* of calmness (*śama*), an absence of passion, not a particular course of external, physical conduct. It is something that occurs internally, transforming the essential self (cf.1:8); i.e. *cāritra* is internalised to a *bhāva* or mental state (see 1:9). *Pravacanasāra* 1:11 goes on to say that if the self which

---

[5] See the *SS* on *TS* 1.1: 'knowledge is mentioned before conduct, for conduct issues from knowledge' - trans. by S.A. Jain p. 4, of: *cāritrāt pūrvaṃ jñānaṃ prayuktaṃ, tatpūrvakatvāc cāritrasya.*

[6] *saṃpajjadi ṇivvāṇaṃ ... jīvassa carittādo daṃsaṇa-ṇāṇappahāṇādo* - *Pravac.* 1:6.

has transformed itself through *dharma* (i.e. through its internal attitude) is united with the pure manifestation of consciousness then it attains to the bliss of *nirvāṇa*.[7]

This definition of *cāritra* as part of the *ratnatraya* may be compared with that given in the *Pañcāstikāya* at gāthā 115, viz.:

> Right faith is belief in the way things are (i.e. in the *tattvas*). Right knowledge is the acquisition of correct knowledge about things (*adhigama*).[8] Right conduct is an attitude of indifference towards things on the part of those who are on the path.

In other words, when you know how things really are you realise that they have nothing to do with the self, and so you maintain a liberating attitude of indifference towards them.[9]

This lack of interest in external conduct is indicative of Kundakunda's attitude throughout these works. Moreover, it is probable that this situation obtains not so much because he takes external practice for granted but because his own development of doctrine has led him to a position where the external is irrelevant. This will become clear when we try to find a place for his understanding of the roles of *jñāna* and *dhyāna* in the standard Jaina categorization of *tapas* (as imperfectly schematised in the *Tattvārtha Sūtra*).

---

7 *dhammeṇa pariṇadappā appā jadi suddhasaṃpayogajudo |*
pāvadi ṇivvāṇasuhaṃ ... Pravac. 1:11.

8 On *adhigama*, see *TS* 1:3 and *SS*.

9 Here 'knowledge' may be being used in the *vyavahāra* or conventional sense, as opposed to the *niścaya* view of *jñāna* which refers to realisation of the self ('self-knowledge'); nevertheless, it is clear that knowledge and conduct are interdependent and inform each other at both levels. The crucial consideration, however, is how *cāritra* is *defined*.

6.2 *Sāmāyika*

Before we deal with *tapas* and *dhyāna* directly, however, it is worth considering some of the associations which cluster around the word *sama / śama*, 'equanimity', and its synonyms in Jaina doctrine. This will provide some indication of how Kundakunda has arrived at his conception of ideal conduct as primarily an attitude of mind rather than specific, physical conduct.[10]

Throughout Jaina literature there occurs the term *sāmāyika*, often translated as 'attaining equanimity'.[11] It is, however, possible to trace a substantial shift in emphasis and meaning between the *sāmāyika* of the early canon and *sāmāyika* as it appears in later works (in, for example, Kundakunda's *Niyamasāra*). An outline of this change will help us to a better understanding of the range and type of mental conduct that Kundakunda recommends in the *Pravacanasāra*.

P.S. Jaini writes that *sāmāyika* is 'first used in canonical texts with reference to a restraint (saṃyama) undertaken by Mahāvīra when he renounced the world'. This involved 'nothing less than the lifetime abandonment of all evil acts'.[12] This usage is evident in the following passage from the *Āyāraṃga Sutta*:

> After the Venerable Ascetic Mahāvīra had plucked out his hair in five handfuls ..., he paid obeisance to all liberated spirits, and vowing to do no sinful act, he adopted the holy conduct.[13]

---

[10] See *Pravac.* 1:7, above.

[11] See, for instance, *JPP* (glossary) p. 350.

[12] *JPP* p. 221.

[13] *tao ṇaṃ samaṇe bhagavaṃ Mahāvīre ... paṃcamuṭṭhiyaṃ loyaṃ karettā siddhāṇaṃ ṇamokkāraṃ karei, karettā savvaṃ me akaraṇijjaṃ pāvakammaṃ ti kaṭṭu sāmāyiaṃ carittaṃ paḍivajjai.* Quoted in *JPP* p. 17, fn. 40 - II.15.23 in Jacobi's trans.; cf. *Utt.* 28.32. Jacobi's trans., 1884, p. 199 is the one used here.

Jacobi's translation of *sāmāyiaṃ / sāmāyikam* in this passage as 'holy' is criticised by Jaini as ignoring the technical meaning of

The important point to note here is that *sāmāyika* is essentially to do with physical conduct (*cāritra*) and so with physical restraint. Moreover, this giving up of all harmful acts is, in effect, a compression of the *mahāvrata*, the five great vows of the ascetic: viz. to desist from *hiṃsā*, *anṛta*, *steya*, *abrahma*, and *parigraha* (injury, lying, taking what is not given, unchastity, and attachment to things). This connection is pointed out by Pūjyapāda in his commentary on *Tattvārtha Sūtra* 7:1 (which enumerates the *mahāvrata*) where he states that, 'From the point of view of *sāmāyika*, which consists of the cessation from everything blameable (i.e. harmful) the vow is one'.[14]

As I have already explained, the earliest understanding of the *mahāvrata* was overwhelmingly in terms of physical restraint; the *sāmāyika-cāritra* of the *Āyāraṃga* must, therefore, be similarly external in its range and focus. However, this very wedding of *sāmāyika* and *mahāvrata* alerts us to the probability that, with the increasing internalisation of the *vrata* - especially of *ahiṃsā* and *aparigraha* (they become at least as significant as attitudes or mental events as they are as physical restraints) -, *sāmāyika* too will be internalised. This does turn out to be the case; the difficulty lies in deciding when - i.e. in what social and religious circumstances - it occurred.

The term *sāmāyika* is also used for what is undoubtedly a very ancient lay practice,[15] namely, the assumption of temporary ascetic status, for periods of up to one *muhūrta* (48 minutes).[16] The purpose of this ritual is, as P.S. Jaini remarks, to lead the layman 'voluntarily and irrevocably

---

sāmāyika-cāritra and so also its wider implications [*JPP* p. 17, fn. 40].

[14] Trans. of: *sarvasāvadyanivṛttilakṣaṇasāmāyikāpreksyā ekaṃ vratam*, *SS* on *TS* 7:1.

[15] One mentioned derisively in the Buddhist *Aṅguttaranikāya* 1.206, quoted in *JPP* p. 223, fn. 42.

[16] See *JPP* p. 223.

into the vows and life of an ascetic'.[17] As the *Āvaśyaka-niryukti* (c.90 C.E.?)[18] remarks, during the time of *sāmāyika*, 'a layman becomes like an ascetic and for that reason it should be performed often'.[19]

The extent to which this practice in its earliest form was fully meditational (i.e. aiming at self-realisation or gnosis through concentration), as opposed to simply a physical restraint, is not clear. P.S. Jaini does not address the problem, giving a largely synchronic analysis of *sāmāyika* based upon Williams' excellent study of the medieval *śrāvakācāra* material.[20] It is reasonable to suppose that lay discipline in this respect would be meditational only to the extent that the corresponding ascetic discipline was also yogic. Yet there is also the possibility that *sāmāyika*, as the mental rehearsal or internalisation of ascetic practice, came to be instrumental in engendering a corresponding internalisation in the very ascetic behaviour it was attempting to concentrate. This process, if genuine, would have been facilitated by the fact that it was the same people who may have been practising in this way, as laity, who would eventually have become *śramaṇas*. Neverthelss, it remains to be shown that the earliest practice of lay *sāmāyika* was anything more yogic than *kāyotsarga*, thought-free physical immobility.[21]

Sāmāyika-cāritra was not, of course, confined to lay practice. For Mahāvīra, as we have seen, it was the one all-

---

[17] Ibid. p. 226.

[18] See Schubring 1962, para. 55.

[19] R. Williams' paraphrase of:
sāmāiyammi u kae samaṇo iva sāvao havai jamhā /
eeṇa kāraṇeṇaṃ bahuso sāmāiyaṃ kujjā - quoted 1963, p. 133.

[20] *JPP* pp. 221-227; cf. R. Williams 1963, pp. 131-139.

[21] Eventually, *sāmāyika* comes to include *pūjā*, 'meditation by worship' and, indeed, is used as a blanket term for all types of spiritual activity. Moreover, according to the later classification of lay spiritual progress, it is the third *pratimā* (out of eleven), and the first of the four lay *śikṣāvrata*. For the relation of these *vrata* to each other and to mendicant practice, see *JPP* p. 182; see also ibid. p. 186-187, p. 190.

embracing ascetic vow; however, the term also appears in canonical texts, not as a comprehensive vow, but simply as one - albeit the first - among six *āvaśyaka* or 'essential duties' of the mendicant, to be performed daily.[22] Here, *sāmāyika* means something like a state of 'mental equanimity' or 'equilibrium' which leads to the end of all sinful activity.[23] In other words, it is an internal state, or 'meditation', initially designed to bring about the cessation of harmful conduct. Schubring sees it as a 'state of inward balance', allied to or manifesting itself in 'an act of devotion to be repeated several times a day'.[24] He characterises the *āvaśya* as 'formulae' which have to be known, and *sāmaīya* as 'a short vow to be brought to one's mind repeatedly during the day promising to shun for life all that is blamable in thoughts, words and deeds ... as well as in all one has personally caused and approved of' (i.e. it corresponds to the 'three restraints' or *gupti*).[25] However, Schubring seems to be reading the term in the light of a particularly mechanised and ritualised context. For, as P.S. Jaini makes clear, these formulae are only the *start* of the practice which leads on to deeper meditation.[26] *Sāmāyika*, therefore, clearly has a more general and primary sense of developing a practice of equanimity towards everything exterior to one's self, with the understanding that the corollary of such an attitude is necessarily good physical conduct. That is to say, the physical restraint connected with Mahāvīra's one great vow has been partially

---

[22] Indeed, before taking the full mendicant vows, the novice Śvetāmbara monk is said to live in the *saṃāiya* state or branch of the monastic order (*-kappa-ṭṭhii*) - see Schubring 1962, paras. 136, 138, 151. For details of the *āvaśyaka*, see Schubring 1962, para. 151; R. Williams 1963, pp.184-5; *JPP* pp. 189-191.

[23] See *Utt*. 28.32, 29 (intro.), and 29:8. Jaini says that the minimum amount of *sāmāyika* required of a monk is three periods a day - *JPP* p. 182.

[24] Schubring 1962, p. 299; see paras. 151, 170.

[25] Ibid. p. 269. On *gupti*, see section 1 above.

[26] *JPP* p. 222ff.

internalised, in recognition of the fact that external action is engendered and sustained by internal attitude. (The inversion of this, of course, is that if one's attitude is pure then, ipso facto, one's external behaviour will be so; the focus of personal practice has thus shifted to the former, since it is the internal attitude which is really instrumental in binding and liberating the soul.)

Pūjyapāda seems to take this further in the *Sarvārthasiddhi*. Starting with the canonical understanding that *sāmāyika* is a *single* great vow, he equates this with the subject becoming one, or concentrated:

> To become one is *śamaya*. *Sāmāyika* is just the same as *samaya*, or it can be analysed as having *samaya* as its purpose.[27]

It is thus made clear that external restraint is the means to a unified internal state, a becoming 'one'. Moreover, it is this inner concentration which is the immediate cause of liberation. This is spelt out elsewhere in the *Sarvārthasiddhi*. At *Tattvārtha Sūtra* 9:2, the causes of *saṃvara* for ascetics are listed; these are *gupti*, *samiti*, *dharma*, *anuprekṣā*, *parīṣahajaya*, and *cāritra* (control, carefulness, virtue / duty, contemplation, victory over the afflictions, and conduct). According to Pūjyapāda, conduct (*cāritra*) is mentioned last to indicate that it is the direct cause of liberation.[28] And foremost, and of most importance, among these five kinds of liberation-causing conduct is *sāmāyika*.[29]

So far we have seen that *sāmāyika* has been characterised chiefly as the development of an attitude of

---

[27] *ekatvena ayanaṃ gamanaṃ samayaḥ, samaya eva sāmāyikaṃ, samayaḥ prayojanam asyeti vā vigṛhya sāmāyikam* - *SS* on *TS* 7:21.

[28] *cāritram ante gṛhyate mokṣaprāpteḥ sākṣāt kāraṇam* - *SS* on *TS* 9:18.

[29] See ibid.: *sāmāyikādīnām ānupūrvyavacanam uttarottaraguṇaprakarṣakhyāpanārthaṃ kriyate*; cf. *Pravac.* 1:7 and *Pañc.* 115, quoted above, pp. 186-187.

restraint or indifference towards the world - an attitude which in turn entails physical restraint. This reading looks, as it were, over its shoulder at that bodily control which is the ultimate factor in liberation. However, the kind of concentration of and on the self, described by Pūjyapāda, looks forward to the self-realisation or *jñāna* of Kundakunda.[30]

When we turn to Kundakunda himself, we find that the only sustained use of the term *sāmāyika*, as such, is in the *Niyamasāra* (although, as we have already seen, in the *Pravacanasāra* there is the crucial equation of *śama* with *cāritra* and *dharma*). There, in the section on *pratyākhyāna* (renunciation), we find the following verses:

> Whatever wrong conduct is in me, I give it all up together with threefold activity and practise threefold equanimity (*sāmāyika*) which is everything and formless, [*Niyamasāra* 103][31]

and

> I am impartial (*sāmya*) towards all living creatures and I have no animosity towards any of them. Having given up all desires, deep meditation (*samādhi*) is attained.[*Niyamasāra* 104][32]

---

30 It is possible, of course, that Pūjyapāda had read Kundakunda; certainly, he must have been aware of some of the latter's source material.

31 *Niy*. 103 trans. by Uggar Sain [Kundakunda (1)], with alterations. The surrounding verses are *ślokas*, but 103 is metrically defective.

32 *Niy*. 104. It is worth noting that commentators generally take verses 77-139 of the *Niyamasāra* to be Kundakunda's version of the six *āvaśyaka*. As Bhargava (pp. 166-167) points out, this particular list of *āvaśyaka* is slightly different from all other versions, before and after Kundakunda. If it is really supposed to be a list of *āvaśyaka* then it is a radically internalised one, in which *pratikramaṇa* (confession), *prāyaścitta* (repentance), etc. are all done by the self to the self through inner discipline, and have no external indicators or emblems; that is to say, they are de-ritualised.

First, it should be noted that *sāmāyika* is equated with inactivity: it is again connected with the threefold restraint (*gupti*) of mind, speech and body. Yet this is viewed not so much as a renunciatory practice as the attainment of 'everything'. It may be asked, what can be meant by a 'threefold equanimity' that is everything and formless? Uggar Sain's modern commentary[33] splits the practice of *sāmāyika* into three tiers (lowest, middle, and highest); however, it seems clear that the threefold *sāmāyika* is simply the restraint of body, speech, and mind, in negation of their threefold activity, and that this practice is viewed as essentially one, a total equanimity rooted in realisation of the self's true relationship (i.e. lack of relationship) with everything else.

Second, equanimity, the condition of impartiality towards everything, is closely connected with the meditational state of *samādhi*, the former apparently being a prerequisite or preliminary form of the latter.

A section of the *Niyamasāra*, called '*parama-samādhi*' (122-133), deals with this relationship in more detail. Here, in gāthā 123, *parama-samādhi* is seen as the result of meditation on the the self through *dharma-dhyāna* and *śukla-dhyāna*.[34] When this is compared with gāthā 133, it can be seen that meditation on the self (through *dharma-* and *śukla-dhyāna*) *is* the practice of *sāmāyika*.[35] Gāthā 133 reads:

> In the teaching of the omniscient, he who continuously practises *dharma-dhyāna* and *śukla-dhyāna*, for him there is lasting equanimity (*sāmāyika*).

Taking these two gāthās together, it becomes clear that

---

[33] Based on Padmaprabha's commentary of c. mid twelfth century C.E., on which see Upadhye p. xl, fn. 1.

[34] ... *dhammajjhāṇeṇa sukkajhāṇeṇa* |
jo jhāyai appāṇaṃ paramasamāhī have tassa - *Niy.* 123.

[35] On *dharma-* and *śukla-dhyāna*, see below.

sāmāyika leads to *parama-samādhi*. Indeed, that they are perceived as virtually synonymous may be inferred from the fact that, barring the first two gāthās (122 and 123) and the last (133), the whole of this '*parama-samādhi*' section is devoted to characterising *sāmāyika*. In selective summary, all external *tapas* and study is useless to one devoid of equanimity (124); but an all-embracing attitude of non-attachment, of *sama* (126), towards all things brings one close to the *ātman* (127) and constitutes *sāmāyika*. In other words, it is not so much a condition resulting from realisation of the self (of its true nature), but a means to engendering that realisation. And it is through such realisation, brought about by meditation on the true nature of the self (= *sāmāyika* [123]), that *parama-samādhi* results. Pure self-awareness or self-knowledge is inextricable from *sāmāyika*, and it is for this, as we shall see, that Kundakunda's ideal ascetic is striving.

It is clearly with definitions such as these in mind that P.S. Jaini refers to *sāmāyika* as meaning both 'attaining equanimity' and 'fusion with the true self', or as 'becoming fixed in *jñāna-cetanā*, pure self-awareness'.[36] This, as Jaini further remarks, amounts to a 'progressive detachment of one's consciousness from all external objects';[37] yet, rather than being mindless, such an attitude - as we shall see - leads, according to Kundakunda, to nothing less than omniscience.

Briefly, we have considered the shift in meaning of '*sāmāyika*' - from being a synonym for the total physical restraint of the *mahāvrata*, via internalised restraint, to an attitude of mind, or development of consciousness through meditation, which leads to pure self-awareness. By doing so, we have charted a line of development through which the ascetic (especially, but not exclusively) has acquired a greater and greater autonomy of means vis à vis his personal liberation.

---

36 *JPP* p. 221.

37 Ibid.

With this rapid sketch of one strand of doctrinal development in mind, we must now return to a more detailed analysis of Kundakunda's internalised mechanism of liberation.

6.3 *Tapas and dhyāna*

The ninth *adhyāya* of the *Tattvārtha Sūtra* deals with *saṃvara* and *nirjarā*, the obstruction of the influx of karmic material and the destruction of that already bound. *Saṃvara* is effected by *gupti* (restraint), *samiti* (carefulness), *dharma*, *anuprekṣā* (reflection), *parīṣahajaya* (victory over the twenty-two afflictions) and *cāritra* (conduct of five kinds) (*Tattvārtha Sūtra* 9:2).[38] *Nirjarā* is effected by *tapas* (austerities / penance) (*Tattvārtha Sūtra* 9:3). The *Sarvārthasiddhi* adds that *tapas* causes both *saṃvara* and *nirjarā*; indeed, it is the chief cause of *saṃvara*.[39] This, says Pūjyapāda, is why *tapas* is mentioned separately here, although it is also included as a sub-category of *dharma* (at *Tattvārtha Sūtra* 9:6). From this it is clear that *tapas* is by far the most important element in the process of achieving permanent liberation from the bondage of *karman*. (There are, of course, degrees of *tapas*, and so also of *saṃvara* and *nirjarā*, but not of final liberation.)

Umāsvāti divides *tapas* into two categories, *bāhya* (external) and *uttara* ('higher', i.e. the internal) (*Tattvārtha Sūtra* 9:19-20). External *tapas* need not detain us here, other than to remark that it consists of:

1) *anaśana* - fasting
2) *avamaudarya* - reduction in food intake
3) *vṛtti-parisaṃkhyāna* - restrictions on the begging of food
4) *rasa-parityāga* - rejection of stimulating or delicious food
5) *vivikta-śayyāsana* - sitting / sleeping in a lonely place

---

[38] On *cāritra*, see *TS* 9:18; cf. p. 185ff. above.

[39] *saṃvaraṃ prati prādhānya pratipādanārthaṃ* - *SS* on *TS* 9:3.

6) *kāya-kleśa* - mortification of the body. [*Tattvārtha Sūtra* 9:19]

According to the *Sarvārthasiddhi*, these are called external 'because they are dependent on external things and these are seen by others'.[40]

Internal *tapas* consists of:

1) *prayāścitta* - repentance of transgressions due to negligence (nine kinds, see *Tattvārtha Sūtra* 9:22)
2) *vinaya* - reverence, especially to elders (four kinds, see *Tattvārtha Sūtra* 9:23)
3) *vaiyāvṛttya* - respectful service to other monks, especially when they are ill (ten kinds, see *Tattvārtha Sūtra* 9:24)
4) *svādhyāya* - study of the scriptures (five kinds, see *Tattvārtha Sūtra* 9:25)
5) *vyutsarga* - renunciation of external and internal attachments (*upadhi* - see *Tattvārtha Sūtra* 9:26)
6) *dhyāna* - meditation (four kinds, see *Tattvārtha Sūtra* 9:28)

[*Tattvārtha Sūtra* 9:20]

These are called 'internal' (*abhyantara*) because of the restraint or limitation of the mind in these cases.[41] In practice, commentators agree that *dhyāna* is the most significant of these internal austerities and the most important feature in the pattern of Jaina ethics.[42]

Dhyāna is first defined (in the *Sarvārthasiddhi* on *Tattvārtha Sūtra* 9:20) as the abandoning of mental confusion (literally, the giving up of the distractions of / to the mind - *cittavikṣepatyāgo dhyānam*).[43] A more technical description follows (at *Tattvārtha Sūtra* 9:27), where meditation is said to be the concentration of thought on one point or object, lasting up to a maximum of one *muhūrta*

---

40 S.A. Jain's trans. of: *bāhyadravyāpekṣatvāt parapratyakṣatvāc ca.*

41 *manoniyamamanārthatvāt* - *SS* on *TS* 9:20.

42 See, for example, *JPP* p. 251, and Bhargava p. 193.

43 On *citta-vikṣepa*, cf. *YS*, 1:30, 1:31.

(forty-eight minutes) for the most robust.[44] The *Sarvārthasiddhi* connects such meditation with *jñāna* by defining *dhyāna* as 'knowledge which shines without quivering like the steady flame of a candle'.[45]

This *dhyāna*, according to Umāsvāti, is of four types:

1) *ārta*	concentration on something painful	
2) *raudra*	concentration on something cruel	
3) *dharmya*	virtuous concentration	
4) *śukla*	pure concentration.	[*Tattvārtha Sūtra* 9:28]

The first two types (*ārta* and *raudra*) are *apraśasta* (not recommended) because they are the cause of the influx of inauspicious karmas.[46] Conversely, the second two (*dharmya* and *śukla*) are *praśasta* (recommended) because they have the power to destroy *karman*.[47] Moreover, *dharmya-* and *śukla-dhyāna* are the causes of *mokṣa* (*Tattvārtha Sūtra* 9:29).

Ārta- and *raudra-dhyāna* are each divided into four types [see *Tattvārtha Sūtra* 9:30-35], characteristic, in the case of *ārta*, of laymen and non-vigilant ascetics (*Tattvārtha Sūtra* 9:34), and in the case of *raudra*, of laymen who have and have not taken the partial vows (*Tattvārtha Sūtra* 9:35). An 'ascetic' who is subject to this spontaneous type of *dhyāna* would, ipso facto, no longer be an ascetic.[48]

Similarly, the liberating kinds of meditation, *dharmya* and *śukla*, are each subdivided into four types (*Tattvārtha Sūtra* 9:36-44). *Dharmya-dhyāna* is divided into:

---

44 *uttamasaṃhananasyaikāgracintānirodho dhyānam āntar-muhūrtāt*. Cf. Patañjali's *YS* 1:2: *yogaś citta-vṛtti-nirodhaḥ*, '*yoga* is the control of the activities of the mind-field'.

45 S.A. Jain's trans. of: *jñānam evāparispandāgniśikhāvad avabhāsamānaṃ* - *SS* on *TS* 9:27.

46 *apuṇyāsravakāraṇatvāt* - *SS* on *TS* 9:28.

47 *karmanirdahanasāmarthyāt* - ibid.

48 See *SS* on *TS* 9:35.

1) *ājñā vicaya* - the investigation of, or meditation on, the teachings of the Jina - especially on what can be known only through those teachings
2) *apāya-vicaya* - meditation on the loss of the true path by others, and the means to their liberation
3) *vipāka-vicaya* - meditation on the effects of *karman* on *jīva*s, and the way to liberation from *karman*
4) *saṃsthāna-vicaya* - meditation on the structure of the universe and the way in which *jīva*s are brought to their particular position.[49]

The *Sarvārthasiddhi* explains that this kind of meditation is attainable by, or characteristic of, laymen of the fourth and fifth *guṇasthānas*, and ascetics of the sixth and seventh *guṇasthānas*.[50]

Śukla-dhyāna is also divided into four:

1) *pṛthaktva-savitarka-savicāra*
2) *ekatva-savitarka-avicārā*

These two 'involve discursive concentration upon the nature of the *tattva*s (existents)'. Each focuses on a single existent, but, in the first, the meditator's attention 'shifts from one of the existent's countless modes to another', whereas, in the second, his attention is applied to a single mode of the existent.[51] They occur between the eighth and twelfth *guṇasthānas*, and the attainment of the twelfth *guṇasthāna* is only possible through their negation of the passions.[52]

---

49 *TS* 9:36 and *SS* - see also *JPP* pp. 252-253; and Bhargava pp. 199-200.

50 See *JPP* p. 253.

51 *JPP* p. 257, based on the *SS* on *TS* 9:39-44.

52 The terminology here is very close to that applied to the first two Buddhist *jhāna*; in the Buddhist case, however, reasoning / conceptual thought (*vitarka*) usually disappears along with discursive thought (*vicāra*) in the second *jhāna* (see Lamotte, pp. 42-43). See also '*Jhāna*' in *Buddhist Dictionary*, and e.g. *Majjhima-Nikāya* I.276. Also

3) *sūkṣmakriyā-anivartin* - the 'meditation' of subtle activity, in which 'all gross and subtle activities of mind and speech, as well as the gross activities of the body, are absolutely stopped'.[53]

4) *vyuparatakriyā-anivartin* - absolute non-motion, in which even the subtle physical activities - breathing, heartbeat, etc.- are stopped. These two - designated *anivartin*, 'that from which there is no falling back'[54] - occur in the final two *guṇasthānas*, immediately preceding physical death and final liberation.

The discussion of *śukla-dhyāna*, in particular, is very limited in the *Tattvārtha Sūtra* and *Sarvārthasiddhi*. A number of problems attend the relevant passages, not least the assertion, at *Tattvārtha Sūtra* 9:37, that the first two types of *śukla-dhyāna* can be attained only by those who know the *pūrvas* (i.e. the original Jaina canon which, at the time of the *Tattvārtha Sūtra*'s composition, was already considered to be 'lost'). These difficulties have been considered by a number of scholars and I shall not enter into a further discussion of them here.[55] Enough, however, has been presented of this standard schema of *tapas* and *dhyāna*, and its relation to the *jīva*'s progress towards liberation, to be able to ask where, if at all, Kundakunda's soteriology of liberation through *jñāna* and liberation fits into this pattern. In order to answer this, we must now look at Kundakunda's gāthās on liberation in greater detail.

---

cf. *Yoga Sūtras* 1:42-44 on *savitarka*, *nirvitarka*, *savicāra*, and *nirvicāra*.

[53] *JPP* p. 269.

[54] Ibid. p. 270.

[55] On *śukla-dhyāna* see Bronkhorst p. 179; Schubring 1962, p. 315 fn. 3, p. 316. On the contradiction between the *TS* and *Bhāṣya* concerning *śukla-dhyāna*, see Zydenbos pp. 34-35. On the later systematisation of *dhyāna*, especially by Haribhadra, see Tatia pp. 283-291.

6.4 *Meditation in the Pravacanasāra*

i) Dhyāna

The first direct reference to 'meditation' (*jhāna / dhyāna*) in the *Pravacanasāra* occurs at gāthā 2:59:

> He, who having conquered the senses etc., meditates on the pure manifestation of consciousness [which is] the self, will not be affected by karmas. How then can the life-essentials (*prāṇā*) follow him?.[56]

The *prāṇā* - the 'life-essentials' or 'animating principles' - do not, as Upadhye explains, 'form the nature of the soul-stuff, but they are the indications or the signs of the presence of the soul in an embodied condition'.[57] That is to say, they are the only available means by which a *jīva* may be detected in *saṃsāra*; or as the *Tattvadīpikā* on *Pravacanasāra* 2:53 puts it, they are the reason for the *vyavahāra* condition of the *jīvā*, as opposed to its condition as it is in itself, its *niścaya* condition.

The *prāṇā* are fourfold - of the senses (*iṃdiya*), of the channels of activities (*bala*) [viz. body, speech and mind], of duration of life (*āu / āyu*), and of respiration (*āṇappāṇa / ānaprāṇā*) (*Pravacanasāra* 2:54). The *jīva* 'lives' in *saṃsāra* (in the past, present and future) by virtue of these *prāṇā*, which themselves originate from material substances (*poggala-davva / pudgala-dravya*) (2:55). As the *Tattvadīpikā* on 2:55 is at pains to point out, the *prāṇā*, because of their material basis, cannot reach the innate nature of the soul.[58] Inevitably, given their materiality, the *prāṇā* are seen as being both the effects and the causes of

---

56 Translation after Upadhye.

57 Upadhye p. 19, fn. 1 on 2:54 (trans.).

58 *tan na jīvasya svabhāvatvam avāpnoti pudgaladravya-nirvṛttatvāt* - *TD* on *Pravac.* 2:55.

material *karman*.[59] The karma-tainted *jīva* supports *prāṇā* again and again (i.e. it is reborn) - *prāṇā* which, by their very nature as active principles, involve the *jīva* in further *hiṃsā*,[60] until it gives up the attitude of possession, of 'mine', towards external objects, especially the body.[61] This, according to the *Tattvadīpikā* on 2:58, breaks the sequence and, having conquered the senses through this renunciation of possession, the person meditating on the pure self achieves *saṃvara*.[62] In other words, there is no rebirth, for the pure soul cannot, by definition, be embodied by material *prāṇā* (themselves the effect and further cause of *karman*); for while the conjunction with material *prāṇā* is the cause of the soul's *vyavahāra* state,[63] from the *niścaya* view the soul is quite separate from material *prāṇā*. As the *Tattvadīpikā* puts it, the cessation of this series of material *karman*

> accrues to him who has conquered all strange substances such as the senses, - like a crystal gem withdrawn from the influence (*anuvṛtti*) of any support, - and who abides in the perfect (*kevala*) and motionless self, completely pure and consisting merely of manifestation of consciousness.[64]

So rather than physical *tapas*, it is meditation on the true nature of the self - that it is pure consciousness - which is instrumental in bringing the cycle of material *prāṇā* and

---

[59] For a full description of the mechanism of this, see *Pravac.* and *TD* 2:56-57.

[60] See *TD* on 2:57.

[61] See *Pravac.* 2:58.

[62] See *Pravac.* 2:59, quoted above.

[63] *vyavahārajīvatvahetavaḥ* - *TD* on *Pravac.* 2:59.

[64] Faddegon's trans. [Kundakunda (3)] p.123, slightly altered, of *TD* on 2:59: *sa (tu) samastendriyādi paradravyānuvijayino bhūtvā samastopāśrayānuvṛttivyāvṛttasya sphaṭikamaṇer ivātyantaviśuddham upayogamātram ātmānaṃ suniścalaṃ kevalam adhivasataḥ syāt*
Note once again the way in which the jewel simile is employed: the material world colours the *jīva* by reflection, there is no real contact.

karma to an end. The classical idea of liberation achieved through the stoppage and shedding of material *karman* through *tapas* fades before Kundakunda's idea of release through *realisation* of the pure self - the *ātman* whose *svabhāva* cannot, by definition, be tainted by *karman* - through meditation.

This is made even clearer at *Pravacanasāra* 2:67, which reads:

> Free from inauspicious manifestation of consciousness, not joined to auspicious (manifestation of consciousness) towards other substance, let me be indifferent (i.e. neutral); I meditate on the self whose self is knowledge.[65]

Introducing this gāthā, Amṛtacandra characterises it as a teaching of 'the destruction of the causes of conjunction with other substance'.[66] By becoming indifferent to *paradravya*, one is released from *aśuddhopayoga* and becomes intent upon the self alone - a state synonymous with *śuddhopayoga*.[67]

The next gāthā (2:68) takes the form of a performative or prescriptive statement, prefaced by the nominative singular of the first person pronoun, with regard to *paradravya*. In other words, it gives what seems to be a paradigm of meditational practice:

> I am neither body, nor mind, nor speech, nor the cause of these, (I am) neither the agent, nor the instigator, nor the approver of doers / actors.

This adds up to a radical reinterpretation of the *gupti* doctrine of classical Jain thought.[68] Freedom from

---

65 Cf. pp. 181ff., above, on *Pravac.* 2:67, etc.

66 Faddegon's trans., p. 127, of: *paradravyasaṃyoga-kāraṇavināśam*; cf. *TD* on 2:65.

67 Paraphrase of the *TD* on *Pravac.* 2:67.

68 See above; *TS* 9:4; *JPP* p. 247.

bondage is no longer a matter of *restraining* or progressively curbing the activities (*yoga*) of body, mind and speech with regard to what is done, caused, or approved by oneself; now it is a matter of realising that body, mind and speech are entirely alien substances (*paradravya*) which, in reality, have no connection with the self whatsoever. A strict dualism applies in which the very instruments and organs of *yoga* (activity) are denied any connection with the essential self; therefore, what body, mind and speech do or do not do is actually irrelevant to liberation. What counts now is knowledge or realisation of the true nature of the *ātman* through meditation, the prerequisite of which is an attitude of indifference (*madhyastha*) to everything not that pure self. (The possible implications of this for Jaina orthopraxy hardly need pointing out.) Thus this gāthā (2:68) may be taken as an apophatic statement about the true nature of the self - a statement which acts, mediately and meditatively, as a means of realising that nature. The *Tattvadīpikā* stresses at length that body, voice and mind - characterised as *acetana-dravya* ('unintelligent / unconscious substance', consisting of *poggala-davva* / *pudgala-dravya*)[69] - act independently of the self; they are autonomous; indeed, the body, taken in its widest sense, is an automaton. For example:

> I am not the unconscious substance which is the cause of body, voice and mind; indeed, these are cause even without me as cause

and

> I am not the unconscious substance which is the independent cause of body, voice and mind; indeed, these are being done even without me as agent, etc.[70]

---

[69] See *Pravac.* 2:69-70.

[70] *na ca me śarīravāṅmanaḥkāraṇācetanadravyatvam asti, tāni khalu māṃ kāraṇam antareṇāpi kāraṇaṃ bhavanti ... na ca me*

All this amounts to saying that the essential cause of bondage is the mistaken belief that the *jīva* has some connection with what is *ajīva*. Such a belief constitutes *aśuddhopayoga*, which is destroyed by the realisation of the *jīva*'s true identity (and thus of the 'mistake') through meditation on its true nature. This seems perilously close to saying that bondage is not simply maintained by delusive behaviour - the product, among other things, of *mohaniyā-karman* - but that it *is* a delusion. If the *jīva*, by definition, cannot act or cause action, if it cannot really have any connection with matter, how can it ever have been bound? Unsurprisingly, the *Pravacanasāra* does not pursue this here, but starts a technical discussion of the nature of atoms (2:70ff.).[71]

ii) Dhyāna and jñāna

Pravacanasāra 2:98-2:108 provides a cluster of gāthās on meditation, the nature of the self and knowledge. I have commented on the significance of some of these for Kundakunda's doctrine of liberation already;[72] here I shall consider their relation to *dhyāna* and *jñāna*.

Pravacanasāra 2:98 states that to identify the self with body and wealth (i.e. with *paradravya*, the not-self) is to resort to the wrong road (*ummaggam / unmārgam*). According to the *Tattvadīpikā*, such identification brings about a transformation into the impure self; it is this which is the 'wrong road'.[73] Thus, 'from the point of view of the

---

svatantraśarīravāṅmanaḥ-kāraṇācetanadravyatvam asti, tāni khalu māṃ kartāram antareṇāpi kriyamāṇāni - *TD* on *Pravac.* 2:68.
What it can mean to characterise *manas* as 'unconscious' or the product of 'unconscious substance' is not made clear. But the physical *manas* of Sāṃkhya, a product of unconscious *prakṛti*, and totally separate from the *puruṣa*, may provide a model here.

[71] Sāṃkhya, of course, has precisely the same problem, one which is inherited by Vedānta.

[72] See above, pp. 140-143, 147-149.

[73] *aśuddhātmapariṇatirūpam unmārgam* - *TD* on 2:98.

impure only the impure self is attained'.[74] Moreover, commenting on the previous gāthā [2:97], Amṛtacandra has already associated this emphasis on the impure with the *vyavahāra* view of the self, i.e. with the point of view that the self is and can be contaminated by *paradravya*.[75] So for Amṛtacandra, at least, when it comes to the question of liberation, the *vyavahāra* view is not simply a theoretical construct - a partial view, or the truth at one particular level - it is actually instrumental in further bondage: to believe that the soul can be connected with and thus contaminated by *paradravya* is to bring about that very contamination.[76] And the self which does not cease to identify with other substances is characterised as one 'whose delusion is produced by the *vyavahāra-naya*'.[77]

'From the point of view of the pure', however, 'only the pure self is attained'.[78] The person who meditates on the *niścaya* view - that there is no connection between the pure self and *paradravya* - actually becomes that pure self, i.e. he is liberated. So, according to this, it is a mental act - meditation - including or allied to another mental act - a particular kind of knowledge about the (non-)relation of the pure self to matter - which is instrumental in liberating the *jīva*. External means and the various kinds of material *karman* are disregarded. This technique is exemplified by *Pravacanasāra* 2:99:

> He who meditates in concentration, thinking 'I am not others' and they are not mine; I am one (with) knowledge', comes to be a meditator on the (pure) self.

---

[74] *aśuddhanayād aśuddhātmalābha eva* - *TD*, intro. to 2:98.

[75] See *TD* on 2:97: *aśuddhadyotako vyavahāranayaḥ* - 'the conventional view which explains the impure'.

[76] Although, at the theoretical level, the *TD* on 2:97 holds to the idea that both views are 'correct': *ubhāv apy etau staḥ, śuddhāśuddhatvenobhayathā dravyasya pratīyamānatvāt.*

[77] *vyavahāranayopajanitamohaḥ* - *TD* on 2:98.

[78] *śuddhanayād eva śuddhātmalābhaḥ* - *TD* on *Pravac.* 2:99.

The *Tattvadīpikā* comments that the person doing this, who

> lets go the non-self and, taking on the self as self, turns away from other substance and confines his thought to the single point, the self, such a one assuredly, confining his thought one-pointedly, will in that moment of confining his thought one-pointedly be pure self.[79]

Here, Amṛtacandra is probably writing under the influence of the synthesis of *yoga* traditions made by Patañjali in the *Yoga Sūtras* and by Vyāsa in his *Yogabhāṣya*. Both these works predate Amṛtacandra by at least several centuries. If Kundakunda himself knew the *Yoga Sūtras* it is not evident in his work, but since he is clearly drawing on the same ancient tradition of meditational and yogic techniques which are systematised by Patañjali, the chronology is not important. (It is interesting to note that Amṛtacandra echoes not only the *yogaś cittavṛttinirodhaḥ* of *Yoga Sūtras* 1:2 but with his stress on *ekāgra*, 'one-pointed thought' or 'concentration', recalls the technical use of this term in Vyāsa as the means by which pure *samādhi* is attained.)[80]

On *samādhi*, the object of *yoga*, Mircea Eliade writes that, in the first place, it is 'the state in which thought grasps the object directly. Thus there is a real coincidence between knowledge of the object and the object of knowledge'.[81] According to Patañjali and his commentators, *samādhi* has a number of stages; by successively accomplishing these, the 'faculty of absolute knowledge' (*ṛtambharāprajñā*) is attained, and this

---

[79] Faddegon's trans. (p.145) of: *anātmānam utsṛjyātmānam evātmatvenopādāya paradravyavyāvṛttattvād ātmany evaikasminn agre cintām nirūṇaddhi sa khalv ekāgracintānirodhakas tasminn ekāgracintānirodhasamaye śuddhātmā syāt* - *TD* on 2:99.

[80] See *Bhāṣya* on *YS* 1:1, etc.

[81] Eliade p. 522.

> is in itself an opening toward *samādhi* 'without seed', pure *samādhi*, for absolute knowledge discovers the state of ontological plenitude in which being and knowing are no longer separated ... Fixed in *samādhi*, consciousness (*citta*) can now have direct revelation of the self (*puruṣa*).[82]

This is similar enough to Kundakunda's concentration on the pure self as knowledge - without, of course, sharing the same technical context or metaphysics - to alert us to the kind of meditational technique the Digambara writer is recommending. The general method has been discussed above (under *'sāmāyika'*); as a technique, it might also be compared with the preliminary form of Theravāda Buddhist meditation - *samatha* or *samādhi*, the development of one-pointedness of mind.[83] But such comparisons merely demonstrate the pan-Indian character of this method; the real interest lies in the way in which Kundakunda applies it and the implications that this has for ascetic practice. And here, the fact that it bears little resemblance to (or at best subsumes) the classical Jaina modes of *dhyāna* as outlined in the *Tattvārtha Sūtra* (see above), with their emphasis on the cessation of all activity, is significant. For Kundakunda has developed a path to liberation which, at least in its later stages, is almost totally hermetic or self-referential. The goal is achieved through the individual's inner concentration on his pure self; this brings about knowledge or realisation of that self which, since the pure self has absolutely no connection with other substances (*karman*, etc.), is synonymous with liberation. The old, semi-materialist model of a soul which is weighted down by material *karman* shedding that *karman* through physical austerities and, in its liberation, ascending to the topmost part of the universe, has been (at least temporarily) superseded.

This becomes clear if we consider the ways in which

---

82 Ibid.

83 See, for instance, Rahula p.68.

meditation is characterised in the *Pravacanasāra*. Gāthā 2:104 reads:

> He, who has destroyed the impurity of delusion, who has no interest in the objects of the senses, and who, having restrained his mind, is fixed in his own nature, is a meditator on the self.

In other words, meditation on the (pure) self is nothing less than realisation of that self; the successful meditator becomes the pure self which is his own nature (*svabhāva*). As the *Tattvadīpikā* on 2:104 puts it: 'Thus meditation, which takes the form of absorption in one's own nature, is the self, because it is nothing other than the self'.[84]

That is to say, the *ātman* has and can have no *dravya* for its substratum (*adhikaraṇa*) other than its own nature; its own nature (as defined by the *Tattvadīpikā*) is 'infinite, innate intelligence' (*anantasahajacaitanya*), and it is the fixing of oneself in this *svabhāva* which constitutes meditation.[85]

Kundakunda himself has already defined the self's *svabhāva* in some detail as being constituted of *jñāna* and *darśana*, an object beyond the senses, eternal (*dhuva*), unmoving (*acala*), without support - so independent (*aṇālamba*), and pure (*suddha*).[86] This is the eternal self, whose 'self' is *upayoga* (2:101), meditation upon which destroys *moha*,[87] and leads to 'imperishable happiness'.[88]

Kundakunda then asks the question (*Pravacanasāra* 2:105), what does the person who has realised his pure self, who has attained *kevalajñāna*, meditate upon (given that he

---

[84] *ataḥ svabhāvāvasthānarūpatvena dhyānam ātmano 'nanyatvāt dhyānam ātmaiveti* - *TD* on 2:104.

[85] See *TD* on 2:104.

[86] At *Pravac.* 2:100-101.

[87] See above, pp. 140-143, 147-149.

[88] *sokkhaṃ akkhayaṃ / saukhyam akṣayam* - 2:103. Note that the *TD* on 2:102 defines *dhyāna* as *ekāgrasaṃcetana*, 'one-pointed awareness'.

is omniscient and, as the *Tattvadīpikā* puts it, does not feel any desire, curiosity or doubt)?[89] The answer is that he meditates on 'supreme happiness' (*param sokkham* 2:106) which, according to the *Tattvadīpikā* (on 2:106), is as much as to say that the self 'continues as simply a one-pointed awareness in a state of calm'.[90] This is the attainment of 'perfection, whose *svabhāva* is innate knowledge and bliss'.[91]

In other words, meditation is not only the instrument of liberation but it also characterises the state of the liberated: path and goal constitute a single practice.

iii) Jñāna

It has been shown that knowledge about the true nature of the self, combined with meditation on that nature, constitutes Kundakunda's path to liberation. However, given the omniscience of the *arhat*, knowledge occupies an even more central place in Kundakunda's soteriology than the above might at first suggest. For he equates knowledge with the knower (i.e. the self); they are co-extensive and omnipresent. This formula, and the relation of knowledge to the objects of knowledge, must now be considered in greater detail.

Śruta Skandha 2 of the *Pravacanasāra* (*jñeyatattva-adhikāra*) ends with the following gāthā:

> Therefore, having thus realised that the self is innately disposed to be a knower, stationed in unpossessiveness, I turn away from the idea of 'mine'. [*Pravacanasāra* 2:108]

The *Tattvadīpikā* comments:

---

89 *abhilaṣitaṃ jijñāsitaṃ saṃdigdham* - *TD* on *Pravac.* 2:105.

90 *anākulatvasaṃgataikāgrasaṃcetanamātreṇāvatiṣṭhate* - op. cit.

91 *sahajajñānānandasvabhāvasya siddhatvasya* - ibid.

For the equation of 'happiness' with knowledge, omniscience and liberation, see *Pravac.* 1:59 and Upadhye's footnote on p. 8 of his translation of 1:59.

This I, qualified for liberation by means of adhering to the idea of 'not mine' and abandoning the idea of 'mine', preceded by full aquaintance with the truth that the self is inherently a knower, devotes itself to the pure self in all its undertakings because there is no gap between them.

That is to say, I am indeed inherently a knower, and as I am one whose knowledge is absolute (i.e. as I am omniscient) I have a relationship - which takes the form of that between a knower and the naturally knowable - with everything, and no other relationship, such as that between possessor and possession. I am, therefore, unpossessive towards all things and attached to nothing.[92]

What does it mean to say that the *ātman* is naturally or inherently a knower (or as the *Samayasāra* puts it of the emotions and the operation of *karman*: 'they are not my own nature; I am exclusively [uniquely] a knower by nature')?[93]

In the first instance, this is a perception which relies upon the teaching that the liberated soul does not simply attain a condition of isolated bliss at the apex of the universe, it is also characterised by omniscience (*kevalajñāna*). (Although, for the sake of precision, one should distinguish between those liberated souls who have already discarded their bodies (*siddhas*) and those *arhats* who have attained omniscience but for the time being remain embodied.) P.S. Jaini renders the term '*kevalajñāna*' as 'knowledge isolated from karmic

---

92 *aham eṣa mokṣādhikārī jñāyakasvabhāvātmatattvaparijñāna-purassaramamatvanirmamatvahānopādānavidhānena kṛtvāntarasyābhāvāt sarvārambheṇa śuddhātmani pravartate* | *tathāhi - ahaṃ hi tāvat jñāyaka eva svabhāvena, kevalajñāyakasya ca sato mama viśvenāpi sahajñeyajñāyakalakṣaṇa eva sambandhaḥ na punar anye svasvāmilakṣaṇādayaḥ saṃbandhāḥ* | *tato mama na kvacanāpi mamatvaṃ sarvatra nirmamatvam eva* | *TD* on *Pravac*. 2:108.

93 *ṇa du te majjha sahāvā jānagabhāvo du aham ikko* - *Sam*. 198 [= 213]; cf. ibid. 207.

interference'. He goes on to say that such knowledge is

> compared to a mirror in which every one of the innumerable existents (*dravya*), in all its qualities (*guṇas*) and modes (*paryāyas*), is simultaneously reflected. These 'knowables' are cognised without any volition whatsoever on the part of the arhat. Furthermore, no activity of senses or mind is involved; there is only direct perception by the soul.[94]

Omniscience is thus the natural state of the soul, in the sense that, when all karmic obstruction is removed, that kind of knowledge automatically obtains. To put it another way, omniscience is not something to be striven for or attained, in the sense of being some quality which is added to or gained by the agent or knower, rather it is something to be realised or revealed (through the shedding of *karman*) as the original nature of the self. Moreover, since the *jīva* has, in reality, no physical relation with anything *ajīva* - their relation is that of the knower and the knowable -, it is apparent that in its fundamental nature the soul has never been anything but omniscient. And to achieve that omniscience it is only necessary to realise it, through meditation on the true nature of the self and its relationship with the world of matter. Again this seems tantamount to saying that karmic bondage - the adherence of matter to the *jīva* - is fundamentally unreal, a mistake or delusion. For while on one level the realisation of the original nature of the self shines through when obstructive *karman* is removed, on another it is that very realisation which is instrumental in removing obstructive *karman*, through the perception that in reality *karman cannot* obstruct the pure self.

Referring to Kundakunda's *Niyamasāra* (159 = 158 SBJ ed.), P.S. Jaini remarks that the defining mark of the omniscient being is 'complete self-knowledge ...; any other

---

[94] *JPP* p. 266.

description is simply a worldly or "conventional" one'.[95] That is to say, 'From the *vyavahāra* point of view the omniscient lord sees and knows everything, from the *niścaya* point of view the omniscient sees and knows the self'.[96] But, according to the *Pravacanasāra*, this exclusive knowledge of the self is not a limitation on or contraction of knowledge; on the contrary, knowledge of the self *includes* knowledge of everything else. As gāthā 1:23 puts it:

> The soul is co-extensive with knowledge; knowledge is said to be co-extensive with the objects of knowledge; the object of knowledge comprises the physical and non-physical universe; therefore knowledge is omnipresent.[97]

It follows from this that the soul too is omnipresent. Although this is admitted as a temporary possibility in certain circumstances by orthodox doctrine, it is not seen as a characteristic of the liberated soul.[98] Kundakunda, however, confirms at *Pravacanasāra* 1:26 that this is how he understands the nature of the *kevalin*:

> The great Jina is everywhere and all the objects in the world are within him; the Jina consists of knowledge, and those referents of words (i.e. objects) are declared his because they are the objects of knowledge.

As the *Tattvadīpikā* on 1:26 states, this means simply that the Jina knows all the objects in the world completely (i.e. he knows the meaning of all words and so he knows

---

95 Ibid. p. 267.

96 *Niyamasāra* 159. Cf. *Niyamasāra* 166: *appasarūvaṃ pecchadi loyāloyaṃ ṇa kevalī bhagavaṃ* ... - '[From the *niścaya* point of view] the omniscient lord sees the real nature of the self, not the universe and non-universe ...'.

97 Upadhye's translation, p. 4.

98 See *JPP* pp. 102-3, and especially p. 269.

their referents). In reality, he has no physical or metaphysical contact with them, or they with him.[99] That is to say, there is no activity on the part of the liberated self, or - as the *Tattvadīpikā* points out - it never leaves its *svatattva*.[100]

This inactivity of the self includes 'knowing'; indeed, there is no 'knowing' as such (in the sense of process) for the pure self; for, since the knower (i.e. the self) has knowledge as its own nature,[101] it does not have to do anything in order to know apart from realise its true nature. This relationship is confirmed by gāthā 1:27:

> The doctrine is proclaimed that knowledge is the self; without the self there is no knowledge. Therefore, knowledge is the self; but the self is knowledge or anything else.[102]

(The *Tattvadīpikā* explains that the self, 'being the seat of innumerable properties',[103] may be knowledge owing to the *dharma* of knowledge, or owing to some other *dharma* it may be something else.[104] In other words, the self and knowledge are co-extensive, but the latter does not define the former, which is actually and potentially much greater.)

The non-knowingness of this *ātman* (= *jñāna*) is further

---

99 *Sarve 'rthās tadgatā ity upacaryante, na ca teṣāṃ paramārthato 'nyonyagamanam asti, sarvadravyāṇāṃ svarūpaniṣṭhatvāt* - '... objects are said metaphorically to belong to him ... but in the real sense of the word there is no mutual going towards each other, since all substances abide in their own characteristic-nature' - Faddegon's trans., p. 16.

100 Ibid. Indeed, at one level, ontological description as such is probably irrelevant to Kundakunda's purpose here which, like that of much, if not all, 'mystical' teaching, is to engender in the audience a particular attitude or transformation of consciousness. In other words, the teaching is itself directly instrumental in self-realisation: conventional or partial knowledge helps to liberate absolute knowledge.

101 *ṇāṇī ṇāṇasahāvo / jñānī jñānasvabhāvaḥ* - *Pravac.* 1:28.

102 Translation after Upadhye p. 4.

103 Faddegon's trans., p. 16, of *anantadharmādhiṣṭhānatvāt* - *TD* on 1:27.

104 *jñānam anyadharmadvāreṇānyad api syāt* - ibid.

stressed by Kundakunda:

> He who knows is knowledge; the self does not become a knower through knowledge; knowledge develops of itself, and all objects are found in knowledge.[105]

As Faddegon puts it in his translation of this gāthā, 'the self does not by the help of its knowledge become something-that-is-knowing (*jñāyaka*)';[106] knowledge is thus the natural or revealed state of the karmically unobstructed *ātman*. The *Tattvadīpikā* explains that this equation obtains because 'the self is an actor of the greatest supremacy and power in whom agency and instrumentality are united'.[107] In other words, the pure self does not *do* anything; despite the confusion of terminology it is not an 'actor' in the ordinary sense of that word, it simply *is*.[108] Moreover, all the objects of knowledge, since they are said to be found or 'stand' (*ṭṭhiya / sthita*) in knowledge, are thus also found in the self which has been equated with knowledge.[109]

It is in this context that passages such as those quoted from the *Niyamasāra* (159; 166 - see above) should be understood. The pure self or *kevalin* knows everything without coming into possessive relation with anything not-self.[110] Knowledge is essentially a matter of indifference or non-attachment, not of possession. That is to say, it is not the result of a process ('knowing') but a permanent state which is revealed and realised through meditation on the true nature of the self. Such meditation focuses on the status of the relationship between *jīva* and *ajīva*, the knower and the known; the full realisation of that

---

[105] Translation after Upadhye p. 5.

[106] Faddegon's trans., p. 21.

[107] *apṛthagbhūtakartṛkaraṇatvaśaktipāramaiśvaryayogitvād ātmanaḥ* - *TD* on 1:35.

[108] Cf. *Niyamasāra* 172.

[109] *Pravac.* 1:23, 1:26-7, 1:36: *tamhā ṇāṇaṃ jīvo.*

[110] See 2:108 and *TD*, above.

relationship is liberation and omniscience. For Kundakunda, an understanding of this is clearly the crucial component in his mechanism of liberation. He reiterates the relationship in a number of similar formulations. For instance,

> The omniscient lord neither grasps nor releases nor transforms the other; he sees all around and knows everything completely,[111]

and

> The knower, who is beyond sense-perception, necessarily knows and sees the whole world neither entering into nor entered into by objects of knowledge, just as the eye sees the objects of sight.[112]

The *Samayasāra* uses a different image to illustrate the relation of the knower (i.e. the self) and the object known (from the *niścaya* view), but with the same meaning:

> Just as chalk does not become the other (i.e. the surface it is applied to) but remains chalk *qua* chalk, so the knower does not become the other (i.e. the object known) but remains the knower *qua* knower. [*Samayasāra* 356 (= 385 J.L. Jaini's ed.)][113]

And again, in a familiar image of the contactless, non-contaminating relation of self and not-self, the *Pravacanasāra* states that 'knowledge operates on objects just as a sapphire, resting on milk, pervades the whole of it with its lustre'.[114]

---

[111] Translation after Upadhye, p. 4, of *Pravac.* 1:32.

[112] Upadhye's trans., p. 4, of *Pravac.* 1:29. Upadhye takes *ṇa paviṭṭho ṇāviṭṭho* as Sk. *na praviṣṭaḥ na āviṣṭaḥ*, as against the commentators who take *na aviṣṭaḥ* (*na apraviṣṭaḥ*) - see fn. 2, p. 4.

[113] Cf. *Pravac.* 1:28 and 1:29, above, where the objects of knowledge are compared to the objects of sight: they are within range of the knower / seer, but, crucially, there is no 'mutual inherence' (Upadhye's trans., p. 4, of *nevaṇṇoṇṇesu*).

[114] Upadhye's trans., p. 4, slightly altered, of *Pravac.* 1:30.

To summarise, one becomes such a knower by rehearsing in meditation this attitude of detachment - which springs from knowledge of the true relation between self and other - towards everything not-self (*ajīva* / *para*). The understanding that the self is a knower rather than a possessor leads to the abandonment of a possessive relationship with anything not-self - indeed, from the *niścaya* point of view, such a relationship is an impossibility, i.e. a delusion, anyway. For, in reality, there is nothing the pure self can do except be itself. In other words, *kevalajñāna* points to the isolation and inactivity of the self; the *ātman* is co-extensive with and yet not of the world; it *is* rather than does. To such an entity, *karman* and the fruit of *karman* are, in the final analysis, irrelevant; they do not bind what, in reality, cannot be bound. Self-knowledge is the sole key to liberation.

6.5 *The rationale for external, ascetic practice, according to the Pravacanasāra*

In the light of this stress on self-knowledge, or self-realisation, and meditation, the question arises of what rationale can be offered for continuing with external practices, i.e. with the identity-defining practices of the Jaina ascetic. Perhaps because his works were composed primarily for those who were already habitually ascetic in their practice, Kundakunda does not address this problem directly. However, in the *Pravacanasāra* and its commentaries there are a small number of significant references which indicate a recognition - albeit a philosophically unsatisfying one - that some kind of answer is required.

In gāthās 3:5-6, Kundakunda lists some characteristics or 'emblems' (*liṅga*) of the Jaina ascetic. First, he states that:

> The mark (of a Jaina ascetic) consists in possessing the form in which one is born, in pulling out hair and beard, in being pure, in

not harming beings, etc., and in not attending to the body.[115]

Then he adds:

> The Jaina mark, which is the cause of the stoppage of rebirths, consists in being free from action based on delusion, in being endowed with purity of manifestation of consciousness and purity of activity, and in being independent of the other (everything not-self).[116]

Considering 3:5 first, the expression 'possessing the form in which one is born' (*jadhajādarūvajādaṃ*) occurs in a slightly different formulation in the previous gāthā (3:4), as *jadhajādarūvadharo*, 'wearing a form similar to that in which he is born'.[117] Upadhye explains that this means that the person wishing to be an ascetic (the subject of these gāthās) 'should give up everything including clothes and remain naked; this is the excellent type of Jaina asceticism'.[118] In other words, this is equivalent to the English colloquial expression 'wearing one's birthday suit', meaning going completely naked (which, of course, is the most obvious characteristic of the Digambara ascetic).

The other components of 3:5 are self-explanatory, except for *śuddha*. The *Tattvadīpikā* describes this 'purity' in material terms, as being due to the negation of 'possessing anything'.[119] As we have seen, in the *Sarvārthasiddhi* (on *Tattvārtha Sūtra* 9:6) 'purity' (*śauca*) is glossed as 'freedom from greed' (*parigraha / lobha*), the defining characteristic of the householder's way of life;[120] it initiates *hiṃsā* and causes bondage. In short, purity both

---

[115] Trans. after Upadhye p. 25; see ibid. p. 25 fn. 2, on *pratikarma*, which he takes as *a-pari-karma*, a reading followed in this translation.

[116] Translation after Upadhye p. 25.

[117] Upadhye's translation.

[118] Upadhye p. 25 fn. 1.

[119] Translation by Faddegon p. 157, of *sakiṃcanatva*.

[120] See above, p. 76ff..

results from and exemplifies non-possession (*aparigraha*).

Śuddha appears again in the next gāthā (3:6), but this time it is connected with *upayoga* ('manifestation of consciousness') and *yoga* ('activity'). In the *Tattvadīpikā* these two are linked as cause and effect: the possession of *aśuddha-upayoga*, coloured by *śubha*- and *aśubha-upayoga*, engenders *aśuddha-yoga* (of body speech and mind); conversely, the negation of *aśuddha-upayoga* leads to purity of *upayoga* and so of *yoga*. In other words, it is the internal condition which informs external behaviour.

The *Tattvadīpikā* claims that these two gāthās (3:5 and 3:6) describe a pair of *liṅga*, 'external' and 'internal', which together characterise the ascetic.[121] There are, however, a number of indications that, rather than a systematic definition of what constitutes *śramaṇa*-status, we have here a conflation of two different classificatory systems, representing two different historical moments in the development of Jaina doctrine. That is to say, there is a certain amount of overlap between the content of the two gāthās which points to a separate origin for each. For instance, although in general the two uses of 'purity' discussed above divide into 'external' and 'internal', we may note that non-possession of material goods springs in the first place from an attitude - freedom from greed -, and that, on the other side, two of the aspects of *yoga*, activity of body and activity of speech, are material in nature and external in operation. Moreover, *mucchā-āraṃbha-vimukkaṃ* / *mūrcchā-ārambha-vimuktam* (3:6), which I have translated as 'freedom from action based on delusion' (i.e. from action based on delusion about the real nature of the self, and thus about its relation to the non-self), is virtually equivalent to the 'purity' (*śuddha*) listed as an 'external' aspect of the ascetic at 3:5. For as I have noted above,[122] *ārambha* is closely associated with *parigraha* in Jaina thought, and denotes a violent action initiated by

---

121 *bahiraṅgāntaraṅgaliṅgadvaitam* - *TD* intro. to *Pravac*. 3:5.

122 See pp. 5, 31, etc., above.

greed and possessiveness. Amṛtacandra's reading of *mūrcchā-ārambha-vimuktam*, as negation of the development of the karmic consequences of the attitude of possession[123] emphasises only one half of the classical theory of the equivalence of *parigraha* and *mūrcchā* as defined at *Tattvārtha Sūtra* 7:17 and *Sarvārthasiddhi*,[124] where *mūrcchā* is both the activity of preserving or acquiring possessions and an attitude of possessiveness towards them.

It is clear from these instances that neither division of the characteristics of the ascetic given at *Pravacanasāra* 3:5 and 3:6 falls exclusively into the 'external' and 'internal' categories which the *Tattvadīpikā* attempts to impose.[125] I suggest that, historically, 3:5 represents an earlier understanding of the *liṅga* of an ascetic, while, given that *upayoga* appears to have originated with him, 3:6 is Kundakunda's revision or further internalisation of that earlier definition. It should also be noted that the next gāthā (3:7) begins with the words 'having taken this characteristic' (*ādāya taṃpi liṃgaṃ*), singular, apparently referring (*pace* Amṛtacandra) to only one set of characteristics. Again, this suggests that 3:6 represents an interpolation by Kundakunda into a traditional description of the way in which one becomes a *śramaṇa*. Moreover, Kundakunda leaves us in little doubt as to which set of characteristics he considers the more important, since he says of the highly if not totally internalised group which make up the Jaina-*liṅga* at 3:6 that they are 'the cause of the stoppage of rebirths' (*apuṇabbhavakāraṇam*).

Kundakunda's view on the relation of internal purity and external practice is, as we have seen, that the physical practice is only of value insofar as it is informed by and proceeds out of the correct internal attitude. To put it

---

123 *mamatvakarmaprakramapariṇāma* - *TD* on *Pravac* 3:6.

124 See above, pp. 73ff.

125 This, of course, is not unexpected, given that Book 3 of the *Pravacanasāra*, in particular, appears to be of a compilatory nature.

crudely, although without significant distortion, if one takes care of the *upayoga* the *yoga* will take care of itself. This returns us to the question of why it should be thought necessary to continue with external practice at all, since the latter is only the reflection of an already-achieved internal state, and it is the internal state which is significant for one's personal liberation. Yet this very phenomenon - that the external reflects the internal - points towards an answer.

Pravacanasāra 3:5-6 deals with the *liṅga*, the characteristic mark, of the ascetic. In logic, a *liṅga* is 'the invariable mark which proves the existence of anything in an object';[126] i.e. given this characteristic or characteristics, there can be no doubt about the nature of the thing examined. In this case we have to do with the *liṅga* which prove that somebody is a true ascetic and so on the route to liberation. The constituents of the external *liṅga* - nakedness, the pulling out of hair and beard, non-possession, *ahiṃsā*, neglect of the body - are, once defined, clear enough and physically evident to anyone who knows what they are looking for. The constituents of the internal *liṅga*, however, are - from the very fact that they are *internal*, relying as they do on pure *upayoga* and attitude - *not* evident to observers; i.e. although they may provide an ideal towards which the individual strives, they are insusceptible to outside verification *in themselves*. And if they are not observable characteristics then, it may be asked, in what sense can they be *liṅga*?

The *internal* are, however, not totally unobservable, for, since external practice is said to reflect an already-achieved internal state, the external *liṅga* of ascetic behaviour imply the inevitable although invisible presence of the pre-defined internal *liṅga*. In other words, there is really only one *liṅga* (or set of *liṅga*) in the strict sense of the term, the external. From the presence or absence of that mark any observer can infer the presence or absence of internal states. And since it has been laid down that what really counts in terms

126 Monier-Williams, *Sanskrit Dictionary*.

of liberation is precisely the internal state, then it becomes clear that, in this teaching, the function of external practice is to provide a *liṅga* - i.e. evidence or proof - of the soteriologically crucial internal condition.[127] That is to say, it is a public demonstration or assurance, chiefly to others but perhaps also to oneself, that one is on the correct road - a visible emblem and reinforcement of Jaina identity.

Nevertheless, from the advanced ascetic's point of view, Kundakunda's stress on the internal makes external conduct karmically (i.e. soteriologically) irrelevant. This is graphically illustrated by *Pravacanasāra* 3:27, which reads:

> He whose self is non-desiring, *that* is asceticism - that is what ascetics seek. Other food, obtained as alms, is not desired (not food); so those ascetics are not takers of food.[128]

It seems that there is a pun here on *eṣaṇa* which can mean either 'desire' or 'alms begged in the correct manner'. The self without desire is foodless, therefore 'other' (i.e. material, actual) food is not food, in the sense that it is not desired (by the desireless self who is the ideal ascetic). In other words, for the true ascetic, external conduct - physical *tapas* - becomes irrelevant: if he is internally pure then what he does physically can have no karmic effects for him.

The *Tattvadīpikā* bears this out:

> Since in essence he is abstinent from food (*anaśana*) and since the alms are devoid of the [fault of desire (*eṣaṇā- doṣa*)] fault against the *eṣaṇā-samiti*, the self-controlled in food is visibly actually foodless. Thus: - if a man is at all times conscious only of the self, which is exempt from the taking of any material sustenance, his

[127] See above, pp. 160-163, for further comments on the external being an emblem of the internal, ref. *TD* on *Pravac.* 3:17.

[128] *Pravac.* 3:27. Cf. *Samayasāra* 405ff. Cf. also Pāli *anesanā*: 'improper alms begging' ('a wrong going for food' - *CPD*); e.g. *DN* III 224.25 - *anesanaṃ appaṭirūpam āpajjati*. The pun that is reflected in my translation is explained in the following paragraph.

innate nature is in itself foodless, inasmuch as it is void of all longing for food. This, namely, is his abstinence from food, his asceticism; for the internal is of more importance (than the external).[129]

Anaśana is given at *Tattvārtha Sūtra* 9:19 as the first of the 'external austerities' (*bāhyaṃ tapaḥ*).[130] Clearly, therefore, Kundakunda and Amṛtacandra are here emptying external *tapas* of any independent soteriological value; for if the *eṣaṇā-samiti* is not infringed, the attitude of non-desire makes even feeding not count as feeding.

This is extreme, but, given the way in which Kundakunda ascribes new values to the vocabulary of begging and fasting, we may surmise that he is here consciously reacting against excessive formalisation, the mechanistic pursuit of physical austerity. That is to say, by giving the 'true' definitions of foodlessness and alms, he provides a corrective to the mindless repetition of a practice whose underlying significance has been forgotten. From the standpoint of personal liberation this may be very necessary, but if taken as a general, social principle it clearly undermines, probably fatally, the rationale for external, ascetic practice. From the point of view of the Jaina community as a whole, it is therefore essential that some reason should be given for continuing with external *tapas*. Such a reason has been outlined above; it may seem philosophically weak but it is socially indispensable. The importance of public display in any religion should not be underestimated; indeed, it is what most obviously characterises a 'religion' as opposed to a private soteriology. Thus, in abstract terms, there is probably a pendulum-like

---

129 Faddegon's trans., p. 169, slightly emended, of:
svayam anaśanasvabhāvatvād eṣaṇādoṣaśūnyabhaikṣyatvāc ca yuktāhāraḥ sākṣād anāhāra eva syāt / tathāhi - yasya sakalakālam eva sakalapudgalaharaṇaśūnyam ātmānam avabudhyamānasya sakalāśanavṛṣṇāśūnyatvāt svayam anaśana eva svabhāva / tad eva tasyānaśanaṃ nāma tapo 'ntaraṅgasya balīyastvāt iti ...

130 See above, pp. 196ff., and *JPP* pp. 250-251, on these.

movement or continuous balancing act in Jainism between excessive formalisation, with its threat to the personal or soteriological, and excessive internalisation, with its threat to the social or corporate identity. Given the compilatory nature of early Jaina texts (including the *Pravacanasāra*), the two extremes may frequently be reached in the same text. It fell to the scholastic commentators to attempt to compensate for and correct this polarisation. The doctrine of the two *naya*, if not conclusive, is at least a holding operation in this struggle. In terms of the present analysis, the *vyavahāra-naya* would thus embody the social view while the *niścaya-naya* would represent the personal or soteriological perspective.

6.6 *Socio-religious roles in the Pravacanasāra*

It remains to comment briefly on the Jaina socio-religious hierarchy implicit in the *Pravacanasāra*, and on Kundakunda's attitude to the laity. (The purpose of this section is simply to make explicit what may be readily inferred from the material already treated.)

The individual's place in the religious hierarchy, and thus his social role, is decided for Kundakunda by his state of consciousness. It is always a particular *upayoga* (manifestation of consciousness) which underlies and informs any external 'emblem' of religious status; and, in theory, it is to the underlying internal state that any question about an individual's status should be referred. In practice, the problem of gauging 'inner-states' leads, of course, to reliance upon external indicators. Nevertheless, Kundakunda is unequivocal about the meaninglessness of external practice unless it derives from and is informed by internal purity.[131]

The equations are as follows: *śuddha-upayoga* is the

131 See above, *passim*.

internal state of the ideal *śramaṇa*, and leads to liberation;[132] *aśuddha-upayoga* covers the full range of inner states short of *śuddha-upayoga*, and leads to a relatively better or worse rebirth. Thus, in terms of socio-religious roles, the latter state characterises virtually the whole community. As we have seen, however, *aśuddha-upayoga* is divided into *śubha-* and *aśubha-upayoga*. *Śubha* is clearly better than *aśubha*, but how positively or negatively the former is viewed depends entirely upon what audience is being addressed. Thus, in Book 1 of the *Pravacanasāra*, which is aimed predominantly at *śramaṇas*, anything less than the attainment of *śuddha-upayoga* is considered unsatisfactory; in Book 3, however, which has a more general (perhaps one should say, less ideal and more realistic) audience in mind, the cultivation and attainment of *śubha-upayoga* can, in itself, be a laudable activity and goal.

Śubha-upayoga is clearly the inner state most open to interpretation and ambiguity in terms of the spiritual value and thus the religious status attached to it. In *Pravacanasāra* Book 1, *śubha*'s *aśuddha* nature is stressed (1:69-1:79): it entails desire, contingency and impermanence, hankering after sense-pleasures, attachment to objects which are dependent and impermanent, and thus it results in misery (see 1:74-77). Even the gods are caught in this trap of contingency (1:71-74). And 'if men, hell-beings, subhuman beings, and gods suffer misery, born from the body, then of what use is (the distinction of) auspicious or inauspicious manifestation of consciousness for souls?'[133] That is to say, if *śubha-* and *aśubha-upayoga* lead alike to rebirth and misery, what is the point of

---

132 See *Pravac.* 1:14; cf. 1:11, 2:103.

133 Translation of *Pravac.* 1:72.

distinguishing between them?[134] The point is clearly to devalue *śubha-upayoga* in the (potential[?]) *śramaṇa*'s mind, and to stress that liberation can only be achieved through *śuddha-upayoga*. This is given full emphasis in gāthās 1:77 and 1:78.

Gāthā 1:77 reads:

> He, who does not think that there is no difference between merit and demerit, wanders about in terrible, unbounded *saṃsāra*, covered in delusion.

In other words, *puṇya* and *pāpa*, associated with *śubha-* and *aśubha-upayoga*, are *both* characterised as totally *saṃsāric*. (Note the emphasis again on knowledge and delusion as the liberating and binding factors.)

In contrast to this, the condition of the *aśuddha-upayogin* (= the ideal *śramaṇa*) is described in the next gāthā [1:78]:

> He who, understanding the nature of things, does not experience attachment or aversion towards objects, his manifestation of consciousness being pure, destroys the suffering which arises from embodiment.

To put this in the terms of the present argument, here Kundakunda is criticising the inner-condition of the laity, probably for a *śramaṇic* or potentially *śramaṇic* audience. That it is indeed the laity he associates with *aśuddha-upayoga* is evident from *Pravacanasāra* 1:69, where the *ātman* which is characterised by *śubha-upayoga* is described in terms of activities associated with lay *vrata*:

> The self which is attached to the worship of gods, ascetics and teachers, to giving, to good morals, and to fasting, etc., is a self

---

[134] See *TD* on *Pravac.* 1:72.

with auspicious manifestation of consciousness.[135]

In this context (Book 1 of the *Pravacanasāra*), therefore, lay-practice is viewed in a negative light.

However, in Book 3 of the *Pravacanasāra*, Kundakunda is apparently much more accommodating to *śubha-upayoga*, and thus, by implication, to the laity (although again he addresses himself directly not so much to the latter as to the average *śramaṇa*). For here it is recognised, realistically, that *śubha-upayoga*, and thus a better rebirth, is also a legitimate goal - albeit a lower one - for ascetics.

Gāthā 3:45 reads:

> In (our) religion there are ascetics who have pure manifestation of consciousness and those who have auspicious manifestation of consciousness. Among them, those with pure manifestation of consciousness are not subject to the influx of karmic matter, while the rest are subject to influx.

The behaviour associated with *śubha-upayoga* is listed at *Pravacanasāra* 3:46ff. This consists mostly of devotion and service to (more) advanced monks and to the ascetic community as a whole. Gāthā 3:54 concludes:

> This conduct is commended for ascetics, but it is said to be the best (or 'the highest form of conduct') for householders; by it alone he (the householder) attains highest bliss.

This is interesting because it seems to hint at the possibility of two routes to the goal of final liberation, associated with the two social and religious roles of ascetic

---

135 On correspondences between this and lay *vrata*, see Faddegon p. 45 fn. 1. But whether it fits into a specific technical pattern or not, the gāthā clearly describes good lay behaviour.

and householder / layman. Perhaps the Hindu idea (most famously expressed in the *Bhagavadgītā*), that the route to salvation is through the conscientious performance of one's *svadharma*, is at work here; more precisely, it may be a concession to expectations within the Jaina lay community which have been aroused by the realisation that, ultimately, their Hindu neighbours expected to be rewarded simply through pursuing their *dharma* as householders.

This interpretation relies, of course, upon taking *paraṃ sokkhaṃ* to mean complete liberation and not some less final state. The *Tattvadīpikā* on 3:54 has no doubt: it explains that good conduct, which is the form of *śubha-upayoga*, is secondary (*gauṇa*) for *śramaṇa*s, but for the laity it is primary (*mukhya*), and even though there is still the existence of passion (*rāga*), the pure self (*śuddhātman*) can be experienced like the sun's heat experienced through the medium of crystal. Such conduct 'gradually brings about the highest happiness of *nirvāṇa'*.[136] In other words, for Amṛtacandra, there is apparently a quick (but difficult) and a gradual (but easier) route to liberation, although it is not clear how gradual the latter is - i.e. whether or not it stretches over many re-births. Whatever the answer, this gāthā clearly reflects a different and more positive attitude to the laity than that evidenced in Book 1 of the *Pravacanasāra*. This suggests that the material in Books 1 and 2, on the one hand, and that in Book 3, on the other, may have been collated under different social circumstances and with a different audience in mind (not to mention by a different hand).[137]

---

136 Faddegon's trans., p. 190, of *kramataḥ paramanirvāṇa-saukhyakāraṇatvāt*.

137 Note 2:97 - cited above, p. 134, - where the teaching of the *niścaya* view (i.e., the view which deals with the real nature of the self) is directed exclusively at *śramaṇas* and *yatis*. See also *Pravac*. 2:102 and *TD*, and Faddegon's trans., p. 147, fn. 1. Jayasena's commentary

All this points to the vulnerability of ascetic territory to invasion by the laity once practice has been largely internalised. The *upayoga* doctrine, with its corollary of internal cultivation, carries within itself the possibility that the condition of *śuddha-upayoga*, and thus of liberation, may be reached by inner development alone. In other words, the attainment of the soteriological goal does not *logically* entail becoming a *śramaṇa*. Indeed, at the end of the *Pravacanasāra*, in gāthā 3:74, there is what looks like a re-definition of '*śramaṇa*' in terms which would not necessarily exclude the laity. Gāthā 3:74 reads:

> He, who is pure, is said to be a śramaṇa; to the pure one belong faith and knowledge; the pure one attains liberation; he alone is a siddha: my salutation to him.[138]

In other words - although perhaps no Jaina would want to put it as bluntly as this -, if you fulfil these criteria through inner-discipline, you are a '*śramaṇa*' regardless of your external, social status.

(*Tātparyavṛtti*) on this gāthā gives a second interpretation of the Prākrit *sāgāro nāgāro* as *sāgārānāgāraḥ*, 'while he is a householder or an ascetic', as an alternative to the first interpretation, viz. *sākārānākāraḥ*, 'with formed or with formless (self-realisation)'. If Jayasena's suggestion were correct, this would mean that meditation on the pure self was considered liberating for both ascetics and laymen. This seems unlikely to be the meaning in the context, but the fact that such a reading could be considered indicates, if nothing else, the status and content of lay religious practice at the time the *Tātparyavṛtti* was composed (second half of the 12th century C.E.? - see Upadhye p. civ).

138 Upadhye's trans., p. 34. The *TD* comments: '*śramaṇa*-hood, which is the manifest road to liberation and is characterised as mental-concentration occupied with a simultaneity of perfect conviction, knowledge and conduct, belongs to the pure alone' - Faddegon's trans., p. 198 of : *yat tāvat samyagdarśanajñānacāritrayaugapadya-pravṛttaikāgryalakṣaṇaṃ sākṣān mokṣamārgabhūtaṃ śrāmaṇyaṃ tac ca śuddhasyaiva.*

However, as we have seen, even within the *Pravacanasāra* itself there are indications of built-in checks to hold back any serious claim on the part of the laity to inner purity for themselves. Put simply, the only evidence of internal purity is external behaviour, and the latter is defined in *śramaṇic* terms. We may speculate that, without this check, a fully internalised and laicised Jaina religious practice, based on what is essentially a pan-Indian meditational technique, would have been likely to prove critical for the cohesion and identity of the Jaina community. Moreover, without the continuing necessity of strict physical (i.e. external) *ahiṃsā* at some level - for whatever reason - there would have been nothing to guarantee the most obvious 'emblem' of Jaina religion or, we may suppose, to retard the tendency towards ethical decay.

I shall now turn to the *Samayasāra*, which provides a test case as to whether Kundakunda can, or even wants to, sustain this tenuous link with external practice in what is his least orthodox work.

PART IV

KUNDAKUNDA: THE *SAMAYASĀRA*

7

Kundakunda: definitions and truths

7.1 *Samayasāra*

i) Introduction

Turning from the *Pravacanasāra* to the *Samayasāra*, we soon become aware of a number of significant differences in terms of content and scope between the two texs. Some of these differences are so great that it is difficult to think that the two works, or even particular parts of them, should be ascribed to the same author (or redactor). (This, of course, does not affect my argument, which is concerned with the practical and historical implications of certain trends in Jaina doctrine.) Three differences are particularly significant. First, there is the absence in the *Samayasāra* of any *upayoga* doctrine. As we have seen, this was Kundakunda's (i.e. the author-redactor's) distinctive means of explaining the mechanism of bondage in the *Pravacanasāra*. The term *upayoga* does occur in the *Samayasāra*, but only in the restricted technical sense employed in, for instance, the *Tattvārtha Sūtra*.[1] Jayasena, in his *Tātparyavṛtti* commentary on the *Samayasāra*, does occasionally employ the *Pravacanasāra*-type *upayoga* doctrine for exegetical purposes (e.g. at *Samayasāra* 210), whereas Amṛtacandra, in his *Ātmakhyāti* is apparently more attached to the immediate text. There is, however, an incompletely formulated *bhāva* doctrine in the *Samayasāra* which fulfils a function similar or identical to that of the *upayoga* doctrine. (This will be considered below.)

The second significant difference is one of degree

---

[1] See above, 4.2(*ii*): *Upayoga according to the Pravacanasāra.*

rather than kind. The use to which the *niścaya-vyavahāra* doctrine is put in the *Samayasāra* is, in a number of gāthās, far more explicitly radical than anywhere in the *Pravacanasāra*, and the implications for ethical conduct are consequently more serious. In fact the *niścaya* view is applied in two different and incompatible ways in the *Samayasāra*.

The bifurcation of the *niścaya* doctrine is probably connected with the third significant difference between the two texts: the fact that the *Samayasāra* is not only more obviously concerned with confronting and refuting other doctrinal positions, particularly Buddhist and Sāṃkhya ideas, but is also more clearly influenced, both in its technical terminology and in its approach to particular problems, by non-Jaina doctrines. It also has a more persistent devotional strain than does the *Pravacanasāra*; of particular note is the conjunction of the (lay) vocabulary of *bhakti* with ascetic concentration on the self (in 'self-devotion') as a means to liberation. (This was, perhaps, an attempt to reduce, through assimilation, the attraction of the Hindu *bhakti* cults for Jains.)

The relative eclecticism of the *Samayasāra* thus indicates the probability that it was compiled from a number of sources, each of which had been subject to a variety of influences. It is not my purpose here to tease out all these threads (although this is an area in which more research could be fruitfully conducted); rather I intend to illustrate the ways in which the *Samayasāra* represents a point of maximum tension between theoretical philosophy and the Jaina tradition of ascetic practice. I shall then consider how certain Jaina philosophical strategies - such as *anekāntavāda* (the doctrine of manifold aspects) and *syādvāda* (the doctrine of qualified assertion) - are used alongside Kundakunda's doctrine of 'two truths' in an attempt to hold together these two strands, the theoretical and the practical.

I shall begin with a general discussion of how the text

views itself, i.e. of how it defines the *samaya* of which it is the essence (*sāra*).

ii) Samaya

Perhaps the most obvious translation of *samaya* would be 'rule' or 'way of life', and thus the *Samayasāra* would be 'the essence of (our) way of life'.[2] However, following Amṛtacandra and Jayasena, modern commentators take *samaya* to mean 'the realised or unified self'. At first sight this seems puzzling. How have they arrived at this apparently idiosyncratic definition?

Without prior knowledge of the way in which the term should be understood all the internal evidence is inconclusive. An external source, however, points us in the right direction. Vātsyāyana's *Nyāyabhāṣya* (dated by Frauwallner to the first half of the fifth century)[3] defines *samaya* as follows:

> The direct meaning of this word (*samaya*) is this referent: this is the application of the rule which connects the designator and the designated. When it is applied the correct understanding of the meaning is derived from the word.[4]

---

[2] The underlying meaning here is 'what is mutually agreed' - so *samaya* would be rules for behaviour rather than doctrinal laws. In Tantra it has the standard meaning of 'the way to behave'. Caillat (1987, p. 508) translates *Samayasāra* as 'Essence of the Doctrine'. Friedhelm Hardy, in a personal communication, points out that, in southern India, 'religion' or 'true religion' developed as the most popular meaning of *samaya*. (See the *Tamil Lexicon*, Vol. 3, pp.1291b - 93b, under '*camaya*'.) I am not, however, persuaded that it should be translated in this way in all or most cases in the *Samayasāra*, for the reasons given in the following pages.

[3] Frauwallner 1973, Pt. 2, p. 8.

[4] *asya śabdasya idam arthajātam abhidheyam ity abhidhānābhidheyaniyamaniyogaḥ* / *tasminn upayukte śabdād arthasaṃpratyayo bhavati* - *Nyāyabhāṣya*. 2.1.55.

The *Nyāyakośa* also gives *nirdeśa* - 'description', 'specification' - as a synonym for *samaya*.

In other words, *samaya* means 'the correct or true definition'. Applying this to the *Samayasāra*, it quickly becomes clear that there too *samaya* has the primary or underlying sense of 'true definition'. Thus gāthā 2 of the *Samayasāra* reads:

> Know that the term '*jīva*' when it has reference to (right) conduct, faith and knowledge is stringently defined; know that when it has reference to material karma it is loosely defined (i.e. it includes that which is essentially alien to it).[5]

There is an analogous gāthā in the *Pañcāstikāya* (162):

> The *jīva* is defined by / in its own nature (*sahāva* / *sva-bhāva*); when it has inessential (non-defining) qualities for its modes it is alienly (loosely) defined (*parasamao* / *parasmaya*) [i.e. it is being 'defined' by what is essentially other than itself]. If one applies the self's own definition one will escape from the bondage of karma.

Returning to the *Samayasāra*, gāthā 3 reads:

> The definition which determines its (the *jīva*'s) unity is universally fine (correct), so talk of bondage when there is only one thing is contradictory.

If what is being referred to here is the astringent definition (*sva-samaya*) of the self then this gāthā appears to contradict the previous one [2], where three things (*cāritra*, *darśana*, and *jñāna*) are mentioned. However, gāthā 7 resolves the difficulty. There it is stated that:

> From the conventional point of view conduct, faith and knowledge are predicated of the knower; but there is neither knowledge,

---

5 Upadhye (p. xlv) gives *sva-samaya* as 'the realisation of the self as identical with Right faith, etc.' and *para-samaya* as identification of the self 'with material karmas'; but this is a gloss rather than a translation.

conduct nor belief, just a pure knower.[6]

As we have seen, (*sva*)*samaya* is the self defined according to its own nature; that is to say, it is defined as one thing, pure knowledge, there being no difference in this context between knowledge and the knower. That is what constitutes the soul's *svabhāva* or essence, as *Samayasāra* 198 makes clear:

> Various types of rising and fruition of karmas have been described by the great Jina(s); but they are not my own-nature. I am one, a knower by nature.[7]

That is to say, the unified self - the self which has realised its own nature - is the pure knower (i.e. the knower *par excellence*, the omniscient, liberated self). And for the pure, liberated knower there is no *ratnatraya* (*samyag jñāna*, *darśana* and *cāritra*) [gāthā 7].

The heterogeneity of the *Samayasāra* has already been commented upon; nevertheless,it is possible to chart the ways in which the meaning of the term *samaya* is extended within the text. As we have seen, the basic meaning of *samaya* is 'true / correct definition'. Thus the *sva-samaya* is the astringent definition of the self, i.e the soul defined or described from the perspective of its essence. This is also precisely the condition of the liberated self. From this basis, the term *samaya* then becomes short-hand for the principal thing it is defining in the *Samayasāra*, namely, the essential or realised self. In other words, we move from the statement that 'The *samaya* (the true definition) of the *jīva* is the realised self' to the understanding that '*Samaya is* the realised self'. Gāthā 151 and its commentaries provide us

---

[6] Cf. *Samayasāra* 16 (18).

[7] Cf. *Samayasāra* 38 where the self is described as follows: 'I am one, indeed, pure, consisting of faith and knowledge (i.e. *upayoga*), always incorporeal. Nothing other is mine whatsoever, not even an atom.' See also *Samayasāra* 31.

with a clear instance of this. The verse reads:

> The true meaning, indeed, the *samaya*, pure, sheer, the seer, the knower - the mendicants who are absorbed in this, their own nature, attain *nirvāṇa*.

These epithets obviously all refer to the pure self, so *samaya* here has become a synonym for the 'unified' or 'realised self'. (Amṛtacandra glosses it in terms of 'entering into the knowledge which is produced from the state of oneness'. Jayasena says he is called *samaya* because 'he attains / transforms (himself) into pure qualities and modes'.)[8] There is also a self-conscious yet ambiguous attempt within the text to define what is meant by '*samayasāra*' itself. Gāthā 142 states:

> Karma is bound or not bound to the self - know these to be points of view. But whatever is said when these alternatives have been transcended, that is *samayasāra* (the true definition of *jīva*).

Is *Samayasāra* therefore a teaching - a 'view' which transcends views? Or is it a condition of the self which reflects its true, transcendental relation to karma?[9] The *Ātmakhyāti* is almost equally ambiguous, stating that he who goes beyond both views and their combination acquires or finds *samayasāra*. And 'if that is the case, then who, indeed, would not activate the alternative-renouncing state of mind?'[10] The fact that alternatives are being definitively discarded lends some weight to the idea that *samayasāra* (essential definition) cannot be another view,

---

[8] *ekībhāvapravṛttajñānagamana* - *Ātmakhyāti* JGM ed. on *Samayasāra* 161 (= Chakra. 151). *śuddhaguṇaparyāyān pariṇamati* - *Tātparyavṛtti* on ibid.

[9] I shall deal with this question from a different perspective when I consider Kundakunda's use of the *vyavahāra-niścaya* doctrine. See below, pp. 239ff.

[10] *yady evaṃ tarhi ko hi nāma pakṣasaṃnyāsabhāvanāṃ na nāṭayati* - *Ātmakhyāti* on *Samayasāra* 142 (152 JGM ed.).

however transcendent; nevertheless, the paradox of a 'definition' that transcends all views cannot be totally discounted.

The text continues:

> One connected to the true definition (*samaya*) knows what is said of the two views, but does no more; he takes neither of the alternative views at all, being without (such) alternative views. [*Samayasāra* 123]

But again *samaya* could be translated here either with the primary sense of 'true definition' or with the extended sense of 'the realised or unified self'. (It should be noted, however, that this gāthā is capable of providing an accurate description of the pure omniscient self that just knows.) This is also true of *Samayasāra* 144, upon which the *Ātmakhyāti* comments:

> Whatever is the practice of the cessation of all views through the non-experience of any point of view, that, indeed, is *samayasāra*.[11]

Modern commentators, however, seem to be in no doubt about the principal meaning of '*samayasāra*'. Chakravarti writes:

> The term *samayasāra* means the essential nature of the Self. This Absolute Ultimate Unity is transcendental in nature. Hence the various appellation based upon different points of view really have no relevancy in that state.[12]

J.L. Jaini concurs: 'Samayasāra is the pure soul in its essence'. The soul is really above all impurities, and 'one

---

[11] *yaḥ khalv akhilanayapakṣākṣuṇṇatayā viśrāntasamastavikalpa-vyāpāraḥ sa samayasāraḥ* - *Ātmakhyāti* on 144 (154).
I shall have more to say about these passages and their relation to the rest of the *Samayasāra* in my discussion of the 'two truths' doctrine.

[12] Commentary on *Samayasāra* 144, p. 101.

who meditates upon this again and again acquires self-absorption, which is *Samayasāra*'.[13] Singh remarks that, in the *Samayasāra*, Kundakunda 'gives instructions how to know the real self (*Sva-samaya*). This *Sva-samaya* (*Samayasāra* 2) or the Ego-in- itself is the pure and ultimate reality'.[14] This is the self which has realised its oneness, a description which 'very much resembles that of the Upaniṣadic and Advaitic Brahman or Ātman'.[15]

In so far as these definitions reflect the principal teaching of the text they are indeed correct. For we have seen how the weight of meaning of the term *samaya* shifts from 'definition', via 'the correct definition of the self', to become synonymous with the self in its true nature, i.e. 'the realised or essential self'. However, the crucial nuance in this conflation of epistemology and ontology is the one which makes knowledge of the true nature (definition) of the self instrumental in realising that pure self, i.e. instrumental in, or indeed tantamount to, liberation. (I shall have more to say about this below.)

Referring to Upaniṣadic doctrine, Gombrich (quoting Malamoud) remarks that, 'The identification of one's *ātman* and *brahman* is "at the same time the truth to be discovered and the end to be attained"'.[16] Rephrasing this formulation to fit Jaina circumstances, we may say that the realisation of the true nature of the self - as totally separate from and untouched by the other (karma, etc.) - is at the same time the truth to be discovered and the end to be attained. Consequently, there are passages such as that at *Pañcāstikāya* 162 [17] which state that the realisation of the correct definition of the self is actually the means to liberation. In other words, the definition or description of the soul from the perspective of liberation - of the soul as it

---

[13] Commentary on 151 (= 144 Chakravarti's ed.).

[14] Singh p. 85.

[15] Ibid. p. 89.

[16] Gombrich 1988, p. 43.

[17] Quoted above, p. 234.

is in its self (*svabhāva*) - is conflated with the idea that that state of the liberated self is actually achieved by realising, i.e. 'knowing', that it *is* the true or real state of the self. And it is in this way that the realisation or 'definition' of the self is seen to be both means and end, the way to liberation and the state achieved.

So whether *samaya* is read as the true condition of the self or as a definition or 'view' beyond alternatives, it comes finally to imply self-realisation and thus liberation. This process in itself illustrates the growing stress on 'self-realisation' in Jaina doctrine, even if some of the gāthās collected under the heading of *Samayasāra* were not originally so gnostic in tenor. It is the gnostic, however, which in the end comes to overlay and alter the meaning of the other layers. A change of context, with its new juxtapositions, inclines some older or more orthodox doctrines towards new meanings. Whether or not one attributes all these shades of meaning to an individual compiler ('Kundakunda') is strictly not relevant to my purpose, which is to explicate a particular doctrinal tendency and its implications for practice.

7.2 *Vyavahāra-niścaya: the two truths doctrine*

We have already seen how the doctrine of two truths was employed in the *Pravacanasāra*. The use to which this *vyavahāra-niścaya* doctrine is put in the *Samayasāra* is more complex and requires some independent discussion before we examine the ways in which it is applied to the mechanism of bondage and liberation.

First, I shall point out a number of apparent contradictions in the text. Gāthā 8 reads:

> Just as a non-Āryan is not able to make another understand [anything] without his non-Āryan speech, so without the conventional truth instruction in the highest truth is not possible.

That is to say, initial instruction has to be couched in

terms which are capable of being understood by those who are spiritually undeveloped. This is the standard reconciliation of the elements in a two truths doctrine: the lower is a means or ladder to the higher. As Frauwallner puts it:

> The common-place consideration (*vyavahāra-nayaḥ)* is necessary in order to make the doctrine intelligible to ordinary men. One can only come to an understanding with a foreigner when one uses his speech [Samayasāro (sic.) v.8]. But one must be clear about the fact that it has validity only in a certain sense. It should necessarily supplement the pure way of thought which alone brings full truth.[18]

This relation is typified in gāthā 16 (19):

> [Right] belief, knowledge and conduct should always be practised by a *sādhu* [from the *vyavahāra* point of view]; but know that these three are, in reality, the self.

Amṛtacandra comments that it is established that the *sādhu*, in talking to other people, must refer to belief, knowledge and conduct. Personally, however, he must cultivate the self with the sentiment that it is at the same time both the means and the end.[19] In other words, the *sādhu* sees through the *vyavahāra* view.

Referring to one of the last gāthās of the *Samayasāra*, Amṛtacandra also states that those who are 'deluded by beginninglessly produced *vyavahāra* views ... do not see the highest truth, the holy *Samayasāra*'.[20]

Similarly, the *Samayasāra* states:

---

[18] Frauwallner 1973, Vol. 2, p. 208.

[19] *yenaiva hi bhāvenātmā sādhyaṃ sādhanam ca syāt tenaivāyaṃ nityam upāsya iti svayamākūya pareṣāṃ vyavahāreṇa sādhunā darśanajñānacāritrāṇi nityam upāsyānīti pratipadyate - Ātmakhyāti* on *Samayasāra* 16 (= 19 JGM).

[20] *te 'nādirudhavyavahāravimūḍhāḥ ... paramārthasatyaṃ bhagavantaṃ samayasāraṃ na paśyanti - Ātmakh* on *Sam* 413 (= 443).

> The knowers of reality say that other substance is 'mine' in conventional parlance, but they know that, from the *niścaya* point of view, not even an atom is 'mine' [324]. Just as when a man says that 'the village, country, town, kingdom are mine' when they are not [really] his, it is his self speaking out of delusion [325], so the knower who takes other substance to be his and makes it his own certainly becomes a wrong-believer [326].

In other words, there is no simple progression from the *vyavahāra* view to the *niścaya* view - an understanding of the former does not automatically lead to an understanding of the latter; on the contrary, if Amṛtacandra is to be believed, it actually prevents it.[21] This seems to conflict directly with the idea that the *vyavahāra* in itself is a means to perfecting the self. (And it should be remembered that the elements of standard Jaina metaphysics - the doctrines concerning the various *tattvas*, *padārthas*, etc. - are included under the *vyavahāra* rubric.) Rather, the crucial step seems to be *the recognition that there are two views*, and that one of them entails delusion and wrong belief. That is to say, you have to realise that the *vyavahāra* view *is* a lower view, that it is just a way of talking about the self for 'practical' or pedagogical purposes, before it can become a means to the higher view. Indeed, it is the recognition of that fact, rather than the doctrinal content of the lower view, which is the real means to achieving the higher, liberating view. It is not surprising, therefore, that the predominant attitude towards the *vyavahāra* viewpoint in these texts ascribed to Kundakunda should be negative. Gāthās such as *Samayasāra* 8 (see p. 239, above) are rare. More typical is *Samayasāra* 156:

> Wise people do not operate in *vyavahāra*, leaving aside the real object (*niccayaṭṭhaṃ*); the destruction of karma is ordained [only] for those ascetics whose refuge is the highest object [i.e. the pure

---

[21] See *Ātmakhyāti* on 413, quoted above.

self, the sole object of the *niścaya* view].

Similarly, gāthā 166 states that there is no influx of karma (*āsrava*) or bondage for the right believer (*samyagdṛṣṭi*).[22] And as we have seen, the 'right-believer' is the person who, rejecting the wrong-belief of the *vyavahāra* view, sees things from the *niścaya* point of view.

Seemingly most radical of all, there is *Samayasāra* 11 [=13]:

> *vavahāro 'bhūdattho bhūdattho desido du suddaṇao* |
> *bhūdattham assido khalu samādiṭṭhī havadi jīvo* ||
>
> The *vyavahāra* [view] does not deal with the really existent, but the pure view (*śuddha-naya*) is taught as the really existent. The living being who depends upon the really existent is, indeed, a right-believer.

Clearly, the significance of this statement depends to a large degree upon the meaning attributed to *bhūdattho* (*bhūtārtha*), translated as 'really existent'. Amṛtacandra offers no real definition.[23] Jayasena, however, glosses *vavahāro* as *vyavahāranayaḥ*, and *abhūdattho* as *abhūtārthaḥ asatyārtho bhavati.* Conversely, *suddhaṇao* is *śuddhanayaḥ niścayanayaḥ* and *bhūdattho* is *bhūtārthaḥ satyārthaḥ* [*Tātparya-vṛtti*. on *Samayasāra* 11(=13 JGM)]. Thus, while the *vyavahāra-naya* has what is false as its object, the *śuddha* / *niścaya-naya* has what is true. In this way, the focus is shifted from the ontological to the epistemological, from things to views about things.

Since the *niścaya-naya* is the view of the unified self, eternally separate from non-self, and the *vyavahāra-naya* is the conventional view, which sees the self as interactive

---

22 *ṇatthi du āsavabaṃdho sammādiṭṭhissa (nāsti tv āsravobandhaḥ samyagdṛṣter)* - *Samayasāra* 166.

23 But see below, pp. 250-251 - *Puruṣārtha* quote.

with the non-self (everything that makes up *saṃsāra*), then it is clear that, according to this *Samayasāra* doctrine, the latter view is 'untrue' in the sense of not reflecting the the real nature of the (lack of) relationship between 'self' and 'other'. (*Bhūtārtha* is thus the 'really existent' in the sense of being the truth about the (non-) relationship between *ātman* and *paradravya*.)

This seems to be the way in which this gāthā [11] should be taken. However, some modern commentators have read *bhūtārtha* in a strongly ontological sense - i.e. they believe it to denote that which actually exists. On this reading, *abhūtārtha* (viz. *paradravya* or *saṃsāra*) is an illusion. Thus Bhatt writes that the contact of *jīva* and *ajīva* is a 'pure fiction' (*upacāra*) and not reality; it brings forth 'illusory experiences constituting the worldly sphere'; consequently, the world is 'a creation of ignorance appearing real only as long as the soul remains ignorant about its true nature'.[24] This is tendentious, not merely in the dubious translation of *upacāra* (a term imported by Bhatt), which might be better rendered as 'metaphor' or 'figure of speech', for Bhatt has jumped from the unreality of a relationship between two categories to the unreality of one of the elements in that relationship (the *ajīva*). Moreover, he claims that the *ajīva* is actually a creation of ignorance - a statement clearly made under the influence of a particular interpretation of late Vedānta. It might be possible to argue that Kundakunda is swaying in that direction, but it can hardly be claimed that he calls the reality of the separate *ajīva* into doubt. Indeed, its reality or unreality is irrelevant to liberation; it is the realisation of its non-relation with the *jīva* which is crucial. That is to say, it is the relation itself which is the 'creation' of ignorance, not the thing. To make *ajīva* unreal would be to make bondage itself unreal, the result of an inexplicable delusion rather than the corollary of an understandable confusion of categories. (That the categories are in reality absolutely

---

[24] Bhatt 1974, pp. 279-291.

separate is, of course, a matter of dogma and the premise upon which the argument is based, not part of it.)[25]

Dixit is closer to the significance of this gāthā [*Samayasāra* 11=13] when he writes of the *Samayasāra* that:

> ... the whole of this text is a standing harangue against all talk of a relationship between a soul and a matter (sic.). Towards the very beginning (v.13) we are told that the practical standpoint is the standpoint of untruth while definitive standpoint is the standpoint of truth - so that even to concede that from the practical standpoint a soul and matter do enter into mutual relationship amounts to saying that they in fact do nothing of the sort.[26]

The radical nature of this gāthā [11=13] thus lies in the fact that it states explicitly that the *niścaya* view is true because it expresses the way things really are, and the *vyavahāra* untrue because it is a false account of reality. The relativity of truth to viewpoint (*syādvāda*), based on the manifold (*anekānta*) nature of reality, seems to have been rejected here in favour of an absolute view of truth. In other words, Kundakunda looks like an *ekāntavādin* here, with a doctrine of 'two truths' which bears a close resemblance to that used in other *ekānta* systems.

Gāthā 272 [=296 JGM] of the *Samayasāra* is equally explicit:

> Know that the *vyavahāra* view is contradicted by the *niścaya* view.

---

25 Here it is useful to bear in mind Matilal's words on 'two truths' in Vedānta and Buddhism, that 'an object can be said to be *not real* in two very different senses'. It can be non-existent or it can be devoid of the 'own-nature or *svabhāva* that it is supposed to possess or that it professes to possess'. Thus, *saṃsāra* is 'not a mere appearance, still less an illusion - it is something that is not quite successful in embodying an own-nature, *svabhāva*' (1986, p. 137). In the terms of the present discussion, it is the self viewed as related to non-self that is not real, because its essence is pure, inactive, isolated consciousness - it is a [self-] knower and nothing else - that is its *svabhāva*.

26 Dixit 1971, p. 134.

Munis absorbed in / adopting the *niścaya* view attain *nirvāṇa.*

The idea of a graduated progression from the *vyavahāra* to the *niścaya* viewpoint does not arise here. Liberation is achieved only by rejection of the former and absorption in the latter (i.e. the self). Amṛtacandra commments:

> The *niścaya* view refers to the self, the *vyavahāra* view refers to the other [the not-self]. The conventional view is prohibited by the *niścaya* view, which blocks for the one who desires liberation all intention which relates to anything other than the self as being a cause of bondage, and because for him intention is no different from being dependent on something other than the self. It is to be rejected because only those are liberated who resort to the *niścaya* view, which refers to the self, and because it is the *abhavya* - one who is definitively incapable of being liberated - who resorts to the *vyavahāra* view which refers to the other.[27]

So even if the *vyavahāra* viewpoint were to be considered a necessary first position, there is clearly no natural progression from there to the liberating *niścaya* view. Indeed, it is difficult to see the *vyavahāra* view positively at all (i.e. as a ladder or raft to the higher view and liberation) when it is precisely the view held by those who can *never* achieve liberation, the *abhavya* souls.[28] In other words, the *vyavahāra* view is essentially a 'wrong-view'. (But note that it is not the view itself which prevents the *abhavya* souls from ever being liberated. Rather that view is their characteristic view; they are incapable of

---

27 *ātmāśrito niścayanayaḥ parāśrito vyavahāranayaḥ | tatraivaṃ niścayanayena parāśritaṃ samastam adhyavasānaṃ bandhahetutvena mumukṣoḥ pratiṣedhayatā vyavahāranaya eva kila pratiṣiddhaḥ, tasyāpi parāśritatvāviśeṣāt |*
pratiṣedhya evaṃ cāyaṃ, ātmāśritaniścayanāyaśritānām eva mucyamānatvāt, parāśritavyavahāranayasyaikāntenāmucyamānenābhavyenāśriyamānatvāc ca - *Ātmakhyāti* on *Samayasāra* 272 (= 296 JGM).

28 On *abhavya* see *JPP* p. 140, and P.S. Jaini 1977.

holding any other.) It should be abandoned as soon as possible.[29]

This feeling is expressed in more purely psychological terms at *Samayasāra* 12 [=14]:

> The pure [viewpoint] which teaches about the pure [substance - i.e. the pure self] should be known by [those whose object it is to be] the seers of the supreme mental state; but the *vyavahāra* teaching is for / employed by those who stand in / employ inferior mental states.

Again the negative formulation indicates that the crucial liberating act is to abandon the *vyavahāra* view. The *śuddhanaya*, which should be adopted instead, is defined at *Samayasāra* 14 [=16]:

> He who sees the *ātman* as neither bound nor touched [by karmic matter], not other than itself, fixed, without differences, and not combined [with anything not self], know that he is one who holds the pure point of view.

On this reading, the difference between the two views is irreconcilable: one cancels out or denies the other.

This is quite a different interpretation of the 'two views' or 'two truths' doctrine from that expressed at, for instance, *Samayasāra* 345-348 [=JGM 357-360]:

> From the point of view of modifications the self is destroyed; from another point of view it is not. Because of this, there is not the one-sided view that the soul acts or that something else acts.
> From the point of view of modifications the self is destroyed; from another point of view it is not. Because of this, there is not the one-sided view that the soul experiences or that something else experiences.
> It should be known that whoever holds the doctrine that the self that acts is the self that experiences [the fruits of that action] is a

29 What this entails in terms of conduct will be considered below.

wrong-believer and not of the Arhat faith.

But it should be known that whoever holds the doctrine that the self that acts is other than the self that experiences is a wrong-believer and not of the Arhat faith.

Here the two views relate to whether an object is viewed with regard to its modes (*paryāya*) or to its substance (*dravya*). To take either perspective as the exclusive truth about an object would be one-sided (*ekānta*) and the mark of a wrong-believer. According to this reading, the self is neither the same as nor different from the doer and experiencer. Right-belief, or 'right-view', entails knowing that both views are valid depending on the perspective taken. Unlike the distinction made above [*Samayasāra* 14, etc.], this is clearly compatible with *anekāntavāda* doctrine; one view (i.e. the *dravya* perspective) is not higher, more 'real', or truer than the other (the *paryāya* perspective); they are complementary. However, the very fact that the *dravya* perspective deals with what is fundamental or essential, while the *paryāya* is a mode of that *dravya*, indicates at least the potential for a logical hierarchy of truth.

It might be thought that the *anekāntavāda*-compatible version of the 'two truths' doctrine opens up the possibility of a 'third' view, one which reconciles or synthesises both statements. However, the strictures of the *syādvāda* doctrine ensure that, rather than a true overview, such a synthesis could only take the form of a perception that the *vyavahāra* and *niścaya* perspectives are *merely* views, and therefore neither is to be taken as exclusively true. Indeed, to ensure this is the function of the classical *sapta-bhaṅgi-naya* formulation as a whole.[30]

On the other hand, such passages as *Samayasāra* 141ff. (=151ff. JGM)[31] are not readily explicable in *syādvāda* terms. Indeed, they seem more like an attempt to discard

---

[30] See *JPP* pp. 94-97; and Dixit 1971 p. 24ff. for the possible historical development of this doctrine.

[31] See pp. 236ff. above, and the following.

the *anekāntavāda* perspective entirely. The relevant section reads:

> From the *vyavahāra* point of view it is said that karma comes into contact with and is bound to the *jīva*; but from the pure (*śuddha*) point of view karma neither comes into contact with nor is bound to the *jīva*. [141]
> 'Karma is bound or not bound to the *jīva*' - know these to be [statements made from] different points of view. But it is said that he who goes beyond alternatives [attains] s*amayasāra*. [142]
> One connected to the true definition knows what is said of the two views, but does no more; he takes neither of the alternative views at all, being without (such) alternative views. [143]
> It is just a statement (*vyapadeśa*) to say that he [the self] attains right perception and right knowledge; he who is said to be free from any alternative views / viewpoint, he has the essential definition (*samayasāra*). [144][32]

The *Ātmakhyāti* on *Samayasāra* 141 and 142 (= 151 and 152 JGM) explains:

> The *vyavahāra* point of view is that karma comes into contact with and is bound to the *jīva* because of the non-existence of any great separateness between them, due to *jīva* and material karma being modes (*paryāya*) of a single bound state. The *niścaya* point of view is that karma does not come into contact with and bind the *jīva* because of the absolute separateness of *jīva* and material karma, due to their being fundamentally different substances (*dravya*). [141]
> The points of view are twofold: the one view is the conceptualization that karma is indeed bound to the *jīva*, the other is that karma is not bound to the *jīva*. Who thus goes beyond, who has altogether overcome conceptualization, having himself become viewless - one whose own-nature has destroyed partial knowledge

---

[32] And so, through the movement from epistemology to ontology outlined above, the person free from alternative views realises, i.e. *is*, the self as correctly defined.

- [for him] the essence of self is evident. Therefore, even he who, going beyond the one-sided view that karma is bound to the *jīva*, conceives that karma is not bound to the *jīva* does not go beyond views. And even he who, going beyond the one-sided view that karma is not bound to the *jīva*, conceives that karma is bound to the *jīva* does not go beyond views. And again, even he who, going beyond these two views, conceives that karma is both bound and not bound to the *jīva* does not go beyond views. Therefore, he who thus goes beyond the combined view, he alone indeed goes beyond choice. He who thus goes beyond all conceptualization, he indeed finds the essence of self. If that is the case, then who indeed would not activate the view-renouncing state of mind (*bhāva*)?' [142][33]

This is strikingly similar to Mādhyamika Buddhism's denial of the ability of doctrines or views to characterize reality. For the Mādhyamika, according to one modern commentator, 'the real as transcendent to thought can be realised only by the denial of the determinations which systems of philosophy ascribe to it'.[34] In other words,

---

[33] *jīvapudgalakarmanor ekabandhaparyāyatvena tadati-vyatirekābhāvāj jīve baddhāspṛṣṭaṃ karmeti vyavahāranayapakṣaḥ* | *jīvapudgalakarmaṇor anekadravyatvenātyantavyatirekāj jīve 'baddha-spṛṣṭaṃ karmeti niścayapakṣaḥ* | (141) |
yaḥ kila jīve baddhaṃ karmeti yaś ca jīve 'baddhaṃ karmeti vikalpaḥ sa dvitayāpi hi nayapakṣaḥ |
ya evainam atikrāmati sa eva sakalavikalpātikrāntaḥ svayaṃ nirvikalpaikavijñānaghanasvabhāvo bhūtvā sākṣātsamayasāraḥ saṃbhavati |
tatra yas tāvaj jīve baddhakarmeti vikalpayati sa jīve 'baddham karmeti ekaṃ pakṣam atikrāmann api na vikalpam atikrāmati yas tu jīve 'baddham karmeti vikalpayati jīvẹ baddham karmetyekaṃ pakṣam atikrāmann api na vikalpam atikrāmati |
yaḥ punar jīve baddham abaddhaṃ ca karmeti vikalpayati sa tu taṃ dvityam api pakṣam anatikrāman na vikalpam atikrāmati |
tato ya eva samastanayapakṣam atikrāmati sa eva samastaṃ vikalpam atikrāmati |
ya eva samastaṃ vikalpam atikrāmati sa eva samayasāraṃ vindati |
yady evaṃ tarhi ko hi nāma pakṣasaṃnyāsabhāvanāṃ na nāṭayati | (142) | - *Ātmakhyāti* on *Samayasāra* 141 and 142 (= 151 and 152 *JGM*).

[34] Puligandla p. 289, fn. 100.

'Rejection of all thought categories [concepts] and views [theories] is the rejection of the competence of reason to apprehend reality. The real [according to Mādhyamika] is transcendent to thought'.[35] '*Samayasāra*' thus looks analogous to that state grasped by Nāgārjuna's *prajñā* and characterized by *paramārtha-satya*, viz. the direct realisation of a higher, ineffable truth, beyond conceptual thought, which is synonymous with liberation. (It is, of course, only an analogy or, at most, a borrowed or shared technique applied to different material; Buddhist and Jain doctrines concerning the nature of 'self', 'not-self', what constitutes liberation, etc., are, it hardly needs to be said, quite different.)

Amṛtacandra highlights this resemblance in another work, the significantly entitled *Puruṣārtha-siddhy-upāya*. There he writes:

> The *niścaya* mode (of statement) they describe as having a real referent; the *vyavahāra* mode as without a real referent. All mundane souls are mostly opposed to knowledge of the reality of things.(5) The great saints (*muni*) teach the mode without a real referent to wake up the sleepy, (6a) (but) who so understands only the *vyavahāra* mode, in him there is no teaching.(6b) As to a man who has not known a lion a toy is the only lion, so a man who knows not the real method takes the practical method itself for reality!(7) That disciple alone who understands both the real and the practical method, and takes a higher view equally distinct from both, obtains the full fruit of the teaching.(8)[36]

---

[35] T.V. Murti, *Central Philosophy of Buddhism*, p. 208, quoted by Puligandla, ibid. fn. 101.

[36] *niścayam iha bhūtārthaṃ vyavahāraṃ varṇayanty abhūtārtham* |
bhūtārthabodhavimukhaḥ prāyaḥ sarvo 'pi samsāraḥ ||5||
abudhasya bodhanārthaṃ munīśvarā deśayanty abhūtārtham |
vyavahāram eva kevalam avaiti yas tasya deśanā nāsti ||6||
māṇavaka eva siṃho yathā bhavaty anavagītasiṃhasya |
vyavahāra eva hi tathā niścayatāṃ yāty aniścayajñasya ||7||
vyavahāraniścayau yaḥ prabudhya tattvena bhavati

First there is the question of what it is the ignorant should understand (6a). Clearly, it is not merely the *vyavahāra* point of view, since in the second half-verse (6b) that is said not to constitute a teaching at all. Rather, it must be the fact that the *vyavahāra* mode is *just* a mode (i.e. that there is a higher view, the *niścaya*) which should be understood. Beyond this, however, both views must be discarded for a position which is neutral (*madhyastha*). In other words, the *vyavahāra-niścaya* distinction is itself simply a means (*upāya*) to approach the highest goal, a means which must itself be discarded in order to attain final liberation.

Such a view sits uneasily among the orthodox Jaina doctrines of *syādvāda* and *anekāntavāda*. For one cannot arrive at such a prescription by adhering to the *syādvāda* analysis.[37] The *vyavahāra-niścaya* doctrine, however (in those cases where the *niścaya* view is said to be the truth rather than merely a different perspective), claims that the view that the self is not really bound leads to self-realisation, a state in which there is no duality of knower and known, and so, by definition, no distinction of viewpoints. The difference between the two views (one congruent with *anekāntavāda*, the other not) is pointed up by a verse in another work attributed to Kundakunda, the *Niyamasāra* [159]:

> From the conventional point of view the omniscient Lord knows and perceives everything; from the absolute [viewpoint] the omniscient knows and perceives [only] the self.[38]

---

madhyasthaḥ |
prāpnoti deśanāyāḥ sa eva phalaṃ vikalaṃ śiṣyaḥ ||8||
Puruṣārtha-siddy-upāya, quoted and trans. (with my alterations) by J.L. Jaini 1940, pp. 107-108.

[37] There is the idea in the fully developed *syādvāda* doctrine that the self is *avaktavya*, but this simply means that '*in some respect* (the ontological situation of) the self is inexpressible' - see *JPP* pp. 95-96.

[38] Quoted by P.S. Jaini, *JPP* p. 267, fn. 33; my translation.

The *anekāntavāda*-compatible *vyavahāra* view points to a state of liberation where the self still has some kind of relation with the not-self (there is a 'knower' and something 'known'), whereas the *niścaya* view envisages a liberated self, totally isolated from the not-self, whose omniscience is identical with self-knowledge.

In other words, even when the *Samayasāra* is apparently rejecting all views (as at 141-144), and so both *anekānta* and *vyavahāra-niścaya* distinctions, it is clear that it is the *niścaya* view, taken as truth, which leads one to the point where views can be abandoned and liberation achieved, i.e. to self-realization. The *niścaya* view indeed characterizes - albeit from an inevitably intellectual rather than experiential perspective - the essence of self. Transcending all viewpoints (the intellectual), one goes on to experience the reality of that state. Here, in the *Samayasāra*, in contrast with the Mādhyamika where the abandonment of views is the chief instrument in the achievement of the goal, it is the espousal of the *niścaya* view which is clearly of prime importance.[39] The idea that the latter should be abandoned too seems to have been added, probably under Mādhyamika influence and perhaps because it was supposed (erroneously) that this was a way of shepherding the absolute, hierarchical distinction of 'two truths' back into the *anekāntavāda* fold.[40] It may also be the case that what was intended merely as a 'description' of '*samayasāra*' ('the realized self') in the text itself was extrapolated by the commentators into a technique for achieving that state.

Furthermore, we can see the fundamental incompatibility between *syādvāda* and the absolute

---

[39] See, for instance, gāthās 11-12, 156, 272, etc., quoted above.

[40] The meaning attributed to '*samayasāra*' ('the essence of self') in *Samayasāra* 141-144, and the fact that these verses conclude a discrete section of the work, point to the likelihood that they were indeed added after the bulk of the text had already been compiled.

vyavahāra-niścaya distinction. The former is essentially an intellectual strategy for evading confrontation with other schools over what appear to be internal contradictions in Jaina metaphysics, as well as for avoiding the logical resolution of such contradictions, with all that that would imply for ethical conduct.[41] The latter, on the other hand, has, like Nāgārjuna's Mādhyamika teaching, a soteriological function.

This is not to say that there may not be an awareness at one level of the text of the dangers to Jaina orthopraxy inherent in doctrines present in another layer; the distinction between the gāthās which are compatible with *anekāntavāda* and those which take an *ekānta* view is frequently and perhaps deliberately blurred. However, once an absolute *niścaya* view has been introduced, its superiority from a logical point of view is unambiguous.[42] Any attempt thereafter to overlay it with *anekāntavāda* must be considered unconvincing. The only real solution would be to exclude the absolute *niścaya* view from the text altogether. The fact that that has not happened only demonstrates its authority within the tradition (whether it derives from an individual called 'Kundakunda', or is merely sanctioned by being attributed to him, is not the point). It therefore falls to the commentators to accommodate it as best they can.

The idea that there are at least two implementations of the *vyavahāra-niścaya* distinction in the *Samayasāra* - one compatible with *anekāntavāda* philosophy, the other (the absolute *niścaya* distinction) not - requires further explication. I shall, therefore, now summarize some of the main ways in which the two patterns are juxtaposed in the text, and suggest some models for their development as contrasting, not to say contradictory, doctrines.

---

[41] The specific nature of the dangers for practice and Jaina identity posed by the absolute *vyavahāra-niścaya* distinction will be discussed below.

[42] See, for example, gāthās 11-12, 156, 272.

7.3 *Two 'two truths' doctrines*

As we have seen, at least two conflicting patterns of application can be outlined for the 'two truths' distinction in the *Samayasāra.* According to one of these (I shall call it 'pattern one') the *vyavahāra-naya* is that viewpoint which considers entities in general, and the *jīva* in particular, from the perspective of modes (*paryāya*). The *niścaya-naya*, on the other hand, is that viewpoint which considers entities from the perspective of pure unified substance (*dravya*). According to orthodox Jaina doctrine, a substance is that which has qualities and modes (*guṇaparyāyavad dravyam*).[43] The substance is the substratum for the qualities, and the qualities undergo modifications (*pariṇāma*) through acquiring new and losing old modes.[44] P.S. Jaini explains :

> Thus, any existent must be seen on three levels: the modes, which last only a moment and belong to the qualities; the qualities, which undergo changes and yet inhere forever in their substances; and the substance, which remains the abiding common ground of support for the qualities and their modes.[45]

Any complete description of an entity's nature needs, therefore, to encompass all three levels, and this is what the *anekāntvāda* purports to do, although at any particular moment 'an ordinary (non-omniscient) person' can only 'be aware of the persistent unity (*ekatva*) of the substance or the transient multiplicity (*anekatva*) of its modes'.[46] Thus, from the *vyavahāra* view, the soul acts and experiences the fruits of action, whereas, from the *niścaya* view, it neither acts nor experiences fruits; yet neither statement contradicts

---

43 *Tattvārtha Sūtra* 5:38.
44 *JPP* p. 90.
45 Ibid.
46 Ibid.

the other while they are sheltered under the *anekāntvāda* umbrella. Both are true from their own particular perspective. There is, therefore, a perspective from which the soul is really bound by karma, for the relation of substance to mode is a real relation.

According to the other 'two truths' pattern ('pattern two'), however, the *vyavahāra*, or conventional view - that the *jīva* acts and is subject to the fruits of action - is essentially a 'wrong view'. For the *niścaya* view, which is 'higher' in the sense of representing the complete truth, not just another aspect of it (it portrays reality), states that, by definition, the *jīva* can have no connection with *ajīva*. Thus any perceived relation between the two is nothing more than a delusion, the product of ignorance.

This second pattern is clearly incompatible with the first, i.e. it is incompatible with *anekāntvāda* philosophy. Moreover, within it the *niścaya* view contradicts the *vyavahāra* view, which is not the case in the first pattern. Thus, from the perspective of pattern one, pattern two is an *ekānta* heresy - a one-sided view; whereas, from the perspective of pattern two, pattern one is in its entirety a 'lower' or *vyavahāra* view, unrepresentative of the truth.

I am not the first to recognise that the *Samayasāra* contains a double 'two truths' doctrine. Bansidhar Bhatt has designated every gāthā in the *Samayasāra* as falling into either a 'mystic' or a 'non-mystic' pattern, the former being attributed by Bhatt to a single individual called 'Kundakunda'.[47] However, for reasons which will become clear, I consider this to be too rigid, not to say tendentious, a division of the text. Moreover, Bhatt makes no specific connection between his 'non-mystic' pattern (my pattern one) and the *anekāntvāda* doctrine; and his interpretation of the *niścaya* view of his 'mystic' pattern (my pattern two) seems to owe more to a wish to claim Kundakunda as a Vedānta metaphysician than to reflect the actual content of the text. I shall, therefore, restrict myself to outlining the

---

[47] Bhatt 1974, pp. 279-291.

different conclusions I draw from my own analysis, rather than offering any detailed criticism of Bhatt's thesis.

The difficulties presented to commentators by the juxtaposition within the text of gāthās containing contradictory 'two truths' doctrines should not be underestimated. Perhaps the most acute problem occurs in the attempt to accommodate the second pattern (where the *vyavahāra* and *niścaya* views contradict each other) to standard Jaina teachings about bondage. If there is really no contact between the self and karma, how is bondage to be explained? (Underlying this is the even more fundamental problem of Jaina philosophy, viz. how can the immaterial [the self] and the material [karma] ever really be said to be in contact?)

From the perspective of practical soteriology it might be objected that the important thing is the non-identification of the self with karmic matter and that the ontological status of the two is not strictly relevant. That is to say, whether or not there is actual contact between them, the liberating 'action' is for the self to maintain an *attitude* of absolute separateness from matter. However, such a claim can hardly be sustained theoretically unless it is also claimed that in reality - i.e. ontologically - there is no relation between them. Liberating knowledge (gnosis) is knowledge of the way things really are; there has to be a correspondence between what is known and what is the case. In other words, transferred to the philosophical or theoretical level (which in the Indian tradition is where they are propagated and defended against criticism) soteriological and ethical doctrines entail ontological or metaphysical counterparts.

The type of problem arising can be illustrated by the following. Gāthā 19 [= 22] of the *Samayasāra* reads:

> So long as there is the understanding 'I am in or I am identical with karmic and quasi-karmic [body] matter, etc. [*no-karman*],' there is

[also] lack of true discriminative knowledge.[48]

One who knows the true nature of things (*bhūdattham* / *bhūtārtham*), however, is not deluded (*asammūḍho* / *asammūḍhaḥ*) in this way [*Samayasāra* 22 (= 27)]. He knows that *upayoga* (*jñāna* and *darśana*) is the *lakṣaṇa* of the *jīva*, so how can such a self become or attribute to itself material substance (*pudgala dravya*) [*Samayasāra* 24 (= 30)]?

In Jayasena's recension, two extra gāthās [23 and 24] are inserted after 19 (= 22), clearly with the intention of providing an explanation of how, if the *jīva* is really separate from *ajīva*, there can be such a thing as bondage. The second of these verses reads:

> Whatever mental state (*bhāva*) the self produces, he (the self) is the agent (*kartā*) of that *bhāva* from the *niścaya* view. From the *vyavahāra* view, it (the *bhāva*) is the agent of material karmas.[49]

In other words, in reality, the self is responsible for its own mental states (*bhāva*), and thus its own bondage or liberation (through attachment or non-attachment to the *ajīva*).[50] This is evidently an attempt to distance the *jīva* from *pudgala-karman* (the *ajīva*) as the direct cause of bondage. From the *niścaya* view the binding state is self-produced, as opposed to produced by *pudgala-karman*. However, this does not explain how what is pure consciousness by nature and definition (the *ātman*) can come to manifest impure mental states (*bhāva*). As we have seen in the *Pravacanasāra*, the standard *vyavahāra-niścaya* distinction of the first pattern would have explained

---

48 On *no-karman* see the *Sarvārthasiddhi* on *Tattvārtha Sūtra* 2:10.

49 The grammar here is odd and the text may be corrupt, but I have translated it as it stands with *kattāraṃ* in line 2 agreeing with *bhāvam* in line 1 (see Appendix).

50 See *Samayasāra* (23).

that the self is the material cause of its own modifications and the instrumental cause of other modifications, whereas the *ajīva* (*pudgala-karman*) is the material cause of its own modifications and the instrumental cause of the *jīva*'s modifications. However, as the commentators are well aware, such an *anekāntvāda*-congruent explanation, which retains a connection with *pudgala-dravya* as the instrumental cause of impure *bhāva*s, is not convincing in the context of the absolute distinction of self and other made by the second *vyavahāra-niścaya* distinction. Thus, what we have here is an open conflict between the two patterns of the *vyavahāra-niścaya* doctrine.

Jayasena attempts to resolve this conflict by positing a new distinction - not found in the text itself, but much used by modern commentators [51] - between *śuddha-niścaya-naya*, 'the pure *niścaya* viewpoint' and *aśuddha-niścaya-naya*, 'the impure *niścaya* viewpoint'. So his *Tātparyavṛttiḥ* on *Samayasāra* 24 (JGM) reads:

> From the pure *niścaya* viewpoint the agent is of pure *bhāva*s, [while] from the impure *niścaya* viewpoint [the agent] is of impure *bhāva*s - so the state of being an agent is just a modification of *bhāva*s from the *niścaya* point of view.[52]

J.L. Jaini explains:

> impure thought-activity is attributed to the soul from the impure real standpoint (Ashuddha Nischaya Naya). From the pure real standpoint (Shuddha Nischaya Naya), the doer is the doer only of its own pure modifications.[53]

This may be clarified further by *Niyamasāra* 18, which

---

[51] Cf. Uggar Sain trans. and comm. on *Niyamasāra* 18.

[52] *ṇicchayado: aśuddhaniścayanayena aśuddhabhāvānāṃ śuddhaniścayanayena śuddhabhāvānāṃ karteti bhāvānāṃ pariṇamanam eva kartṛtvaṃ* | *Tātparyavṛttiḥ* on *Samayasāra* 24.

[53] SBJ ed., p. 17 - J.L. Jaini's comments on *Samayasāra* 24.

reads:

> From the *vyavahāra* view the self is the agent and experiencer (of the effects) of material karma; but from the *niścaya* view the self is the agent and experiencer through mental states which have arisen from karma.

This differs from *Samayasāra* (24) (see above) in that it makes it clear that, according to this *niścaya* view, particular *bhāva*s which arise in the self, of which it is the agent or material cause, and which, in turn, are the causes of bondage, only do so through the instrumental influence of *pudgala-karman*. That is to say, the *niścaya* view presented here [*Niyamasāra* 18] corresponds to what Jayasena calls the *aśuddha-niścaya-naya*. In this way the connection between material karma and the self is kept, but mediated or attenuated through mental states (*bhāva*). Such a reading clearly belongs to the first *vyavahāra-niścaya* pattern.

None of this, of course, comes any closer to explaining how pure consciousness (self) can be subject to impure thought-activity in the first place; all it does do is offer an apparently arbitrary explanation of how the soul, *from the niścaya point of view,* can be said to be both pure and impure at the same time. In other words, faced in the same text with the two *vyavahāra-niścaya* patterns outlined above, Jayasena tries to run them together by designating as *aśuddha-niścaya-naya* what would be considered a *vyavahāra* view from the perspective of the second pattern. But logically - as perhaps Amṛtacandra recognised in avoiding the juxtaposition of these gāthās (*Samayasāra* 19-24 and [23]-[24]) - this makes no difference. The contradictions are unresolved and the problem is left hanging.

Why then did Jayasena feel it so important to attempt to reconcile the two views instead of following what would be a logical solution, that of pattern two - viz. to maintain that in reality the self does not have and cannot have impure *bhāva*s, that it is not bound, and that it is only necessary to realise the truth of that (non-) relation of the self and karma (the not-self) in order to achieve liberation? Apart from the obvious answer, that he is writing a commentary on a received text and so has to make sense of the contents as he finds them (and he is probably working on the assumption that, despite the disparate nature of the gāthās, he is dealing with a work by the revered *ācārya* Kundakunda), there is another, more compelling reason. Put simply, because the material covered by the first *vyavahāra-niścaya* pattern comprises the whole socio-ethical content of Jainism, it is essential for the survival and cohesion of the Jaina community to maintain a connection between that content and the soteriological goal. (I shall return to this below.)

7.4 *Dvikriyāvāda*

Despite the apparent impossibility of resolving it in orthodox terms, Jaina thinkers were periodically forced to confront directly the problem outlined above - namely, what can be the relation between an immaterial conscious self and material unconscious matter, and how can the latter bind or have contact with the former? One of their strategies for dealing with this involves rejection of the *do-kiriyāvāda / dvi-kriyāvāda* doctrine, the assertion that one cause can produce two different effects (in this case, the idea that the soul can be the agent of its *bhāvas* and also of *pudgalakarma* or karmic modification). An examination of the way *dvikriyāvāda* is dealt with in the *Samayasāra* thus helps to clarify the difference between the two *vyavahāra-niścaya* patterns given above.

Samayasāra 83-86 [=89-92] reads:

> From the *niścaya* view the *ātman* acts on itself alone. And again know that the *ātman* experiences itself alone [83].
> From the *vyavahāra* view the *ātman* acts on various kinds of *pudgalakarma*. Likewise, it experiences [the fruits of] the various kinds of *pudgalakarma* [84].

If the *ātman* acts on this *pudgalakarma*, and likewise experiences it[s fruits], it will lead to the doctrine that a single cause can produce two different effects; that [teaching] is repudiated by the Jina [85].
Because they make a pair of the state of the self and the state of matter, the *dvikriyāvādins* are wrong believers [86].

This passage concludes a familiar argument (given at *Samayasāra* 80-82 [86-88]). There it is stated that the *jīva* is the instrumental cause (*nimitta*) of *pudgala* being transformed into *karman*, in the same way that *pudgalakarma* is the instrumental cause of transformation in the *jīva* [80]. Neither *jīva* nor *karman* produce changes in the quality of the other, but the modification (*pariṇāma*) of each is produced by the other acting as an instrumental cause [81]. Consequently, the *ātman* is said to be the agent (*kartā*), i.e. the material cause, of its own modifications through its own psychic states (*bhāva*), but it is not the agent (material cause) of any modifications of karmic matter [82], and vice versa.

Here we have Jaina orthodoxy's attempt to reconcile the doctrine of the strict duality of soul and matter with the fact of bondage. The argument is that the *jīva*, through its own agency, causes modifications to its psychic state, and these are somehow instrumental in causing matter to modify itself in a particular way. Similarly, matter, through its own agency, causes modifications to its own states, a process which is somehow instrumental in causing the *jīva* to modify itself. In other words, although neither is acting materially on the other they are, nevertheless, mutually bringing about changes in each other. The exact mechanism or metaphysics of this circular process remains, however, unexplained.

To summarise, according to Jaina philosophy, 'two distinct and conflicting effects cannot be produced by identically the same cause nor, conversely, can the identically same effect be produced by two entirely different causes'.[54] For if this were possible, it is claimed that the effect would be to make the original cause in itself one thing or the other. So here, if the original cause is identified with the *acetanā* effect the *cetanā* self ceases to be; and if it is identified with the *cetanā* effect matter ceases to be. According to the Jains, this is erroneous since the first situation would lead to materialism (the *ātman* as *cetanā-dravya* would be unreal), and the second would lead to monism (the material world or *acetanā-dravya* would be unreal).[55] To avoid these two extremes they adopt the *anekāntavāda* / *syādvāda* congruent position outlined above.

This, however, is only one of four possible 'solutions'. The first two have been rejected by Jaina orthodoxy - namely, that (1) both karma and the *jīva* are material or that (2) the material is unreal. We may note in passing that 'solution' 1 - that both the *jīva* and karma are material - is not necessarily 'materialist' in the sense we understand it and in which orthodox Jains came to represent it, viz. that there is no such thing as salvation or liberation. Indeed, this 'solution' may well have been the original (i.e. pre-textual) Jaina view, the difference between the self and matter being one of quality not kind. That is to say, both are material, but the soul, consisting of subtle matter, can achieve liberation by refining itself from grosser matter and ascending to the top of the (physical) universe. (And according to orthodox Jaina doctrine, even in liberation the soul remains part of a physically or materially conceived universe.) Such a doctrine would not only be compatible with other archaic Jaina beliefs but would remove the intractable problem of how to account for bondage and liberation without undermining the rationale for ethical behaviour (although without, of course, alleviating the extreme difficulty of achieving liberation by this path). A

---

[54] Chakravarti's commentary on *Samayasāra* 85 (p. 75).

[55] See ibid., and *Samayasāra* 137-140 for the gāthās expressing this argument in full.

return to this position, which would naturally have ruled out any gnostic practices, was hardly a possibility for Kundakunda, given the philosophical sophistication of his times. Consistency loses its attractions when the alternative is credibility.

Returning to the four possible 'solutions', the third is the *anekānta* one - that the *jīva* and matter are quite different and totally separate from one point of view, and yet, at the same time, from another point of view they are interactive. That leaves a fourth possibility, one which is followed by Kundakunda in the second *niścaya* pattern. This has a similar effect to solution 2, but it is not (as Bhatt thinks) identical to it in substance. For rather than positing the unreality of one of the pair of *jīva* and matter, it simply stresses the unreality or illusory nature of the relationship between them. Thus bondage is a question of ignorance and liberation becomes a matter of knowledge - a realisation of the true (non-) relation. This, of course, is very close to the Sāṃkhya view. It is also clearly just as inimical as the first two 'solutions' to the *anekānta* perspective (i.e. it is an *ekānta*, 'one-sided', view).

Sheerly as a matter of logic, any one of the 'solutions' 1, 2 and 4 is more convincing than the orthodox solution (3). Thus, while the second *vyavahāra-niścaya* pattern breaks out of the *anekānta* circle and pushes the Jaina conceptions of self and karma towards a logical resolution in its own doctrine of bondage and liberation, orthodoxy's adherence to the *anekānta* doctrine may be identified as one of the reasons for the Indologist's old cliché that Jaina doctrine and philosophy have remained largely static. For *anekāntavāda* suspends the various elements of Jaina doctrine before the contradiction between the material and the spiritual, which lies at the heart of the teaching, forces a further logical development. It has, as we have seen, good social reasons for doing so. A logical solution, such as that offered by the second *vyavahāra-niścaya* pattern, has potentially fatal consequences for the ascetic practices which provide the Jainas with their social identity.

However, in an age when religious rivalry was conducted at the level of philosophical debate, there were clearly some individuals or 'schools' who, under a variety of influences and for a mixture of defensive, offensive, or sheerly intellectual reasons (and probably in tandem with the development of meditational techniques), felt compelled to propound a 'one-sided' (*ekānta*) solution.

To approach this from a slightly different angle, we may characterize *anekāntavāda* and the second *vyavahāra-niścaya* pattern as two different and incompatible ways of dealing with the same problem, resolving into alternative solutions. That problem is to account for the connection between material karma and an immaterial soul. For orthodox Jainism, the resolution of this is essentially a philosophical rather than a soteriological problem: the important fact for religious practice is that the soul is, by definition, really bound. *Anekāntavāda* and *syādvāda* are thus strategies for defending or evading criticisms of this dogma which may arise in debate with proponents of non-Jaina doctrines. To be counted a Jain at all requires, in the orthodox view, assent to this proposition (i.e. that the soul is really bound). Consequently, *anekāntavāda* actively affects religious practice (soteriology) only in the indirect sense that it contributes to *ahiṃsā* through promoting tolerance of other views.[56] Negatively, it preserves the status quo and thus the full range of ascetic and ethical practices.

Taking as a starting point what originally may have been simply a description of the self from the perspective of liberation (i.e. the self viewed synchronically), the second *vyavahāra-niścaya* pattern takes this to be the true (i.e. complete or real) definition of the soul at all times and in all circumstances. Understanding this then becomes crucial for soteriology and religious practice: liberation becomes a matter of gnosis, the realisation of the real

---

56 *Pace* Matilal (1981), I see this as merely a side-effect and not, in *anekāntavāda*'s developed form, its primary function.

nature of the self, its *samayasāra*. Thus the *niścaya* view is no longer simply a description of the state of the (already) liberated soul, rather it is the *means* by which the soul achieves that liberation. It can, therefore, no longer be said to be one among a number of equally valid views, for unless you believe that it is *the* correct view you cannot achieve liberation. If, on the other hand, the *anekāntavāda* continues to be followed, then the *vyavahāra-niścaya* distinction loses its soteriological power, becoming merely a philosophical view as opposed to a religious means.[57]

In short, it is one of the features of the *Samayasāra* that it takes established doctrines and, by means of a technique which seems to have been largely borrowed from competing Buddhist and Vedāntic systems, devalues their practical significance in the hierarchy of spiritual progress. Bhatt's portrayal of the 'Kundakunda' of his 'mystic' pattern suggests an individual religious innovator as the source of this process.[58] However, evidence of the progressive internalisation of doctrine prior to Kundakunda's time, his reliance on stock Jaina teachings, the development of his ideas by later commentators, as well as his position as the virtual initiator of the Digambara scriptural tradition, suggest that it is more fruitful to view these works as heterogeneous repositories of accumulated Digambara teaching, including relatively new as well as traditional material, rather than the imperfectly preserved work of an individual heterodox philosopher. Viewed as products of a broad historical movement these works are less easy to discount as mere curiosities or aberrations, something

---

[57] There are, as we have seen, some indications in the *Samayasāra* that once the heteroprax implications of the second *vyavahāra-niścaya* pattern were understood attempts were made to disarm it by re-imposing the first *vyavahāra-niścaya* pattern. The incompatibility of the two solutions is, however, too radical for this to succeed in a logically satisfying way. Once the absolute *niścaya* (2) view is admitted, the *anekāntavāda* is irretrievably discredited.

[58] Bhatt 1974, p. 289.

which their continuing popularity would argue against anyway. In the absence of other reliable evidence, the effects or potential effects on religious practice of particular teachings can only be deduced by modern scholars; but it is easy to underestimate such effects if the teaching is ascribed to the inspiration of just one person. It is the very variety of texts like the *Samayasāra*, the disparate doctrinal strands they attempt to weave together, and the emergence within this fabric of dominant patterns, which make their study so important for any reconstruction of Jaina religious history.

8

The mechanism of bondage according to the *Samayasāra*

In its essentials the mechanism of bondage according to the *Samayasāra* does not differ significantly from that found in the *Pravacanasāra* [1] Nevertheless, some of the technical terminology is different, and a brief summary of the main principles not only clarifies the question of what is thought to be really instrumental in bondage (already discussed to some extent in the 'Two Truths' section above) but also prepares the ground for an understanding of the central teachings of this text concerning liberation and the means to attaining it.

i) Bhāva

The *bhāva* doctrine is not so clearly defined as the *Pravacanasāra*'s *upayoga* doctrine, but it functions in much the same way. A *bhāva*, in this context, is a state of the *jīva* - specifically, a state of mind or consciousness. In other words, it is a modification or mode (*paryāya*) of the quality of consciousness. So the basic dichotomy still obtains between the modal and the substantial self, between *paryāya* and *dravya*; and in this dichotomy *bhāva* falls on the *paryāya* side. It is differentiated or limited consciousness, i.e. consciousness modified by various degrees of impurity, as distinct from pure consciousness or omniscience, the natural state of the *jīva*. The liberated self is thus essentially *bhāva*-less, although it is sometimes referred to as being the *parama*- or *śuddha-bhāva* (e.g. at *Samayasāra* 12 and Commentary), in the same way as it is described in the *Pravacanasāra* as 'possessing' *śuddha-upayoga*.

What brings about this apparent limitation of the soul's

---

[1] See above, p. 124ff.

pure omniscient nature?

Samayasāra 89 [96] - 100 [107] explains that because of its beginningless association with delusion (*moha*) the soul's pure consciousness is modified [89], and it produces - i.e. is the agent of - *bhāva*s which in turn are the instrumental cause of *pudgala-dravya* modifying itself into karma [90-91]. That is to say, an individual, through the *bhāva* of ignorance (*ajñāna*), confuses the self with non-self and vice-versa, and so, via his *bhāva*s, becomes the instrument of karmas. Thus the soul binds itself. Conversely, the knowing self does not become the agent of karmas [92-93]. It is modified or 'false' consciousness - the *bhāva* of ignorance - which produces the false-notion (*vikalpa*)[2] that the self and not-self (*jīva* and *ajīva* / *para*) are related [94-96]. In short, the soul is not really responsible for the binding of knowledge-obscuring karma, rather it is *bhāva*s which bring about the modification of matter into karma, and so bondage is essentially the product of *bhāva*s [101-102]. Furthermore, *bhāva*s are produced by ignorance, itself the product of (knowledge-obscuring) karma.

As *Samayasāra* 185 [178 JGM] puts it:

> Thus the knower knows [his true nature - see 184]. [But] the one who doesn't know, ignorant of the true nature (*svabhāva*) of the soul, covered with the darkness of ignorance, supposes that attachment (*rāga*) itself is the soul.

In other words, karma produces ignorance, ignorance produces *bhāva*s, and *bhāva*s in turn produce (via karma) more ignorance, including ignorance of the true relation of *bhāva*s such as *rāga* to the soul.[3]

---

[2] Cf. *Samayasāra* 288 JGM.

[3] It is interesting to note that this effectively subsumes the *kaṣāya* doctrine under the *bhāva* and 'ignorance' doctrine: emotional involvement with the not-self - with the objects of the senses, etc. - is based upon ignorance of the fundamental separateness of self and

Partial or limited knowledge is knowledge with *bhāva*s, whereas pure knowledge or omniscience is *bhāva*-free. Thus *Samayasāra* 183 [JGM 176] reads:

> When the *jīva* has this true (non-perverse) knowledge, then the self, which is pure consciousness, produces no *bhāva*s whatsoever.

This true or non-perverse (*aviparīta*) knowledge is, as the previous two verses (181 and 182) have made clear, the realisation that the pure soul really has nothing to do with any emotions or karmas whatsoever. So pure knowledge - i.e. unmodified pure consciousness or *upayoga* - produces no *bhāva*s. To put this in terms of the *vyavahāra-niścaya* doctrine, it is only from the *vyavahāra* viewpoint - the viewpoint of the modified self - that the soul produces *bhāva*s; from the *niścaya* view the soul is *bhāva*- and karma-free.

The important point, however, is that ignorance binds and knowledge does not. *Samayasāra* 127 [JGM 137] spells this out:

> The *bhāva* of an ignorant person consists of ignorance; through that he / it produces karmas. But the knower's *bhāva* consists of

---

matter. Such emotional attachment arises through experiencing the objects of the senses through the medium of modified or false consciousness (ignorance), and it is that *bhāva* which is the root cause of the mistake which leads to attachment and bondage. In other words, *rāga*, *dveṣa* and *moha* are modifications of consciousness brought about by ignorance (*ajñāna*). Consequently, when ignorance disappears attachment, etc., will also disappear. The objects of the senses - the contents of the material world - towards which this attachment is directed - in reality have, and can have, no effect on the self. (See *Samayasāra* 366-381, especially 371 and *Ātmakhyāti* [JGM 384], cf. *Samayasāra* 22, 69, 113-115, for a lengthy exposition of this argument. For a version of the standard *kaṣāya* doctrine given through the simile of dust clinging to an active oil-smeared body - it is the oil (attachment) not the action which is instrumental in bondage - see *Samayasāra* 237ff.).

knowledge and therefore he does not produce karmas.[4]

This passage continues with a number of verses [132-136] showing that ignorance is due to the operation of various karmas. But as we have just seen [*Samayasāra* 127], ignorance itself produces karmas. The argument is thus circular, closed by the idea that *moha* is beginningless. The soul is ignorant of its real nature; such ignorance leads to the production of *bhāva*s which in turn give rise to karma. Karma includes knowledge-obscuring karma which causes the soul to be ignorant of its true nature, and so on.

It should be noted, however, that within this circle the *bhāva* of ignorance, which is instrumental in bondage, is caused by knowledge-obscuring karma, i.e. by something material and *para* or 'not self'. This is spelt out at *Samayasāra* 300 [328 JGM] which asks the question:

> What wise man, indeed, knowing all *bhāva*s to have arisen from non-self (*para*), and knowing that the self is pure, would utter the words, 'This is mine'?[5]

And in the following three verses [301-303], the self that identifies with *bhāva*s is compared to a thief moving about guiltily, perpetually in fear of arrest (bondage). However, the 'guiltless' soul (the one that realises it has no connection with *bhāva*s) has no fear of bondage because it knows that it cannot really be bound.

So if one asks what constitutes the real cause of bondage, the reply must be that it is the identification of the self with the not-self through ignorance of their true

---

4 Cf. *Samayasāra* 128 and 129, where it is said that for a knower all *bhāvas* consist of knowledge, whereas for the non-knower they consist of ignorance.

5 Cf. *Samayasāra* 46 [JGM 51] which states that: 'That all these states (*bhāvas*) such as intention (*adhyavasāna*), etc. (belong to) *jīvas* is declared by the Jinas to be a statement teaching the *vyavahāra* view.' From the *niścaya* point of view, the *jīva* is unitary [*ekko nicchido jivo* - *Samayasāra* 48]; it has no *bhāvas*.

relation. And when it is asked what causes such ignorance, the answer is that it is caused by that karma which has arisen in the first place from ignorance (via *bhāva*s).

Two things follow from this. First, the self has, in *essence*, no place in this closed circle of cause and effect. It is a chain of self-perpetuating delusion: ignorance produces *bhāva*s, which produce karmas, which produce more ignorance, etc. This is because *bhāva*s, although seemingly products of the self, actually arise from the non-self (see *Samayasāra* 300, quoted above). The soul, therefore, is not really bound; it is simply suffering from the delusion that bondage is its condition.

The second point to arise is that this now tenuous connection of the soul and karma (via delusion) is broken altogether once it is realised that binding ignorance is precisely ignorance of the true (non-) relation of self and karma. For karma, because it is nothing more than the term for *pudgala-dravya* which has come into contact with the *jīva*, must itself be a delusion - for such contact (that of *jīva* and *ajīva*) is, in reality, not possible. In other words, once bondage is seen to be basically a mistake or delusion, material karma loses its force as an explanatory factor anywhere in the chain of cause and effect. Not only is it discounted as the direct cause of bondage, but it cannot even convincingly claim to be the cause of the delusion of contact between *jīva* and *ajīva*, since it is only itself thought to be real because of the delusion that the *jīva* and *ajīva* can actually come into contact with each other.

To put this in more general terms, the point of soteriological focus has now been shifted irrevocably away from action and inaction as the binding and liberating factors towards internal states, i.e. towards ignorance and knowledge. The role of karma theory in this is finally irrelevant and, for that reason, logically unconvincing. Once again the implications of Kundakunda's argument carry him beyond the bounds of Jaina orthodoxy. For if karma is not important then what is done or not done in the world (by the ascetic and by others) is not important either.

What does matter is knowledge (gnosis), inner realisation of the true nature of the self.

This potential crisis for asceticism is, as we have seen, a direct product of the second *vyavahāra-niścaya* pattern, where the *niścaya* view about the (non-) relation of self and other is taken to be the exclusive truth. However, the fact that the two *niścaya* patterns co-exist in the same text obscures and tempers to some extent the radical implications of the second pattern; one strand of the *Samayasāra* still holds to karma and its removal as being instrumental in bondage and liberation.[6]

ii) The role of intention (adhyavasāna) in bondage

Verses 262 [JGM 280] - 265 [JGM 283] of the *Samayasāra* state that:

> Bondage is brought about by what is resolved (determined / intended - *adhyavasita*) whether one kills beings or not. This is the succinct statement of the bondage of *jīvas* from the *niścaya* point of view [i.e. according to *niścaya* pattern one] (262).
> Similarly, the resolution (*adhyavasāna*) to lie, to take what is not given, to be unchaste and to acquire property leads to the bondage of bad (*pāpa*) karma (263), whereas the resolution to be truthful, to take only what is given, to be chaste and not to acquire possessions leads to the bondage of good (*puṇya*) karma (264).
> For *jīvas*, resolution occurs with reference to an object, but bondage is not caused by that object; bondage is caused by resolution [i.e. by the attitude towards the object] (265).

In other words, it is a mental event, an attitude (*adhyavasāna*), which is really instrumental in bondage.

---

[6] The equation that knowledge is the (true) nature of the self (epistemology = ontology), inevitably leads to problems of expression such as those outlined above: ignorance (*avidyā*, *moha*, etc.) is a state, condition, modification, etc.; but is its opposite the best state or a non-state? In Buddhism this problem arises with *diṭṭhi*: does Enlightenment amount to *samma-diṭṭhi* or no *diṭṭhi*? (See Collins, Chapters 3 and 4.)

The *mahāvratas* have thus been internalised - a process familiar to us from Umāsvāti's *kaṣaya* doctrine. Here, however, the scope is widened to make *any* kind of intention, will or resolution binding to a greater or lesser degree; mental events in themselves are thought, ultimately, to be counter- productive. So it is no longer simply the case that passionate or negative mental states entail bondage, but even states free of these bring about bondage of *puṇya-karma* if they are willed or determined in any way. Intention in itself, rather than simply negative intention, keeps one in *saṃsāra*. The extent of this is made clear by the *Samayasāra* when it lists the synonyms for *adhyavasāna* at 271 [JGM 295]:

> *Buddhi* (intellect), *vyavasāya* (resolve), *adhyavasāna* (determination), *mati* (thought), *vijñāna* (discrimination), *citta* (wish), *bhāva* (mode of thought), *pariṇāma* (modification) - all these have the same meaning.

So any kind of thought or intention is a *bhāva* and is thus considered to be a modification or transformation (*pariṇāma*) of self. In that sense it is also an activity, a falling off from the ideal state of non-active, motionless omniscience. Thus soteriologically speaking, the *quality* of intention can only be of secondary importance; the Jains, even when they have internalised the mechanism of bondage, continue to keep their distance from the Buddhists, for whom it is precisely the quality of intention which is soteriologically crucial. In other words, there can, ultimately, be no middle way to liberation for the Jains. Only *munis* who are free from *adhyavasāna*, etc. are entirely free from further bondage.[7]

However, we have seen that, according to the second *niścaya* view, this freedom from *adhyavasāna* is only to be obtained by realising that, in reality, the *jīva* has and can have nothing to do with such modified mental states, since

---

[7] See *Samayasāra* 270 (JGM 294).

the latter arise from what is *para*, other than the self.[8] So when it comes to liberation (the concern of the advanced monk), as opposed to just a better rebirth, it is knowledge or realisation of the fact that the *jīva* and *adhyavasāna* cannot in reality come into contact, rather than the stopping of mental activity as such, which is crucial according to the second *niścaya* pattern. I shall now look at this mechanism of liberation in more detail.

---

[8] See *Samayasāra* 46, 48, and 300, quoted p. 270 above.

9

The mechanism of liberation according to the *Samayasāra*

9.1 *Liberation in the Samayasāra*

i) Knowledge and the knower

Near the end of the *Samayasāra*, Kundakunda goes to the trouble of listing a number of specific things which are *not* knowledge (*jñāna*) and which, presumably, he fears may be confused with it. This passage starts with the verse [390]:

> Texts are not knowledge, because texts do not know anything. The Jinas say that knowledge is one thing and texts another.

The same formula is repeated for sound or word (*śabda*) [391], form (*rūpa*) [392], colour (*varṇa*) [393], smell (*gandha*) [394], taste (*rasa*) [395], touch (*sparśa*) [396], *karma* [397], the medium of motion (*dharma*) [398], the medium of rest (*adharma*) [399], time (*kāla*) [400], space (*ākāśa*) [401], and will or resolution (*adhyavasāna*) [402].[1]

This does not seem to be a conventional list of, for instance, means to or objects of knowledge. The purpose behind it, however, is clear: to discount what is 'known' through the sense organs (including mind, which has *śāstra* as its object) as true knowledge. This includes the five *ajīva dravya*, non-sentient substances which constitute the physical universe (*karma* = *pudgala* here), and attitude or intention (*bhāva*, represented here by *adhyavasāna*). In other words, everything is excluded except the *jīva* itself.

The *Samayasāra* [403 = JGM 433] then goes on to state that:

---

[1] The verse treating *adhyavasāna* has a slightly different form - it is said to be *acedaṇa* / *acetana* (unconscious) - perhaps for metrical reasons, or because it is a later addition.

As it always (*nitya*) knows, so the *jīva* is *the* knower, the wise. And it should be realised that knowledge (*jñāna*) is not separate from the knower (*jñāyaka*).

This may be compared with *Samayasāra* 198 (= JGM 213):

Various types of rising and fruition of karmas have been described by the great Jina(s); but they are not my own-nature *(sahāva / svabhāva).* I am one, a knower by nature *(jāṇagabhāvo du aham ekko).*[2]

In other words, the defining characteristic or quality of the *jīva* is that it knows - that is its essence. Moreover, as Chakravarti points out in his commentary on *Samayasāra* 404, according to Jaina metaphysics, a *dravya* and its *guṇa* are an inseparable, indivisible unity; neither can be present without the other. So in this case, *jīva* and *jñāna*, self or knower and knowledge, are not different categories brought together by a third category, they are identical: the knower is essentially one with knowledge.[3]

To put it slightly differently, the pure self is a knower by nature and par excellence; it is not to be differentiated from what it knows. Indeed, it is only the self which can know anything because it is only the self which has knowledge for its *svabhāva*. Moreover, because of this it does not *do* anything in order to know - it has no need to *act* in order to obtain knowledge, knowledge is its condition. And what it knows is precisely itself. Thus knowledge is not a matter of knowing something beyond or external to the self, but of realising or knowing one's own true nature. The greater one's knowledge of self (the purer the self), the greater one's knowledge of everything. Eventually, complete knowledge of the self brings omniscience: the self realises itself as unobstructed

---

[2] Also quoted, p. 235, above.

[3] Chakravarti's commentary, pp. 232-233.

knowledge.

In the light of this equation of knowledge, the knower, and the self, it is revealing to look at *Samayasāra* 404 (= JGM 434). This is the verse which follows that which equates knowledge and the knower or self (403). It reads:

> Knowledge is right belief; self-restraint; the *sūtras*, consisting of *aṅgas* and *pūrvas*; merit and demerit; and asceticism [i.e. *pravrajyā* - formal assumption of the *mahāvrata*, and so initiation into mendicancy].[4] The wise agree on this.

There is some confusion here about the form of *sammādiṭṭhi,* 'right belief'. Chakravarti and Jaini both give *sammādiṭṭhi / samyagdṛṣṭih* (misprint in Prākrit?, nominative singular in Sanskrit); the JGM edition gives *sammādiṭṭhī / samyagdṛṣṭiṃ* (nominative singular Prākrit, accusative singular Sanskrit), which is having it both ways, although it at least conforms to the metrical need for a long syllable. I have translated the verse in accordance with the reading of the commentators and translators, who take *jñāna* to be the subject. Such a reading certainly conforms to the context. However, it is possible that verse 404 is an imported traditional gāthā whose original subject was *samyag-dṛṣṭi*, right belief. If this is so, then by the time it was incorporated into the *Samayasāra* it must already have been very ancient, for the *pūrvas* had long since been lost.[5] Thus if knowledge of the *pūrvas* is still considered a necessary part of *samyag-dṛṣṭi*, which in turn is the prerequisite of the religious life, then, without reinterpretation, this verse is little better than a counsel of despair. Similarly, the idea that full renunciation is necessary for *samyag-dṛṣṭi* is very ancient. Therefore, whatever the original meaning of this verse, it is both more

---

4 See *JPP* p. 243.

5 If the context were not Jain, however, the obvious interpretation of *pūrva(kaṃ)* would be simply 'with -', and that may be the meaning here.

meaningful and more compatible with the new context to take *jñāna* as the subject. Indeed, knowledge, which has just been equated with the knower (the self), is clearly too important to the overall significance of the text to revert here to being just another sub-category.

In this context, therefore, *Samayasāra* 404 states that knowledge - i.e. the knower, the self - *is* all these things, viz. right belief, restraint, the *sūtras*, *dharma* and *adharma*, and full renunciation. Consequently, to know or realise the self is to know - that is to say, be - all these things. In other words, (self-) knowledge is the whole of the religious life, the *mokṣa-mārga*. Through a radical internalisation a single principle subsumes all the rest, and both the path and the goal are found within the self. *Jñāna*, which is self-realisation or gnosis, supersedes all external discipline. (It is also interesting to note how this internalisation removes the problem of the *pūrvas*: that is to say, their loss is no longer a bar to liberation, since if you know your self you will necessarily 'know' all the *sūtras* - *jñāna* contains them.) Liberation is thus a function of the autonomous self, i.e. of the cultivation or purification of the self through the development of greater and greater (self-) knowledge. And, as Chakravarti puts it, on perfection of knowledge the self 'becomes perfect and knowledge becomes completely co-extensive with reality'. The self is then both *sarvajña* and *paramātma*, the omniscient and absolute self.[6]

ii) Self-realisation

We have seen that according to the *Samayasāra* the self (the knower) and knowledge are in essence one. This is, as it were, the omniscient perspective. But to attain this state, to become the pure self, it is necessary to realise, i.e. to experience, this theoretical truth in the self. In more abstract terms, a description of an ontological condition is both the end of and the means to a new epistemology, the full implementation of which leads back to that ontological

[6] Chakravarti p. 233.

state at a new level of personal experience or attainment. And this liberation (omniscience) through self-realisation or knowledge has been made possible precisely through the equation of self and knowledge. As the *Niyamasāra* puts it:

> From the *vyavahāra* point of view the omniscient lord sees and knows everything, from the *niścaya* point of view the omniscient sees and knows the self.[7]

The clear implication is that by knowing the self one knows everything, and thus one is a liberated soul, a *kevalin*.

The self to be known is, of course, the pure self, i.e. the self as it is in its essence or *svabhāva*, the self as knowledge. For 'realising the pure self the *jīva* becomes pure; but knowing the impure self it becomes impure' [*Samayasāra* 186].

Indeed, according to the *Samayasāra* it is only through pure (self-) knowledge that one can attain liberation. The five standard media of knowledge - sense perception, scripture, clairvoyance, telepathy, and omniscience - all refer to the one thing (or state). That is reality *(paramaṭṭha / paramārtha)*. Having attained that, one attains liberation.[8] Moreover, 'the many who are without these kinds of knowledge do not achieve this state. If you desire complete liberation (*parimokkham*) from karma then you must obtain this superior state' [*Samayasāra* 205].[9]

The *Samayasāra* stresses that without concentration, i.e. without at least the attempt to realise this one reality which is the realised self, all religious discipline is useless. Or as *Samayasāra* 152 (= JGM 162) puts it:

---

[7] *Niy* 159 [= SBJ 158]. Also quoted pp. 212-213, above.

[8] See *Samayasāra* 204.

[9] That *paramaṭṭho / paramārtha* in the *Samayasāra* refers to the pure, unified or realised self - that it is the condition of 'entering into knowledge which is produced from the state of oneness' - has been established above. See p. 235ff. above, ref. *Samayasāra* 151.

> One who performs *tapas* and (observes) *vrata* without being fixed in reality [*paramaṭṭha* - the pure self], the all-knowing call that (practice) foolish *tapas* and foolish *vrata*.

So even when they are 'observing vows, rules and restraints, and practising *tapas*, such people are devoid of knowledge because they are outside *paramārtha*' [*Samayasāra* 153]. Outside *paramārtha*, and ignorant of the cause of liberation, they long for merit (*puṇya*) which can only keep them in *saṃsāra*.[10]

Knowledge or realisation of the self is thus crucial to liberation, but how is it to be attained? It has already been suggested that partial knowledge is the indispensable means to realisation of absolute knowledge, but what form does such knowledge take?

As we have seen, the ignorant self binds itself through identifying with what is not self. As *Samayasāra* 92 [= JGM 99] puts it:

> The soul (*jīva*) that is full of ignorance, (mis)taking the non-self (*para*) for the self (*ātman*), and the self for what is non-self, is the agent of karmas.

Conversely,

> The soul which consists of knowledge, not (mis)taking the non-self for the self, or the self for what is non-self, is not the agent of karmas [*Samayasāra* 93 = JGM 100].

The essential mental act is therefore discrimination based on knowledge of the true nature of the self. Again we see the mixture of ontology and epistemology: the pure self cannot, by definition, come into contact with anything not self, yet it is precisely knowledge of this which is instrumental in separating self and not-self - i.e. such knowledge causes the self to relinquish its 'unreal' or

---

10 See *Samayasāra* 154 (= JGM 164).

delusory contact with the other and thus realise its real condition.

As we have seen, with increasing stress on the essential purity of the self and its equation with knowledge (omniscience), the idea arises that the *ātman*, in its essence or *svabhāva*, cannot by definition ever really come into contact with any material substances. And what was originally true just of the individual who had attained *kevala-jñāna* is now predicated of every *ātman*.

This points us towards something which is implied but never made explicit in Kundakunda's reformulation of the relationship between self and matter - namely, that it is impossible that the soul could ever be or ever have been really bound. Naturally, this is closely allied to the shift away from the importance of physical karma and the concomitant rise of the idea that the pure self is something to be attained by realisation of its true ontological status. It should be stressed, however, that because of the eclectic nature of the *Samayasāra* the direct link with the path of physical austerity is never finally broken. Thus, for instance, while gāthā 71 (= JGM 76) states that:

> When the absolute difference between *āsravas* (inflowing karmic matter) and the self (*ātman*) is known by this *jīva*, then there is no bondage for it,

the following verse (72 = JGM 77) tempers this with the statement that:

> Having known the impurity of *āsravas*, their contrary nature (to the self), and that they are the causes of misery, the *jīva* abstains from them.

In other words, the *jīva* that knows the true relationship between the self and *paradravya* does not act in an *āsrava*-causing way and so is not bound. Thus in these verses, it is implied that knowledge is still at least nominally subsidiary to conduct as the means to liberation. Nevertheless, given the overall trend of thought in this text, such qualifications seem little more than a holding operation in a pass which, in principle, has already been sold.

If the state of purity, of omniscience, is the eternal condition of the *ātman* (i.e. in reality it cannot and can never have been associated with the impure, knowledge-restricting not-self), and the knowledge of this truth realises or brings it about in fact (i.e. engenders liberation), then this comes very close to saying that every individual is now and always has been a *kevalin*. In other words, there are the same kind of premises here which gave rise in Mahāyāna Buddhism to the *tathāgatagarbha* or 'Buddha-Nature' theory.[11] For, in the Jain case, there is the barely concealed proposition that everyone has the Jina- or *kevalin*-nature (i.e. each person's *ātman* is really omniscient), and that knowledge of this realises it ontologically. Kundakunda, of course, does not go so far as to say that *saṃsāra* and *nirvāṇa* are really the same thing; it is still assumed that with physical death the liberated *ātman* is released to a nirvāṇic place or condition. However, the logic of this physical liberation, which was tied to the material view of the universe (and perhaps originally to the idea of a material soul), is now very vague and, significantly, no attempt is made to explicate it. Emphasis now falls upon the *state* of liberation rather than upon its location. (Again, the concept of liberation as a state of pure consciousness or knowledge is reminiscent of Mahāyānist beliefs.)

One can only speculate on the effect of such ideas on the Jaina layperson, even supposing that they were disseminated to him. But it is clear that any changes must have been largely in terms of expectation rather than practice. That is to say, if the link with physical asceticism cannot be broken without risking the identity of the community as a whole, such theoretical possibilities as that

---

[11] On the *tathāgatagarbha*, see, for instance, P. Williams 1989, pp. 96-115.

of a 'Jina-nature' nevertheless make liberation *seem* closer. They are affectively satisfying. (This, of course, still leaves room for the [heretical] suspicion that practice may not be quite so important as had previously been thought, given that in reality the self is even now liberated.) And one can continue to defer realisation of the inherently liberated and omniscient self alongside an increased hope of ultimately attaining the ideal religious goal.

iii) Discriminative knowledge

Returning now to the concern of the ascetic or advanced layperson - i.e. the way to obtain or realise liberation in practice - it is useful to examine in more detail what is meant by discriminative knowledge.

Samayasāra 202 (not found in the JGM ed.) asks:

> How can one, not knowing the self (*ātman*) and not knowing the non-self (*anātman*), not knowing the *jīva* and *ajīva*, be a right-believer (*samyag-dṛṣṭi*)?

In other words, one cannot even get on to the first rung of the ladder to salvation without such knowledge;[12] and yet such knowledge in itself constitutes liberation. This, however, is not an impenetrably vicious circle, as becomes clear if we draw an analogy with early Buddhism's *sammā diṭṭhi* or 'Right Understanding'. For the Buddhist, Rahula tells us, 'Right Understanding is the understanding of things as they are ... [it] is the highest wisdom which sees the Ultimate Reality'. This understanding is, however, of two kinds:

> What we generally call understanding is knowledge, an accumulated memory, an intellectual grasping of a subject according to given data. This is called 'knowing accordingly' (*anubodha*). It is not very deep. Real deep understanding is called 'penetration' (*paṭivedha*), seeing a thing in its true nature... This

---

[12] See *JPP* p. 272 on *samyag-dṛṣṭi* as the fourth *guṇasthāna*.

> penetration is possible only when the mind is free from all impurities and is fully developed through meditation.[13]

For the Jains too, partial, intellectual knowledge puts one on the ladder which leads to absolute knowledge and liberation.

It is interesting to note that, with the developing stress in Jaina theory on knowledge and self-realisation as the means to liberation, there is an increasing tendency to borrow Buddhist terminology; for Buddhism clearly has a more developed and sophisticated ready-made vocabulary for describing inner discipline and experience. One example of this which is significant in the present context occurs at *Samayasāra* 293-299. The relevant passage reads:

> Having clearly known the nature (*svabhāva*) of what binds and the nature (*svabhāva*) of the self (*ātman*), he who has no attachment to what binds attains liberation from karma [293].
> The *jīva* and bondage are differentiated [lit. 'cut'] by their own essential and distinctive characteristics. Cut by the knife of discriminative wisdom (*paṇṇā / prajñā*), they fall apart [294].
> [When] the *jīva* and bondage are differentiated by their own essential and distinctive characteristics, bondage should be cut away and the pure self grasped [295].
> How is the self grasped? The self is grasped by discriminative wisdom (*prajñā*). Just as [the self] is separated (from bondage) by *prajñā*, so it should be grasped by *prajñā* [296].
> The conscious being (*cetayitā*) to be grasped by *prajñā*, I am that in reality; whatever mental states (*bhāva*) make up the remainder should be known to be other than mine [297].
> The perceiver (*daṭṭhā / dṛṣṭā*) to be grasped by *prajñā*, I am that in reality, etc. [298]
> The knower (*nādā / jñātā*) to be grasped by *prajñā*, I am that in reality, etc. [299].

---

13 Rahula p. 49.

Gāthā 293 makes the usual distinction between the *svabhāva* of the self and everything else, and relates liberation to non-attachment to, or separation from, the latter. This is the inescapable (i.e. ontological) separation of the *jīva* and what (apparently) binds it (294a), but it is *prajñā* which is instrumental in realising that gulf between *jīva* and *ajīva* (294b). Such realisation of the pure self is liberation (295).

In other words, separation of the *jīva* and what binds it is no longer a physical matter - i.e. it is not a matter of burning off karma through *tapas* and preventing further influx (*āsrava*) through inaction - it is now an intellectual or mental concern. One realises the true nature of the self through *prajñā* (discriminative wisdom), and that in itself releases the pure self; it enables it to attain to its true condition.

The use of the term *prajñā* here is almost certainly borrowed from Nāgārjuna or from Buddhist *prajñāpāramitā* literature in general. For Nāgārjuna, *prajñā* is the means by which the higher truth (*paramārtha-satya*) is grasped - it is 'direct, intuitive insight into reality as it is in itself'.[14] For Kundakunda, the reality of the self is that it is absolutely unconnected with what is not self, and *prajñā* isolates, in the first instance, that pure self. It is the initial and crucial intellectual means of discriminating between *jīva* and *ajīva*, self and bondage. In this sense, it is synonymous with *samyag-dṛṣṭi* (see above). But as in the Buddhist case, *prajñā* has, according to the *Samayasāra*, another facet. This is spelt out in gāthā 296 (see above), where it is said that just as the *ātman* is differentiated (*vibhakta*) from the not self or from 'bondage' by *prajñā*, so it is also to be realised or attained (*gṛhītavya*) by *prajñā*. In other words, there are two stages or kinds of *prajñā*: the intellectual knowledge of the way things are in reality, and the means to the personal realisation or attainment of that reality. This seems to correspond to the early Mahāyānist

---

[14] Puligandla p. 95; see also P. Williams 1989, pp. 42-45.

distinction between *prajñā* which is knowing intellectually, through deep or meditative analysis, the way things must really be, and 'paranormal experience of a meditative absorption directed towards the results of such analysis'.[15]

In summary, *prajñā* is conceived of in two interlinked ways: as deep intellectual analysis, and as something less conceptual, the direct realisation or achievement of that state which has previously been isolated by analysis. The fact that for the Jains the liberated self is omniscient does not conflict with the non-conceptual or non-intellectual form of liberating *prajñā* (*prajñā* 'two'), for omniscience cannot be attained by a conscious attempt to expand one's normal limited knowledge. Rather it is only to be achieved by removing the obstacles to one's natural state of omniscience, i.e. by purifying the self, and especially by divesting oneself at a deep level of the delusion that the self is really in any way connected with what is not self. It is the *experience* of the pure self, rather than simply intellectual knowledge of it, that is liberating.

In contrast to the Buddhist texts, this division between, on the one hand, the intellectual and conceptual, and, on the other, the meditative and non-conceptual, is never systematically analysed or even described by Kundakunda in the *Samayasāra*. Nevertheless, the use of the term *prajñā* in the passage given above (especially in gāthā 296) implies precisely such a distinction. And what we saw when we considered *dhyāna* in the *Pravacanasāra* [16] is no less evident in the *Samayasāra*; namely, that liberation is to be attained by *meditation* on the pure self. For instance, we have already seen (in a different context) gāthā 151, where it is said that mendicants who are absorbed in the realised self, their *svabhāva*, attain *nirvāṇa*.[17] Similarly, gāthās 187-189 state that:

---

[15] P. William's description (1989), pp. 43-44.

[16] See p. 201ff., above.

[17] *tamhi ṭṭhidā sahāve muṇiṇo pāvaṃti ṇivvāṇaṃ* - *Samayasāra* 151. For the complete verse, see p. 236, above.

> The self which, having restrained itself by itself with regard to both meritorious and demeritorious actions, is fixed in perception and knowledge and is free from desire for other things, which, free from all combination [i.e. free from all attachment to what is not self], meditates on the self through the self and disregards karma and *nokarma* - (that) sentient being reflects upon the state of oneness [187-188].
> Meditating on the self, consisting of perception and knowledge and not consisting of anything else [OR 'not thinking (*manāḥ*) of anything else'], he very quickly realises the self which is completely free from all karma [189].[18]

In other words, it is meditation on the pure or unified self which is itself instrumental in realising or attaining that pure self. You know or identify the pure self (conceptually) and then you realise (i.e. attain it) by meditating on it. Moreover, meditation on the self comes to be seen as both the acme and index of right conduct. As two gāthās only found in Jayasena's recension of the *Samayasāra* put it:

> Indeed, meditation should be practised on knowledge, belief (/ perception) and conduct. But these three are the self; therefore practise meditation on the self [JGM 11].
> The ascetic who is constantly engaged in practising this meditation on the self attains liberation from all suffering quickly [JGM 12].

The term used for 'meditation' here is not *dhyāna* but *bhāvanā*. In early Jaina texts *bhāvanā* is connected with the five *mahāvrata*. It has a range of meanings, from the underlying mental disposition which leads to the right understanding of the vows, to their specific observance.[19]

---

[18] On *nokarma* - quasi-karmic matter which makes up the *jīva*'s bodies, etc. - see *Tattvārtha Sūtra* 2:10.

[19] See Schubring paras. 45,167,171; cf. *JPP* p. 243, fn. 3, and *TS* 7:3.

In the present context, however, the meaning of the term is significantly closer to the standard Buddhist use of *bhāvanā*, namely, as mental development or mental culture in general and meditation in particular.[20]

The important point to note here is the stress on meditation on the self as the means to liberation:[21] right conduct has been redefined as *ātmabhāvanā* (meditation on the self), and thus internalised. (There is probably also the implication that if one meditates on the self then one's external conduct is automatically correct.)

iv) Renunciation of bhāva

In a similar way renunciation is also internalised: stress now falls upon the renunciation of all (mental) states or *bhāva* (with the exception, of course, of *ātmasvabhāva*). Gāthā 34 (= JGM 39) reads:

> As (self-) knowledge renounces all (mental) states (*bhāva*), knowing them to be other (than the self), so (self-) knowledge should be considered to be the real / definitive definition of renunciation.

In other words, knowing the self, one recognises and renounces or rejects everything not self, all *parabhāva*.[22] And it is reiterated that knowledge is the *svabhāva* of the self:

> The holy men, who know absolute reality, call that holy man a conqueror of delusion who, having overcome delusion, realises that the self has knowledge for its own-nature (*svabhāva*).

Seen correctly, therefore, the self, untouched by anything else, is in a natural state of renunciation. It does not have to *do* anything to renounce since, having no other

---

[20] See *CPD* p. 36, entry on *bhāvanā*, and Rahula p.68.
[21] Cf. *Samayasāra* 151, above.
[22] See *Samayasāra* 35 (= JGM 40).

states and being in contact with no other states, there is nothing to renounce. Again knowledge of one's true nature leads to attainment of that true nature; renunciation of *parabhāva* - i.e. the realisation that they *are* other (*para*) - leads to the state of renunciation. For the delusion (*moha*) which is overcome is precisely that the self has anything to do with other substances. This is made clear by gāthās 36 and 37 (JGM 41 and 42). The first of these states that:

> (When) it is realised that 'delusion has nothing whatsoever to do with me; I am one, consciousness (*upayoga*)', the knowers of the true definition of self (*samaya*) call that the state of being free from delusion.

The second gāthā (37) repeats this formulation with '*dharma* etc.' *(dhammādi / dharmādi)* substituted for *moha.*

In other words, the self, when truly defined, has nothing to do with the other *dravya* (viz. *dharma*, *adharma*, *pudgala*, *akāśa*, *kāla*, and other *jīva*), and to realise that is to be free from delusion.[23]

That the knower, the pure self, is naturally a renunciate is borne out by a further passage in the *Samayasāra*. Gāthā 210-214 read:

> Non-possession (*aparigraha*) is said to be desirelessness. The knower does not desire merit (*dharma*). And it is by the non-possession of (i.e. the lack of desire for) *dharma* that he becomes / is a knower [210 = JGM 225].

The next three gāthās [211-213 = JGM 226, 228-229] repeat this formulation, substituting demerit (*adharma*) [211], and food (*aśana*) [212] and drink (*pāna*) [213] for *dharma*.

The passage continues:

---

[23] At least, Amṛtacandra interprets *dharma* here as the principle of motion, one of the five *ajīva* substances - see *Ātmakhyāti* on JGM 42. It could, however, simply mean 'merit'.

> Thus the knower does not desire all these various states (*bhāva*), for in reality his nature (*bhāva*) is knowledge, and he is independent of everything [214 = JGM 230].

As we have already seen, both meritorious and demeritorious actions keep one in *saṃsāra*. Here, the *desire* for the fruits of such actions has the same result. More interesting in this context, however, is the internalisation of *aparigraha* with regard to eating and drinking. Now it is the attitude, the lack of desire for food and water, which defines fasting. The stress has been shifted from the material fact of non-consumption, so closely tied to physical *ahiṃsā*, to the underlying state, or mental attitude. And *aparigraha* itself is defined as desirelessness, an attitude.

Thus the indices of the religious life - physical renunciation and non-possession (*aparigraha*) - are, through internalisation, drawn into the equation of self-knowledge and liberation. And the condition of renunciation is no longer something to be achieved through action or inaction but, being the natural state of the self, it is therefore something to be realised. In other words, the barrier to full renunciation and thus liberation is, in effect, a delusion with regard to what is not self: the delusion that it is possible in reality to have a relationship with it. Consequently, it is not the physical objects which make up the *ajīva* world themselves which are to be renounced, but the attitude towards those objects. As *Samayasāra* 210 puts it, 'a person who has no *parigraha* is said to be desireless' [*apariggaho aṇiccho bhaṇido*]; and it is by this kind of non-possession or desirelessness that one is a knower, i.e. liberated.[24] The concomitant of this is that it is attachment or desire, an attitude, which prevents self-knowledge and thus liberation. So according to *Samayasāra* 20 (= JGM 214):

---

24 See p. 289, above.

If as much as an atom of desire / attachment (*rāga*), etc., is found in someone, he does not know the self even if he knows all the scriptures.

Absence of desire (*rāga*) is the indicator of self-knowledge because only someone who knows the self, and thus the real relation of self to not self, knows that to desire is pointless, since in reality it is impossible to possess anything at all. In fact this works both ways: desire obstructs omniscience and liberation, but (partial) knowledge leads to the abandonment of desire and thus ultimately to liberation (total knowledge).

How does this treatment of desire (*rāga*) relate to the standard *kaṣāya* doctrine as found in the *Tattvārtha Sūtra* ? According to the *kaṣāya* doctrine, it is the negative emotions or passions underlying action which cause karmic particles to adhere to and thus bind the soul. And this seems to be precisely the meaning of a simile employed by Kundakunda at *Samayasāra* 237-241 (= JGM 255-264). There, it is said of a man with an oil-smeared body, who is performing martial exercises in a dusty place and doing damage to the surrounding foliage, that the real (*niścayataḥ*) cause of the dust sticking to his body is the oil, not his bodily activity. In the same way, a wrong believer engaged in activity, who has *rāga*, etc., as his *upayoga*, is smeared by karmic dust (*rajasā*) [241 = JGM 259]. On the other hand, when a man performs exercises with a body which is oil-free, whatever the physical destruction he causes, no dust sticks to him. Similarly, a right-believer, even though he is engaged in various activities, is not smeared by karmic dust because of the absence of *rāga*, etc., as his *upayoga* [246 = JGM 264].

Chronologically, however, this passage evidently belongs to an early layer of the *Samayasāra*, given its emphasis on the suppression of passion rather than on *jñāna* as the means to liberation. And considering the broader context, it becomes clear that Kundakunda's other teachings have entailed significant modifications to the *kaṣāya* doctrine.

At one level a temporary accommodation of the *kaṣāya* and *jñāna* doctrines is possible: the necessity of controlling the passions is recognised but the means to achieving that control is through knowledge of the true state of the *jīva* - its fundamental isolation. This leads to the realisation that the desire for a relationship between the self and anything else is bound to be frustrated, and thus to the abandonment of *rāga*, etc. This accommodation can only be temporary, however, since such a formulation itself contains the doctrinal basis of Kundakunda's second *niścaya* pattern - the physical isolation of the self from all matter. Thus, karma and the self being totally separate and incompatible, the idea that the self is or can be bound, even by passionate behaviour, is itself a delusion. From this perspective the *kaṣāya* doctrine is intrinsically false.

This illustrates very well the fact that the diverse nature of the material collected in the *Samayasāra* leads to an ambiguity in the meaning of some individual gāthās which can only be partially resolved by examining them in their immediate context. To take a further example, gāthā 247 (= JGM 265), apparently continuing the passage I have summarised above (*Samayasāra* 237-246), reads:

> He who thinks 'I kill' [√*hiṃs*] and 'I am killed by other beings' is deluded and ignorant; but the knower is opposed to (i.e. knows other than) this.

Taken as it stands, this seems to belong to the second *niścaya* pattern - i.e. the self is neither an agent nor a patient but simply a knower. In other words, in so far as they both stress the absolute isolation of individual souls, the difference between this and the Sāṃkhya view, expressed famously in the *Bhagavadgītā* (quoting *Kaṭha Upaniṣad* 2:19-20), is nominal. The *Bhagavadgītā* verse - almost certainly the formal model for Kundakunda's gāthā - states that:

> He who thinks that it (i.e. the *puruṣa*) kills and he who thinks that it is killed, neither of them understands; this neither kills nor is killed.[25]

However, the next gāthā of the *Samayasāra* (248 = JGM 266), which immediately ties the connection between death and karma, makes it clear that there is to be no overt abandonment (i.e. transcendence) of ethics. Action is not about to lose its moral significance, and there can, of course, be no karma-transcending theological solution. In context, therefore, gāthā 247 means that what one apparently does or what one has done to one is exclusively the result of one's own karma. Specifically, an individual's death is determined by the expiry of his *āyus*- or age-determining karma.[26] Moreover, according to Jaina doctrine a person's *āyuṣ-karma* (i.e. his longevity) in this life is fixed definitively at some moment during the last third of his *previous* life.[27] In these circumstances, the belief that you are really instrumental in killing others or that they can be really instrumental in killing you is a delusion. The moment of your death has been fixed by karma long before you were (re)born.

More generally (and moving away from the difficulties posed by this quasi-fatalistic doctrine), what happens to individuals is determined solely by their own actions; each is entirely responsible for his or her own karma.[28] And it is precisely the deluded belief that one can affect or be affected by others which causes one to be bound by *puṇya*

---

[25] *ya enaṃ vetti hantāraṃ yaś cainaṃ manyate hatam* |
ubhau tau na vijānīto nāyaṃ hanti na hanyate || *Bhagavad Gītā* 2:19 ||

[26] *Samayasāra* 248-252 = JGM 266-270.

[27] See *JPP* p. 126. The strong element of fatalism in this has been discussed by P.S. Jaini (1977).

[28] See *Samayasāra* 253ff. = JGM 271ff.

and *pāpa* karma.[29] (This does not undercut the ethical imperative of *ahiṃsā* because, as we have seen,[30] it is combined with the idea that the determination (*adhyavasāna*) to kill is enough to bind one [*Samayasāra* 262, etc.]. It does, however, make accidental *hiṃsā* non-binding.)

To summarize, the distance between Jainism and Sāṃkhya is maintained in orthodox Jaina doctrine (in Umāsvāti, for instance) by the connection between the self and karma. For, at some level, according to the orthodox position, there can be a real relation between the soul and karma, between self and not-self. (Such a conjunction of *puruṣa* and *prakṛti* is, of course, an ontological impossibility for the Sāṃkhya.) However, when that connection is abandoned as being ultimately untrue (which is the contention of Kundakunda's second *niścaya* pattern), then the gap between the Jaina and Sāṃkhya positions closes. And the verses on karma we have just considered are undercut by statements such as:

> Thus the right-believer knows the self, whose own-nature (*svabhāva*) is to be a knower; knowing reality (*tattva*), he renounces both the arising and fruition of karma. (*Samayasāra* 200 [= JGM 212])

In other words, the right-believer realises that karma and the *bhāva*s it produces have, in reality, nothing to do with his self, so he rejects them. Then, he is instructed:

> Having given up the impermanent substances (*dravya*) and modes of thought (*bhāva*) in the self, grasp this, your eternal, permanent, single *bhāva*, realizable through / as your own-nature (*svabhāva*). (*Samayasāra* 203 [= JGM 219])[31]

---

29 *Samayasāra* 259-261 = JGM 277-279.

30 See p. 272ff., above.

31 Cf. 297-299 = JGM 325-327, quoted p. 284, above.

Negatively, therefore, renunciation is the rejection of delusion and wrong attitude (i.e. of alien *bhāvas*); positively, it is the realisation of the true nature of self, of *svabhāva*.

Once again, if all the doctrinal elements examined above are directly juxtaposed (i.e. if they are viewed synchronically rather than diachronically) then they are clearly incompatible. *The self is not an actor; it is karma which is the real agent. But in reality karma does not and cannot have any effect on the self; therefore, not only is any action by the self a delusion but so too is bondage. That is what one must realise in order to attain liberation.* Clearly this threatens both the ethical basis of Jainism and the ascetic practice of physical *ahiṃsā* derived from it. In conclusion, therefore, I shall examine the *Samayasāra*'s final verses, which attempt to deal with this question of the significance of ascetic and lay practice.

9.2 *Liṅga, practice and the path to liberation*

The *Samayasāra* concludes with the following eight gāthās:

> The deluded, having assumed the characteristic marks of ascetics (*pāsaṃḍiya*) or householders, which are of many kinds, say: 'This characteristic mark is the path to liberation'. (408)
> A characteristic mark is certainly not the path to liberation; in that the Arhats who are indifferent to the body, having given up distinguishing characteristics, devote themselves to insight, knowledge and conduct. (409)
> The characteristic marks belonging to ascetics and householders are not this path to liberation. The Jinas say that insight, knowledge and conduct are the path to liberation. (410)
> Wherefore, giving up the marks adopted by householders or ascetics, draw the self onto the path to liberation, which consists of insight, knowledge and conduct. (411)
> Establish the self on the path to liberation, (know it,) meditate on it,

and always dwell there; do not dwell among other substances. (412)

The essential self is not known by those who are attached to the various kinds of ascetic or householder characteristic marks. (413)

Although the conventional view holds that there are two (kinds of marks) on the path to liberation, by the absolute view one does not wish for any marks on the path to liberation. (414)

That conscious being who, having read this *Samayaprābhṛta* and understood its true meaning, holds to that meaning, will attain the highest bliss. (415)

In our examination of *Pravacanasāra* 3:5 and 3:6,[32] we saw that the end of rebirth, and thus the attainment of liberation, is brought about by the adoption of certain pure modes of thought and behaviour. It is these which constitute the defining characteristic (*liṅga*) of the Jain. We also noted that, although Amṛtacandra splits *liṅga* into two categories, the external (*bahir*) and the internal (*antara*),[33] in social terms there can only really be one set of *liṅga*, the external, since an individual's internal state can only be demonstrated and evaluated through his external behaviour. With that in mind, it becomes clear that when both Amṛtacandra and Jayasena, in their commentaries on this concluding passage from the *Samayasāra*, say that the *liṅga* being referred to are simply *dravyaliṅga*, they do little to temper the radical social implications of Kundakunda's total abandonment of *liṅga*.[34]

The first question to be asked of the *Samayasāra* passage quoted above is who is being referred to by the term *pāsaṃḍiya* [408 = JGM 438], Jaina or non-Jaina ascetics? According to Monier-Williams, *pāṣaṇḍa* is a

---

[32] See pp. 217-222, above.

[33] See p. 219.

[34] Jayasena makes the distinction between *bhāva* and *dravya liṅga*, i.e. what belongs to the self and what does not, and perhaps also with the sense of 'internal' and 'external' - see *Tātparyavṛttiḥ* on JGM 438 and 439.

'heretic'; that is to say, for Hindus it is 'one who falsely assumes the characteristics of an orthodox Hindu' (i.e. a Jaina, a Buddhist, etc.). On first consideration therefore, this would seem to be a term of denigration referring to non-Jaina ascetics (or even to non-Jains in general). Gāthā 411 (= JGM 441), however, uses *anagāra* (literally, 'homeless', and so mendicant or ascetic) as a synonym for *pāsaṃḍiya*, and *anagāra* is a standard term for a Jaina ascetic. This may be an example of older verses taking on new meanings in a new context, for gāthā 409 (439) makes it clear that *all liṅga* are to be abandoned. In other words, the *Samayasāra* is not simply making a distinction here between Jaina ascetics and everybody else (perhaps the original meaning of 408 [438]), but between everybody else (lay people and ascetics) and those who have attained *kevala-jñāna*, the Arhats (see 409 [439], above). This is supported by the *Ātmakhyāti* on 414 (444) which refers to two kinds of *dravyaliṅga*, divided between Jaina ascetics and their lay followers,[35] both of which are *vyavahāra* views and to be abandoned in favour of the *liṅga*-less *niścaya* view which is the ultimate truth (*paramārtha*) (see 414 [444] and *Ātmakhyāti*).

Crucially, the purpose of this passage is not primarily descriptive but injunctive: those addressed are likewise enjoined to give up all *liṅga* (i.e. attachment to *liṅga*) and thus attain liberation. But who are those addressed? Clearly, they are advanced ascetics who are being urged on by Kundakunda to arhatship, *kevala-jñāna* and liberation. They are linked by gāthā 414 (= JGM 444) with the *niścaya* view, i.e. the view that the self in its *svabhāva* cannot be touched by matter and therefore cannot be bound. So even attachment to ascetic conduct is classified as the product of a *vyavahāra* view and does not lead one to the highest religious goal. Only self-knowledge - self-realisation - can do that.

---

[35] *śramaṇaśramaṇopāsakabhedena dvividhaṃ dravyaliṅgaṃ* - *Ātmakhyāti* on *Samayasāra* 414 (444).

To expand on this: the essential self (*samayasāra*) cannot be realised by those who identify with any *liṅga* whatsoever (413 = JGM 443), but it is realised by those who devote themselves to *darśana*, *jñāna* and *cāritra*, which constitute the path to liberation (409 = JGM 411). The vocabulary here is that of the orthodox definition of what comprises the *mokṣamārga*, given by Umāsvāti at the beginning of his *Tattvārtha Sūtra*.[36] The meaning though carries a substantially different weight; for Kundakunda, as we have seen, has redefined the *ratnatraya* in terms of self-knowledge: in reality there are no such things as faith (insight), knowledge and conduct, there is just the pure knower.[37] So when he enjoins devotion to faith, knowledge and conduct as the means to liberation (409, etc.), it is understood that this means self-devotion, i.e. concentration and meditation on the self (412). As the *Ātmakhyāti* on Sam. 410 (= JGM 440) puts it:

> (Attachment to) *dravyaliṅga* is not the path to liberation because, in being dependent on the (material) body it is (attachment to) other substance (*paradravya*). Therefore, it is faith, knowledge and conduct which are the path to liberation, because in being dependent upon the *ātman* they are one's own substance.[38]

What appears to be a punning allusion to *vihāra* in gāthā 412 (= JGM 442) makes the internalisation clear: it is the self which is the true *vihāra*, the real monastery, temple and sacrificial enclosure. Prākrit *vihara* could be either *vihāra* or *vihara* (*vi √hṛ*) in Sanskrit. The allusion may be intentional; Monier-Williams gives *vihāra* as a word for a Jain monastery or temple, but the term does not seem to have been widely used by the Jains themselves at this

---

36 *samyagdarśanajñānacāritrāṇi mokṣamārgaḥ* - *TS* 1:1

37 *Samayasāra* 16 (=18) - see pp. 234-235, above; cf. pp. 279ff.

38 *na khalu dravyaliṅgaṃ mokṣamārgaḥ śarīrāśritatve sati paradravyatvāt | tasmād darśanajñānacāritrāṇy eva mokṣamārgaḥ ātmāśritatve sati svadravyatvāt* - *Ātmakhyāti* on JGM 440.

period, so perhaps the main target here is the Buddhists. The meaning, however, is clear: it is the self alone which constitutes the path to liberation; attachment to external conduct is attachment to what is alien to the self and soteriologically counter-productive.

The essential question now arises: does this mean that the seeker after *kevala-jñāna* should actually abandon the forms of Jaina ascetic life to concentrate undistractedly on the self? That would be radical indeed, going well beyond the statement of *Samayasāra* 152-153 (quoted pp. 279-280, above) that *tapas*, etc., are useless without self-realisation, and taking Kundakunda's perception that ultimately *only* self-realisation or meditation on the self is soteriologically effective to a logical if not necessary conclusion. The key, however, seems to be that it is *attachment* to *liṅga* that is to be abandoned, not *liṅga* itself.[39] It is reification that is to be avoided, and the promotion of form over underlying significance. In other words, the ascetic can obtain freedom from *liṅga* through internal discipline, the cultivation of an attitude, without having to make external changes. Thus, although internalisation or concentration on the self makes external practice largely irrelevant, the fact that its full logic is not developed until the ascetic is close to *kevala-jñāna* preserves the formal structure of monastic life.

This emphasis on attachment to the thing rather than the thing itself helps us to understand what, at first sight, appear to be the two most radical, not to say antinomian, gāthās in the *Samayasāra*, namely, 306 and 307 (= JGM 334 and 335):

> Repentance, pursuit of the good, rejection of evil etc., concentration, non-attachment to external objects, self-censure, confession of faults, purification (by expiation) - this is the eightfold pot of poison. (306)
> Non-repentance, non-pursuit of the good, non-rejection of evil etc.,

---

[39] See *Samayasāra* 413 = JGM 443.

non-concentration, non-abstinence from attachment to external objects, non-self-censure, non-confession of faults, non-purification - this is the pot of nectar. (307)

Clearly this eightfold list (306) constitutes a description of the conduct expected of the good ascetic. Although in this form it does not correspond exactly to any formula that I can discover, each of its elements must have been part of monastic practice from an early date.[40]

What then can be meant by, for instance, describing the practice of *pratisaraṇa* (glossed by Jayasena as 'the turning towards qualities such as 'right belief')[41] as 'the pot of poison' and its non-performance as 'the pot of nectar'?

The modern commentator, J.L. Jaini,[42] explains that, although all eight practices are commendable for ascetics,

> for one who is bent solely on the realisation of the self, they are hindrances, and therefore like poison, because they produce bondage of good karmas which keep the soul in Samsara, and stand in the way of its self-realisation.[43]

He then goes on to state that the practice of self-absorption

---

40 In my translation of this list I have followed Jayasena's *Tātparyavṛttiḥ* on JGM 334-335. On *pratikramaṇa* as 'ritualized confession', see *JPP* p. 349; see also Schubring para. 159. According to the *TS* (9:22) *pratikramaṇa* comes under *prāyaścitta* (repentance), which itself is one of the subdivisions of internal *tapas*. Kundakunda's *Niyamasāra* states that meditation (*jhāṇa* / *dhyāna*) on the self constitutes the repentance of all transgressions (*pratikramaṇa*). See also *Niyamasāra* 83-91. On *parihāra*, see Schubring para. 161, and *TS* 9:22, where it occurs in the technical sense of expulsion from the order; cf. Bhargava pp. 185, 189-190. On *dhāraṇā*, see Schubring para. 72; it is also given at *TS* 1:15 as one of the four divisions of sensory knowledge. On *nindā*, see Schubring para. 160. On *pratikramaṇa*, *nindā* and *garhā*, see Bhargava p.169.

41 *samyaktvādiguṇeṣu preraṇaṃ* - *Tātparyavṛtti* on *Samayasāra* 306 [= JGM 334].

42 On *Samayasāra* 306 (= JGM 334, and 327 in Jaini's SBJ ed.)

43 p. 174, SBJ ed.

is 'to remove the perverse belief that practical conduct of saints, i.e. repentance, etc., will lead to Liberation from bondage of karmas'.[44] In other words, these gāthās describe an attitude to be adopted by those on the verge of pure knowledge and liberation; and they are articulated in a way which is probably designed to shock ascetics out of attachment to those elements of their religious life which they hold most dear. (In this respect these gāthās are perhaps comparable in method to the *kōans* of Ch'an Buddhism.) Moreover, the eight practices given at *Samayasāra* 306 are connected with lapses from perfect monastic conduct: the need for them implies lack of perfection on the part of the ascetic. Similarly, when they are not needed it is because perfection has been attained. (And once again ontology and epistemology do their dance: the state of perfection, where prescribed ascetic practices are transcended, is finally achieved by non-attachment to - i.e. by transcendence of - precisely such practices.)

Another modern commentator, Chakravarti, takes these gāthās to be descriptive (i.e. broadly philosophical) rather than prescriptive (religious) in tenor; he sees them as representing the perspective of the already purified 'transcendental Self', beyond good and evil, for whom the question of discipline or non-discipline is quite meaningless. For Chakravarti, the term *apratikramaṇa* does not imply the mere opposite of *pratikramaṇa* (which would imply the removal of discipline and giving full reign to the impure emotions), rather the negative prefix (*a*-) 'must be taken to signify the absence of necessity to practise the discipline'.[45] For the self absorbed in its own pure nature impure psychic states are brought to a stop, so it is unnecessary to practise the various kinds of discipline.[46]

This interpretation saves him from the potentially

---

[44] Ibid.

[45] p.190, Chakravarti's ed. of *Samayasāra*.

[46] See ibid. pp. 189-190.

embarrassing concession that it is possible, even necessary, to give up orthodox ascetic practices short of actual liberation. The purpose of the *Samayasāra*, however, is religious; and both here (*Samayasāra* 306 and 307) and in the concluding gāthās (408-415) the intention is clearly to engender an attitude of total non-attachment in the listener. Indeed, in the very last verse (415) it is stressed that those who understand and hold to the true meaning will, for those very reasons, attain the highest bliss. This implied devaluation of actual ascetic practice - from the highest perspective (the second *niścaya* view) it too is a hindrance to liberation - obviously has the potential to threaten that conduct which is the defining basis of Jaina religion. (In soteriological matters the inessential quickly becomes the irrelevant: what is no longer *essential* for liberation becomes a hindrance to be abandoned.)

It is little wonder, therefore, that the *Samayasāra* was at one time considered a text 'too sacred to be read by householders'.[47] Upadhye states that 'the spiritual statements from Niścaya-naya may prove socially and ethically harmful to the house-holders who are almost absolutely lacking in spiritual discipline'.[48] But it is also clear that, unless tempered by other instruction, such teachings must have also posed a threat to ascetic behaviour. The full extent of that threat perhaps only becomes apparent in such Apabhraṃśa works as Yogīndu's *Paramātmaprakāśa* (c. 900 C.E.?), and research is clearly required in that field before the limits of Jaina orthodoxy can be accurately defined.

In the works attributed to Kundakunda, and in the *Samayasāra* in particular, a point of maximum tension is reached between soteriological theory and social necessity, between the inner state and the outer discipline, between *ātman* and *liṅga*. But by the time of Yogīndu, the connection seems to have snapped for some, and orthodoxy

---

47 Upadhye p. xlvii.

48 Ibid.

(i.e. external religious practice) has been largely abandoned; for others, ascetic practice retains its dominance as the emblem and preserver of Jaina identity. The significance of Kundakunda's works is that at one level they point in the direction that was to be taken by Yogīndu while at another they prescribe largely conventional practices. Their eclectic nature entails internal contradictions, but it is these very contradictions which give commentators scope to temper the full (heretical) implications of the *niścaya* strand in Kundakunda's thought. Thus it is ensured that, in practice, the threat to Jaina conduct and social identity is circumscribed and remains latent rather than actual.

9.3 *Liberation according to Kundakunda: some conclusions*

As we have seen, in Kundakunda's soteriological theory liberation is a matter of knowledge (*jñāna*), of realisation of the true nature of the self through meditation. But in Digambara as in Śvetāmbara practice it remains a matter of largely external asceticism, the maintenance of (physical) *ahiṃsā*. This is because it is external practice that distinguishes 'Jainism' as a religious tradition. Whatever the philosophical rationale for doing so, such practices cannot be abandoned without threatening the Jaina's sense of identity. Jainism's life crisis rituals, which strictly speaking are irrelevant to soteriology, are largely taken from Hindu models;[49] its doctrines, if taken to their logical conclusions (as they sometimes are by Kundakunda), become so internalised and karma is so dematerialised that the dividing line between such doctrines and those, for instance, of Sāṃkhya and Vedānta becomes attenuated to the point of non-existence (except for a few, logically arbitrary points). It becomes crucial, therefore, to retain at some level the reality of the connection between the soul

---

49 See *JPP* pp. 291-304; R. Williams 1963, pp. 274-287; Sangave pp. 243-252, 381.

and physical *karman*, and so keep *tapas* as the primary means to liberation, otherwise the link with tradition is broken and the monk's discipline pointless. It is the logicians or scholastics, obliged to express themselves in broadly philosophical terms, who are confronted by the full force of this problem.[50]

Jaina doctrines and ascetic practices were originally formulated in the context of physicalist or materialist ideas, probably including the notion of a material or quasi-material soul. Later, the soul is conceived of as fundamentally immaterial, but the means of bondage (*karṁan*) remains unambiguously material. The logical tensions which arise from this juxtaposition of the material and the non- material are stripped bare at times of dispute and philosophical 'system-building'. The scholastics have to retain the tradition, embodied in the practices of the ascetic, and at the same time provide a justification or doctrinal rationale for such behaviour. They also have to deal with the accumulated and accumulating rationalisation and internalisation of doctrine, derived ultimately from the contradiction between the material and immaterial at the heart of that teaching. Such a contradiction invites extreme solutions. But given prevailing Indian beliefs about the nature of the soul, and the inherent tendency of doctrines to become more rather than less sophisticated - to move from ethics to metaphysics - a return to the idea of a material soul was unlikely. In addition, there were other, perhaps more important reasons why the movement should have been towards greater and greater internalisation, since, at

---

[50] By logicians or scholastics I mean fifth century (?) writers such as Siddhasena and Samantabhadra (see *JPP* p. 83ff.) and those who followed them. For a list of such writers and summaries of their main works through to the seventeenth century, see Dixit 1971, pp. 88-164. Dixit characterises this period as the 'Age of Logic'. Undoubtedly, some of the works attributed to Kundakunda were at least compiled in this period (Dixit includes him in his list), but in terms of content they are far less orthodox, as Dixit himself points out when he refers to the *Samayasāra* (see pp. 93-94, 132-135).

least on the surface, this strategy provides the 'easier' or graded route to liberation, and, as we have seen, lowers the soteriological ladder into the territory of the laity. However, as has been made clear, to take this process to its logical conclusion threatens to disintegrate the tradition, and with it 'Jaina' identity. The scholastics, therefore, have to maintain the tension without falling into either camp (the real danger, of course, being from the kind of total internalisation, with its attendant 'dematerialisation' of *karman*, which Kundakunda approaches in parts of the *Samayasāra*). Given this, I would suggest that a major reason for the peculiar content and form of what is technically considered to be 'Jaina philosophy' - *syādvāda*, *anekāntavāda*, and the (orthodox) *naya* doctrine - is precisely the need to retain a raison d' être for the ascetic practices which constitute Jaina identity in the face of a progressive tendency to rationalise and internalise doctrinal formulations.

In the works ascribed to Kundakunda, however, internalisation threatens at times to break the controls imposed by Jaina philosophy. If the 'orthodox' *naya* doctrine allows neo-Vedāntic teachings to be propagated (at one level) without precipitating a collapse into the vacuum created by the implications of a non-material soul doctrine, Kundakunda's heterodox reading of the *niścaya-vyavahāra* distinction (in the *Samayasāra*) removes that philosophic restraint. By doing so it provides a glimpse of the full, 'heretical' implications for Jaina practice and doctrine of radical internalisation deriving from the conviction that the soul really has no connection with matter whatsoever. For the predominant view in Kundakunda is that what counts soteriologically is what happens internally, in consciousness. Instrumental in this are *upayoga* (in the *Pravacanasāra*) and *bhāva* (in the *Samayasāra*); stress thus falls on meditation (*dhyāna*) leading to realisation (*jñāna*) of the self's total separation from matter - indeed, the pure self is defined in both the *Pravacanasāra* and the *Samayasāra as* (such) knowledge - rather than on the practice of *tapas*. Consequently, *cāritra* comes to be seen in terms of 'attitude' rather than physical action / inaction.

For ascetics, *hiṃsā* is redefined as harm caused (internally) to the *self* through neglect of or offence against the monastic rules. This is significant for two paradoxical, although ultimately complementary reasons. On the one hand, it permits the 'formalisation' or 'ritualisation' of the monks' conduct: that is to say, it is now fulfilment of the role, not behaviour as such, that counts, for by following the prescribed rules the desired end will inevitably be achieved. On the other hand, it opens the way for *intention* to become the the chief instrument of bondage and liberation. To put it differently, *hiṃsā* is only *hiṃsā* if it is intended; but, by definition, as long as one's behaviour accords with the rules laid down for ascetics then *hiṃsā* cannot be intended. Therefore, as the texts remark, there can be no *hiṃsā* for proper ascetics regardless of the harm done to living creatures. When this formulation is combined with Kundakunda's *upayoga* doctrine - and to some extent the former clears the way for the latter - then, from that internalised perspective, it becomes clear that it is impure consciousness which leads to wrong intention and thus ultimately to violation of the ascetic rules. There can be no violation by accident; transgression has to be preceded by intention, and thus by impure consciousness. So *aśuddhopayoga* is at the root of all *hiṃsā*, and all *hiṃsā* is *hiṃsā* to one's self.

Seen from this perspective, external, physical behaviour in the world is essentially irrelevant to soteriology: bondage and liberation begin and end with consciousness, external conduct is merely the outward sign of an inner state. Thus on the one hand there is the belief that simply by following the external rules to the letter one will achieve the religious goal, and on the other there is the belief that the only soteriologically significant behaviour is that which brings about inner purity. But by asserting that if the monk is following his rules exactly then ipso facto he must be internally pure, one brings about a meeting or balance between the extremes of total internalisation and total externalisation; one becomes a reflex of the other, and depending upon which component is given causal preference or emphasised, the external or the internal, a different view is obtained of the institution of renunciation.

We may call these views the 'social' and the 'personal'; the former is to do with questions of Jaina identity (for the Jains themselves, and therefore necessarily vis à vis the wider community), the latter is a question of personal soteriology for individuals (*śramaṇas* and advanced laity). In Kundakunda and his commentators, when the question is raised of why one should go on with physical asceticism when everything of soteriological significance is internal, a matter of realisation, the reply is that one should continue to behave in the prescribed ways because they provide an outward sign of inner purity. Philosophically this is less than compelling, but it is a line of argument with an underlying social imperative; for, as we have seen, what distinguishes Jainism as a religious tradition is the behaviour of its ascetics. So to behave in such a way is not merely the external sign of an ideal Jaina religious, it is actually to embody and perpetuate the unique socio-religious identity of the Jaina community. From the point of view of the laity, therefore, the function of the ascetic is to provide them with a symbol or emblem of their own tradition, one which it is essential to preserve. And this is probably the underlying motivation for the laity's diligence in ensuring that the *śramaṇas* perform their ascetic practices to the letter.[51] (The ascetic also, of course, provides the laity with a constant reminder of the soteriological ideal towards which they may more or less urgently aspire.)

This is the 'social' view of renunciation which I have connected with external ascetic behaviour. The 'personal' view I see as being concerned with internal transformation and gnosis, as exemplified in the teachings of Kundakunda,

---

51 See *JPP* p. 208.

i.e. with soteriology. These two views do not necessarily coincide with the further distinction between the views of the laity and those of the *śramaṇas* themselves. It is clear that both originally and throughout most of Jaina history the soteriological emphasis for ascetics and advanced lay followers falls upon external practice. Thus internal practices may be taken on as extra *vrata*, or because the correct internal attitude is required before external practice is effective, but they do not replace external *tapas*. One may surmise that for the majority of ascetics the practical implication of the internalisation of doctrine - viz. liberation through self-realisation - itself remained an ideal, to be achieved or even attempted only by the most advanced *śramaṇas* . Most hoped to approach liberation and attain at least a better rebirth by following the rules for ascetics to the letter (from the 'social' view their proper role), a formidably difficult undertaking even in its ritualised form.

There are indications in the texts that this process of ritualisation started at a relatively early date.[52] From one perspective this may be seen as a quest for greater autonomy on the part of the renouncers, the need for their soteriological progress to be in their own hands and less subject to the fortuitous and accidental. The drive towards greater and greater control over the process of one's own liberation is probably also one of the contributory reasons for a progressive internalisation of practice. Furthermore, it may be remarked that through 'ritualising' external behaviour the way is cleared for a greater concentration on obtaining inner purity. For simply by following the rules the monk's external considerations are taken care of; he does not have to 'think' about his behaviour, and so his consciousness can be engaged elsewhere, in the realisation

---

[52] E.g. in *Viyāhapannatti*, *Sarvārthasiddhi* and in Book 3 of the *Pravacanasāra*, parts of which are probably derived from older material.

of his own inner nature or self. And it may be that the doctrines expounded by Kundakunda were in part intended as an antidote to excessive 'ritualisation', a reformation through radical internalisation, emphasising that it is not the external form that counts but the internal transformation of consciousness. Such a reading is borne out by the fact that this teaching was aimed specifically at *śramaṇas*, i.e. at those who had to some extent already mastered the external forms.

We can see from the above that, although doctrines such as Kundakunda's undercut external asceticism at a theoretical level to the extent that the rationale for such asceticism becomes slender, there are overriding social reasons which ensure the retention of traditional practice. For it is the practice of ascetics which carries the tradition and which provides the Jainas with their socio-religious identity. With the acknowledged loss of most of their original canon, such ascetic practice is thus a particularly important vehicle for the Digambaras. Consequently, although Kundakunda is acknowledged and revered as being virtually the initiator or compiler of their 'new' scriptural and doctrinal tradition, the implications of his less orthodox teachings are not permitted to destabilise or threaten established ascetic practice; for the tradition that provides the Digambaras with their identity is already in place, embodied in that same ascetic practice, in the behaviour and monastic rules of the *śramaṇas* themselves. So while *śuddhopayoga* or the pure self may become the inner emblem or ideal of the aspiring ascetic, it does not replace or negate the outer emblem of ascetic practice. The new philosophical and doctrinal reasons for this retention may be weak but the social or communal reasons are stronger.

In addition, it should be remembered that the spiritually advanced laity also undertake numerous ascetic practices, so they too carry the tradition. Thus although internalisation of doctrine gives them a foothold on the soteriological ladder, the actual ascent requires external practice, with the full 'logic' of internalisation coming to the fore only for those to whom external ascetic practice is already second nature. To put it another way, it may be the case that external practice itself represents the path to inner purity for the laity and less advanced ascetics, while for the ideal ascetic it is merely the outer sign of an already achieved inner state. In this fashion the recurrent ambiguity of ritual is demonstrated, for the question of whether it is instrumental or expressive is not answered: it is simply ambiguous.

Table

						krodha (anger) *māna* (pride) *māyā* (deceitfulness) *lobha* (greed)
				oneself	**due to**	
		bodily activity	**can be done by**	one's agent	**due to**	**ibid**
				others with one's approval	**due to**	**ibid**
saṃrambha (impulsion / determination to do violence)	**can be done by the 3 *yogas***	speech activity	**can be done by**	**ibid**		
		mind activity	**can be done by**	**ibid**		
samārambha (collecting means / preparation to do violence)	**can be done by the 3 *yogas***					
			ETC.			
ārambha (actually undertaking violence / commencement of violence)	**can be done by the 3 *yogas***					

[= 108 ways in which a *jīva* is counted as the *adhikaraṇa* of *āsrava* - i.e. 108 ways in which the *jīva* can cause injury]

Appendix 1

Niyamasāra

18

kattā bhottā ādā poggalakammassa hodi vavahāro |
kammajabhāveṇādā kattā bhottā du ṇicchayado ||

103

jaṃ kiṃci me duccarittaṃ savvaṃ tiviheṇa vosare |
sāmāīyaṃ tu tivihaṃ karemi savvaṃ ṇirāyāraṃ ||

104

sammaṃ me savvabhūdesu veraṃ majjhaṃ na keṇavi |
āsāe vosarittāṇaṃ samāhi paḍivajjae ||

133

jo du dhammaṃ ca sukkaṃ ca jhāṇaṃ jhāedi ṇiccasā |
tassa sāmāigam ṭhāī idi kevalisāsaṇe ||

159 (SBJ 158)

jāṇadi passadi savvaṃ vavahāraṇaeṇa kevalī bhagavaṃ |
kevalaṇāṇī jāṇadi passadi ṇiyameṇa appāṇaṃ ||

Appendix 2

Pañcāstikāya

115

sammattaṃ saddahaṇaṃ bhāvāṇaṃ tesim adhigamo ṇāṇaṃ |
cārittaṃ samabhāvo visayesu virūḍhamaggāṇaṃ ||

147 (SBJ 154)

jaṃ suhamasuham udiṇṇaṃ bhāvaṃ ratto karedi jadi appā |
so teṇa havadi baṃdho poggalakammeṇa viviheṇa ||

148 (SBJ 155)

jogaṇimittaṃ gahaṇaṃ jogo maṇavayaṇakāyasaṃbhūdo |
bhāvaṇimitto baṃdho bhāvo radirāgadosamohajudo ||

162

jīvo sahāvaṇiyado aṇiyadaguṇapajjao dha parasamao |
jadi kuṇadi sagaṃ samayaṃ pabbhassadi kammabaṃdhādo ||

Appendix 3

Pravacanasāra

1:7

cārittaṃ khalu dhammo dhammo jo so samo tti ṇiddiṭṭho |
mohakkhohavihīṇo pariṇāmo appaṇo hu samo ||

1:9

jīvo pariṇamadi jadā suheṇa asuheṇa vā suho asuho |
suddheṇa tadā suddho havadi hi pariṇāmasabbhāvo ||

1:11

dhammeṇa pariṇadappā appā jadi suddhasaṃpayogajudo |
pāvadi ṇivvāṇasuhaṃ suhovajutto va saggasuhaṃ ||

1:23

ādā ṇāṇapamāṇaṃ ṇāṇaṃ ṇeyappamāṇaṃ uddiṭṭhaṃ |
ṇeyaṃ loyāloyaṃ tamhā ṇāṇaṃ tu savvagayaṃ ||

1:26

savvagado jiṇavasaho savve vi ya taggayā jagadi aṭṭhā |
ṇāṇamayādo ya jiṇo visayādo tassa te bhaṇiyā ||

1:27

ṇāṇaṃ appa tti madaṃ vaṭṭadi ṇāṇaṃ viṇā ṇa appāṇaṃ |
tamhā ṇāṇaṃ appā appā ṇāṇaṃ va aṇṇaṃ vā ||

1:29

ṇa paviṭṭho nāviṭṭho ṇāṇī ṇeyesu rūvam iva cakkhū |
jāṇadi passadi ṇiyadaṃ akkhātīdo jagam asesaṃ ||

Upadhye takes *ṇa paviṭṭho nāviṭṭho* as Sanskrit. *na praviṣṭaḥ na āviṣṭaḥ*, as against the commentators who take *na aviṣṭaḥ (na apraviṣṭaḥ)* - see his fn. 2, p. 4.

1:30

rayaṇam iha iṃdaṇīlaṃ duddhajjhasiyaṃ jahā sabhāsāe |
abhibhūya taṃpi duddhaṃ vaṭṭadi taha ṇāṇam atthesu ||

1:32

geṇhadi ṇeva ṇa muṃcadi ṇa paraṃ pariṇamadi kevalī bhagavaṃ |
pecchadi samaṃtado so jāṇadi savvaṃ ṇiravasesaṃ ||

1:35

jo jāṇadi so ṇāṇaṃ ṇa havadi ṇāṇeṇa jāṇago ādā |
ṇāṇaṃ pariṇamadi sayaṃ aṭṭhā ṇāṇaṭṭhiyā savve ||

1:43

udayagadā kammaṃsā jiṇavaravasahehiṃ ṇiyadiṇā bhaṇiyā |
tesu vimūḍho ratto duṭṭho vā baṃdham anubhavadi ||

1:46

jadi so suho va asuho ṇa havadi ādā sayaṃ sahāveṇa |
saṃsāro vi ṇa vijjadi savvesiṃ jīvakāyāṇaṃ ||

1:52

ṇa vi pariṇamadi ṇa geṇhadi uppajjadi ṇeva tesu aṭṭhesu |
jāṇaṇṇavi te ādā abaṃdhago teṇa paṇṇatto ||

1:69

devadajadigurupūjāsu ceva dāṇammi vā susīlesu |
uvavāsādisu ratto suhovaogappago appā ||

1:72

ṇaraṇārayatiriyasurā bhajaṃti jadi dehasaṃbhavaṃ dukkhaṃ |
kiha so suho va asuho uvaogo havadi jīvāṇāṃ ||

1:77

ṇa hi maṇṇadi jo evaṃ ṇatthi viseso tti puṇṇapāvāṇaṃ |
hiṃḍadi ghoram apāraṃ saṃsāraṃ mohasaṃchaṇṇo ||

1:78

evaṃ vididattho jo davvesu ṇa rāgam edi dosaṃ vā |
uvaogavisuddho so khavedi dehubbhavaṃ dukkhaṃ ||

1:85

aṭṭhe ajadhāgahaṇaṃ karuṇābhāvo ya maṇuvatiriesu |
visaesu a ppasaṃgo mohassedāṇi liṃgāṇi ||

2:29

ādā kammamalimaso pariṇāmaṃ lahadi kammasaṃjuttaṃ |
tatto silisadi kammaṃ tamhā kammaṃ tu pariṇāmo ||

2:30

pariṇāmo sayam ādā sā puṇa kiriya tti hodi jīvamayā |
kiriyā kamma tti madā tamhā kammassa ṇa du kattā ||

2:58

ādā kammamalimaso dharedi pāṇe puṇo puṇo anne |
ṇa cayadi jāva mamattaṃ dehapadhānesu visayesu ||

2:59

jo iṃdiyādi vijaī bhavīya uvaogam appagaṃ jhādi |
kammehiṃ so ṇa raṃjadi kiha taṃ pāṇā aṇucaraṃti ||

2:63

appā uvaogappā uvaogo ṇāṇadaṃsaṇaṃ bhaṇido |
so vi suho asuho vā uvaogo appaṇo havadi ||

2:64

uvaogo jadi hi suho puṇṇaṃ jīvassa saṃcayaṃ jādi |
asuho va tadhā pāvaṃ tesim abhāve ṇa cayam atthi ||

tadha (line 2) emended to *tadhā*

2:65

jo jāṇādi jiṇiṃde pecchadi siddhe taheva aṇagāre |
jīvesu sāṇukampo uvaogo so suho tassa ||

2:67

asuhovaogarahido suhovajutto ṇa aṇṇadaviyamhi |
hojjaṃ majjhattho 'ham ṇāṇappagam appagaṃ jhāe ||

2:68

ṇāhaṃ deho ṇa maṇo ṇa ceva vāṇī ṇa kāraṇaṃ tesiṃ |
kattā ṇa ṇa kārayidā aṇumaṃtā ṇeva kattīṇaṃ ||

2:80

arasam arūvam agaṃdhaṃ avvattaṃ cedaṇāguṇam asaddaṃ |
jāṇa aliṃgaggahaṇaṃ jīvam aṇiddiṭṭhasaṃṭhāṇaṃ ||

2:81

mutto rūvādiguṇo bajjhadi phāsehiṃ aṇṇamaṇṇehiṃ |
tavvivarīdo appā bajjhadi kidha poggalaṃ kammaṃ ||

2:83

uvaogamao jīvo mujjhadi rajjedi vā padussedi |
pappā vividhe visaye jo hi puṇo tehiṃ saṃbaṃdho ||

2:86

sapadeso so appā tesu padesesu puggalā kāyā |
pavisaṃti jahājoggaṃ ciṭṭhaṃti hi jaṃti bajjhaṃti ||

2:87

ratto baṃdhadi kammaṃ muccadi kammehiṃ rāgarahidappā |
eso baṃdhasamāso jīvāṇāṃ jāṇa ṇicchayado ||

2:88

pariṇāmādo baṃdho pariṇāmo rāgadosamohajudo |
asuho mohapadoso suho va asuho havadi rāgo ||

2:89

suhapariṇāmo puṇṇam asuho pāva tti bhaṇiyam aṇṇesu |
pariṇāmo ṇaṇṇagado dukkhakkhayakāraṇaṃ samaye ||

2:90

bhaṇidā puḍhavippamuhā jīvaṇikāyādha ṭhāvarā ya tasā |
aṇṇā te jīvādo jīvo vi ya tehiṃdo aṇṇo ||

2:91

jo ṇavi jāṇadi evaṃ paramappāṇaṃ sahāvam āsejja |
kīradi ajjhavasāṇaṃ ahaṃ mamedaṃ ti mohādo ||

2:92

kuvvaṃ sabhāvam ādā havadi hi kattā sagassa bhāvassa |
poggaladavvamayānaṃ ṇa du kattā savvabhāvāṇaṃ ||

2:93

geṇhadi ṇeva na muṃcadi karedi na hi poggalāṇi kammāṇi |
jīvo puggalamajjhe vaṭṭaṇṇ avi savvakālesu ||

2:97

eso baṃdhasamāso jīvāṇaṃ ṇicchayeṇa ṇiddiṭṭho |
arahaṃtehiṃ jadīṇaṃ vavahāro aṇṇahā bhaṇido ||

2:98

ṇa cayadi jo du mamattiṃ ahaṃ mamedaṃ ti dehadaviṇesu |
so sāmaṇṇam cattā paḍivaṇṇo hodi ummaggaṃ ||

2:99

ṇāhaṃ homi paresiṃ ṇa me pare santi ṇāṇam aham ekko |
idi jo jhāyadi jhāṇe so appāṇaṃ havadi jhādā ||

2:101

dehā vā daviṇā vā suhadukkhā vādha sattumittajaṇā |
jīvassa ṇa saṃti dhuvā dhuvovaogappago appā ||

2:102

jo evaṃ jāṇittā jhādi paraṃ appagaṃ visuddhappā |
sāgāro 'ṇāgāro khavedi so mohaduggaṃṭhiṃ ||

2:104

jo khavidamohakaluso visayaviratto maṇo ṇirumbhittā |
samavaṭṭhido sahāve so appāṇaṃ havadi jhādā ||

2:108

tamhā taha jāṇittā appāṇaṃ jāṇagaṃ sabhāveṇa |
parivajjāmi mamattiṃ uvaṭṭhido ṇimmamattammi ||

3:5

jadhajādarūvajādaṃ uppāḍidakesamaṃsugaṃ suddhaṃ |
rahidaṃ hiṃsādīdo appaḍikammaṃ havadi liṃgaṃ ||

3:6

mucchāraṃbhavimukkaṃ juttaṃ uvajogajogasuddhīhiṃ |
liṃgaṃ ṇa parāvekkhaṃ apuṇabbhavakāraṇaṃ jeṇhaṃ ||

3:16

apayattā vā cariyā sayaṇāsaṇaṭhāṇacaṃkamādīsu |
samaṇassa savvakāle hiṃsā sā saṃtattiya tti madā ||

3:17

maradu va jiyadu va jīvo ayadācārassa ṇicchidā hiṃsā |
payadassa ṇatthi baṃdho hiṃsāmetteṇa samidassa ||

All editions have *jiyadu*, although the chāyā gives *jīvatu*.

3:17b

uccāliyamhi pāe iriyāsamidassa ṇiggamatthāe |
ābādhejja kuliṃgaṃ marijja taṃ jogam āsejja ||

3:17c

ṇa hi tassa taṇṇimitto baṃdho suhumo ya desido samaye |
mucchā pariggaho cciya ajjhappapamāṇado diṭṭho ||jummaṃ||

3:18

ayadācāro samaṇo chassu vi kāyesu vadhakaro tti mado |
caradi jadaṃ jadi ṇiccaṃ kamalaṃ va jale ṇiruvalevo ||

3:19

havadi va ṇa havadi baṃdho madamhi jīve 'dha kāya-ceṭṭhamhi |
baṃdho dhuvam uvadhīdo idi samaṇā chaḍḍiyā savvaṃ ||

3:20

ṇa hi ṇiravekkho cāgo ṇa havadi bhikkhussa āsayavisuddhī |
avisuddhassa ya citte kahaṃ ṇu kammakkhao vihio ||

3:20c

vatthakkhaṃḍaṃ duddiyabhāyaṇaṃ aṇṇaṃ ca geṇhadi ṇiyadaṃ |
vijjadi pāṇāraṃbho vikkhevo tassa cittammi ||

3:27

jassa aṇesaṇam appā taṃ pi tavo tappaḍicchagā samaṇā |
aṇṇaṃ bhikkhaṃ aṇesaṇam adha te samaṇā aṇāhārā ||

3:45

samaṇā suddhuvajuttā suhovajuttā ya hoṃti samayamhi |
tesu vi suddhuvajuttā aṇāsavā sāsavā sesā ||

3:54

esā pasatthabhūdā samaṇāṇaṃ vā puṇo gharatthāṇaṃ |
cariyā paretti bhaṇidā tāeva paraṃ lahadi sokkhaṃ ||

3:74

suddhassa ya sāmaṇṇaṃ bhaṇiyaṃ suddhassa daṃsaṇaṃ ṇāṇaṃ |
suddhassa ya ṇivvāṇaṃ so cciya siddho ṇamo tassa ||

Appendix 4

Samayasāra

Text compiled from Chakravarti's and JGM editions, following Chakravarti's numbering system unless otherwise stated. The bracketed numerals refer to the *Sanātana Jaina Grantha Mala* (JGM) and, in one instance, the *Sacred Books of the Jainas* (SBJ) equivalents.

2 (2)

jīvo carittadaṃsaṇaṇāṇaṭṭhido taṃ hi sasamayaṃ jāṇa |
poggalakammuvadesaṭṭhidaṃ ca taṃ jāṇa parasamayaṃ ||

3 (3)

eyattaṇicchayagado samao savvattha sundaro loge |
baṃdhakahā eyatte teṇa visaṃvādiṇī hodi ||

7 (7)

vavahāreṇuvadissadi ṇāṇissa carittadaṃsaṇaṃ ṇāṇaṃ |
ṇavi ṇāṇaṃ ṇa carittaṃ ṇa daṃsaṇaṃ jāṇago suddho ||

8 (8)

jaha ṇavi sakkam aṇajjo aṇajjabhāsaṃ viṇā u gāheduṃ |
taha vavahāreṇa viṇā paramatthuvadesaṇam asakkaṃ ||

11 (13)

vavahāro 'bhūdattho bhūdattho desido du suddhaṇao |
bhūdattham assido khalu samādiṭṭhī havadi jīvo ||

11 (JGM only)

ṇāṇamhi bhāvaṇā khalu kādavvā daṃsaṇe caritte ya |
te puṇa tiṇṇi vi ādā tamhā kuṇa bhāvaṇaṃ āde ||

12 (14)

suddho suddhādeso ṇādavvo paramabhāvadarisīhiṃ |
vavahāradesido puṇa je du aparame ṭṭhidā bhāve ||

12 (JGM only)

jo ādabhāvaṇam iṇaṃ ṇiccuvajutto muṇī samācaradi |
so savvadukkhamokkhaṃ pāvadi acireṇa kālena ||

14 (16)

jo passadi appāṇaṃ abaddhapuṭṭhaṃ aṇaṇṇayaṃ ṇiyadaṃ |
avisesam asaṃjuttaṃ taṃ suddhaṇayaṃ viyāṇīhi ||

16 (19)

daṃsaṇaṇāṇacarittāṇi sevidavvāṇi sāhuṇā ṇiccaṃ |
tāṇi puṇa jāṇa tiṇṇi vi appāṇaṃ ceva ṇicchayado ||

19 (22)

kamme ṇokammamhi ya aham idi ahayaṃ ca kamma ṇokammaṃ |
jā esā khalu buddhī appaḍibuddho havadi tāva ||

24 (JGM only)

jaṃ kuṇadi bhāvam ādā kattā so hodi tassa bhāvassa |
ṇicchayado vavahārā poggalakammāṇa kattāraṃ ||

32 (37)

jo mohaṃ tu jiṇittā ṇāṇasahāvādhiyaṃ* muṇadi ādaṃ |
taṃ jidamohaṃ sāhuṃ paramaṭṭhaviyāṇayā viṃti ||

*All editions give *ādhiyam*, which looks doubtful.

34 (39)

ṇāṇaṃ savve bhāve paccakkhādi ya pare tti ṇādūṇa |
tamhā paccakkhāṇaṃ ṇāṇaṃ ṇiyamā muṇedavvaṃ ||

36 (41)

ṇatthi mama ko vi moho bujjhadi uvaoga eva aham ekko |
taṃ mohaṇimmamattaṃ samayassa viyāṇayā viṃti ||

38 (43)

aham ekko khalu suddho daṃsaṇaṇāṇamaio sadārūvī |
ṇavi atthi majjha kiṃcivi aṇṇaṃ paramāṇumittaṃ pi ||

46 (51)

vavahārassa darīsaṇam uvadeso vaṇṇido jiṇavarehiṃ |
jīvā* ede savve ajjhavasāṇādao bhāvā ||

* Although the texts print *jīvā*, nominative, this makes no real sense and should, I suggest, be emended to *jīve*.

71 (76)

jaiyā imeṇa jīveṇa appaṇo āsavāṇa ya taheva |
ṇādaṃ hodi visesaṃtaraṃ tu taiyā ṇa baṃdho se ||

72 (77)

ṇādūṇa āsavāṇaṃ asucittaṃ ca vivarīyabhāvaṃ ca |
dukkhassa kāraṇaṃ ti ya tado ṇiyattiṃ kuṇadi jīvo ||

83 (89)

ṇicchayaṇayassa evaṃ ādā appāṇam eva hi karedi |
vedayadi puṇo taṃ ceva jāṇa attā du attāṇaṃ ||

84 (90)

vavahārassa du ādā poggalakammaṃ karedi aṇeyavihaṃ |
taṃ ceva ya vedayade poggalakammaṃ aṇeyavihaṃ ||

85 (91)

jadi poggalakammam iṇaṃ kuvvadi taṃ ceva vedayadi ādā |
dokiriyāvādittaṃ pasajadi so jiṇāvamadaṃ ||

86 (92)

jamhā du attabhāvaṃ poggalabhāvaṃ ca do vi kuvvaṃti |
teṇa du micchādiṭṭhī dokiriyāvādiṇo honti ||

92 (99)

param appāṇaṃ kuvvadi appāṇaṃ pi ya paraṃ karaṃto so |
aṇṇāṇamao jīvo kammāṇaṃ kārago hodi ||

93 (100)

param appāṇam akuvvī appāṇaṃ pi ya paraṃ akuvvaṃto |
so ṇāṇamao jīvo kammāṇam akārago hodi ||

127 (137)

aṇṇāṇamao bhāvo aṇāṇiṇo kuṇadi teṇa kammāṇi |
ṇāṇamao ṇāṇissa du ṇa kuṇadi tamhā du kammāṇi ||

141 (151)

jīve kammaṃ baddhaṃ puṭṭhaṃ cedi vavahāraṇayabhaṇidaṃ |
suddhaṇayassa du jīve abaddhapuṭṭhaṃ havai kammaṃ ||

142 (152)

kammaṃ baddham abaddhaṃ jīve edaṃ tu jāṇa ṇayapakkhaṃ |
pakkhātikkaṃto puṇa bhaṇṇadi jo so samayasāro ||

143 (153)

doṇha vi ṇayāṇa bhaṇidaṃ jāṇai ṇavariṃ tu samayapaḍibaddho |
ṇa du ṇayapakkhaṃ giṇhadi kiṃci vi ṇayapakkhaparihīṇo* ||

*Sheth gives *parihīna.*

144 (154)

sammaddaṃsaṇaṇāṇaṃ eso [= edaṃ JGM] lahadi tti ṇavari vavadesaṃ |
savvaṇayapakkharahido bhaṇido jo so samayasāro ||

151 (161)

paramaṭṭho khalu samao suddho jo kevalī muṇī ṇāṇī |
tamhi ṭṭhidā sahāve muṇiṇo pāvaṃti ṇivvāṇaṃ ||

152 (162)

paramaṭṭhammi ya aṭhido jo kuṇadi tavaṃ vadaṃ ca dhārayadi |
taṃ savvaṃ bālatavaṃ bālavadaṃ viṃti savvahṇu* ||

Savvahṇu looks odd. Pischel, para. 105, gives *savvaṇṇu* for *sarvajñā*. He also gives an instance of *savvaṇhu*, which should perhaps be the form here.

153 (163)

vadaṇiyamāṇi dharaṃtā sīlāṇi tahā tavaṃ ca kuvvaṃtā |
paramaṭṭhabāhirā jeṇa teṇa te hoṃti aṇṇāṇī ||

156 (166)

mottūṇa ṇiccayaṭṭhaṃ vavahāre ṇa vidusā pavaṭṭhaṃti |
paramaṭṭham assidāṇaṃ du jadīṇa kammakkhao vihio ||

JGM 166 prints *hodi* for *vihio*. I have printed *pavaṭṭhaṃti* as this is the version given in all editions and commentaries, although there seems to be no linguistic explanation for the presence of the aspirate.

183 (176)

edaṃ tu avivarīdaṃ ṇāṇaṃ jaiyā du hodi jīvassa |
taiyā ṇa kiṃci kuvvadi bhāvaṃ uvaogasuddhappā ||

185 (178)

evaṃ jāṇadi ṇāṇī aṇṇāṇī muṇadi rāgam evādaṃ |
aṇṇāṇatamocchaṇṇo ādasahāvaṃ ayāṇaṃto ||

186 (179)

suddhaṃ tu viyāṇaṃto suddham evappayaṃ lahadi jīvo |
jāṇaṃto du asuddhaṃ asuddham evappayaṃ lahadi ||

187 (180)

appāṇaṃ appaṇo ruṃbhidūṇa dosu puṇṇapāvajogesu |
daṃsaṇaṇāṇaṃhi ṭṭhido icchāvirado ya aṇṇamhi ||

188 (181)

jo savvasaṃgamukko jhāyadi appāṇaṃ appaṇo appā |
ṇavi kammaṃ nokammaṃ cedā ciṃtedi eyattaṃ ||

189 (182)

appāṇaṃ jhāyaṃto daṃsaṇaṇāṇamao aṇaṇṇamao |
lahadi acireṇa appāṇam eva so kammaṇimmukkaṃ ||

198 (213)

udayavivāgo viviho kammāṇaṃ vaṇṇido jiṇavarehiṃ |
ṇa du te majjha sahāvā jāṇagabhāvo du aham ekko ||

200 (212)

evaṃ sammāiṭṭhī appāṇaṃ muṇadi jāṇagasahāvaṃ |
udayaṃ kammavivāgaṃ ca muadi taccaṃ viyāṇaṃto ||

201 (214)

paramāṇumittiyaṃ pi hu rāgādīṇaṃ tu vijjade jassa |
ṇavi so jāṇadi appāṇayaṃ tu savvāgamadharo vi ||

202 (-)

appāṇam ayāṇaṃto aṇappayaṃ ceva so ayāṇaṃto |
kaha hodi sammadiṭṭhī jīvājīve ayāṇaṃto ||

203 (219)

ādamhi davvabhāve athire mottūṇa giṇha tava ṇiyadaṃ |
thiram ekam imaṃ bhāvaṃ uvalabbhaṃtaṃ sahāveṇa ||

204 (223)

ābhiṇisudohimaṇakevalaṃ ca taṃ hodi ekkam eva padaṃ |
so eso paramaṭṭho jaṃ lahiduṃ ṇivvudiṃ jādi ||

205 (224)

ṇāṇaguṇehiṃ vihīṇā edaṃ tu padaṃ bahū vi ṇa lahaṃti |
taṃ giṇha supadam edaṃ jadi icchasi kammaparimokkhaṃ ||

210 (225)

apariggaho aṇiccho bhaṇido ṇāṇī ya ṇicchade dhammaṃ |
apariggaho du dhammassa jāṇago teṇa so hodi ||

211 (226)

as 210, except *adhamma* is substituted for *dhamma*

212 (228)

as 210, except *asaṇa* is substituted for *dhamma*

213 (229)

as 210, except *pāṇa* is substituted for *dhamma*

214 (230)

evamādu* edu vivihe savve bhāve ya ṇicchade ṇāṇī |
jāṇagabhāvo ṇiyado ṇīrālaṃbo du** savvattha ||

Jayasena has * *ivvādu* and ** *ya*

247 (265)

jo maṇṇadi hiṃsāmi ya hiṃsijjāmi ya parehiṃ sattehiṃ |
so mūḍho aṇṇāṇī ṇāṇī etto du vivarīdo ||

262 (280)

ajjhavasideṇa bandho satte māreu mā va māreu |
eso bandhasamāso jīvāṇaṃ ṇicchayaṇayassa ||

263 (281)

evam aliye adatte abramhacere pariggahe ceva |
kīrai ajjhavasāṇaṃ jaṃ teṇa du bajjhae pāvaṃ ||

264 (282)

tahavi ya sacce datte baṃbhe aparigahattāne ceva |
kīrai ajjhavasāṇaṃ jaṃ teṇa du bajjhae puṇṇaṃ ||

265 (283)

vatthuṃ paḍucca jaṃ puṇa ajjhavasāṇaṃ tu hodi jīvāṇaṃ |
ṇa ya vatthudo du baṃdho ajjhavasāṇeṇa baṃdho tti||

270 (294)

edāṇi ṇatthi jesiṃ ajjhavasāṇāṇi evam ādīṇi |
te asuheṇa suheṇa va kammeṇa muṇī ṇa lippanti ||

271 (295)

buddhī vavasāo vi ya ajjhavasāṇaṃ madī ya viṇṇāṇaṃ |
eyattam eva savvaṃ cittaṃ bhāvo ya pariṇāmo ||

272 (296)

evaṃ vavahāraṇao paḍisiddho jāṇa ṇicchayaṇayeṇa |
ṇicchayaṇayassidā puṇa muṇiṇo* pāvanti ṇivvāṇaṃ ||

*JGM has the alternative reading: *ṇicchayaṇayasallīṇā muṇiṇo*

293 (321)

bandhāṇaṃ ca sahāvaṃ viyāṇio* appaṇo sahāvaṃ ca |
baṃdhesu jo virajjadi** so kammavimokkaṇaṃ kuṇai ||

JGM has *viyāṇiduṃ* and ***jo ṇa rajjadi*

294 (322)

jīvo baṃdho ya tahāchijjaṃti salakkhaṇehiṃ ṇiyaehiṃ |
paṇṇāchedaṇaeṇa u chiṇṇā ṇāṇattam āvaṇṇā ||

295 (323)

jīvo baṃdho ya tahā chijjaṃti salakkhaṇehiṃ ṇiyaehiṃ |
baṃdho cheyayavvo suddho appā ya ghittavvo ||

296 (324)

kaha so ghippai appā paṇṇāe so u ghippae appā |
jaha paṇṇāe yibhatto taha paṇṇā eva ghittavvo ||

297 (325)

paṇṇāe ghittavvo jo cedā so ahaṃ tu ṇicchayado |
avasesā je bhāvā te majjha pare tti ṇāyavvā ||

298 (326)

paṇṇāe ghittavvo jo daṭṭhā so aham ... ibid. ||

299 (327)

paṇṇāe ghittavvo jo ṇādā so aham ... ibid. ||

300 (328)

ko ṇāma bhaṇijja buho ṇāuṃ savve paroyaye bhāve |
majjham iṇaṃ ti ya vayaṇaṃ jāṇaṃto appayaṃ suddhaṃ ||

306 (334)

paḍikamaṇaṃ paḍisaraṇaṃ parihāro dhāraṇā ṇiyatti ya |
ṇiṃdā garuhā sohī aṭṭhaviho hoi visakumbho ||

307 (335)

apaḍikkamaṇaṃ apaḍisaraṇaṃ aparihāro adhāraṇā ceva |
aṇiyattī ya aṇiṃdā agaruhā 'sohī amayakuṃbho ||

324 (-)

vavahārabhāsieṇa u paradavvaṃ mama bhaṇaṃti vidiyatthā |
jāṇaṃti ṇicchayeṇa u ṇa ya mama paramāṇumettam avi kiṃci ||

325 (-)

jaha kovi ṇaro jaṃpai amhā gāmavisayaṇayararaṭṭhaṃ |
ṇa ya honti tassa tāṇi u bhaṇai ya moheṇa so appā ||

326 (-)

em eva micchadiṭṭhī ṇāṇī ṇissaṃsayaṃ havai eso |
jo paradavvaṃ mama idi jāṇaṃto appayaṃ kuṇai ||

345 (357)

kehi ci du pajjayehiṃ viṇassae ṇeva kehi ci du jīvo |
jamhā tamhā kuvvai so vā aṇṇo va ṇeyaṃto ||

346 (358)

kehi ci du pajjayehiṃ viṇassae ṇeva kehi ci du jīvo |
jamhā tamhā vedadi so vā aṇṇo va ṇeyaṃto ||

347 (359)

jo ceva kuṇai so ceva vedako jassa esa siddhaṃto |
so jīvo ṇāyavvo micchādiṭṭhī aṇārihado ||

348 (360)

aṇṇo karei aṇṇo paribhuṃjai jassa esa siddhaṃto |
so jīvo ṇāyavvo micchādiṭṭhī aṇārihado ||

356 (385 SBJ):

jaha seṭiyā du ṇa parassa seṭiyā seṭiyā ya sā hoi |
taha jāṇao du ṇa parassa jāṇao jāṇao so du ||

390 (420)

saṭṭhaṃ ṇāṇaṃ ṇa havai jamhā saṭṭhaṃ ṇa yāṇae kiṃci |
tamhā aṇṇaṃ ṇāṇaṃ aṇṇaṃ saṭṭhaṃ jiṇā viṃti ||

403 (433)

jamhā jāṇai ṇiccaṃ tamhā jīvo du jāṇao ṇāṇī |
ṇāṇaṃ ca jāṇayādo avvādirittaṃ muṇeyavvaṃ ||

404 (434)

ṇāṇaṃ sammādiṭṭhi du saṃjamaṃ suttam aṃgapuvvagayaṃ |
dhammādhammaṃ ca tahā pavvajjaṃ abbhuvaṃti buhā ||

408 (438)

pāsaṃḍiyaliṃgāṇi va* gihaliṃgāṇi va bahuppayārāṇi |
ghittuṃ vadaṃti mūḍhā liṃgam iṇaṃ mokkhamaggo tti ||

*JGM ed. has *pākhaṃḍiya* - see Pischel para. 265: *pākhaṃdi* is the erroneous writing of *kha* for *ṣa*.

409 (439)

ṇa du hoi mokkhamaggo liṃgaṃ jaṃ dehaṇimmamā arihā |
liṃgaṃ mucittu daṃsaṇaṇāṇacarittāṇi sevaṃti ||

410 (440)

ṇavi esa mokkhamaggo pāsaṃḍīgihamayāṇi liṃgāṇi |
daṃsaṇaṇāṇacarittāṇi mokkhamaggaṃ jiṇā viṃti ||

411 (441)

jamhā jahittu liṅge sāgāraṇagāraehiṃ vā gahie |
daṃsaṇaṇāṇacaritte appāṇaṃ juṃja mokkhapahe ||

412 (442)

mokkhapahe appāṇaṃ ṭhavehi taṃ ceva jhāhi taṃ ceva* |
tattheva vihara ṇiccaṃ mā viharasu aṇṇadavvesu ||

* JGM ed. reads: *ṭhavehi vedayadi jhāyahi ceva*, which is preferable.

413 (443)

pāsaṃḍiliṃgesu va gihaliṃgesu va bahuppayāresu |
kuvvaṃti je mamattaṃ tehiṃ ṇa ṇāyaṃ samayasāraṃ ||

414 (444)

vavahārio puṇa ṇao doṇṇi vi liṃgāṇi bhaṇai mokkhapahe |
ṇicchayaṇao ṇa icchai* mokkhapahe savvaliṃgāṇi ||

* JGM ed. reads: *ṇiccayaṇao du ṇicchadi*

415 (445)

jo samayapāhuḍam iṇaṃ paṭhiūṇa atthataccao ṇāuṃ* |
atthe ṭhāhidi ceyā so hohi** uttamaṃ sokkhaṃ ||

* JGM ed. reads: *paṭhidūṇaya acchataccado nāduṃ* and ***pāvadi*, which must be right.

Bibliography

Primary Sources and Translations

Apabhraṃśa

Yogīndu — *Paramātmaprakāśa* and *Yogasāra*, ed. A.N. Upadhye, Bombay, 1937.

Pāli

Dhammapada — S. Radhakrishnan (ed. and tr.), Oxford, 1950.

Majjhima-nikāya — Pali Text Society edition, London.

Saṃyutta-nikāya — Pali Text Society edition, London.
- trans. V. Fausboll [Sacred Books of the East, Vol. X, Pt. 1] Oxford, 1881.

Suttanipāta — Pali Text Society edition, London.

Vinaya-piṭaka — Pali Text Society edition, London.
- *Suttavibhaṅga* tr. I.B. Horner in *The Book of the Discipline* (*Vinaya-Pitaka*), Vol. I [Sacred Books of the Buddhists, Vol. X] London, 1938.

Visuddhimagga — Pali Text Society edition, London.

Prākrit

Āyāraṃga Sutta — in Puppha Bhikkhu (ed.), *Suttāgame* I, Gurgaon, 1953, pp. 1-99.
- H. Jacobi (ed.), *The Āyāraṃga Sutta of the Śvetāmbara Jains*, London [Pali Text Society], 1882.
- tr. with an intro. by H. Jacobi as 'The Ācārāṅga Sūtra', in *Jaina Sūtras* Pt. I, [Sacred Books of the East, Vol.XXII] Delhi, 1980 [reprint of 1st ed., Oxford, 1884], pp. 1-213.
- M. Jambuvijaya (ed.), *Āyāraṅga-*

suttam, Jaina-Āgama Series No. 2(1), Bombay, 1976.

- W. Schubring (ed.), *Ācārańga-Sūtra:Erster Śruta Skandha* (Text, Analyse und Glossar), original ed. Leipzig, 1910], reprint Liechtenstein, 1966 [Abhandlungen für die Kunde des Morgenlandes herausgegeben von der Deutschen Morgenländischen Gesellschaft, Band XII, No. 4].

Sūyagaḍaṃga Sutta in Puppha Bhikkhu (ed.), *Suttāgame* I, Gurgaon, 1953, pp. 101-182.

- *Studien zum Sūyagaḍa: die Jainas und die anderen Weltanschauungen vor der Zeitwende. Textteile, Nijjutti, Ubersetzung und Anmerkungen*, W.B. Bollée, [Schriftenreihe des Südasien-Instituts der Universität Heidelberg, Band 24] Teil I, Wiesbaden, 1977.

- *Studien zum Sūyagaḍa. Textteile, Nijjutti, Ubersetzung und Anmerkungen*, W.B. Bollée, [Schriftenreihe, etc., Band 31] Teil II, Stuttgart, 1988.

- M. Jambuvijaya (ed.), *Sūyagaḍaṃga-suttaṃ*, Jaina-Āgama Series No. 2(2), Bombay, 1978.

- tr. with an intro. by H. Jacobi as 'The Sūtrakṛtāṅga Sūtra' in *Jaina Sūtras* Pt. II, [Sacred Books of the East, Vol. XLV] Delhi, 1973 [reprint of 1st ed., Oxford, 1895], pp. 235-435.

Dasaveyāliya Sutta in Phulchandji Mahārāj (ed.), *Suttāgame* II, Gurgaon, 1954, pp.

947-976.
- tr. by K.C. Lalwani, Delhi, 1973.
- E. Leumann (ed.), W. Schubring (tr.), Ahmedabad, 1932.

Uttarajjhayaṇa Sutta in Phulchandji Mahārāj (ed.), *Suttāgame* II, Gurgaon, 1954, pp. 977-1060.
- tr. with an intro. by H. Jacobi as 'The Uttarādhyayana Sūtra' in *Jaina Sūtras* Pt. II, [Sacred Books of the East, Vol. XLV] Delhi, 1973 [reprint of 1st ed., Oxford, 1895], pp. 1-232.
- J. Charpentier (ed. with an intro., critical notes and a commentary), *The Uttarādhyayanasūtra*, Uppsala, 1922.

Viyāhapaṇṇatti (*Bhagavaī*) in Puppha Bhikkhu (ed.), *Suttāgame* I, Gurgaon, 1953, pp. 384-939.
- J. Deleu (intro., critical analysis, commentary and indexes), Belgium, 1970.

Kundakunda (1) *Niyamasāra*, Prākrit text, ed. and tr., with intro., notes and comm. by Uggar Sain, [Jagmandarlal Jaini Memorial Series, Vol. V] Lucknow, 1931.
- *Niyamasāra* - reprint of above, critically edited by Padmashri Sumatibhai Shah, Solapur, 1988.

Kundakunda (2) *Pañcāstikāyasāra*, Prākrit text, ed. and tr., with intro., notes and an original comm. in English by A. Chakravartinayanar, [The Sacred Books of the Jainas, Vol. III] Arrah, 1920.

Kundakunda (3) *Pravacanasāra*, Prākrit text, tr. and ed. with an intro. by A.N. Upadhye (includes Sanskrit commentaries of Amṛtacandra (*Tattvadīpikā*) and Jayasena (*Tātparya-vṛtti*), and Pande Hemaraja's Hindi commentary), (2nd ed.) Bombay, 1935.

- *The Pravacana-sāra of Kunda-kunda Ācārya, together with the commentary, Tattva-dīpikā, by Amṛtacandra Sūri*, English tr. by B. Faddegon, ed. with an intro. by F.W. Thomas, Cambridge, 1935.

Kundakunda (4) *Samayasāra*, Prākrit text, ed. and tr. with intro. and comm. by A. Chakravarti, Banaras, 1950.

- *Samayasāra*, Prākrit text, tr., comm. and intro. by J.L. Jaini, [Sacred Books of the Jainas, Vol. VIII] Lucknow, 1930.

- *Samayaprābhṛtam*, G. Jain (ed.) [includes Sanskrit commentaries of Amṛtacandra (*Ātmakhyāti*) and Jayasena (*Tātparya-vṛtti*)], (Sanatana Jaina Grantha Mala 3) Benares, 1914.

Sanskrit

Amṛtacandra - see Kundakunda (3), *Tattvadīpikā*.

- see Kundakunda (4), *Ātmakhyāti*.

Bhagavadgītā R.C. Zaehner (ed.), Oxford, 1969.

Jayasena - see Kundakunda (3), comm. on *Pravacanasāra*.

- see Kundakunda (4), comm. on *Samayasāra*.

Patañjali *Patañjala Darshana (Yoga Sūtras)*, (with the commentary of Vyāsa), J. Vidyasagara (ed.), Calcutta, 1940.

Pūjyapāda (Devanandin) — *Sarvārthasiddhi*, P.S. Shastry (ed.), [Sanskrit Grantha No. 13] Banaras, 1955.
- *Reality*, tr. of *Sarvārthasiddhi* by S.A. Jain, Calcutta, 1960.

Umāsvāti — *Tattvārthādhigama Sūtra*, ed. and tr. by J.L. Jaini, [Sacred Books of the Jains, Vol. II] Arrah, 1920.
- *Tattvārthādhigama* (with *bhāṣya*), ed.. K.P. Mody, Calcutta, 1903.
Tattvārtha Sūtra, ed. Pt. Sukhlalji with his comm. and tr., with an intro. by K.K. Dixit, [L.D. Series 44] Ahmedabad, 1974.

Vātsyāyana — *The Nyāya-Sūtras with Vātsyāyana's Bhāṣya*, ed. G.S. Tailanga [Vizianagram Sanskrit Series, Vol. IX] Benares, 1896.
- *Gautama's Nyāyasūtras (With Vātsyāyana-Bhāṣya)*, tr. G. Jha, Poona, 1939.

Dictionaries and Reference Works

Ardha-māgadhī koṣa — Ratnachandra (ed.), intro. by A.C. Woolner, Vol. I, Ajmer, 1923.

Buddhist Dictionary — compiled by Nyanatiloka, 4th revised edition, Kandy, 1980.

A Critical Pāli Dictionary — begun by V. Trenckner, revised, continued and edited by D. Andersen, H. Smith and H. Hendricksen, Vol. I, Copenhagen, 1924-1948.

A Grammar of the Prākrit Languages — R. Pischel, tr. from the

German by S. Jha, 2nd revised edition, Delhi,1981.

Pāia-Sadda-Mahaṇṇavo: A Prakrit-Hindi Dictionary compiled by H.D.T. Sheth, Calcutta, 1928.

A Sanskrit-English Dictionary M. Monier-Williams, Oxford, 1979 (reprint).

Works Cited

(excluding primary sources in classical languages and dictionaries, for which see above)

Alsdorf, L.

1958 'Itthīparinnā: A Chapter of Jain Monastic Poetry, Edited as a Contribution to Indian Prosody', *Indo-Iranian Journal*, Vol. II, The Hague, pp. 249-270.

1962-1963 'Uttarajjhāyā Studies', *Indo-Iranian Journal*, Vol. VI, The Hague, pp. 110-136.

1965 *Les Études Jaina*, College de France.

1966 *The Āryā Stanzas of the Uttarajjhāyā*, Wiesbaden.

1977 'Jaina Exegetical Literature', in A. N. Upadhye, *et al.* (ed.), *Mahāvīra and His Teachings*, Bombay, pp. 1-8.

Basham, A.L.

1951 *History and Doctrine of the Ājīvikas*, London.

Bhatt, B.

1974 'Vyavahāranaya and Niścayanaya in Kundakunda's Works', *Zeitschrift der Deutschen Morgenländischen Gesellschaft*, Suppl. 2, Leipzig, pp. 279-291.

Bhargava, D.
1968 *Jaina Ethics*, Delhi.

Bollée, W.B.
1977 *Studien zum Sūyagaḍa: die Jainas und die anderen Weltanschauungen vor der Zeitwende. Textteile, Nijjutti, Ubersetzung und Anmerkungen* [Schriftenreihe des Südasien-Instituts der Universität Heidelberg, Band 24], Teil I, Wiesbaden.
1988 *Studien zum Sūyagaḍa. Textteile, Nijjutti, Übersetzung und Anmerkungen* [Schriftenreihe, etc., Band 31], Teil II, Stuttgart.

Bronkhorst, J.
1985 'On the Chronology of the Tattvārtha and some Early Commentaries', *Wiener Zeitschrift für die Kunde Südasiens*, Band XXIX, Vienna, pp. 155-184.

Caillat, C.
1974 'Jainism', in C. Caillat, A.N. Upadhye, B. Patil (ed.), *Jainism*, Bombay, pp. 1-48.
1975 *Atonements in the Ancient Ritual of the Jaina Monks*, Ahmedabad.
1987 'Jainism', in M. Eliade (ed. in chief), *The Encyclopedia of Religion*, Vol. 7, New York, pp. 507-514.

Chatterjee, A.K.
1978 *A Comprehensive History of Jainism*, Vol. I, Calcutta.

Collins, S.
1982 *Selfless Persons*, Cambridge.

Deleu, J.
1970 *Viyāhapannatti (Bhagavaī): Introduction, Critical Analysis, Commentary and Indexes*, Belgium.
1977 'Lord Mahāvīra and the Anyatīrthakas', in A.N. Upadhye *et al.* (ed.), *Mahāvīra and His Teachings*, Bombay, pp. 187-193.

Deo, S.B.
1956 *History of Jaina Monachism*, Poona.

Dixit, K.K.
1971 *Jaina Ontology*, [L.D. Series 31] Ahmedabad.
1978 *Early Jainism*, [L.D. Series 64] Ahmedabad.

Doshi, S.
1985 *Masterpieces of Jaina Painting*, Bombay.

Eliade, M.
1988 'Yoga', in M. Eliade (ed. in chief), *The Encyclopedia of Religion*, Vol. 15, New York, pp. 519-523.

Frauwallner, E.
1953 *Geschichte der Indischen Philosophie*, Band 1 [Band 2, 1956], Salzburg.
1973 *History of Indian Philosophy*, (2 Vols.), trans. V.M. Bedekar, Delhi.

Glasenapp, H. von
1942 *The Doctrine of Karma in Jain Philosophy*, trans. G.B. Gifford, Bombay.

Gombrich, R.F.
1971 *Precept and Practice: Traditional Buddhism in the Rural Highlands of Ceylon*, Oxford.
1984 'Notes on the Brahmanical Background to Buddhist Ethics' in G. Dhammapala, R. Gombrich, K.R. Norman (ed.), *Buddhist Studies in Honour of Hammalava Saddhatissa*, Sri Lanka, pp. 91-102.
1988 *Theravāda Buddhism: A Social History from Ancient Benares to Modern Colombo*, London.

Jacobi, H.
1884 See *Āyāraṃga Sutta*.
1895 See *Sūyagaḍaṃga Sutta* / *Uttarajjhayaṇa Sutta*.

Jaini, J.L.
1940 *Outlines of Jainism*, Cambridge.

Jaini, P.S.
1977 'Bhavyatva and Abhavyatva: A Jain Doctrine of "Predestination"', in A.N. Upadhye, *et al.* (ed.),

Mahāvīra and His Teachings, Bombay, pp. 95-111.

1979 *The Jaina Path of Purification*, Delhi.

1980 'Karma and the Problem of Rebirth in Jainism', in W. O'Flaherty (ed.), *Karma and Rebirth in Classical Indian Traditions*, California, pp. 217-238.

Jain, S.A.

1960 *Reality: (English translation of Shri Pūjyapāda's Sarvārthasiddhi)*, Calcutta.

Johnston, E.H.

1974 *Early Sāṃkhya*, Delhi (reprint of original edition, 1937, London).

Keith, A.B.

1936 Review of A.N. Upadhye's edition of the *Pravacanasāra* in *The Journal of the Royal Asiatic Society*, London, pp. 528-9.

Lamotte, E.

1988 *History of Indian Buddhism: From the Origins of the Śaka Era*, trans. S. Webb-Boin, Paris (original French edition, 1958, Paris).

Matilal, B.K.

1981 *Central Philosophy of Jainism (Anekānta Vāda)*, [L.D. Series 79] Ahmedabad.

1986 'The Logical Illumination of Indian Mystiçism', in N.J. Allen, R.F. Gombrich, T. Raychaudri, G. Rizvi (ed.), *Oxford University Papers on India*, Vol. 1, Pt. 1, Oxford.

Norman, K.R.

1977 'Kāvilīyaṃ: A Metrical Analysis of the Eighth Chapter of the Uttarādhyayana-Sūtra', in A.N. Upadhye *et al.* (ed.), *Mahāvīra and His Teachings*, Bombay.

Ohira, S.

1982 *A Study of Tattvārtha Sūtra with Bhāṣya*, [L.D. Series 86] Ahmedabad.

Olivelle, P.

1974 *The Origin and Early Development of Buddhist Monachism*, Ceylon.

Pischel, R.

1981 *A Grammar of the Prākrit Languages*, tr. from the German by S. Jha, 2nd revised edition, Delhi, 1981.

Poussin, La Vallée

1923-1931 *L' Abhidharma de Vasubandhu*, IV, Paris.

Puligandla, R.

1975 *Fundamentals of Indian Philosophy*, New York.

Rahula, W.

1978 *What the Buddha Taught*, [2nd edition] London and Bedford.

Rice, B.L.

1914 *Epigraphia Carnatica I, Coorg Inscriptions No. 1*, [revised ed. 1972], Madras.

Sangave, V.A.

1980 *Jaina Community: A Social Survey*, Bombay.

Schubring, W.

1935 *Die Lehre der Jainas*, Berlin and Leipzig.

1957 'Kundakunda echt und unecht', *ZDMG*, Vol. 107, Leipzig, pp. 537-574.

1962 *The Doctrine of the Jainas*, trans. W. Beurlen [of *Die Lehre der Jainas*], Delhi [reprint 1978].

1966 *The Religion of the Jainas*, Calcutta.

Singh, R.J.

1974 *The Jaina Concept of Omniscience*, [L.D. Series 43] Ahmedabad.

Tatia, N.

1951 *Studies in Jaina Philosophy*, Ahmedabad.

Tieken, H.

1986 'Textual Problems in an Early Canonical Jaina Text', *Wiener Zeitschrift für die Kunde Südasiens*, Band XXX, Vienna, pp. 5-25.

Upadhye, A.N.
1935 'Introduction' to *Pravacanasāra* [see *Kundakunda* (3)], Bombay, pp. i-cxxvi.

Williams, P.
1989 *Mahāyāna Buddhism: The Doctrinal Foundations*, London.

Williams, R.
1963 *Jaina Yoga: A Survey of the Mediaeval Śrāvakācāras*, London.
1966 'Before Mahāvīra', *Journal of the Royal Asiatic Society*, London, pp. 2-6.

Zydenbos, R.J.
1983 *Mokṣa in Jainism, According to Umāsvāti*, [Beiträge zur Südasienforschung, Band 53] Wiesbaden.

Glossary and Index

A

abhavya - souls incapable of attaining liberation, 245-246
ācārya - religious teacher, 260
acetanā - non-consciousness, 262
acetanā - non-conscious substance, 262
activity (of body, speech and mind), 7-12, 15-16; in the *Tattvārtha Sūtra*, 47-90; *see also yoga*
ādāna-nikṣepana-samiti - care in picking things up and putting them down, 69-70
adharma - demerit, 289
adhikaraṇa - substratum (of karmic influx); of *jīva* type, 64-66; of *ajīva* type, 67-72; 68, 209
adhyavasāna - intention, resolution, will, 272-274; synonyms for, 273, 275, 294
Ādipurāṇa, 89
ahiṃsā - non-injury, non-violence, 1, 11, 20, 25, 63, 73, 81, 83-84, 89, 156, 158, 166, 169, 177-179, 182, 189, 221, 230, 264, 290, 294-295, 303
ajīva - insentient, 64, 67-68, 103, 120n, 129, 139, 142, 146, 148, 150, 161, 170, 173, 205, 212, 215, 217, 243, 255, 257, 268, 271, 283, 285, 290; five *ajīva-dravya*, 275
Ājīvikas, 41
ajñāna - ignorance, 111, 268
akusala - karmically unwholesome, 13
alms, 27-29, 222-223
Alsdorf, L., 4, 14
Amṛtacandra, 94, 113-114, 116, 129-130, 133, 157, 160-161, 164, 168, 170-171, 173, 175, 179-180, 203, 206-207, 220, 228, 231, 233, 236, 240-242, 250, 259, 289n, 296
anagāra - homeless (ascetic), 297
anaśana - fasting, 223
anekānta(vāda) - (doctrine of) manifold aspects, 103, 137, 183n, 232, 244, 247-248, 251-255, 258, 262-265, 305
anubhāva - fruition of karma, 55
aṇukaṃpā - *see* compassion
anuprekṣā - reflection, 192, 196
aṇuvrata - partial vows (taken by laity), 73-74, 74n, 78; *see also mahāvrata*
Apabhraṃśa, 302; use of, 93, 95
aparigraha - non-possession, non-possessiveness, non-attachment (fifth *aṇuvrata* of lay person), 74-75, 74n, 88, 169, 219, 289-290
appamāda - mindfulness, 52
ārambha - 'undertaking', premeditated action, violence, 5-6, 26, 31-33; meaning of, 38-40; 65-66, 66n, 72, 154, 173-174, 220, 311
arhat - 'worthy of worship', omniscient being, Jina, 35, 172, 210, 211, 247, 295, 297
asat - unreal, 142, 148

B

E

F

R

S

T